The publisher and the University of California Press Foundation gratefully acknowledge the generous support of the Robert and Meryl Selig Endowment Fund in Film Studies, established in memory of Robert W. Selig.

Archipelagic Cinemas

TRANSPACIFIC STUDIES

Series Editors

Janet Alison Hoskins, University of Southern California
Viet Thanh Nguyen, University of Southern California

Editorial Board

Brian Bernards, University of Southern California
Adrian De Leon, New York University
Nancy Lutkehaus, University of Southern California

In recent years, the issue of how regions are connected and what kinds of cultural exchanges take place on a global scale has become of increasing importance. The term *transpacific* has come to signify the nexus of these flows of culture, capital, ideas, and labor across the Pacific. Drawing from Asian Studies, American Studies, and Asian American Studies, a new generation of scholars is developing new models for considering the geopolitical struggle over the Pacific and its attendant possibilities for inequality and exploitation. The word and concept of the transpacific can be harnessed for purposes of both domination and resistance.

The Transpacific Studies series seeks to publish monographs that look at cultural and political movements and artistic works that have arisen to contest state, corporate, and military ambitions and attempts to place them in a context that should be more dynamic than older ideas of the "Asia Pacific" or the "Pacific Rim" of global trade.

1. *Becoming Global Asia: Contemporary Genres of Postcolonial Capitalism in Singapore*, by Cheryl Narumi Naruse

2. *Archipelagic Cinemas: Screening Southeast Asian Modernity*, by Dag S. Yngvesson

Archipelagic Cinemas

Screening Southeast Asian Modernity

Dag S. Yngvesson

UNIVERSITY OF CALIFORNIA PRESS

University of California Press
Oakland, California

Suggested citation: Yngvesson, D. S. *Archipelagic Cinemas: Screening Southeast Asian Modernity*. Oakland: University of California Press, 2025. DOI: https://doi.org/10.1525/luminos.247

Library of Congress Cataloging-in-Publication Data

Names: Yngvesson, Dag S. author
Title: Archipelagic cinemas : screening southeast asian modernity /
   Dag S. Yngvesson.
Description: Oakland, California : University of California Press, [2025] |
   Series: Transpacific studies ; vol. 2 | Includes bibliographical references
   and index.
Identifiers: LCCN 2025006680 (print) | LCCN 2025006681 (ebook) |
   ISBN 9780520424852 cloth | ISBN 9780520416796 paperback |
   ISBN 9780520416802 ebook
Subjects: LCSH: Motion pictures—Southeast Asia—History |
   Regionalism in motion pictures | Southeast Asia—In motion pictures
Classification: LCC PN1993.5.S644 Y54 2025 (print) |
   LCC PN1993.5.S644 (ebook)

LC record available at https://lccn.loc.gov/2025006680
LC ebook record available at https://lccn.loc.gov/2025006681

GPSR Authorized Representative: Easy Access System Europe,
Mustamäe tee 50, 10621 Tallinn, Estonia, gpsr.requests@easproject.com

34   33   32   31   30   29   28   27   26   25
10   9   8   7   6   5   4   3   2   1

CONTENTS

ACKNOWLEDGMENTS

This book and the long research and writing processes that preceded it have been made possible by the generosity and collaboration of many different colleagues, friends, and family members. Over the past several years, Thomas Barker, Gaik Cheng Khoo, Sandeep Ray, Fuad Rahmat, Sumit Mandal, and other colleagues and admin staff at the University of Nottingham, Malaysia, have helped create a conducive working environment and platform of operations that inspired and supported this work in numerous ways. I am especially grateful to Gaik Cheng Khoo for also founding and continually fostering the Association for Southeast Asian Cinemas Conference (ASEACC), which has been a crucial source of ideas, inspiration, and experiences that have contributed to this book over the course of more than a decade. Roland Tolentino, Mariam Lam, Adam Knee, Patrick Campos, Jasmine Nadua Trice, Philippa Lovatt, Kei Tan, Quirine van Heeren, Soyoung Kim, Rosalind Galt, Bliss Cua Lim, Antonio Sison, David Hanan, Alicia Izharuddin, and many other members and contributors have made ASEACC gatherings among the most anticipated, enjoyable, and intellectually stimulating academic events I've experienced. ASEACC also connected me to Brian Bernards, whose encouragement and support for my work and, as a member of the Transpacific Studies series board, for this book, I immensely appreciate. I am also very thankful for the support of Janet Hoskins as series editor along with Viet Thanh Nguyen. My journey with the University of California Press has been a generative and relatively stress-free one thanks to the generosity, support, and guidance of Enrique Ochoa-Kaup. Joe Abbott's detailed and light, but firm, stylistic hand as copy editor has also been a great asset, as has Jeff Anderson's helpfulness and flexibility as production editor. In addition, I would like to express my appreciation for the three anonymous peer reviewers and one UC board reviewer whose comments encouraged and helped shape and develop this project in many impactful and important ways.

From long before I officially began my career as an academic, my film, and later scholarly, collaborations and many, many conversations with Koes Yuliadi have been a continual source of knowledge and inspiration. During dissertation research and filming trips to Indonesia, Koes and Yusma Kaye have also welcomed me time and again as a long-term guest in their homes in Jakarta and Yogyakarta; for this, and the continuing exchanges that occur there and elsewhere, I am incredibly thankful. Decades of conversations, drinks, jokes, and discussions with Degung Santikarma and Alit Ambara in Yogyakarta, Bali, the U.S., and elsewhere have enriched and shifted my understandings of Indonesian history and politics and life in general in innumerable ways. Alit's collaboration and generosity (and unbelievable speed) with his artistic skills have also contributed immensely to my films, to my sense of aesthetics and politicized humor, and to the cover of this book. Thank you, Bung. Leslie Dwyer, John Roosa, Gung Ayu Ratih, Hilmar Farid, Baskara T. Wardaya, and Rachmi Diyah Larasati have been important teachers, mentors, and friends from early on in my work in Indonesia.

I am also grateful for the long-term camaraderie and collaboration of Yogya and Jakarta denizens Tito Imanda, Ekky Imanjaya, Eric Sasono, Intan Paramaditha, Alia Damaihati, Kurnia Gembul Yudha, Dhimas Aryo Vipha Ananda, Hafiz Rancajale, Otty Widasari, and other Forum Lenteng members, and Lulu Ratna, Adrian Jonathan Pasaribu, Umi Lestari, and many more. Tito deserves special mention as an ASEACC member who also founded the Association of Indonesian Film Scholars (KAFEIN), a group that has provided me with numerous opportunities for learning and exchange over the years. Stimulating and fun interactions with members IGAK Satrya Wibawa, Mundi Rahayu, Evi Eliana, Budi Irawanto, Dina Herlina, Sazkia Anggi Anggraini, Novi Kurnia, Rosalia Engchuan, Zaki Habibi, Panji Wibowo, Chris Woodrich, Ratna Erika Suwarno, Shadia Pradsmadji, Agus Mediarta, Muh Bahruddin, and others have contributed greatly to my overall perspectives on Indonesian and Southeast Asian cinemas, while providing inside jokes for my films. KAFEINer and Netherlands-based scholar-practitioner Ari Purnama has been a long-term friend and has generously shared his thoughts on edits of my last film, as well as on the proposal for this book.

Akhlis Suryapati, Budi, Andas, Martono, Firdaus, Niya, Adisoerya Abdi, Dany, and other staff members of Sinematek Indonesia, the Indonesian film archive in Jakarta, have been unflaggingly helpful and generous with their time and resources, providing me access for many months of archival research, including clearance to view films on 35 mm, as well as on video. Niya's singularly detailed knowledge of the contents and organization of the library was also an especially invaluable resource from which my work benefited immensely. My heartfelt thanks go to Sanchai Chotirosseranee and the Thai Film Archive, and to Simon Santos and Video48 for providing images from Thai and Filipino film histories for use in the book. Discussions, conversations, and collaborations with Yogyakarta- and Jakarta-based filmmakers Anggi Noen, Riri Riza, Makbul Mubarak, Aryo Sweta, Bayu Prihantoro Filemon, and others have enriched both my research on local filmmaking and my own local filmmaking.

I am forever grateful to my graduate dissertation advisers Shaden Tageldin and John Mowitt, as well as committee members Jason McGrath, Alice Lovejoy, and Keya Ganguly at the University of Minnesota. I am especially thankful for the continuing support, guidance, and friendship from Shaden and Jason. Faculty, staff, and graduate colleagues at Cultural Studies and Comparative Literature, Asian and Middle Eastern Studies, and other departments helped create a supportive network from which I was able to launch my initial research for the book. Before, during, and after graduate school, friendship and intellectual exchanges with Emily Ng have provided a regular source of inspiration, humor, and encouragement. Fieldwork for my dissertation and this book have been funded by several university and national grants, most recently a 2018 American Institute for Indonesian Studies/Henry Luce Foundation Research Grant.

Perhaps most important, this book would never have been possible without the generosity, love, and support of my family. Barbara Yngvesson, my mother, has tirelessly read and commented on numerous drafts and versions of chapters, proposals, and other elements. Hers has probably been the most crucial editorial contribution to the book, and to say I am grateful is insufficient. I am very lucky to be surrounded (if digitally much of the time) by not only one but two scholars and thinkers who, despite coming from different fields, are able and willing to engage with my work. My father, Sigfrid Yngvesson's "scientist" perspectives and questions have also been very helpful in trying to make this book as accessible as possible to nonspecialists (at least the patient readers among them :p). My brother Finn has also read, encouraged, and asked generative questions along the way, and we have held numerous discussions about various aspects of Indonesia life and politics, including on cinema. Last but most, with her patience, support, love, questions, criticisms, discussions, ideas, jokes, and unusually broad, down-to-earth perspective on Indonesian and Southeast Asia media, culture, and politics, my wife and life partner, Windi Wahyu Ningtyas, has contributed to this book on a daily basis for the last decade (and also to numerous film projects). For this I am truly blessed and grateful, as I am for the presence of our daughter, Siti Alengka Rang Yngvesson, who has been an endless source of joy, wonder, inspiration, and much-needed distractions for the last six years. I am also deeply indebted to my family-in-law, *Ibu* Sumiyati, the late *Bapak* Anwar, *Mas* Agung, *Mas* Arief, and *Mas* Teguh for the open arms with which I have been accepted and for their exposing me to new methods and centers of critical thought and practice that have further broadened my view as a scholar and human being.

Prologue

Over the last two decades, cinema as we knew it has been transformed by a new technological milieu, the effects of which reach back into the past even as they push forward into the future. Mushrooming virtual archives have given new life to cinema's former selves, illuminating historical crossroads where debates over key sources and triggers for the global development of motion pictures linger unresolved. My long-term work in and around Indonesia and Southeast Asia has been driven by questions about the derivation and politics of cinematic form and style outside the West and by the diverse methodological permutations such inquiries inspire: sifting through piles of disks and uncountable browser tabs, hovering over flatbed editors, squinting at yellowing newspapers, and lurking around rituals and semiabandoned theaters. Through repetition and openness to apparent coincidence, patterns emerge, divulging clues to some of film studies' most divisive missing links—in this case, especially around the formation, function, and approach of cinemas based in the Global South.

This book takes filmmaking in Southeast Asia as one such link. The project's dual archaeological and "archipelagic" approach is provoked by the media flows that characterize a region of *tanah air* (land-water) where common strategies of representation have circulated for centuries. Looking past the modern, nationalistic focus of film studies, I show how these strategies inflect the development of basic cinematic approaches and conventions while overflowing the domestic boundaries that have served as a key organizing principle for nearly every study of film in the region so far. Reading across, within, and before national cinemas in Southeast Asia, I uncover a dense, intermedial amalgam of styles and modes of expression. Foremost among them are the negation of naturalism, the lauding of symbolism and abstraction over direct exposition, and a formative tendency to incorporate reflections or metacommentary on processes, media, and politics of representation. Unlike their association with avant-gardes and radical aesthetics elsewhere in the world, in Southeast Asia these conventions are generally considered populist and lowbrow. This points to a particular set of habits and expectations that characterized the tastes of regional audiences throughout much of the twentieth century. Popular films here normally preclude binary interpretation of good and evil or self vs. other and frequently engage grave political stakes with a collective show of exuberance and mockery—an especially notable feature of early Southeast Asia cinemas. Together these modes of expression inscribe a defiantly local yet hybrid and cosmopolitan archipelagic imagination—a vanguard of non-Western visual politics that emerged decades earlier than the celebrated "oppositional" tactics of postcolonial and Third cinemas elsewhere in the Global South.[1] How and why this occurred are key questions driving the book's initial chapters.

Based on the island of Java in Indonesia, but tracing comparative circuits around the region and across the Pacific, I track the progression of these emergent modes and conventions of representation as they adapt to rapidly changing historical conditions—especially the institution of rigid structures of gender and power that are understood to accompany the development of modern nations. I take up the staging of radical shakeups of official patriarchal regimes and dictatorships on the region's screens in detail in chapters 4 and 5, where I identify a pattern of reflecting—and profoundly refracting—the positive images and claims proffered by regional authoritarians through the eyes of Southeast Asian women. This pattern, I argue, points to one of the most crucial features of archipelagic representation in the region: a symbolic order that resists the imposition of a single, sovereign point of reference or authority. A narrow modernist, male gaze is thus often subordinated to what that gaze is structurally prevented from seeing: the more "realist" view of those who are living in poverty, facing single motherhood, or engaging in prostitution (and often all three). As I show, the more depersonalized perception of female ghosts and spirits also serves as an important tool in disrupting the imposition of a constrictive, yet allegedly universal, patriarchal vision. The gendered perspective produced between spirits and those living under inhuman conditions is eminently archipelagic, revealing the yawning fissures and holes that dot the images, narratives, and logic on which dictators and their minions stand. I position the paradoxical truth of such a view—"complete" because it encompasses the actual fragmentation of reality—as an unruly source of empowerment, but also of risk, and potentially trauma and shock.

At the heart of my analysis is an exploration of the ways that emergent technologies often appear to be pulled *backward* in time as they are made to interact with older media, challenging standards of what can be counted as an intervention in film form per se. Paradoxically, what I see as the regional hauling "back" of film, with its alleged modern singularity, into a sphere of demonstrably greater inter- and multimediality, mirrors the current dismantling of established cinematic norms brought about by the myriad proliferating screens, chips, and platforms of the digital era. Strategies like "breaking the fourth wall" are hence deprived of subversive potential as such, even as the movie screen is opened and transformed into a transmedial space where divergent ideas, genres, and technologies comingle, braiding together multiple times, locales, and political interests in the process. In this way, I position Southeast Asia—and the Pacific Ocean as key "outer" region of Southeast Asian cinematic exchange and comparison—as a dynamic lens through which to expand theories of non-Western development, media histories, and conceptualizations of national identity.

A COMMON AESTHETIC THEORY?

Dance and art scholar Kapila Malik Vatsyayan has made a similar argument about historically embedded conventions of theater, architecture, and painting in the region, which she extends to include India. "It is clear," she writes, "that the fresh ground which the West has just broken was in some ways an accepted principle of an age-old Asian . . . tradition," especially in terms of Euro-American modernist breaks "from realism and naturalism" in the twentieth century (1971:19). For Vatsyayan, the earlier, enduring interest in indirect, nonfigurative representation in India was driven by "a common aesthetic theory [which] governed all the arts, both performing and plastic, in South and South East Asia. Roughly speaking . . . [this involves] the establishment of a hierarchy of realities where the principle of suggestion through abstraction is followed [along with] . . . the manifestation in the arts of the belief that time is cyclic rather than linear. . . . This tradition of the arts appears to have been persuasive from Afghanistan and India to Japan and Indonesia over two thousand years of history" (1971:26).

Vatsyayan's argument about historical continuities between Asian and Southeast Asian art forms was echoed by film scholars like Roy Armes (1987:135) and Ella Shohat and Robert Stam (2014:295) in relation to Southeast Asian cinemas. These scholars, however, provide little evidence of such continuities and little or no analyses of actual Southeast Asian films to support their argument.[2] In the decades since Armes's and Shohat and Stam's studies, subsequent work has focused explicitly on Southeast Asian, rather than non-Western or Third World, cinemas, producing a wealth of more detailed information about how filmmaking took root and developed in much of the region.[3] Yet at the same time, most of these studies have focused on individual Southeast Asian nations or areas within them. All but two of them are also edited volumes written by multiple authors with varying focuses and usually specializing in only one Southeast Asian nation, thus reducing the possibility of establishing clear connections across chapters. Few studies, if any, have made a concerted effort to compare and identify similar aesthetic patterns across the region that common historical aesthetic approaches may have contributed to. Despite the tantalizing earlier references and the greater wealth of information that now exists, what Vatsyayan refers to as a "unity through infinite multiplicity" (1971:22) in Southeast and South Asian arts has yet to be shown in the region's cinemas.

The lack of a thorough, comparative written account of regional filmmaking does not, however, indicate the absence of broad, regional thinking on the part of scholars and practitioners. The Association of Southeast Asian Cinemas Conference (ASEACC), an organization founded by Malaysian film scholar Gaik Cheng Khoo in 2004, has allowed for a regional view to be constructed, discussed, disputed, and variously reconstructed by film academics, critics, and filmmakers via its biennial meetings, held in various Southeast Asian locales. Although even at ASEACC events, most papers are focused on a single nation or area, comparisons are inevitably made through discussion and questions from specialists in other parts of the region. The majority of the attendees are based in Thailand, the Philippines, Indonesia, or elsewhere in Southeast Asia. In addition to papers, each conference involves a selection of films from around the region, presented by their makers whenever possible, inviting further efforts to draw connections among them, while also noting key distinctions.

After attending my first ASEACC in Singapore as a graduate student in 2012, I have been a regular presenter, committee member, and organizer—experiences that have contributed to the gradual development of the regional perspective on which I have based this book. I was also fortunate to be offered a teaching position in Malaysia upon completion of my dissertation, and my years here have exposed me to a host of new films, scholars, and filmmakers from outside Indonesia, where my dissertation work was focused. Teaching in the region has also provided a base of operations where the importance of Southeast Asian cinemas is taken for granted, something that is not the case in the U.S. and Europe. In 2020, I was invited by a group of ASEACC regulars to contribute to a special section of the *Journal of Cinema and Media Studies* entitled "Theorizing Region: Film and Video Cultures in Southeast Asia."[4] Each of the six essays continued the practice of focusing on a single nation or part thereof. But at the same time, coeditors Philippa Lovatt and Jasmine Nadua Trice premised the project on interrogating and deconstructing the concept of national cinemas. Across the various contributions, the result evokes a fragmented, archipelagic view of a region composed of closely interrelated subnational hubs of aesthetics and media production. From this perspective, the nations around these subcenters become readable as interdependent and, in certain ways, inseparable from each other rather than from the national borders that would divide them.

ASEACC members Brian Bernards (2015) and Elmo Gonzaga (2016, 2024) have also broken important new ground with explicitly supranational, regionally focused studies across various Southeast Asian media. Comparing the region with other archipelagic areas such as the Caribbean, Bernards examines its postcolonial literatures through the lens of the "Nanyang imagination," applying the term often used by Chinese migrants to Southeast Asia. Doing so not only implies the diverse interconnections that make up the region's "insides" but foregrounds the constant, formative circulations of people and ideas from elsewhere in Asia and the world. For Bernards, this opens the conception of national cultures, viewing them in terms of larger networks that "prioritize contact, exchange, heterogeneity, and creolization instead of racial, ethnic, or linguistic uniformity and singularity" (2015:13). Gonzaga, following Édouard Glissant, argues that an archipelagic perspective, transcending national borders and reaching out over connective (rather than constraining) bodies of water, "enables the juxtaposition of seemingly unrelated objects within the same geographic location or historical period" (2024:21). In Gonzaga's work, such highly charged yet "tenuous affinities" point to the particular potential of regions like Southeast Asia to produce novel or radical convergences among otherwise distinct media forms, including newer digital and older analog ones (Gonzaga 2016).

These collective views of contemporary regional cinemas, screen cultures, digital media, and literatures provide further inspiration for the supranational, archipelagic approach that I take in this book. In relation to Lovatt and Trice's compilation, I apply it "backwards" here as a historical lens with which to gather evidence and look more closely into the possibilities of Southeast Asian cinemas emerging and developing along the lines of what Vatsyayan calls a "common aesthetic theory"—one that, for Vatsyayan, especially links the region's modes of representation to past waves of "globalization" that spread India's religions, languages, and classical narratives throughout East and Southeast Asia. These older conventions and theories, she argues, position South and Southeast Asian artistic traditions as having long ago anticipated "the inadequacy of the 'word,' the dissatisfaction with the theoretical dependence on Aristotle's mimeses" (1971:19), and other modern revelations around which artists in Europe and the U.S. found inspiration to break with naturalism in the nineteenth and twentieth centuries.

As I will show in the chapters ahead, signs of the influence of South Asian aesthetics, religions, and philosophies are indeed widespread in much of Southeast Asia. Yet with few exceptions, one does not encounter such elements in obvious or pure forms. Owing to the constant forces of historical change and the fact that they were heavily localized from the beginning, Indian spiritual, intellectual, and formal aspects of Southeast Asian societies (and now cinemas) are present mainly in fragments that are combined with other traces and layers of local, regional, and global ideas, genres, and forms. As Gaik Cheng Khoo (2006), Rosalind Galt (2021), and Arnika Fuhrmann (2016) have argued about Malaysian and Thai cinemas, for example, local *adat* customs, embedded strains of animism, and vernacular adaptations of Buddhism and Islam have exercised significant influences on the form and content of films, both historically and on those made during the post-1998 spate of "new waves."

Building on these and other studies, I argue that long-historical frameworks of spiritual, social, and political thought and practice have produced a set of common regional permutations of South Asian influences, among many others. Indian influences began to arrive around the first century A.D. and were added to existing local-regional beliefs and aesthetic forms. The attitudes and philosophies of representation constituted by the subsequent amalgamation of conventions and active historical remnants appears to have made an especially lasting impression on much of the region. The result, as we will see, was critical to how further waves of globalization were received and processed—especially those from the Middle East and Ottoman Empire beginning in the thirteenth century and Europe around three hundred years later. The interaction of these further shifts with extant layers produced the set of archipelagic aesthetics, approaches, and flourishes that I position as the basis from which Southeast Asian films have been constructed from the early twentieth century. Geography, and the region's preeminent bodies of water, have played an especially important role in this process of development.

MANDALAS, REGIONAL HISTORIES, AND ARCHIPELAGIC NATIONALISMS

In his classic *History, Culture, and Region in Southeast Asian Perspectives*, O. W. Wolters argues that in premodern times, the Indian Ocean functioned as the region's "single ocean" (1982:46), indicating its dominant importance as an arena of exchange—a status that would later shift to the Pacific as trade with other areas increased. Across its waters, Indian religions, literatures, and political and cultural concepts traveled into the archipelagic expanses of Southeast Asia and then on to landlocked areas. For Wolters, these new ideas and practices were critical to the region's historical development but were adapted without causing massive epistemic shifts. Indian influence—particularly the idea of the spherical *mandala* as an ideal political structure—added to existing tendencies in which authority was based on multiple, shifting loci of power that would form and re-form around the agency of formidable and charismatic leaders. Such leaders were believed to be spiritually powerful, a quality that followers held they could absorb and develop in themselves through association, loyal service, and close study (1982:18–19).

What Indian religions and political concepts crucially added to these extant structures, Wolters argues, was the concept of such spiritually based authority as broadly applicable beyond the limited spheres of the "men of prowess" whose domains dotted the archipelago at the time (given historical patterns of gender and power in the region, women of prowess would likely have emerged as well). Would-be leaders hence began to construct their paths to power by developing a "unique claim to 'universal' sovereignty" (1982:27). Yet at the same time, political authority in the region was divided among *mandalas*, "patchwork[s] of often overlapping . . . 'circles of kings,'" each of which held claim to power "derived from a single and indivisible divine authority" (27). In practice, each such circle of power was also inherently mutable, including in terms of the geographic area/s over which its authority extended, which would "expand and contract in concertina-like fashion" (27) over time. This occurred as Indian and other ideas were moved, modified, and divided across a region comprising these multiple, competing political "centers"—an archipelagic array of mandalas, often composed of actual islands that dotted and defined the fluid expanse of water and land that would come to be known variously as Nanyang, Nusantara (especially the maritime parts), the East Indies, and later, during World War II, Southeast Asia.

Some of these loci were small and had a limited individual influence in the region as a whole. Victor Lieberman refers to semiautonomous, "self-replicating microcultures" that surrounded larger concentrations. These, he argues, helped ensure that attempts to impose a more homogeneous "standard imperial culture" would also normally face resistance and modification from multiple directions at once (2010:42). Especially in the oceanic areas most critical to the region's internal and external relations, the combination of archipelagic geography and mandalas, or "solar polities" as Lieberman calls them, helped to amplify and embed these patterns of political flux over time. In the transition to the early modern age of commerce, for example, Barbara and Leonard Andaya argue that "the nature of the Southeast Asian land and seascapes limited the growth of large empires, allowing for the proliferation of numerous small and largely independent polities" (2015:5) to continue.

Under certain conditions, however, a particular mandala or authority figure might also succeed in greatly expanding its influence. Wolters sees larger kingdoms such as the East Java–based Majapahit Empire (1293–1597) as examples of expanding and contracting mandala-type polities that attained a greater permanence, etching themselves more deeply into historical memory (1982:27–28). Such polities, with their storied abilities to negotiate difference, continued to be explicitly referenced, claimed, and appropriated into the spheres of authority that followed them, informing political structures and aesthetic conventions in direct and indirect ways. The strategic location of the region and its various mandalas along established and emergent trade routes also facilitated their growth as "active and dynamic participants" (Andaya and Andaya 2015:5) in the global spread of goods and technologies between the fifteenth and nineteenth centuries. For Wolters, modernizing Southeast Asian mandala societies would "expect the continuous flow of foreign merchandise but also . . . absorb the mondial perspectives" of successive global shifts like Buddhism, Arab-Muslim modernism, and subsequent transpacific waves of influence from Europe and then the U.S. (1982:47). As they strove to be constantly "up-to-date" and were unusually "accepting of new ideas," leaders and their mutable circles of power also showed a high degree of self-confidence and a "remarkable capacity to localize incoming influences" (Andaya and Andaya 2015:9).

As I show in various ways throughout this book, what emerges as most important in the context of these interlocking and mutating spheres of authority is the continuity of certain deeply embedded patterns that have retained a significant influence—in large part owing to the patterns' inherent flexibility and adaptability.

Observed over the course of decades or centuries, the work of such patterns out-shines the seemingly transformative adoption of one specific religion, technology, or idea from a particular place outside the region or even from a single, especially powerful sphere of authority like Majapahit or Ayutthaya—any single one of which is outweighed by the collective archetype of the mandala itself. For Elmo Gonzaga, "the looseness of the *mandala* configuration" has continued to be expressed in "the contemporary form of archipelagic nations such as the Philippines." As in the rapid entrance of new languages, literatures, or other technologies of communication in the region's past, the inevitable appearance of novel and potentially "incongruent media modalities" among its present array of political economic loci remains unlikely to "entail sudden rupture or irreversible alteration" (2016:96–97). Alongside and within the more fixed political borders of contemporary modern nations, as this suggests, authority in the region continues to be divided among multiple, mandala-like spheres. Some have existed for centuries and practice "old" forms of politics and statecraft; others, like the urban media hubs that dot and inscribe their own networks of aesthetics and exchange across the region, combine local narratives and modes of expression with regional and global ones via the most current technologies of representation.

The historical prominence of subnational regions like West or Northern Sumatra and the influence of smaller, yet wealthy and powerful polities like Brunei and Singapore exemplify this regional-systemic continuity. Malaysia's status as a "federal constitutional elective monarchy" is perhaps especially clear in the continuing influence of multiple political loci, each corresponding to "universal" ideas of authority associated with different historical times. The country's thirteen states, nine of which are based on historical Malay kingdoms and ruled by unelected royalty, share power with the democratically elected prime minister and other centralized government officials. All have their own written constitution and a high degree of autonomy on certain matters, especially regarding religion. On a rotating basis, each ruler also sits as the nation's centralized king or Yang di-Pertuan Agong, serving as a balance and at times corrective force vis-à-vis the elected prime minister and ruling coalition. As in similar arrangements in Thailand and Indonesia (which has a number of "special regions" ruled by local royalty or subject to *sharia* law, among other things), the results of such power-sharing with ostensibly anachronous "premodern" modes of authority can be surprising.

In my own experience living in Malaysia during the Covid 19 pandemic (2020–23), frequent movement-control orders were exploited by party officials to temporarily do away with elections, resulting in the prime minister being replaced twice in three years. This appeared to most observers as a way to put things "back in order" after an opposition victory in 2018 upset the dominance of a conservative, ethnonationalist coalition (Barisan Nasional) that had been in power since 1957. Just when things had begun to look quite bleak, the Agong stepped in and ordered a stop to the ongoing government declarations of emergency powers (which he had also previously approved), thereby severely reducing the shadowy, backroom political dealings that had characterized much of the pandemic in Malaysia. The result was the restoration of democracy, at least such as it had been during pre-Covid times. The potential for a much broader political crisis was averted and Anwar Ibrahim—an opposition candidate who, over a lengthy career, had been consistently blocked from the prime minister's seat and even jailed by opponents—was elected. Malaysia, like most other nations, remains rife with various problems. Yet this episode of political reality-drama brought into stark relief the ways in which decisions, despite the outward image of centralized and unified ethnic Malay authority, are in fact made via a tangled interplay of multiple spheres and "centers" of power operating within it. This process can at times lead to unexpected outcomes in national-level politics, while consistently offering spaces for varied interests and practices that operate beneath the homogeneous surface of official images and narratives.

In the past, as well, "precisely because the same texts and symbols meant different things to different people, negotiation and exchange" (Lieberman 2010:40)—in effect communication and various modes and technologies thereof—were strengthened and intensified by constant efforts to achieve consensus. As Wolters argues, high levels of regional communicativity and interactivity shaped the nature of authority. A regional king, queen, or "man of prowess," dependent on negotiation with various centers and peripheries was "not an autocrat; he was a mediator" (1982:18)—one with heightened sensitivity to information and changes happening along borders and arriving via waterways both near and far. For better and at times for worse, modern nationalist leaders have shown a similar level of self-assurance and ability to communicate with and mediate between multiple local and foreign entities at once. Indonesian president Soekarno's (r. 1945–66) famed skill at playing the Eastern and Western poles of the Cold War off each other while negotiating with myriad other, nonaligned points between is one example. As detailed in chapter 4, in the later years of Soekarno's rule and in successors like Soeharto or the Filipino dictator Ferdinand Marcos, however, these qualities can also be seen to ossify and fade. The result is the emergence of "strong men" who defy expectations and therefore are more likely to face power struggles, regular mass public demonstrations, and simultaneous attacks from urban centers and far-off peripheries with military force and other violent means.

For the Andayas, the enduring necessity for leaders to show a certain openness and flexibility was influenced not only by geographic factors per se but by the fickle, frequently deadly, behavior of nature in the region—a force that time and again carries massive political, economic, and social ramifications. Often further amplified by global patterns of climate change, this dynamic has continued into the modern present. Numerous active volcanoes dot the region's stormy seas; along with other perils like earthquakes and constant storms, these have impressed a deep, transhistorical respect for the particular features of Southeast

Asian *tanah air* on most peoples in the region. This has also produced strong, enduring modes of engagement with nature, including spiritual communion, in ways that influenced the reception and adaptation of various world religions. Reliance on the environment and natural resources, the Andayas argue, also "fostered a deep respect for the protective influences of the ancestors, which was reflected in indigenous cosmologies and incorporated into local understandings of incoming religious teachings" (2015:4–5). Considering the importance of spiritual and philosophical prowess for leaders, these beliefs and practices were then applied to associated political, economic, and social shifts and modes of exchange. In many cases, religious institutions or figures acquired a mandala status and influence that rivaled that of kings.

An example of how the regional entanglements of nature and geography with spirituality, communication, and politics have continued to be expressed in the era of nations is taken up in chapter 5, where I examine ongoing cinematic manifestations of the mythical Javanese spirit queen of the South Sea, Kanjeng Ratu Kidul. Often linked by scholars to older Hindu, Buddhist, and animist figures, she emerged most forcefully in the legends and royal historiographies of sixteenth-century Java. According to those narratives, in the late 1500s, the queen entered into an alliance with a prince who had high aspirations to establish a new sphere of influence with himself at its center. With the support of spirit armies and the forces of nature, over which she holds sway, the prince prevailed, launching a kingdom, now known as the Mataram Dynasty, that has lasted until the present. In the form of the Yogyakarta sultanate, the dynasty was a key participant in the nationalist movement and war for independence against Dutch rule (1945–49) and still holds political power over a large and influential "special region" in Java. In exchange for the mystical/religious support believed to have enabled this especially lengthy and influential mandalahood, the rebellious prince-turned-king and all his future heirs would enter into a spiritual "marriage" with the queen. An assortment of offerings continues to be brought once a year, with much ceremonial pomp, to a nearby gateway of her underwater realm, on the beach at Parangkusumo just south of Yogyakarta.

This persistent relationship between human authority figures, spirits, and nature points to another enduring aspect of how authority is understood and practiced in Southeast Asia, one that I take up in chapters 3, 4, and 5. The positioning of the queen, together with the lineage of kings and sultans spiritually pledged to her in perpetuity, expresses a basic symbolic pattern in which male and female signifiers or representatives are positioned to work, think, and act together. Each is associated with distinct qualities of roughly equal value that can at times be appropriated or deployed by either sex (and various genders). Mandalas and their structural-political descendants are typically constituted by amalgamations of differing religious, political, and historical aspects collectively populating a "multicentric landscape of 'universal' sovereigns'" (Wolters 1982:50) who maintain constant conversations with various borders and peripheries. Following from this, the modern, generally Western, logic of a single basic reference or point of authority—whether masculine-phallic, epistemological, political, spiritual, or otherwise—can only loosely and problematically be applied. In this context, we might imagine Vatsyayan's regional aesthetic theory based on showing "a hierarchy of realities" using "the principle of suggestion through abstraction" (1971:26) holding sway. As I show throughout the book, various recent attempts at deploying a more singular masculine or "realist" perspective have encountered reflexive, systemic forms of resistance, even while in some cases succeeding in creating the appearance of universal, patriarchal rule.

As I argue in chapter 3, one of the factors that makes this the case is the continuity of traditions of matrifocality across the region. I contend that popular films and other media (along with ritual, spiritual, and other practices) help to reembed these traditions, in appropriately modified forms, in the changing circumstances of modern nationhood. Women's historical roles as controllers of household finances and as equal recipients of inheritance (and as subject to bride prices rather than dowries that elsewhere in Asia make female children a financial burden on families) have long facilitated their mobility outside the home. What Wolters calls the "relative unimportance of [genetic] lineage" (1982:18) throughout the region also dilutes or complicates the growth of customs like the centering of patrilineage and passing down of the "Name of the Father" in much of the West. Especially in middle and lower classes, Southeast Asian women are commonly positioned as partners and breadwinners working alongside, or at times in place of, male family members. While such power is often household-based, the mobility afforded by women's key economic roles, including buying and selling in local markets and beyond, radiates influence outside the home and into the social and inevitably political lives of communities and at times of regencies and states. Reading across studies of Southeast Asia, repeating patterns of women's agency in local societies frequently come to the fore in terms of what defines Southeast Asia as a region with certain basic commonalities.[5] In relation to this, in chapters 4, 5, and 6, I discuss how images of strong women in the films of the 1950s and 1960s contrast with the statistical dominance of men behind the camera at the time. But I contend that the transfer of historically embedded ideas of gender and power from traditional arts to commercial stages and onto regional screens prepared the way for the early entrance of a few influential female directors, writers, and producers. This development was followed by a far greater influx of gender diversity in the last three decades of filmmaking in Southeast Asia, in many cases rivaling or even exceeding what is found in the West.

Another regional commonality that I position as a key influence on modern patterns of representation is the understanding and expression of history. As I have mentioned, Southeast Asia's proto- and early states were made up of varied collections of conventions, religions, and styles of political authority that emerged in, and are associated with, distinct time periods. Older techniques and strategies were combined with newer ones such that the newer ones were "fractured and restated and therefore drained of their original significance" (Wolters 1982:55). Yet at the same time, they often still bore a recognizable connection to something originating outside the region. The effect of these typical mixtures of divergent styles, philosophies of statecraft, and times produces a complicated picture of regional development, especially in how history is understood and narrated by Southeast Asian societies. This has in turn spawned confusion and speculation among early scholars of Southeast Asia, like historian C. C. Berg, who worked to "make [the] . . . continuity clear" in what he termed "queer" local modes of historiography, with their penchant for treating past and present events as simultaneous and constructing "imaginary genealogies" that were recorded as fact (1955:126–27, 123).[6]

The diverse layers of regional and world history combined in narratives produced by regional societies often gave the impression of Southeast Asians living in a present made up of multiple eras at once. Similar to the way film technologies are "hauled backward," it appeared to scholars like Berg that cultures and polities were also simultaneously moving backward and forward through time. Benedict Anderson (1983) and others have argued that while fluctuating ideas of time, space, and power held sway for centuries among polities based on islands like Java, the rise of Western-style nationalism in Southeast Asia in the late nineteenth and early twentieth centuries resulted in a formative epistemic break—one that altered how regional communities imagined themselves developing over time. The result, for Anderson, was a sense of consistent chronological progression in which time became "homogeneous," expressed along the regular intervals of modern calendars and the pages of daily and weekly newspapers.

Building on archipelagic and mandala-based perspectives, this book offers a somewhat different view of the expression and collective imagination of history and time during the years of anticolonial movements and rapid national development. On one hand, audiences for the periodicals and novels that Anderson and others analyze were mainly literate elite minorities. On the other hand, the regionally produced films that I examine (and the touring, supranational vernacular theaters that I position as a key influence on them) catered to lower-class viewers. While their wealthier counterparts preferred the clear chronological representations of time in Hollywood and European screen-fare, these far larger, poorer, and generally less-educated audiences delighted in a different view of modernity: images that revealed the national present filled with legends and conventions of the past, even as it was shot through with exciting, emergent technologies, ideas, and aesthetics from across the Pacific and elsewhere.

This book builds on this contemporary understanding of region, connecting it to what Vatsyayan positions as a longer, shared history of political, social, religious, and aesthetic multiplicity (1971:22). I investigate how the emergence of modern mass media in Southeast Asia functioned to challenge, rather than bolster, the violent and arbitrary imposition of national borders in the periods during and after decolonization (or in some cases, the gradual reduction of Cold War–level imperial engagement with Western powers). Doing so has required close, long-term study of a sprawling array of audiovisual and other texts and contexts, searching them for fragments and traces of diverse and often radically distinct places and times. This process has in turn called for an open and variable set of methodologies. My years of research in Indonesia (2008–15) that provided the original basis for this book combined formal analysis, language study, archival work, and ethnographic observation and participation with considerable doses of theory, historiography, and literature. In expanding my scope to include as many other parts of the region as possible, the resulting chapters have been organized by combining particular topics, films, narratives, and historical periods around a theme. To best address these topics and themes, the methods that inform each chapter are mixed and at times differ from one chapter to the next. While allowing these constructive inconsistencies to determine important parts of the book's structure, I have also attempted to make the flow of information across the chapters as clear and engaging as possible. At the same time, I have endeavored to avoid reliance on a singular perspective, the imposition of a homogeneous chronology, or other similar conventions that might lead to a reductive picture of this complex, and at times convoluted, milieu.

As I show, the conditions that linked emergent regional cinemas to traditions of archipelagic representation retained a deep resonance throughout the twentieth century. I argue that current archipelagic attitudes and styles have been further amplified by global shifts and splits associated with the rise of digital media in the twenty-first century. Although I attempt to identify patterns that are valid throughout much of the region, I do not claim that these are absolute or universal in the context of Southeast Asia. Regional cinemas share numerous conventions, qualities, and approaches, but as one would expect, these do not constitute an "iron cage" that restrains filmmakers as if by force; numerous examples of films that do things differently can be found. It is also beyond the scope of this book to look in detail at the cinemas of every country in Southeast Asia. I have therefore focused mainly on Indonesia, Malaysia, Singapore, Thailand, and the Philippines. I hope that others will be inspired to expand on this study with further comparisons outside the regional locales that it covers.

CHAPTER BREAKDOWN

Chapter 1

Chapter 1 drops readers into Southeast Asia of the 1950s—a key formative period for much of the region's national cinemas—via a close analysis of the 1957 Indonesian film *Tiga Buronan* (*Three Fugitives*, dir. Nya Abbas Akup). The film's seemingly compelled, yet ultimately playful, repetition of global and local genres and tropes is underscored by its ironic inclusion of *latah*, a socioneurological condition in which startled victims involuntarily repeat the words or movements of their provokers. Following James Siegel's (1986) analysis of latah as a layered and purposely disruptive response to imposed hierarchy, I show that Akup's film, like similar efforts from Malaya and Thailand, addresses the issue of local, regional, and global aesthetic copying with a patently obvious form of "bad" imitation. The effect is precisely like a jerky, impulsive cinematic "syndrome" that afflicts popular films across the entire region. The conscious application of this antinaturalist style, I argue, defines a regionally specific set of basic, "archipelagic" cinematic approaches. This seemingly compulsive, nervous style is belied by the relatively self-possessed attitude of filmmakers who deploy it to engage the myriad challenges and "shocks" of nationalization and globalization. The result, as I highlight throughout the book, is an unconventional narrative of development that sets Southeast Asia cinemas, and their respective nations, apart from much of the rest of the Global South.

Chapter 2

In chapter 2, I juxtapose the formative regional influence of vernacular theaters like Malayan *bangsawan* and Javanese *opera stambul* with Miriam Hansen's (1999, 2000, 2012) view of classical Hollywood cinema as a widely circulating "vernacular modernism" on a global scale. For Hansen, the term *vernacular* signals the role and perception of Hollywood as a "low" and accessible aesthetics of modernity that allowed its products a broader influence than those of more exclusive, high-modernist movements. Yet in Southeast Asia, Hollywood was generally positioned and priced at a more elevated level, in the realm of educated urban elites. The dynamic and cosmopolitan but "low" and accessible sphere of vernacular theaters hence exerted a far greater modernizing influence on Southeast Asian publics. This, I argue, produced the conditions of possibility for the emergence of regional cinemas around established aesthetic and economic circuits that were *separated a priori* from the elite "Class A" venues where Hollywood and European fare dominated.

Chapter 3

Comparing conceptions of nationalism to decentered ideas of gender and power in Indonesia, Malaysia, and the Philippines, I show how regional cineastes came to define a key archipelagic pattern in Southeast Asian films: a "matrifocal gaze" positioning women as prominent agents and actors onscreen in ways that distort and displace the "universal" centrality of men elsewhere. Building on studies of women's historically strong economic and social roles in the region, I argue that films use camera angles, editing, and mise-en-scène to visualize the continuity of these roles in the modern spaces of developing nations. I highlight the seemingly paradoxical, "undecided" identities of young women who position themselves between home- and family-based traditions of feminine influence and the social and political shifts shaping emergent public spheres. As I demonstrate, the formal elevation of such characters over more typically elite, modernist men mirrors, yet often inverts, offscreen debates over "proper" modes of development according to Western patriarchal paradigms. The role of gender in the formulation of nationalist identities, I suggest, also led to some of the starkest differences among the region's national cinemas, in some cases leading to decades of cinematic "blindness" with little or no film production. I compare these patterns with the negative fates attached to more visibly progressive "modern girls" in Hollywood and East Asian cinemas and with venerated, but mainly passive, women in popular Hindi social films around the same time. In doing so, I return to the histories of vernacular modernist aesthetics that I argue underpin the convergence of class, gender, and cinematic style in regionally specific ways.

Chapter 4

Chapter 4 focuses on the crucial shifts beginning in 1965, when three of the region's most notorious, anticommunist strongmen—Soeharto, Lee Kuan Yew, and Ferdinand Marcos—"coincidentally" came to power at the outset of the American war in Vietnam and two years after the rise of right-wing military dictator Thanom Kittikachorn in Thailand. Through close, comparative readings of films of the 1970s and early 1980s, I build on the previous chapter's formulation of a matrifocal gaze, focusing on the fate of this trope in radically shifted political circumstances. I show how expanded censorship and government oversight steered emergent critical impulses into indirectly politicized, thickly gendered spaces of urban poverty and prostitution. In numerous Indonesian, Thai, and Filipino films, "fallen" women, separated by political or economic circumstances from their traditional bases of power, emerge as the most effective populist vehicles—and melodramatic veils—for critiques of status quos across the region. The result, I argue, is akin to a particular regional variant of what Ernesto Laclau (2005) calls a "grey area of contamination," commodification, and ethical complexity that also constitutes "the very essence of the political." In this case, the films I analyze contribute to a pervasive atmosphere of informal authority and dissent that surrounds and works to diffuse the exclusively masculine agency promoted by the region's rising patriarchal-developmentalist states.

Chapter 5

Chapter 5 deepens the previous analysis of gender and power, focusing on the feminine ghosts and spirits at center stage in the region-wide phenomenon of supernatural or "mystical horror" films running from the mid-twentieth century to the present. I argue that this genre's unruly alliance of market forces and archipelagic undercurrents offers a closer look at the structural-historical undergarments of the previous chapter's cinematic prostitutes. As I show, the still human, but suprapatriarchal, powers of chapter 4's fallen women are eerily similar to, if more limited than, the superhuman abilities of a regional pantheon of female spirits. This includes the Malaysian *pontianak*, the Thai *phi mae maai*, the Filipino *manananggal*, and the aforementioned Ratu Kidul, the goddess-like Javanese queen of the South Sea. My analysis interweaves ethnographic observations of ongoing rituals in Java with regional histories of feminine spiritual authority and close readings of mystical-horror films and their narrative and sociopolitical sources. Connecting the dots, I position the dynamically gendered supernatural worlds on Southeast Asian screens as emanations of a contested yet enduring pluralist symbolic order—a regional conception of authority that returns to challenge the ever-more vigorous imposition and exploitation of patriarchy in the 1980s and 1990s. The potential for agency, I argue, is divided among dual masculine and feminine basic signifiers, the powers of which are often combined in, or alternated between, distinct genders and sexes.

Chapter 6

Following the euphoric tides that swept away regional dictators from the late 1980s to the early 2000s, my concluding chapter examines the triadic entrance of cinematic new waves, representative governments, and streaming digital media in much of Southeast Asia. Assessing these shifts in historical context, I begin to account for the continuities of certain established patterns that have emerged alongside triumphal departures. Young upstarts in Bangkok, for example, led the way to unprecedented international acclaim through a series of prescient cinematic returns. Even as the success of these efforts dashed hopes for slick, Hollywood-esque "upgrades" to local form and style, I show that industry paradigms were radically shifted in another way: with cheaper digital equipment; loosened restrictions on production; and money from festivals, foundations, and private investors, many aspiring filmmakers were even better positioned than earlier generations to resist the national gravitational pulls of Jakarta, Bangkok, or Manila.

Following the overall focus on temporal and formal "backward"-ness and intermediality, I conclude the book by examining the return and expansion of archipelagic fragmentation via a steep rise in high-budget, popular, and politically charged horror films throughout the region after 2015. These works, I argue, use older, established approaches and spirit characters to engage with new problems, especially those posed by the vast regional expansion of neoliberal corporate influence. In the face of what is elsewhere understood as a postmodern crisis of affect, I propose that regional filmmakers forge new emotional connections and strategies by reclaiming the archipelagic features and plural symbolic structures of the region's past.

BEYOND ACADEMIA

Coming from and starting a bicultural family, living in Sweden during formative moments of my childhood, living in Russia during one of the most important political transitions of the twentieth century, and working in Indonesia and Malaysia over the last two decades have indelibly impressed on me the importance of paying attention to, and learning to see the world through, unfamiliar perspectives. My long, parallel career as a media producer has been profoundly informed by these insights and has facilitated my engagement with groups and audiences far outside the borders of academia—borders I have always perceived as porous or illusionary.

My creative work in closest conversation with this book is the hybrid ethnofiction *Banyak Ayam Banyak Rejeki* (*Many Chickens Lots of Luck*, 2021),[7] which I codirected and produced with Indonesian scholar-practitioner Dr. Koes Yuliadi (Indonesian Institute of Arts, Yogyakarta). Set in central Java and produced in parallel with my doctoral studies, the film became an opportunity to experiment with and apply the basic archipelagic features and techniques that I was uncovering in my research. Following my research, the film engages contemporary debates about gender politics, deploying an exuberant and absurd, yet carefully gauged, satire of the increasing practice and promotion of polygamy in Java and elsewhere in the archipelago. Similar to the book, but in a different mode, the film deploys regional cinematic themes and approaches of the 1950s to the 1970s. It reflects how current shifts in media technology can be exploited to amplify enduring, pluralist structures of authority, disturbing continual attempts to institute narrow or simplistic patriarchal visions. In both festival-based and academic discussions and screenings, the film offers a platform to present my scholarly ideas in different ways and to audiences who are less familiar with film studies or other academic discourses.

On a final and more personal note, my immersion in skateboard media, as young fan and then professional filmmaker, is another, perhaps less-obvious, source of connection to my current scholarly work. My formative immersion as a teenager in the fragmented presentation and mocking imitation of mainstream media that are classic features of skateboard aesthetics has come to play an unexpected role in my career as a scholar. It was especially crucial in recognizing and decoding the deeply political aspects of similar populist tactics used by Southeast Asian filmmakers engaging waves of globalization and nationalization in the 1950s and 1960s. My earlier documentary on the American pornography industry, *Rated X: A Journey through Porn* (2000) also broadened and challenged my understandings of gender and power in ways that profoundly informed this book. Engaging in discussions with and absorbing the life experiences and perspectives of sex workers in Los Angeles helped me to perceive and understand how agency can be embedded outside of traditional patriarchal or other official spheres in a context as different as Southeast Asia.

1

"Culture Bound" Aesthetics and Archipelagic Form

TANAH AIR AND CINEMATIC PATCHWORKS

Affixed to the walls of a house in Bandung, West Java, in the early postindependence years of 1950s Indonesia are scraps of an exotic modernity. Pieces of photographs and advertisements from *Life* magazine have been carefully selected, cut, and pasted in strategic locations throughout the house, while others are archived in thick scrapbooks. The images are classic 1950s Americana: blond women in bathing suits; fair-skinned babies; large, fuel-guzzling cars; shining pots and pans; and high-heeled shoes, among other treasures. Their local curator, Laila (Dhalia), a lower-class Javanese woman in her late twenties (fig. 1), has most likely never touched or seen such objects up close. Yet she seems drawn to the images, which she claims are "needed." Her pimp, an ex-revolutionary soldier named Puja (Bambang Hermanto), mocks her, ordering her to focus instead on entertaining the men who come to the house to gamble. But whenever she has a free moment, Laila returns to her task of cutting and pasting.

The house, one of the main locations for the 1954 Indonesian film *Lewat Djam Malam* (*After the Curfew*, dir. Usmar Ismail), conveys a typical mixture of old and new. Its foundations and the lower half of its walls are cement, while its upper walls consist of *gedhek*, a material of woven bamboo that facilitates Laila's compulsive pinning. Chairs and tables are of loosely contemporary style, made with then-abundant hardwood, and the overall layout is modern, indicating, among other things, the influence of Dutch colonial designers. Yet traditional printed fabrics take the place of most doors, their zigzagging patterns disrupting the otherwise squared logic of the interior. The Western pinup images stand out in a similar way, their uneven shapes and alien content contrasting with the local regularity of

FIGURE 1. The actress Dhalia as Laila in *Lewat Djam Malam*,
positioned in front of images she has clipped from *Life* magazine and
pinned to the woven bamboo sections of the wall in the house where
she works as a prostitute. Courtesy of KAFEIN.

the *gedhek*'s gridding. The contrast is heightened by various other wall hangings,
such as a hand-drawn *batik* image featuring expressionistically rendered horses. In
the next room, a realistic painting appears at first to depict cowboys riding into the
sunset of the American West—perhaps a reference to director Ismail's completion
of a yearlong cinema program at the University of California, Los Angeles, in 1953,
the previous year.[1] On closer inspection, however, the horses are camels, the image
typical of souvenirs brought back from an Islamic pilgrimage to Mecca. The interior of the house as a whole conveys a subtly impish humor that appears aimed at
preempting expectations of the dominance of foreign imports or of their supposed
dilution or sullying of local patterns and configurations.

Laila's clippings are only the latest addition to what is already a dense assortment of objects and styles, offering attentive viewers a trip through a collection of
local, regional, and transnational forms that speak of ongoing encounters between
disparate aesthetic, economic, and political systems. What can the form and patterning of these images and the film in which they are arranged be understood to
offer the study of cinema and other mass media as transnational phenomena that
are also local and, in this case, regional? In my reading, Laila's impulse to clip
and embed the imported American pictures within a veritable archive of traces of
other engagements with foreign image-regimes conveys a certain cool-headedness
around such meetings. The sense of amazement, terror, or "shock" conventionally
associated with the global spread of Western modernity via mass media appears

attenuated in this case. In the hands of an ostensibly lowly prostitute, these new and alien figures from across the Pacific Ocean are reflexively, almost compulsively, subjected to a process of selection and modification and then positioned within a preexisting patchwork that gives the impression of "expecting" them. Even as they reveal a certain patterning of desire, the woman's impulses unlock a playful mode of subversion that rechannels the established power of its objects.[2]

At the same time, the patchworks produced by the clipping imbue the film's modern imagery with the importance of other, older media and the histories attached to them. On one level, the film's collages mitigate the radical nature of the changes under way in postindependence Bandung and elsewhere in the newly minted nation. Indonesia's independence was declared in 1945 but only fully realized in 1949 after four years of armed struggle against Dutch colonizers. As the curfew in the title of *Lewat Djam Malam* suggests, by the early 1950s, things were still far from settled.[3] While acknowledging the triumph against colonialism, the film's fragmented images and dark, tragic narrative highlight fissures already appearing in the ideals on which Indonesia had only just been founded. Most of the male characters in *Lewat Djam Malam* seem to be in the process of sinking through these elongating cracks. Laila, too, as her pimp repeatedly points out, is a "fallen" woman. Yet her impulse to engage with the processes she, the nation, and much of the region are swept up in imbues her with an allegorical glimmer. It is Laila, and not the former freedom fighters around her, who provides a sliver of hope in an otherwise remarkably dismal view of the aftermath of revolution.

Taken together, *Lewat Djam Malam*'s form, narrative, and mise-en-scène express a subtle preference for the play of multiple perspectives, spaces, and times over the "classical" illusion of a continuous, all-encompassing view. In this sense, although it catered to an audience that was largely illiterate at the time, a film like *Lewat Djam Malam* can be seen as engaging in the kind of archipelagic imaginary that Brian Bernards argues Southeast Asian novelists "deploy to rethink colonial and national paradigms that contrive their cultural genealogies" (2015:13–14). I position this aesthetic attitude as an expression, in a different yet related media, of the basic archipelagic approach to cinema that I argue is a common feature of motion pictures and other mass media produced in Southeast Asia from the early to mid-twentieth century on. As an Indonesian film set in Bandung and written and directed by two West Sumatran intellectuals working in the capital, Jakarta, *Lewat Djam Malam* enunciates another important feature of archipelagic aesthetics: nationality that is not taken or presented as the source of a homogeneous outlook but is marked and specifically inflected by numerous subnational, regional, global, and, especially in the case of cinema and print media like *Life* magazine, transpacific points of influence. As shown by many other regional films, such points do not easily or necessarily align themselves with the imposed, hegemonic view of a single "center" or point of reference.

In this vein, while the island of Java on which *Lewat Djam Malam* is filmed and set is of vital importance to my study, it is positioned as one among numerous sources of the archipelagic perspective that I trace across the region. While Java too often plays the role of an imposed political, economic, and cultural locus in Indonesia, at the same time, it has always been subject to internal incoherence, atomized into several distinct and often conflicting regions, like a miniature archipelago in itself. It is also filled with influential migrants like Usmar Ismail and Asrul Sani, Lewat Djam Malam's screenwriter, (as well as more far-flung migrants like me), who bring with them the habits, languages, and outlooks of other Islands or other countries entirely.

Taken together, the disparate features, strategies, and interests that make up an archipelago, a region, or a single island can be seen to reflect Southeast Asian (and historically Malay) approaches to representation that are, in their lauding of multiplicity, necessarily not uniform. Even so, I show that by reading across regional texts, media, and subcenters of production, it is possible to detect an underlying set of representational traits and techniques forged by common historical experiences and processes. Within these processes, geography is an undeniable if paradoxical force that has shaped "unities" in local and regional outlooks through the continual imposition of radical fragmentation and fluidity. Outside of a few significant landmasses, Southeast Asia is a region of *tanah air* (Malay for "land-water"), consisting of thousands upon thousands of distinct islands, languages, and cultural groups for whom the accident of physical proximity has led to a reality in which the potential for encounters with strange or foreign entities is constant.

What is shared in the region is thus the experience of incessant change and the need to engage with—and, if possible, make use of—the ever-present potential for transformation brought by continual exposure to novelties from near and far. Perhaps not surprisingly, this need has at times led to the entanglement of creative pursuits with impulses or even compulsions to act, react, or manipulate in particular ways, as in *Lewat Djam Malam*'s scene of clippings above. In this chapter and others, I highlight different aspects of the work of this drive to engage and play with the constant arrival, and at times imposition, of foreignness and difference. I also focus on the aesthetic innovations and particular conventions such politically loaded play has helped to foster over time. These conventions, I argue, produce a loose but palpable concurrence of regional approaches to communication and representation. What I term Southeast Asia's archipelagic cinemas hence reflect a reality in which collective perceptions, and cinematic and other mass-media representations, rarely settle into a homogeneous view.

In light of this state of affairs, I position European and transpacific imperialism and colonialism in the region as an important but irregular and unpredictable influence—one that has undeniably changed the course of development throughout Southeast Asia in distinct and indelible ways but that can also be seen as consistent with the shifting nature of historical experience more broadly. In the study of mass media, my analysis departs from conventional understandings of imperialism and colonialism, the entrance of motion picture technologies, and the importation and exhibition of classical Hollywood films as the primal, formative "shocks" that triggered the emergence of regional modernities or national cinemas. Those who take for granted that "most national cinema producers have to operate in terms of an agenda set by Hollywood" have also remarked that in comparison to almost anywhere else, South and Southeast Asian cinemas "significantly maintain their own terrain" (Crofts 1993:50).

As I established in my prologue, particularly in the case of Southeast Asian cinemas, such broad studies are inevitably light on the details of how and why this occurs and what the result of such a rare ability to overlook or disregard American cinema might be. As I show in this chapter and in chapter 2, Hollywood is not so much ignored by regional filmmakers as knowingly decoupled from the exalted, economically dominant (and therefore often singularly demonized) status it enjoys elsewhere. For mainstream Southeast Asian audiences, films from the U.S. are generally less important than other imports, especially those from elsewhere in the region. This is not to say, however, that American cinematic influence or products are absent. In the aftermath of independence, mass media in many ways did embrace the inevitability of modern nations (including national cinemas and Hollywood imports) as an enduring legacy of colonial mapping and geopolitical reorganization according to Western patterns. But at the same time, filmmakers and other artists reflexively cracked and denaturalized the form and content of films, nations, and the collective identities formed between them. Many of Southeast Asia's emergent countries and their cinemas were hence embedded into the shifting, archipelagic connections and divisions that underpin regional experience. While the broader realities of Indonesian or Thai or Philippine cinemas inevitably remain visible as such, I contend that each is premised on addressing the nation as a construct—at times fake—best understood in terms of the collision and intersection of local, regional, and transnational planes that serve as formative patchworks to which Southeast Asian filmmakers continually return. As we will see, references to Hollywood are often an ingredient in such typical aesthetic mixtures but rarely, if ever, a dominant one.

The result is a series of aesthetic eddies that, while not immune to Americanisms, perceptibly alter the direction and intensity of the transnational and transpacific media flows that carry them around the world. Doing so sends familiar genres, technologies, and formal flourishes spinning off course, while pulling expansive theories of global cinematic development beyond their effective depth. As regional cineastes struggled to survive in challenging conditions while simultaneously providing meaningful commentary on the experience of modernization, their conventionally "idiosyncratic" works began to reveal not a collective ignorance but a shared awareness of and approach to a new medium. Myriad variations and differences from the typically archipelagic approaches I identify here have of course also arisen, including attempts to recreate a Hollywoodian approach. But for reasons to be elaborated below, such efforts constitute a minority. From an outside perspective, and at times even a local one, Southeast Asian cinemas can take on the appearance of having been stricken by a regionally bound "syndrome"—one that can appear lacking to some or "wrong" in its contravention of mainstream global patterns. As I will show, however, this ostensible affliction offers its own often enjoyably unruly brand of creative expression.

THE AFFLICTED APPARATUS

The idea of Southeast Asian cinemas as afflicted by a syndrome is borne out well by an early scene in the 1957 comedy-action-satire *Tiga Buronan* (*The Three Fugitives*), the third film and first major hit for director Nya Abbas Akup, an East Javanese of Sumatran parentage who would later be called the "father of Indonesian comedy."[4] A young man named Maman has just returned to a small West Javanese village after a decade of seeking his fortune and fighting in the war of independence from the Dutch (1945–49). Like *Lewat Djam Malam, Tiga Buronan* focuses on the aftermath of revolution, but it does so in a rural setting and with a deceptively light-hearted air. Entering his childhood home, Maman spies an elderly auntie squatting in front of a fire with her back to him. As if struck by a sudden impulse, instead of calling out a greeting, he sneaks up and taps the old woman from behind, startling her. This produces a reaction that viewers outside of Southeast Asia may find strange. Turning around to face Maman in an agitated state, the woman blurts out a meaningless string of curses ("*mati mati mati!*" [die die die]) and then appears helpless to do anything but mimic the words and gestures of her nephew. Her complete surprise overrides any ability she may have to formulate a more coherent response (fig. 2). As she begins to come to her senses, it also becomes clear that the woman no longer recognizes Maman. The curses, abetted by aggressive swipes of a wooden spoon, begin to suggest acts aimed at fending off an alien intruder.

What has in fact occurred is neither a random anomaly nor a simple instance of self-defense. The auntie's reaction would be familiar to most local and regional viewers as *latah*, a pattern of behavior mainly associated with the rural lower classes. Often, as in the scene described above, it is purposely triggered as a source of cheap entertainment for those in the vicinity of the victim. In urban upper-class contexts, people often attempt to suppress latah's potentially embarrassing outbursts. In medical and anthropological literature, *latah* is defined as a hyperstartle response that, as Akup's scene shows, consists of a short, involuntary burst of cursing or obscene gestures. This is often combined with uncontrolled mimicry of the words or movements of those surrounding the person in whom latah has been triggered. Many researchers refer to latah as a "culture bound syndrome"—a pattern of behavior that occurs only in a certain area, in this case in Southeast Asia.[5]

In the context of *Tiga Buronan*, the early entrance of latah, with its connotations of lowbrow village humor, serves as a comedic signifier for the film's rural locale.

FIGURE 2. As Maman (Bambang Irawan), the film's erstwhile hero, returns home after the revolution, writer-director Akup introduces the theme and trope of "culture bound" repetition, here in the form of *latah*. The uncontrolled reaction Maman provokes in his aunt at first appears to represent the epitome of rural (and, until recently, colonized) backwardness. Later in the film, however, it takes on the appearance of a prescient, if involuntary, "reading," signaling an upcoming threat. As viewers are gradually given to understand, Maman, the former country boy, is now in fact a military spy whose arrival will actualize a bloody conflict that has been brewing since long before independence from the Dutch.

Akup, however, rarely deploys jokes in a simple or cheap manner and generally uses physical comedy or stereotypes as an entrance to something more complex. Here, the latah scene sets the tone for a weightier theme running through much of the film: an escalating series of surprise entrances and attacks that implicate the rural in the national, the regional, and the geopolitical (and vice versa), suggesting rural isolation to be a deceptive ruse. Attempts to restore calm and order after each disruption are, as in the auntie's case, beset by pauses, stutters, and seeming compulsions. These occur as characters, and at times the film itself, encounter a variety of foreign "intruders." This includes not only villains but also incongruous cinematic conventions that are inserted into scenes, linguistic neologisms that are suddenly blurted out by characters, or other seemingly incompatible elements imposed on the narrative context.

In the crowded, often chaotic story-world that results, latah is positioned as both a particular, local habit and an allegory for a problem faced by myriad "developing" locales. It signals the ever-present threat of losing control and defaulting to base imitation when facing a new or alien presence, whether in the form of persons, ideas, or images. In this sense, Akup's deployment of latah in a film is perhaps less idiosyncratic than it seems. As I have indicated, the term, and the habit it depicts, are well known throughout the region (although it has different names in Thailand and the Philippines), and latah is in fact frequently used as a metaphor outside of the rural or lowly contexts where it is mainly thought to occur. It has been applied by Jakartan film critics in *Tempo*, a national news magazine, for example, to mock what was seen as a knee-jerk tendency among Indonesian filmmakers to mimic

FIGURE 3. Two stills from the early scene in *Tiga Buronan* that momentarily appears to identify the film as a musical.

popular local and regional trends (*Tempo* 1974:45).[6] In a related way, the use of latah in *Tiga Buronan* reflects ironically on challenges shared by Southeast Asian and other Global South filmmakers who face a constant flow of allegedly higher quality transnational products; this includes Hollywood imports, although here, as we will see, the filmic competitors of greatest concern do not necessarily come from the West.

Appropriate to its various metaphorical applications, "lowly" latah is also a more complex phenomenon than it might at first appear. As the auntie's outburst begins to demonstrate, despite the inevitable ridicule latah's victims are subjected to, its furious mimicry can imbue it with the sense of a strong and potentially subversive reaction. For Hildred Geertz, latah's "compulsive obedience of commands" in fact constitutes "acts which are at base unconscious parodies of the social relationship between inferior and superior" (1968:99). The *Encyclopedia of Multicultural Psychology* similarly calls latah "a mechanism by which lower-status individuals can demonstrate socially inappropriate behavior in a culturally acceptable manner" (Jackson 2006:140). In the case of *Tiga Buronan*, once latah is introduced into the film's narrative world, its signature blend of compulsive mimicry and passive-cum-active aggression quickly spreads, infecting characters and even seeming to embed itself in the film at the level of form and style—especially in Akup's deployment of references to globally popular genres and tropes.

Almost immediately following the initial latah scene, for example, we are treated to a more overtly pleasant and, for those from outside the region, likely more familiar introduction to life in an agrarian village in Southeast Asia. Contrasting with a previous scene announcing the impending arrival of a murderous gang of fugitives, a gleaming paddy-full of conical-hatted rice farmers spontaneously break into a song-and-dance routine about the joys of rural life (fig. 3). At first, the abrupt stylistic and tonal shift appears to transport onscreen villagers and viewers alike to an ideal transnational intersection where the globe-trotting paths of Fred Astaire, prancing Soviet collective farmers, and their equally exuberant Indian (and in fact Malayan)[7] counterparts have collided, as if discovering a mutually intelligible, "traditional" modernity.

From one angle, the scene's broad familiarity could be read as Akup's own latah-like reaction to the transpacific export and circulation of Hollywood products and tropes and especially to a growing global pile of impressions thereof. In this view, dancing farmers in Southeast Asia could be a result of the "shock" of pressure put on local filmmakers by the popularity and established legitimacy of tropes like song and dance, pushing them toward base mimicry in order to succeed in a local marketplace saturated with foreign imports.

Here, however, considering the stylistic deviation of the scene from the segments surrounding it, the effect is also to produce a sense of incompatibility or absurdity, calling attention to the strangeness of the shift. In Akup's and his collaborators' hands, the abrupt, unprecedented appearance of song and dance functions in a way that is not unlike the sudden exclamation or repetition of something otherwise "random" in latah. Further mirroring the auntie's latah outburst, the film also appears to quickly recover from its entrancement with song and dance, after which the scene's distinctive style and break into fantasy are not repeated or echoed elsewhere in the narrative (although other kinds of outbursts continue). With the interlude left as a glaring anomaly, a sly metacommentary begins to emerge from the stylistic incongruence of the scene. Even while momentarily looking silly and easily seduced by the transnational, the film's mimicry positions the typical tropes of song and dance as if *they* were the silly ones: "low" filmic impulses similar to rude gestures or curses that would normally be suppressed. As the song-and-dance scene is thus implied not to be of a piece with the local puzzle on the screen,[8] its ostensibly clear, universal readability is interrogated.

As this begins to show, *Tiga Buronan*'s engagements with the transnational can also be read as a more formalized version of the strategy deployed in *Lewat Djam Malam* three years earlier. Similar to how the prostitute Laila compulsively yet creatively clips and processes the imagery of *Life* magazine in Usmar Ismail's film, in *Tiga Buronan* (also produced by Usmar Ismail and Perfini), Nya Abbas Akup "cuts and pastes" popular tropes from globally circulating films traveling around the Pacific and beyond, positioning them as part of a heterogeneous patchwork. As in *Lewat Djam Malam*, this stylistic appropriation implicitly lowers the status of such tropes, modifying their form and diminishing their potential dominance by comparison to the local and regional images and concepts with which they are surrounded. If the song-and-dance scene is nonetheless still a geopolitical, market-compelled form of cinematic latah, its controlled, subtly ironic mimicry is also differentiated from the auntie's knee-jerk, spoon-waving curses.

While latah is framed in scholarly and medical literature as a "syndrome" or neuropsychiatric disorder, I follow James Siegel (1986), Hildred Geertz (1968), and others, interpreting it as a facet of local and regional symbolic processes that, while often looked down on, is generally not seen as an illness. Clearly, Akup understood it as a phenomenon both highly localized and connected to fundamental problems of representation and expression manifesting in Indonesia and throughout the region in the mid-twentieth century. At stake in Akup's cinematic latah is something closer to the shock typically attributed to the experience of rapid modernization following the imposition of Western industrial paradigms of development. The conventional language used to describe encounters with new and foreign technologies, techniques, or agents—"an overwhelming sense of grandeur and awe . . . in which the immaterial workings of God and his spirits were subordinate" (Larkin 2008:7), for example—is in fact quite similar to the discourse around latah in which a victim is temporarily "possessed" by startlement. While Akup's use of latah aims to engage with this type of experience, as I will elaborate further below, the intimate locality of his metaphor radically reframes the shock of the foreign and the modern as something familiar and almost expected.

For Siegel as well, latah constitutes one of the most visible parts of an important complex of behaviors, habits, and strategies that mediate shock and generally aim to avert full-blown, involuntary mimicry. Their function, he argues, is to prevent those confronted by something new or unexpected from falling into an unthinking, imitative posture that reads as possession by an intruder. The most common defense against such base imitation "without the pretense of reply" (1986:124) is the deployment of an easily discernible artificiality in the reaction triggered by an encounter with the foreign—even, or especially, if it involves mimicry. An example of this is the engagements observed by Siegel with actual foreigners on the streets of Surakarta, Central Java, in the 1980s. The presence of tourists, expats, or European businessmen was of course not so unique as to be actually shocking to most. Yet locals, especially youth, seemed to feel compelled to act out when they encountered foreigners (in my own experience in villages, and sometimes also cities, this is still the case, and is not limited to young people). Often, the youth would blurt strange words or phrases taken from obscure English-language media or slang, such as "Hallo, Mac!," inevitably confusing their targets. While precluding an actual conversation and potentially making themselves look foolish, Central Javanese hecklers are, for Siegel, effectively issuing a preemptive linguistic strike. The underlying aim is to label strangers as strange from a local perspective (even as much of the world considers them uniquely powerful), confirming that "such foreigners are outside the discourse of Javanese; there is no way to speak to them properly" (125).

As I read Siegel, in the impulse to draw language borders around them, foreigners are not banished but rather "cut out" and embedded as strange in the picture of the local that emerges. The foreigners' ability to thoroughly shock is thus purloined, even if they are still capable of triggering a disturbance such as the interaction described above. In the process, a deft, if somewhat blunt, geopolitical intuition is revealed on the part of the Javanese youth. Their knowingly "broken"

English adds something to the encounter with the foreign, imbuing the stranger's language with an absurd or false air and banishing the specter of base imitation (in a similar way, I've been greeted with a rousing "Good morning!" in late afternoon, followed by uproarious laughter). While perhaps outside the targets' awareness, an implicit reading of the "original" foreign trigger for the interaction is also produced: it must be hiding some inherent lack or falsity that the process of mimicry brings out and highlights.

COLLIDING REGIONS, JUMPY COWBOYS,
FOREIGN NATIONS

The above interactions and semiformalized responses could be seen as a kind of impromptu "street theater" that recalls other, more formalized but also improvisational practices elsewhere in the region. Vicente Rafael, for example, sees Filipino appropriation and vernacularization of colonial Spanish *comedia* theater as similarly offering "venues for expressing and conventionalizing fantastic identifications with alien places and alien sources of power that lay at the basis of colonial-Christian authority" (2005:117–18). At the same time, Filipino *comedias*' "citation and . . . circulation of foreign images" functioned to give European conventions and references the appearance of "stereotypes," which also came to seem "vaguely absurd" (2005:119–20). In my analysis, repurposing foreign conventions in ways that deconstruct and alter their meaning or status is part of an important region-wide trend in vernacular theaters, something I discuss at greater length in chapter 2. As this suggests, the reception and strategic fragmentation of imported genres and modes of representation links the regional practice of cinema—understood as a new and foreign technology—with that of other arts, deflating and placing motion pictures on the same level as older, traditional forms.

In the realm of visual art, for example, Siegel also sees a strategic repositioning or "breaking" in Indonesian historical encounters with foreign aesthetics, as when Western landscape paintings were popularized in nineteenth-century Java and as a result began to take on new, localized "spatial arrangements" (1986:127). For Siegel, such altered compositions continued to influence artistic trends well into the twentieth century, including an approach to pastoral scenes that by the 1980s had become what he calls "the most common picture in Java today" (126). In the endless iterations of the same basic scene and style that crowded local art markets and adorned the walls of village farmers and wealthy urbanites alike, thickets of trees were generally depicted framing rice fields or water with a mountain in the background (fig. 4). The arrangement evokes a ubiquitous rural scene that can still be found outside of city centers almost anywhere in Java or much of Indonesia. In Siegel's reading, the painting employs typically naturalist elements but arranges them in ways that seem at odds with the goal of creating realistic dimensionality, shifting and deforming the basic premises of popular Western conventions. While

FIGURE 4. Siegel does not include an example of the "most common" painting he describes. In lieu of an "original," this quite ordinary Javanese landscape (2024), of which one still can find numerous variations in art markets and online, appears to fit the bill. Used by permission of Cerah Art and Bambang Sastra Wiguna, the artist.

the only source of illumination is the sun, for example, the light appears to come from opposing angles and sides of the picture, as if different objects in the painting were illuminated at different times of day, or the space imagined is one in which the laws of physics are altered (127).

The effect suggests a series of planes (simultaneously overlaying as in foreground, middle, background) and intersecting with each other. The planes "gape open in front and close up toward the back," paradoxically receding into the distance while also invoking a sense of flatness and never allowing for a single vanishing point to be identified. "Instead of being drawn into the picture," writes Siegel, "the viewer thus bumps up against a plane confronting him" (129). In a formal sense, the painting delivers a patchwork of multiple points of view, pierced by darker or black areas that coincide with the juncture of distinct planes. Siegel's informants interpreted these as sites where things that are "strange" or "foreign" hold sway, including spirits, which inhabit the obscured spaces behind the dark gaps where visual logic breaks down in the meeting of incongruous planes and perspectives. Yet the painting's porous formal borders do not imply separation from the world of viewers, who are invited to see the realities they inhabit (both visible and normally unseen, as in strangers and spirits) as coincident with the image. For Siegel, the image is a translation of a daily reality always already imbued with the possibility of disturbance; his informants found the illustration to be "nice," while also containing elements that are "terrifying." The overall effect, however, was "tranquil" (129–30).

As a complex product of ongoing processes of development and globalization, the painting and Siegel's interpretation of it resonate with how I see films working to mediate (or perhaps, indeed, "tranquilize") the constant shock of incursions by strange, alien forces—in this case especially those of modernization. The fragmented, sometimes violent, view of pastoral tranquility in *Tiga Buronan*, for example, could be said to express a similar attitude, although in more openly dramatic, provocative terms. This attitude is revealed not only in the arrangement of individual shots or scenes but especially in the formal, narrative, and tonal incongruities across the film as a whole. For example, the song-and-dance sequence described above offers an ostensibly calming generic reference that, lacking further repetition of its tropes, is eventually identified as a strange anomaly that bumps against other, more "realistic" views of the rural. The effect is to challenge spectators' easy identification of or with a single point of view into which the film's visual, narrative, and formal contradictions might slip and vanish. Here the result is perhaps more rousing and humorous than calming per se, but the overall effect suggests that dealing with foreign incursions of various sorts can be fun and generative instead of just tense, confounding, or overwhelming. As in the painting, the fragmenting, archipelagic mode of resistance to a unified view that I identify in the film functions almost like a pleasurable form of "training" or reinforcement for audiences facing wave upon wave of change and globalization.

Another scene goes further, deepening the sense of the film as a performative response to the pressures of the time and place in which it was produced. This scene, too, begins by positioning the sphere of transnational aesthetics as if it were an alien force that imposes itself on the movements and affect of characters, opening and highlighting seams and inconsistencies in the local-cum-national spaces on the screen. It begins with another classic modern-global setup: the eponymous three fugitives make their grand entrance, while terrified villagers scatter in all directions, emptying the small town's main drag. Clad in black, the villains stride purposefully into the deserted street, as if they were expecting a lone, gunslinging sheriff to step into their path, signaling an impending shoot-out (fig. 5). In David Hanan's analysis, the scene does precisely this, evoking one of the most typical generic signatures of westerns. It does so, he writes, "just sufficiently for an audience to sense they are 'seeing double', and that this may be Indonesia, but it is also reminiscent—through elements of its staging and framing—of American cinema" (2017:133–34).

There are no sheriffs in most West Javanese villages, however, and the sequence of events typically triggered by such scenes in westerns is humorously subverted: the familiar setup of the villains' entrance ends with them menacingly shaking hands with *Pak* Haji (Udjang), a wealthy landowner who has completed the

FIGURE 5. The gazes of Akup's fugitive bad guys constantly shift from their surrounds to each other as they seem to be trying to assess whether they're making a properly ominous cinematic entrance. The idea of compulsive mimicry is also underscored as the sidekicks repeatedly look to their leader (played by Bing Slamet, *center*) for the most appropriate evil facial expression.

Hajj and is thus seen as a pillar of Islamic values. But this alone is perhaps too simple and clear to be genuinely subversive or funny for a filmmaker like Akup. Reviewed more carefully, the staging of the villains' introduction prompts viewers to go beyond a "mere" doubling of perspectives. As the they stride into the village, they look typically mean, but also a bit unnatural, almost like human puppets manipulated by an unseen hand, leaving them not fully in control of their bodies. While their status as actual, menacing outlaws is part of the film's reality, so, too, is their gawky posturing, which exceeds any easy association with something "Indonesian" or "Hollywood," or even typically theatrical or cinematic.

In the scene of their entrance, and at times elsewhere, the fugitives appear as if they are consciously trying, and often failing, to act like the typical bad guys one might see in a transnational genre film like a western (as Hanan points out, their movements and appearance also reference West Javanese *lenong* theater). The humor comes from the resultant undermining of any sort of authenticity, local or global. What rings "true" or familiar is hence a certain mode of representation in which multiple genres and styles are combined yet marked as distinct from each other, producing strange junctures and repercussions in the image and offering a fragmented, archipelagic field of identification to viewers. More so than the song and dance, and not wholly unlike the Javanese youths above, Akup's scene uses a combination of complex body movements, facial expressions, camerawork, and setting to draw "lines" around the foreign/transnational elements that have been cut and pasted into the film's jumble of local and transpacific references. Evoking the basic structure of the Javanese landscape painting described above, the film as a whole continually highlights the crags and shadowy gaps that appear when different modes of representation associated with distinct, potentially conflicting, points of view are combined. The sense of the "strange" that lurks in the painting's formal incongruities functions in the film as an ever-present source of productive absurdity.

In its layered performance of being compelled by a conflicted morass of social, political, and market forces, *Tiga Buronan* evokes what Siegel terms a Javanese penchant for locating and exploiting "manufactured absences" or silences in encounters with strange foreign objects or media otherwise characterized by the experience of shock (1986:123–24). In Akup's crosshairs, westerns and musicals, along with the various local and regional forms and references with which the film surrounds them, are exploited for their recognizable audience draw while also implicated as fungible products that don't quite fit when applied to something more historically specific (cinema itself, in its classical taboo against flaunting its inherent fakery and constructedness, has a key manufactured silence outed). As in Rafael's analysis of Filipino *comedias*, the foreign is unveiled as a stereotype and rendered absurd in a way that simultaneously supports, overflows, and interrogates the local and the national.

For all its jumping around among conventions, genres, and identities, *Tiga Buronan* has a clearly defined beginning, middle, and end. Yet in scenes such as the fugitives' entrance, narrative flow is subordinated to the clash of genres and styles and the sense of strangeness it produces, which become as integral to the film as its story. Working in parallel (and at obtuse angles) with the narrative, Akup's manufactured absurdities open the diegesis to reflections on the politics of form. The cracked and strange approach to cinematic storytelling that results, while full of playful experimentation and awkward pauses, stutters, and repetitions, was also popular. *Tiga Buronan* was a hit, and its clever forgery of westerns was reprised by Akup to even more farcical effect a year later in *Djendral Kantjil* (*General Mouse Deer*, 1958).[9] The faux-western mode was also soon adopted by other regional filmmakers and was expanded by Akup as the main theme of several entire films in the 1970s and 1980s. Numerous other Jakarta-based directors followed suit, leading the *Tempo* critics to cry *latah*.[10] In latah-like fashion, the trend also expanded throughout the region. The Malayan actor-director P. Ramlee's 1962 film *Labu dan Labi* (*Labu and Labi*), for example, makes similar transnational fun of "fake" cowboys in an extended dream sequence that resembles an adult version of *Djendral Kantjil*'s mock-up. Popular deconstructive takes on westerns and action films also emerged in the Philippines and Thailand in the 1960s, the latter famously reprised in the Thai new wave classic *Fa Thalai Jone* (*Tears of the Black Tiger*, dir. Wisit Sasanatieng, 2000).

Despite the regional scope of the habit it refers to, however, Jakarta-based *Tempo* magazine's charge of cinematic latah was focused on a critique of filmmaking at the national level. This points to a further paradox in *Tiga Buronan*'s performative engagements with locally, regionally, and globally circulating genres and tropes, which appear to flagrantly disregard the hallowed boundaries of the then newly formed nation. As if to muddy things further, Perfini was among the most vocal production companies in explicitly positioning its products as "national cinema" (Ismail 1983:84). When examined more closely, this claim, too, does not easily align with continental Euro-American ideals of the modern nation as a self-enclosed "'fortress and landmass' safeguarding internal homogeneity" (Bernards 2015:13). In Akup's and most of Perfini's other films, "Indonesia," like everything else placed into the archipelagic patchworks onscreen, is implied to be an awkwardly artful, formally overconstructed project-product. Always already fake and fragmented, the nation is imagined as a site where transnationally circulating forms and ideas collide with each other and, as in *Tiga Buronan*, with particular local and regional forms of theater and music and with embarrassing regional "culture bound" conditions like latah.

On one level, this reads as a self-deprecating acknowledgment of the power of both foreign and intimate invaders and of the political economic inevitability of the impulse to mimic or react to them in historically proscribed ways. Chains of simulation and comparison extending to and from various cut-and-pasted fragments visibly weight the form of scenes like the villains' entrance, as actors wear borrowed references like bulky, ill-fitting clothes. Yet on another level, as I have suggested, it is precisely with their clumsy blurting of inauthentic, excessive gestures that such scenes deflect the nagging menace of rote imitation, or what Benedict Anderson calls the "spectre of comparisons": the haunting feeling that the nation and its various components and operating procedures are part of a standardized "series"—essentially a chain of copies—stretching from West to East (1998:29, 33).

In vanquishing such specters, regional films of the 1950s and 1960s imbue the nation with a Frankensteinian materiality that is a far cry from the lofty political ideals associated with official national identity. Yet the strange, archipelagic "realism" of Indonesia, Malaya, Thailand, or the Philippines onscreen in the 1950s was familiar enough to viewers to make it successfully marketable. As I will show in the next sections, the impulses to create this experimental-yet-popular national aesthetics and the regional-historical factors driving them starkly separate the history and development of cinemas in Southeast Asia from the trajectories of film in other regions, nations, and influential locales in the Global South.

ARCHIPELAGIC AESTHETICS, THE NATION, AND FISSURED POSTCOLONIAL IMAGES

A question that is repeatedly raised across this book is how the materiality, aesthetics, and discourses of Southeast Asian film history can be used to critically expand the established conventions and theoretical paradigms of film studies and other fields. In the most basic sense, my findings in Southeast Asia suggest an intriguing distinction from conventional scholarly narratives of technocultural astonishment and stark epistemic shifts wrought by the arrival of motion pictures on the world's Eastern and Southern shores. In Ella Shohat's and Robert Stam's survey and analysis of the aesthetics and politics of global cinemas, for example, films are understood to create a fraught, alienating double consciousness across the decolonizing world. Via imported Hollywood and European movies, cinema proffers a "linear, comprehensible destiny" (2014:102) as a shining symbolic tool of liberation that is in fact illusory: the ideal images of smooth, homogeneous modernity it sells are at odds with the messy, fragmented realities of decolonizing societies. The mismatch, furthermore, implies a lack in such "underdeveloped" audiences for their seeming inability to achieve or comply with imposed Western standards. Especially for the many groups who were brought together by European conquest in the first place, Shohat and Stam argue that cinema's clarity of vision is premised on hiding the facts of its underlying paradoxes and conflicts of interest.

The result is what they term a "fissured colonial spectator" (103), one goaded by mass media to recognize and conquer a "foreignness" that, in most of the imported films that dominated markets in the Global South, is associated with how non-Europeans are presented on the screen. What is ostensibly foreign in the modern discourse of films consumed by colonized spectators is thus the colonized themselves, leading to a crisis of identification. Brian Larkin's more geographically targeted study of Nigeria makes a concurrent point. He argues that the implementation of electricity, radio, and mobile cinema units in Northern Hausa regions in the 1930s and 1940s functioned as an irresistibly alluring "colonial sublime"—a politically charged spectacle of technological achievement (and liberation) that caused much local conflict and consternation on its arrival but then quickly cast its spell on Hausa society, triggering a broad epistemic shift. For Larkin, the Westernized technoaesthetic regime that resulted was especially influential on nationalist leaders, who initially fought its implementation but soon reversed course and "internaliz[ed] . . . its logic" (2008:8). The result was long-standing cultural, political, and identitarian divisions similar to those identified by Shohat and Stam elsewhere in the Global South.

As Larkin, Shohat and Stam, Miriam Hansen (1999, 2000, 2012), and many others understand broader processes of development and contestation throughout the world, cinema has consistently been a medium through which the spread of Western modernity, and the sublime technological advances associated with it, are experienced as a series of "shocks." Packaged and exported together with other emergent technologies and Western conceptions of modernization and rationalization, cinema is capable of disrupting the continuity of older aesthetic patterns, exerting a "levelling impact on indigenous cultures" while "challeng[ing] prevailing social and sexual arrangements and advanc[ing] new possibilities of identity and cultural styles" (Hansen 2000:12).[11] Among the most important sources of disruption and shock, in which cinema and various other mass media are heavily implicated, is the reorganization of postcolonial and non-Western parts of the world into nation-states that are assumed to impose a Western epistemic outlook in their basic design and function. For Shohat and Stam, the eventual emergence of what they call "Third Worldist" filmmaking represents a broad critical response to the psychological, political, and aesthetic schisms instituted by the rapid formation of modern nations in the Global South and of the more-or-less homogeneous national cinemas that correspond to them.

If the majority of Third Worldist films then come to construct "a peculiar realm of irony where words and images are seldom taken at face value [and] . . . techniques of metacinema and reflexivity have been virtually ubiquitous" (Shohat and Stam 2014:279), it is the result of an accumulated lack of trust in the fissured images and unreconcilable identities proffered by Hollywood and Europe and by the national films that are argued to take after them. The tactic of decoding and deconstructing classical Western imagery is in some ways similar to what we have seen so far in Southeast Asia. Yet the experience of real shock and sense of lack, trauma, and other negative psychic complexes that Shohat and Stam and others attach to the coming of cinema and nation appears distinct from the playful, subversive reflections on political, economic, and aesthetic compulsion that characterize the films of Akup or the Malayan writer-director-actor P. Ramlee, for example. From the first inklings of Southeast Asian "national" cinemas in the 1920s, 1930s, and 1940s, the work of regional filmmakers displayed a presumption that cinematic imagery is characterized by fakery and construction and should be taken and enjoyed as such. In Shohat and Stam's analysis, by contrast, it is normally only after decades of overdetermined nationhood and co-opted film production that the psychic splits associated with Third Worldism can "reappear in a liberatory, anticolonialist register" in the form of conscious hybridity and politically barbed syncretism (8). The eventual emergence of these "oppositional" aesthetic regimes, understood to be immersed in a common global struggle against the influence of Hollywood, is what also finally contributes to the questioning of the imported-yet-inexorable logic of the nation itself.

The immediate questioning of national ideals, sly self-reflexivity around formal and generic borrowing, and demonstrably "calmer" (if still jumpy and compulsive) reception of cinema that my study shows throughout Southeast Asia thus stands as something of a global anomaly. Very few Southeast Asian examples of "Third Worldism" are cited by Shohat and Stam; outside of India, Asian films overall are sparse in their otherwise broad study. Krishna Sen, among the most influential nonnative scholars of Indonesian cinema, concurs: "Indonesian radicalism and 'Third Cinema' (both as movements and as sets of ideas) seem to have by-passed each other" (Sen 2003:147). Yet despite this distinction, in the broader picture of Indonesian cinema that emerges in Sen's work, its development is painted in more familiar strokes. In her seminal *Indonesian Cinema: Framing the New Order* (1994), for example, Sen frames the arrival of motion pictures in Indonesia in the conventional terms set by other studies of film and globalization: as a modern process of "changes, interruptions and disruptions" (1994:3) that bring about epistemic shifts and sharp departures from the past. The question I take up here—why Indonesia and other Southeast Asian nations have not responded to such disruptions in the more typically "Third Worldist" manner outlined by Shohat and Stam and others—is left open by Sen.

Perhaps the problem is indeed a "national" one. Sen's exclusive focus on Indonesian cinema as a product of modern nationhood leads her to view the possibility of links with the historical conditions of media and aesthetics in the region with suspicion. To do so, she argues, would be to imagine film or other mass media as drawing on a "putative national cultural past." This, furthermore, "may well mean that we fall into an essentialist . . . mistake of emphasizing continuities and universalities within a national cinema" (1994:3). For Sen, the formation of a nation relegates the cultural and aesthetic logics of the past to the status of archaic myths and artifacts. In the modern present, these are, if anything, decontextualized beyond recognition or co-opted by the state to support its image of national identity. "In what sense," she asks, "is the ancient, pre-colonial available to the [contemporary] popular audience?" (1994:3). In Sen's analysis, the past has largely vanished from the visual regimes of modern nationhood.

Seeking to move beyond this impasse, this book looks at aesthetics in the archipelagic context of nations that are understood to be shaped by regional histories and powerful subnational territories, as well as by conventional trends of development and Westernization.[12] Looking at Southeast Asia in relation to its formative transpacific struggles and alliances, I follow Viet Thanh Nguyen and Janet Hoskins in their focus on the trajectory of emergent nations outside the binaries of East and West by producing "new sets of relationships based on heritage that may be even stronger than those of nation and citizenship." Similar to my analysis of Southeast Asia, the translocal and regional spaces defined by such connections are seen by Nguyen and Hoskins as inseparable from "a complicated history of competition, conflict, and negotiation with the west, with each other, and with their own minorities" (2014:12).

As I have begun to show, from a regional—and, indeed, transregional or transoceanic—perspective, procedures and understandings of cinema function in complex and conventionally unpredictable ways. They attach themselves to discourses, texts, and practices that reach beyond, before, deep within, and potentially *after* the nation and its expected role as a mirror or specter of Western influence. Looking at cinema and other media this way aims to interrogate the lingering myth in which nation formation is understood as an absolute historical cut—one into which potentially useful and relevant elements of the past are too often understood to simply vanish, leaving important questions about the status of national cinemas unanswerable. Engaging the cataclysmic, "leveling" incursions of cinema and nation in terms of regional *continuities* of long, prenational histories filled with various disruptions, I position the coming of modernity and national cinemas in Southeast Asia as an enabling paradox: a disruption that is always already expected.

As Hassan Muthalib puts it in the context of Malaya, because of the pervasive influence of local/regional aesthetic strategies and patterns, "the link with [our] historical and cultural past was . . . maintained and so the arrival of cinema did not result in a cultural shock for the locals" (2013:2). Seen in this way, Southeast Asian films of the 1950s might be more comparable with what Shohat and Stam term the "Post-Third Worldist" (2014:292), a state of aesthetics that follows and builds on an earlier "stage" characterized by a more direct oppositional stance toward Hollywood (and other Western) cultural products. This is especially salient if Southeast Asia is seen as part of a larger transpacific region encompassing both South and North America, in which cinema is an active site of political and economic contestation. With its self-conscious "aesthetics of garbage" and structure made up of a "compilation of pastiches, [like] a kind of cinematic writing in quotation marks" (Shohat and Stam 2014:310), the Brazilian *Bandido da Luz Vermelha* (*Red Light Bandit*, dir. Rogerio Sganzerla, 1968), for example, takes an approach and style closer to that of Southeast Asian films in the 1950s. Yet unlike them, *Bandido* still smacks of works aimed at audiences steeped in the logic of emergent global "alternatives" to Hollywood heralded by intellectual elites and screened at international festivals. In comparison, Southeast Asia's geographic and cultural distance from North America, combined with its historically robust regional aesthetic practices, appears to have diminished, if not completely eliminated or ignored, the influence of Hollywood. The region's cosmopolitan, yet distinctly lowbrow, archipelagic approach to film aesthetics has also generally been spurned by elites and, especially prior to the 1990s, is far less recognized or appreciated in the spheres of international art and oppositional cinemas.

Many early Southeast Asian filmmakers, like their contemporaries in the cinematic new waves of Europe, South America, and elsewhere, were intellectuals well-versed in the world's various cinematic movements, styles, and politics. Many wrote and translated prolifically alongside other creative outputs like painting and theater. Yet unlike their internationally lauded, post–Third Worldist comrades in South America, the primary audiences for films like *Tiga Buronan, Tamu Agung* (*Honored Guest*, dir. Usmar Ismail, 1955), *Labu dan Labi*, the Filipino hit *Juan Tamad Goes to Congress* (dir. Manuel Conde, 1959), or the Thai *Mae Nak Phra Khanong* (*Mae Nak from Khanong*, dir. Rungsri Tasapayak, 1959) were understood to be much less engaged in high modernist or intellectual spheres. The implicitly elevated status of "garbage" films like *Bandito*, touted for their radical aesthetic "cannibalism" (as opposed to imitation) of mainstream cinema is largely absent from early Southeast Asian films. While regional movies, as I have begun to show, were equally engaged in the politics of globalism through "eating" and regurgitating popular genres and conventions in satirically modified forms, they traded on their potential to appeal to much larger, popular audiences (see chapter 2 for more details on the economics of Southeast Asian films).

This populist potential was both a blessing and curse, as locally made films were generally seen by critics and much of the educated elite as actual trash, blighting the ideals and pretentions that they—unlike typical audiences—attached to national cinema. Politicians and official custodians of national purity often derided Southeast Asian films as cheap, incoherent, or, in the films' complex and darkly critical views, even "counterrevolutionary."[13] Ironically, had critics succeeded in pressuring regional producers to make their films more "properly" aligned with elite ideals of national representation, Southeast Asian cinemas might well have fallen into the same "fissured" relationships with audiences that plagued many other areas of the Global South in the 1950s and 1960s. In this context, the fate of makers of popular films in India in the 1950s and 1960s was perhaps most similar to those in Southeast Asia.

DISRUPTION VS. HAPPY ENDINGS IN INDIA AND HOLLYWOOD

Indian filmmakers, too, relied on the patronage of popular audiences mainly from the lower classes. Their works—with ubiquitous genre-bending, self-referentiality, and similarly excessive levels of humor and emotion to Indonesian, Malayan, Thai, or other regional fare—were likewise distinct from, and resistant toward, Western classical approaches. Steven Crofts, for example, sees the unique relationship Indian and Southeast Asian cinemas built with Hollywood as "an accomplishment managed by few" (1993:50). But Indian popular films, like their Southeast Asian counterparts, were generally dismissed by elite viewers and critics as "alarmingly noisy and nonsensical, if not dangerously seductive and utterly vulgar" (Sunya 2022:14). In some ways, as Samhita Sunya (2022) suggests, things were even harder for mainstream Indian filmmakers owing to the emergence of what became known as parallel cinema. This more independent, self-consciously experimental or intellectual wave of films was driven by a new crop of independent writer-directors like the Bengali Satyajit Ray in the 1950s, the likes of which did not emerge in a concerted fashion in Southeast Asia until the late 1990s. Such parallel Indian films generally spurned popular conventions, instead relying heavily on acceptance from international festivals and hence winning elite approval by "put[ting] Indian cinema on the world map" (Sunya 2022:16).

The elite perception of popular filmmakers and their work suffered even more as they were increasingly compared to their less commercially oriented colleagues in the parallel movement. As if to muddy the field further, because of the self-referential, antinaturalist styles of most popular Indian films, early parallel cinema efforts like Satyajit Ray's *Pather Panchali* (*Song of the Little Road*, 1955) resisted these conventions by taking a realist approach heavily influenced by European films of the time (later parallel films employed a variety of different styles). Only more recently have studies such as Sunya's begun to broadly reappraise mainstream Indian cinema, citing the immense appreciation and love for such movies showed by nonelite audiences both locally and internationally. Sunya argues that mainstream Hindi films like *Awaara* (*The Vagabond*, dir. Raj Kapoor, 1951) helped to create extensive aesthetic and political economic networks based entirely outside the West, exceeding the films' oft-derided status as fungible products defined by market forces. She positions such works as part of an alternative global canon—one that made Bombay, in particular, an influential "nodal point" of 1960s world cinema (Sunya 2022:15), whether critics and intellectuals at the time liked it or not. In this vein, *Awaara* not only had long theatrical runs in India and numerous other countries but played to the "immeasurable delight" of officials and university students, for example, when it was sent with the first Indian film delegation to the Soviet Union in 1954 (Sunya 2022:11).

Sunya also notes that many popular Indian films were and are, in fact, very concerned with social and political issues, something that is often seen as the exclusive purview of alternative cinemas. In the 1950s and 1960s, Indian films brought perspectives that were often highly critical of national policies and their effects on commoners to immense numbers of working-class and peasant viewers, many of whom were illiterate. In line with Sunya's study, Rosie Thomas contends that despite the much-maligned status of this demographic and the films that cater to them, such audiences were and are "ruthlessly discriminating" about their cinema (1985:120)—a fact that, as in Southeast Asia, many Indian filmmakers and studios were made constantly and painfully aware. Catering to elites was effectively not an option, but a truly "bad" film would quickly be sniffed out and rejected by the so-called masses.

In this vein, Ashish Rajadhyaksha argues that despite the appreciation heaped on a lineage of self-consciously experimental films "from Eisenstein to Brakhage" (in which "parallel" Indian luminaries such as Mrinal Sen or Satyajit Ray are included), it was Indian popular films that more systematically developed and expanded "the ways by which the celluloid screen can, directly and unmediatedly, conduct a transaction with the spectator to provide a 'fourth look' to the cinema" (2009:37). For Rajadhyaksha, the frequent scholarly use of terms like *primitive* to describe qualities in Indian popular cinema that were elsewhere lauded as oppositional vis-à-vis the global hegemony of Hollywood demonstrates a broad lack of understanding of the context and tastes of its audiences and of the corresponding set of conventions and styles standardized and deployed by filmmakers (15). Consistent economic troubles, despite demonstrable popularity, have also contributed to the labeling of Indian cinema as "pre-industrial" (Rajadhyaksha:15) and to its long-standing lack of legitimacy in the eyes of the state. This, in turn, has fostered an enduring animosity between film producers and government authorities. The result, among other things, is to undermine the identity of Bollywood, along with the linguistically and geographically fragmented field of Indian filmmaking as whole, as constituting a proper "national cinema" (Rajadhyaksha:16).

In some sense, then, Indian cinema in the 1950s and 1960s is like a bigger, more globally circulated, version of Southeast Asian filmmaking. Although landlocked, it shares an archipelagic configuration of many distinct loci and languages of production linked by a common set of "excessive" conventions and a strained relationship with elites and critics. Kapila Vatsyayan's (1971) theory, discussed in the prologue, of a larger aesthetic region in which Indian approaches to representation have historically influenced and been adapted throughout much of Southeast Asia appears to resonate with this view. The conscious and circumstantial Indian resistance to the idea of a "pure" national cinema at the levels of form, narrative, and industrial-, audience-, and market-structures further mirrors aspects of Southeast Asian cinemas that I have taken up above and, especially in regard to market conditions, will explain further in the next chapter. But among all the similarities posed here, I contend that there is one key commonality among Southeast Asian films that is *not* shared with most South Asian ones. What distinguishes the overall effect of the similarities among Indonesian, Malaysian, Thai, and Filipino films from those of India is *a general lack of closure* in the Southeast Asian variants, while formal and narrative resolution is argued to be broadly enforced through various means in Indian popular cinemas.

As Ravi Vasudevan understands the exuberant, melodramatic and self-reflexive qualities of popular Indian social issue films in the 1950s, "the [film] text undertakes a narrative and performative operation which allows for forbidden, transgressive spaces to be opened up" (1989:38). But at the end of the narrative, as Vasudevan and many others have argued, the Indian social film "closes these spaces, re-instituting a moral order" (38). This provides something that more closely resembles a so-called Hollywood ending, and, although nationalists were still rarely satisfied, gestures toward the solidity of an Indian identity. In this combination of disruption and reintegration, I suggest, Indian social films are not so unlike the Hollywood genre of "comedian comedy" that emerged in the early sound era, building on the popularity of live comedy troupes such as the Marx Brothers. Referring to how the genre's rampant "intertextuality and fragmentation . . . destroys the classical illusion of a unified, self-contained, and coherent text," Henry Jenkins categorizes comedian comedy as an oft-ignored, but surprisingly common "nonhermetic tradition" within classical Hollywood (1992:10, 12).

Long before the recent efforts to critically reappraise Indian popular films, as Jenkins shows, the purposeful disruptiveness of these tendencies vis-à-vis mainstream Hollywood convention was labeled a form of modernist cinema. Among others, in the late 1960s, actor-director Jerry Lewis's numerous forays into comedian comedy were hailed by critics in the journal *Cahiers du Cinéma* as building on an alternative "tradition of subversion" (13) running through Hollywood's otherwise conservative and highly regulated filmmaking system. Yet as in the Indian films mentioned above, for Jenkins, the genre ultimately appears to reveal an inseverable attachment to just such a system. Despite catering to the "primitive" and potentially subversive tastes of their popular audiences, producers of comedian comedy still appear reticent to offer something more thoroughly destabilizing to mainstream conventions and the values associated with them, including national identity. Jenkins cautions that despite flaunting formal, narrative, and characterological wildness, comedian films are not able to completely free themselves from or negate classical Hollywood norms. As in Indian cinema, this is especially clear in the unspoken edict to resolve the seeming paradoxes and subversions posed by a film in its conclusion.

Take, for example, the 1952 comedian comedy *Son of Paleface*, written and directed by Frank Tashlin, one of the genre's most ubiquitous figures. Initially it might be seen as an apt, transpacific analogue of *Tiga Buronan* (or vice versa, since *Tiga Buronan* was released five years later). *Paleface* is wild, experimental, metacritical, and self-referential in its form. Like *Tiga Buronan*, it spoofs westerns, and it stars comedian Bob Hope as a "fake" cowboy dressed in loud pinstripe suits. It begins with a shot in which the image, a close-up of Hope's character with his back turned to the camera, is presented as a still, as if "paused" owing to a technical error. When the picture finally moves, it soon freezes again, then continues to start and stop at key moments, such as when Hope is about to kiss the woman in front of him. The result is a formal cat-and-mouse game that openly addresses the audience, toying with their expectations and desires. Not unlike a projectionist-cum-announcer from the early days of the Euro-American "cinema of attractions" (1895–1908; see Gunning 1986) (or from the classical days of Thai cinema, about which more below), Hope cracks jokes via voice-over underneath the jerky imagery, making light of various movie conventions while introducing the basic premises of the story. This multilayered, technologically reflexive approach sets the tone for the pranks, asides delivered directly into the camera, and other formal disruptions of classical norms that continue through most of the narrative. These are positioned as one of the film's main attractions for viewers, at times overtaking the importance of the narrative.

Despite its mocking manner, however, *Paleface* begins to diverge from the commitment of a film like *Tiga Buronan* to mocking and sending up globally and locally circulating conventions and sociopolitical values. It soon introduces the typically straight-and-narrow Roy Rogers, playing himself: a "real" cowboy, albeit a dandyish, singing one, against which Hope's hopelessly absurd wrangler is positioned as a foil. This begins to hint at the film's grounding in classical cinematic tropes and values, toward which it increasingly gravitates as the narrative unfolds. In the end, Hope's character, whose loud pinstripes are red, white, and blue, stops bumbling so much and joins the cheery, wholesome Rogers in slaughtering hordes of movie Indians and bringing black-clad, horse-mounted villains to justice. Through the struggle, both Hope's character and his brigand cowgirl love interest (Jane Russell) are reformed into "proper" people (and, perhaps more important, proper male and female movie characters), after which they marry. Before the credits roll, the new couple drives off into a sunset against which Rogers, atop his rearing steed, is prominently silhouetted. In the final tally, it is the jokes and disruptions that are mainly paused in favor of narrative and sociopolitical resolution: the West is won (again) and the nation, its white citizens and their patriarchal families, appear set to live happily ever after.

As I have noted elsewhere (see Yngvesson and Alarilla 2020), the ending of Akup's *Tiga Buronan* flirts with, but then subverts, a similar brand of closure-effect. Its protagonist, Maman, turns out to be an army spy who returned to his rural home not for nostalgic reasons but to foil the mission of the black-clad Mat Codet and his gang to take control of the village and its profitable, rice-producing fields. In the end, not unlike the plot of *Paleface*, Codet and his men are captured or killed in a shoot-out with soldiers. But buildup to the final conflict and the presentation of its aftermath are quite distinct. For one, the victory is not presented as the direct result of Maman's actions, which undermines the sense of him as classical, goal-oriented male protagonist. For most of the ending, Maman remains trapped by Mat Codet, and even his trusty, modern radio provided by the government refuses to work. Outside of his knowledge, his love interest, Ginah (Chitra Dewi), takes it on herself to outrun a henchman and call in the military, saving the day.

When the soldiers arrive, Maman, who is undercover and not in uniform, is at first assumed to be one of the bandits and held at gunpoint. Undaunted, he soon takes his place in a military jeep set to ride off into the sunset but then suddenly realizes he's forgotten something, stopping the film again just as it seems poised for a triumphant finale. Running back into the village, Maman emerges together with Ginah and her father, the cowardly religious pillar *Pak* Haji. Maman then reclaims his place in the sunset-bound jeep, while Ginah holds up her finger, now adorned with a ring. Nothing is directly said about marriage, and because the custom of giving engagement rings was all but unknown at the time in Indonesian society, this appears to be yet another nod to global convention: Maman "forgot" one of the key ingredients of a typically Holly- or Bollywood happily ever after: marriage (or at least a proposal). Having made a show of checking this box, Maman and his cronies can safely steer their jeep into the distance, where the sun is setting. While the resulting shot now does evoke a classical ending, the film isn't finished yet. It adds a further reverse angle that I argue undermines the formulaic sense of closure that Maman has worked so hard to ensure: as Ginah and her father stand and wave in an extreme long shot, the image around them is still filled with machine-gun toting soldiers who, unlike Maman, don't seem to be going anywhere soon. It almost looks as if they're "guarding" the film's optimistic conclusion.

The implication returns the film to what it *really* needed to remember before concluding matters onscreen: its engagement with the idea of the nation. The aggressive-looking, uniformed gunmen surrounding the better half of the film's now indefinitely deferred happy couple raise the question of whether the "West," or in this case the rural East, can in fact be won. If peace in Indonesia's dynamic, yet far from idyllic, villages cannot be sustained without the continual threat or active presence of centralized force, what of the even more complex and fragmented newly minted country around it? In this case the "bad guys," Mat Codet and his gang, have also been identified as former revolutionary fighters in the war to end Dutch colonialism a decade prior. Their guns, taken as spoils from that conflict, are further reminders of the pitfalls, paradoxes, and internal factions that emerged during nationalist struggle, however good or necessary the fight. Not coincidentally, 1957, the year of *Tiga Buronan*'s release, was also when Soekarno, Indonesia's first president, briefly declared martial law in order to institute his infamous "guided democracy" policy. The policy was a decidedly authoritarian response to Indonesia's extreme political fragmentation, and it effectively ended elections only two years after the first-ever opportunity for citizens to vote in 1955. As this and other Indonesian films at the time suggest, the problems of revolution embed themselves in the nation that follows, visibly cracking its grand hermetic facade of unity in diversity until it resembles an "archipelagic" region of disparate interests, factions, and locales.

SOUTHEAST ASIAN CINEMAS AND REVOLUTION

This context-based refusal of closure—one that could be termed "realist" but not naturalist or classical in a Hollywood sense—arguably puts popular Southeast Asian films on a formal/structural footing that is closer to independent or "parallel" offerings in South Asia (although, in fact, the more self-consciously experimental, radically fragmented Indian films like those of Mrinal Sen, Basu Chatterjee, or Ritwik Ghatak were made later, in the 1960s and 1970s). Among other factors, such as market conditions and audience taste, the anticlosure attitude of a film like *Tiga Buronan* also appears intimately tied to the experiences associated with the recent armed revolution against Indonesia's colonizers and with its complicated aftermath in the early years of nationhood. What, then, of the films of other Southeast Asian countries, not all of which had violent, anticolonial revolutions that their cinemas could reflect on? Malaysia, Singapore, and the Philippines, for example, negotiated independence deals with their colonizers (Britain and the U.S. respectively at the time of independence, although the Philippines had experienced an American-assisted revolution against Spanish colonizers half a century earlier), while Thailand was never officially colonized. Yet what these countries shared with their revolutionary neighbors was an almost unbelievably rapid transition to modern nationhood that I argue left deep impressions on regional cinemas, along with most other areas of life.

Things began in earnest over the fifty years preceding 1940, as the still-colonized region was put through an "extraordinary burst of state-making" (Reid 2015:251) at the hands of British, Dutch, French, and American authorities seeking to modernize their colonial possessions. Only Siam's monarchy was officially free—yet not from the constant need to negotiate with Western interests. From the mid-nineteenth century, it, too, was ensnared in a series of European treaties that helped move it rapidly toward a bloodless revolution and the shift to constitutional monarchy (and the name Thailand) in 1932. As Anthony Reid (2015) argues, this period of imposing modern state structures across the region laid the basic framework for the far more rapid and "astonishing time of crisis and transformation" (306) that followed. During the brief, disruptive window of World War II and its immediate aftermath, these artificial colonial states suddenly disintegrated and were conjured—now with massive doses of nationalist political "alchemy"—as independent nations.

This double transformation, experienced in such tight historical synchronicity, not only produced nations very quickly but also worked to reembed a sense of regional identity in the diverse set of new, geographically proximate countries that resulted. As Reid shows, the Japanese occupation of Southeast Asia during the war was among the most important factors driving this collective shift. Over a brief, three-month period between 1941 and 1942, the Nippon army destroyed all the colonial empires built by Europeans and Americans across Southeast Asia during the previous few centuries. Japanese forces then began training local recruits to better organize and fight to protect the "Greater East Asia Co-prosperity Sphere" that was envisioned as an extension of Imperial Japan. In a veritable flash, "the status of European government, law, and manners was abruptly punctured by European failure on the battlefield" (Reid 2015:312), replaced by an East Asian vision of modernity. At the same time, large numbers of native Southeast Asians were placed in urban offices in governing roles (and were also trained as directors, cameramen, and other high-level film crew), although still under tight Japanese control. Only three years later, in 1945, Japan would surrender to the Allied forces, leaving a region devastated by the former's brutality but also better trained and ideologically prepared to fend off the attempted returns of European imperialists.

For Reid, this unforeseeable series of events opened the door for an especially turbulent, at times almost ad hoc, transition to independent nationhood that set Southeast Asia's experience apart from that of other colonized areas, including in East and South Asia. This was particularly the case for those, like Indonesia, who would enter into bloody, yearslong conflicts with returning colonizers, while working to radically sweep away the subjugated ways of the recent past. In terms of economic infrastructures and foreign investment, the fates of Singapore, Malaysia, Thailand, and the Philippines were much better than their revolutionary neighbors in Indonesia, Vietnam, and Burma. But, Reid argues, those who fought to end colonialism succeeded in creating "the most well-defined national moral communities" (332). Despite their relative prosperity, those who negotiated freedom politically, like Malaysia, lacked a harrowing-yet-potentially unifying struggle and thus "failed to produce a single idea of the nation" (333). But the divisions and associated problems were often less clear than Reid suggests. As Nicholas Tarling argues, those who fought for independence used tactics that drew on their experiences under Japanese occupation, hurriedly cobbling together and expanding armies with little time for training, while also engaging guerilla tactics and forces, as well as "forming youth movements [and] employing bully-boys"—effective strategies that also "deferred or worsened the problems [a national revolution] would face when it succeeded" (2004:143).

These are precisely the kind of complications reflected in *Tiga Buronan* (as well as in *Lewat Djam Malam* and many other contemporary films), around which it refuses to offer viewers a stable sense of closure in its final moments. As Reid also contends, the more cohesive ideas developed in nationalist struggle too easily became a false chimera around which internal struggles continued for decades, ensuring that "military rule, corruption, and arbitrary dictatorship became common in the post-revolutionary countries" (2015:332). Complicating matters further, hanging over many of the region's well-deserved triumphs was the fact that, owing to the very brief window of time for reconstruction offered by World War II, the borders of so many proud new countries were "created out of imperial convenience" (Tarling 2004:142)—inherited with little modification from the boundaries set by colonizers.

As I have begun to show, although political will and centralized controls might strive to create smooth and forward-looking, modernist "imagined communities" (Anderson 1983), matters on popular screens, as in life, would be otherwise. In both the region's revolutionary-ideological successes and its economically advantageous, politically negotiated "failures," nations would mainly be visualized in terms of the paradoxes that defined them, not in the globalized conventions of nationalism or of a "Hollywood ending" to colonialism. For example, in the mystical horror genre, one of the most popular in Malaysian cinema of the 1950s and 1960s, divisive racial splits between politically dominant Malays and local Chinese and Indians (a big part of the national failure Reid identifies) were obsessively addressed but left open and unsolved. As Rosalind Galt argues, the disruptive presence of female monsters like the *pontianak* in such movies (see chapter 4) "preempts the status of the patriotic [Malay] hero in favor of a figuration of Malayness that is both monstrous and ambiguous" (2021:128). The result was numerous hit films in which, in the earliest years of the nation, key national-ideological precepts were challenged or made to appear unreliable, unmodern, or even duplicitous.

When comparing these patterns to other filmmaking traditions, it is important to keep in mind that Southeast Asia's individual film industries are much smaller than India's, America's, or other global centers of production. While regional producers have large potential audiences at home, the far lower number of screens has often limited profitability. As I mentioned above, Southeast Asian films are also relatively unknown outside the region, so there is both less at stake financially and less political impetus for governments to control national representation to the point of enforcing something as specific as closed endings, although concerted attempts have at times been made. One can also identify differences in patterns of showing physical or military contestation (including from traumatized or criminal former freedom fighters) between postrevolutionary Indonesia, for example, and Malaysia or Thailand. But I argue that the common and exceptionally quick transition to modern nationhood across the region was engaged by filmmakers using similar approaches to representation. These approaches generally deemphasized formal and generic consistency and continuity, visual naturalism, or necessary narrative closure.

The reasons for this are of course also more complex than just a shared, quick, and fraught transition to independence. As I take up in more detail in the next chapter, during the key processes of state- and nation-building from the late nineteenth century to the mid-twentieth, aesthetic ideas and conventions were undergoing their own, equally rapid and radical, process of movement from traditional and ritual-based arts to emergent commercial performance styles, from whence they embedded themselves in local cinemas. Not unlike their Indian counterparts, regional filmmakers riding these waves of change faced the thorny but generative problem of being caught between the heady ideals produced by elite education and the meaner social and aesthetic realities grounding and economically sustaining their work. While many Southeast Asian cineastes held key positions in emergent national processes, their work was consumed almost exclusively by lower-class audiences with particular expectations—aesthetic principles that often contradicted elitist tastes and political ideals. Yet the region's national cinemas did not generally become a source of trauma or disillusionment in the ways that Shohat and Stam see throughout much of the Global South. Despite numerous limitations and drawbacks, I contend that regional viewers were more often able to see "themselves" onscreen, however split, distorted, or intentionally mocked by the aesthetic conventions they preferred.

Despite, and often precisely because of, this situation, filmmakers saw themselves as engaged in politically important processes of nation building but also of actively reflecting the gaps and lacks that both plagued and enriched national life. Inexorable paradoxes, including the fact that the work of filmmakers was almost uniformly met with the upturned noses of their own intellectual peers, were frequently incorporated as gestures of self-reflexivity or self-deprecating humor. In this context, it is the canny incorporation of disorderly or "primitive" formal flourishes and other ostensible shortcomings that I position as defining features of an emergent archipelagic "classicism" across Southeast Asia. As we move our focus beyond postrevolutionary Indonesia and into the uncolonized, but still rapidly shifting, sphere of Thailand, the difference from typical Third Worldist (and scholarly) ideals of either Hollywoodization or its direct opposition only becomes more apparent.

CLASSICAL, NATIONAL, REGIONAL, GLOBAL, AND VERSIONS THEREOF

Among the most generative regional examples of the debate over "proper" modes of national representation and its aesthetic effects is the Thai practice of live film dubbing, or "versioning." As May Ingawanij (2012, 2018), Mary Ainslie (2014, 2018), and others have shown, voice-over artists, or what local English-language media called versionists, dominated popular cinema in Thailand from the 1930s to the 1970s. Their particular modes of exhibition profoundly shaped not only the consumption but the production of cinema and the critical and popular discourses surrounding it. In full view of delighted audiences, versionists created or replaced films' entire soundtracks live (including dialogue, music, and sound effects), improvising with the assistance of basic scripts and a variety of technical tools including microphones, mixers, and record players. Locally produced films as well as foreign ones (especially from India and China), were exhibited in this way, the latter with their soundtracks muted and replaced by patchworks of voices and music that responded to, but were flagrantly out of synch with, the films' imagery.

Like elsewhere in the region, then, Thai exhibitor-practitioners reacted to the arrival of new technologies of representation, and the circulation of local and global genres and styles, by making countless local "versions" thereof. All of these contained recognizable similarities to their Thai and foreign sources, but none could be said to be a precise copy. This is because each time a particular film was exhibited, its dialogue and soundtrack would be altered spontaneously (or simply added spontaneously), often in ways that addressed the specific linguistic, geographic, or social contexts of audiences in diverse Thai locales. Versioning was in high demand in centers of modern urbanity and distant points of rural or island exhibition alike. As Ingawanij stresses, the distinction from the conventional Western/classical setup of a hushed, darkened movie theater with the projector hidden behind viewers in an enclosed room is stark. In the machinery, processes, and ideas underlying Thai versioning, which she also terms "makeshift cinema," the imported filmic apparatus was pulled apart, reconstructed, and exhibited along with the films and other multimedia elements added to them. The result, not unlike the archipelagic aesthetics of Akup and others working in Java, was a complex marriage of the human and the mechanical, the local and the transnational, showcasing "the interfacing of 'new' and '(very) old' media practices and medium ontologies in Southeast Asia" (2018:11).[14]

Lines of exchange around and across the Pacific also play an especially important role here. As Ainslie and Ingawanij emphasize, the fragmented Thai approach to the conception, exhibition, and consumption of films emerged in the context of a divided audience, the upper-class minority of which viewed mainly Hollywood and Chinese fare in expensive cinemas in Bangkok or Chiang Mai. These spectators also generally lauded the few internationally regarded domestic 35 mm sound productions made during the same period. The vast, less-affluent and educated majority of viewers, however, preferred the versioned screenings that treated various Thai locales as "centers" of transpacific engagement where Hollywood, Chinese, and Indian products and aesthetics were sent to be transformed. While some of these screenings also took place in large, expensive venues, Ingawanij shows that the customary realm of versionists was in smaller theaters on the outskirts of big cities or in rural areas with no standalone cinemas. The latter were served by mobile, "itinerant" troupes who often spent months at a stretch on the road, traveling by "van, truck, rickshaw, boat or on foot, and in some cases even on elephant back" (Ingawanij 2018:10).

As the practice became increasingly established, a postwar industry grew up around these majority, lower-class viewers, producing films cheaply on silent 16 mm stock and relying on the versionists to add sound and use their fame as performers to promote and sell particular films. Along with the standard provision of an empty space or "hole" where the soundtrack would otherwise be, the visual style of these films can be said to match the fragmented, improvised nature of their mode of exhibition, emphasizing performativity. According to Ainslie, Thai 16 mm films often appeared "jerky and disjointed, immediately disrupting the diegetic world of the viewer and so . . . reinforcing the artifice of the film" (Ainslie 2018:313–14). In certain ways, Ainslie's analysis also reflects the pervasive distaste of Thai upper classes for the voluminous, "degenerate" 16 mm films. She refers to the ad hoc nature of their form as an "inadvertent" development that is largely the result of mistakes and "technical flaws" that were simply "not a concern for the audience" (314). While not going as far as the critics who called Indian popular cinema around the same time "primitive" (Rajadhyaksha 2009), in a similar way, Ainslie implicitly positions Hollywood classical form as a global standard of comparison—one predicated on smoothing joints and jerks in order to hide the inherent artifice of films. The style created by Thai filmmakers with a huge audience base and sustained across at least four decades is hence tacitly relegated to the status of an inadequate derivative or perhaps indeed of unintentional aesthetic garbage.

Yet even if the form of Thai popular cinema is to some extent the result of chance or coincidental innovations, we might also think of it in terms of how the complex "involuntary"-yet-politicized blurtings and mimicries of film-latah have shaped movies elsewhere in the region—always without, I would argue, taking Hollywood as the final yardstick or reducing the work of local cineastes to a cinema of random mistakes. As Ainslie also acknowledges, several local film scholars have begun to approach the 16 mm era in a different way. Patsorn Sungsri, for example, refers to such films as adhering to an established, "conventional" Thai style adapted from locally embedded theatrical and other narrative forms. Most viewers, she argues, actively enjoyed and were "satisfied" with this approach (2004:55). Others have retrospectively positioned 16 mm films as the height of "classical" Thai cinema in light of their vastly greater distribution and impact compared to Hollywood-influenced 35 mm sound films (or to Hollywood or other foreign films themselves) (Ainslie 2018:304). In my reading, the local scholars' intervention is crucial, as it imbues Thai popular cinema with an air of greater intentionality, while highlighting the contemporary influence and continuity of what Ingawanij calls its "interfacing" of distinct "media ontologies." This in turn reflects what Gonzaga (2016) and others see as the region's typical "intermedial" tendencies, inspired by historically embedded networks of communication linking vastly different groups across archipelagic expanses of islands and water. What the Thai critics see in this extensive body of filmic work is the emergence of a standard: a basic formal approach to production and exhibition that is constitutively distinct from Hollywood, European, and other global styles.

While popular Indonesian films of that era are not always explicitly labeled "classical," they, too, like the 16 mm products of Thai filmmakers in the 1950s and 1960s, are implicitly positioned as such by critics and scholars.[15] As foundational works from the early years of independence, like their Thai counterparts, the "classicalness" of films produced in Jakarta at the time is entangled with the troubled ideal of a national character emerging through mass media. In this context, Ingawanij's view of Thai versionists as mimicking—but more importantly "profaning" or bringing down "to common usage what had been set apart through consecration" (2018:21)—has strong regional echoes, not the least of which is the complex and literally profane simulations of latah.[16] Further distinguishing Southeast Asian cinemas from oppositional movements elsewhere in the Global South, her analysis will be of help in processing how 16 mm films in Thailand, and the work of popular cineastes elsewhere in the region, are constitutive of national cinemas and at the same time anathema to idealist (or at times any) concepts of the nation.

This is not to say, however, that cinema and conventional nationalism were *never* aligned in Thailand or elsewhere in the region. Ingawanij shows that the openness and malleability of the 16 mm versioning apparatus allowed for it to be appropriated and deployed not only by freelance versionists or those sponsored by business interests (often selling various forms of medicine) but also by Thai government propaganda troupes. These troupes were tasked with incorporating and repeating "hypernationalistic announcements" that "ritualistically and affectively create[d] the bond of patriotic love between the villagers and the mobile troupe, as a symbolic embodiment of the state" (2018:21). In line with the heavy U.S. presence and influence in Thailand at the time, the films shown were often also saturated with anticommunist ideology, creating, along with the versionists' more rigidly structured performances, a "boundary separating Thainess from communism" (Ingawanij 2018:21). Unlike some of the other, more "makeshift" or even "inadvertent" aspects of Thai versioning, this function appears in step with the view of cinema more broadly as a transnational delivery system for the political goals of one or the other side of the Cold War. As in Benedict Anderson's *Imagined Communities* (1983), the view also supports a particular understanding of the modern world as a group of essentially comparable nations, each projecting its surface particularities and its underlying, homogeneous similarities via globalized mass media technologies.

In Indonesia, the production house PFN, or Perusahaan Film Nasional (National Film Company), also made short instructional films for the government, as well as fictional features with explicitly nationalist themes set by the state. One such film was *Dewi dan Pemilihan Umum* (*Dewi and the Public Elections*, 1955), which was helmed by Indonesia's first female director (see chapter 3 for more details), Ratna Asmara, and combined a dramatic story with explanations and instructions on how to participate in the first public elections, held in 1955 (Lestari 2022:56). Yet even in this seemingly straightforward case of national cinema, the plot highlights attempts by businesses and individuals to further their own interests by influencing voters, foreshadowing the actual severe political fragmentation that would result from the election. Certain Malayan films of the 1950s, such as the heroic drama *Sergeant Hassan* (dir. Lambretto Avellana and P. Ramlee, 1958) centered on armed Malay resistance to the Japanese occupation and also conformed to and conveyed a more closed, unquestioning nationalist perspective. As Gaik Cheng Khoo (2006:99) points out, however, such films invariably failed to attract a broader, multiracial (if also lower-class) local audience, appealing mostly to Malays while alienating racial others.

The production and reception of representative "national" films was generally less successful than that of more ideologically and socially open or inconclusive efforts. As Ingawanij also makes clear, in Thailand the strictly controlled hypernationalist strain of 16 mm cinema was a version of a version: a tiny minority of cinematic practice in Thailand at the time. For Ingawanij, like the scholars who termed it classical Thai cinema, versioning is defined not by following global cinematic paradigms but by its celebrated ability to "profane the technical tools of cinema and their associated ideological underpinning" (2018:21). What is classical, then, and, in a truer sense, "national," mainly involves taking apart and reformulating the global and the local into shifting patchworks of elements ideally aimed to address heterogeneous regional audiences. In Thailand these patchworks allude to particular, and often highly distinct, *versions* of Thainess, the majority of which eschew centrally established ideas of national purity, even while a few work to construct it. Often, these versions involve employing local dialects and using particular references to cater to the specific experiences and perspectives aligned with them, effectively addressing Thailand in terms of its multiple subnational regions and "centers" and mirroring the fragmentation of form, genre, locale, language, and other references in the exhibition of the films themselves. This basic approach to cinema production and exhibition, which I term *archipelagic*, also functions to alter, divide, and profane the unified, homogeneous Thai nation as conceived and promoted by the central government.

BOENG, AJO BOENG!

Throughout the region, cinema has constituted one of the most important ways both to imagine and to deconstruct the nation. Yet filmmakers were not alone in inheriting this difficult and paradoxical task. As I have begun to show (and will expand on in the next chapter), the reproduction of archipelagic aesthetics in Southeast Asia was and is an eminently multi- and intermedial endeavor in which cineastes are entangled in complex media histories and with the work of other artists, writers, and performers. Thai versioning stands among the clearest examples of the deconstruction of a national imaginary using a multimedia approach based in the radical reconfiguration of cinematic technologies. Figure 6, for example, depicts one of the most apt and recognizable symbols of Indonesian artists' analogous, archipelagic impulses to playfully subvert and desacralize nationalist iconographies in the mediums of painting and text.

Requisitioned by Soekarno, the poster was created by a team of artists based in Batavia (now Jakarta) at the beginning of the nationalist struggle against the Dutch (1945–49) in 1945. At first glance, the image of a native man breaking free of his shackles against the background of the red and white Indonesian flag appears as a typical example of a globally comparable nationalist aesthetics. Yet in this case, the artists felt an image alone was not sufficient: the poster needed to call out to would-be Indonesians through multiple channels, inciting them to struggle but also addressing them in a more particularized manner—one in which they might recognize something collectively of "themselves," even if the result would at one level be a kind of self-mockery. As fate would have it, the noted poet Chairil Anwar happened to pass by. After briefly considering the image, he offered "Boeng, Ajo Boeng!" or roughly, "Brother, Let's Go Brother!"—the now-famous tagline. The words he chose, deploying the egalitarian neologism *boeng* (now spelled *bung*), by which Soekarno himself was known, were a perfect fit, and the poster was an instant classic, canonized as a symbol of national struggle against colonial oppression.

FIGURE 6. The famous nationalist poster created by painter Affandi, working together with the artist Sudjojono and SIM (Seniman Indonesia Muda [Young Indonesian Artists]). The deceptively simple and serious tagline "Boeng, Ajo Boeng!" (Brother, Let's Go Brother!) was supplied by notorious modernist poet Chairil Anwar.

Perhaps the poster's creators were indeed caught up in a fervent spirit of nationalism, driven in part by the oncoming armed struggle against the Dutch, in which many of them would participate. But the words also conveyed a different meaning, and as they were applied to the image in large, capital letters, the artists couldn't help but chuckle. Anwar, a radical new innovator in the then-emergent national language, Indonesian, was also known for haunting Jakarta's brothels in search of both pleasure and inspiration. As his colleagues discerned, Anwar had taken the tagline from the calls of local prostitutes (Sembiring 2010), who used them to incite passing men to join a far briefer, more commercialized union than what the poster was otherwise promoting.

Among the most sacred emblems encapsulating Indonesian nationalism and modernism (and patriarchy), the poster was believed by its creators to be incomplete until the utterances of a "profane" feminine source were added to the artistic strokes of the capital city's emergent master-painters. The addition implicitly linked them, and all who viewed the poster, to the seamier, illicit sides of urban life inherent in all nations but normally excluded from nationalist imagery. The earnest struggle for an ideal unity that the poster symbolizes simultaneously offers a satirical commentary on its own meaning and address, rendering a fittingly multiplex, paradoxical icon of the nation as a whole. The "fake" or misappropriated nationalist utterances of prostitutes were—even in the final, officially sanctioned, image of the poster—not separable from the real thing. The artists, having absorbed the complex milieu surrounding them in what would be the capital city, and drawing on their own diverse experiences with nationalist struggle, were driven to question the nation even as they gave birth to one of its classical visual cornerstones.

This image, and its glorious, nefarious call to action, resonated throughout the various spheres and genres of nationalist art. Soon after independence, Usmar Ismail, later to be dubbed the "father" of Indonesian cinema, wrote that nationalist artists should position "their souls as a radar that captures every detail . . . in the lives" (1983:10) of the vast ethnically and geographically divided peoples that had suddenly become "Indonesians." As Ismail and his colleagues-in-celluloid demonstrated in distinct but related ways, the convoluted signals emitted by the people would drive filmmakers to imagine and project the nation onscreen as a politically, socioeconomically, culturally, and temporally inconsistent, heterogeneous entity. By pointedly imagining Indonesia as a false or "bad" copy of the (Western) geopolitical ideal of nations constituting a homogeneous, modern series, filmmakers paid homage to the archipelagic realities of local and regional histories. Doing so also implied that from a local perspective, global ideals simplistically advocating unity and homogeneity would themselves ultimately appear fake or contradictory, just as they did in the rigidly (ethno)nationalist tenor of the Malayan film *Sergeant Hassan*.

Building on this analysis and its focus on multimedia approaches to cinema and nation-cum-region, chapter 2 will begin by exploring the critical role of Malay, Thai, Filipino, and Javanese vernacular theaters in anticipating and bringing together the emergent modern/regional public that would help define the lowbrow-yet-cosmopolitan aesthetics of the films produced in the 1950s and 1960s. I position theatrical forms like *bangsawan, stambul, sarsuela,* and *likay,* which emerged in parallel with motion pictures in the late nineteenth and early twentieth centuries, as a bridge between the forms and habits of traditional media and those of film. As I show, one especially important result of this process was a formative split—not only in the style but also in the audiences for films produced in the region and those made elsewhere. Drawing on, and radically expanding, Miriam Hansen's (1999, 2000, 2012) idea of classical Hollywood as a global "vernacular modernism," I examine the similar role of a set of regional vernacular theaters in setting the tone (and gathering the audiences) for the region's cinemas.

2

———

The Emergence of
Archipelagic Aesthetics

Vernacular Theaters and Regional Modernisms

The opening of the 1956 Indonesian film *Tiga Dara* (*Three Sisters*), directed, produced, and cowritten by Usmar Ismail, may be somewhat surprising given the sardonic, allergic, or simply uninterested reactions of regional cineastes to the global influence of Western movies highlighted in the last chapter. A musical romantic comedy-drama, *Tiga Dara* centers on the trials and tribulations of Nunung (Chitra Dewi), a woman whose family is pushing her to marry as soon as possible. On Nunung's twenty-ninth birthday, at once somber because of her gradually advancing age and, owing to her prominent position as the eldest of three daughters, also jubilant, the sisters agree that the best way to celebrate is *nonton* (watching). For the three upper-middle-class girls, this means traveling to a fancy urban screen where ticket prices are high and the films on display are imported—mostly from Hollywood (when we eventually see the outside of the theater, its parking lot, like its screen, is full of rare modern imports, in this case large American cars).

Perhaps in anticipation of what they will see on that screen, the three sisters immediately burst into a routine that evokes classic musicals from the opposite side of the Pacific (fig. 7). The resulting scene's lighting is typically high key (bright and uniform), whereas the family's home at first appears rather plain and unadorned, with few of the obviously local flourishes of the sets and locations I mentioned in chapter 1. The nondiegetic soundtrack combines jazz-pop arrangements with Latin rhythms in a way that evokes Westernized takes on global trends, at least for the moment. Driven by these sounds, *Tiga Dara*'s opening number follows the girls singing and dancing their way from the kitchen, where their simple celebration has just taken place, into the private areas of their home. There, they

54

FIGURE 7. Chitra Dewi, Mieke Widjaya, and Indriati Iskak (*left to right* in the right-hand still) as Nunung, Nana, and Nenny, the three sisters at the center of Usmar Ismail's film *Tiga Dara*. The left-hand still shows the culmination of Nunung's birthday party, after which the girls agree to go see a movie. The smooth, alluring visuals and choreography of the opening number evoke Hollywood musicals of the 1930s and 1940s, including the otherwise rare American (but common regional) habit of looking into the camera (not depicted here).

don outfits more befitting an exotic, elite trip to the movies, with viewers vicariously in tow. As they shake and shimmy, Nunung and her sisters do engage in a certain amount of typically regional flouting of the conventions of classical Hollywood, such as when they "break the fourth wall" by looking into the camera, signaling the performed, constructed nature of the world onscreen. But in this case, they do so in one of the few ways that is generally accepted in American movies: during a musical sequence that temporarily immerses the film in a space of unrealistic fantasy.

As this brief description already begins to suggest, *Tiga Dara* appears to differ in important ways from many of the films I analyzed in chapter 1, especially in how it approaches globally dominant foreign influences such as Hollywood. As I argue throughout this chapter, while this is in some sense the case, the film's complicated engagements with, and careful calculations involving, signifiers of American movies point to something distinctly Southeast Asian: the starkly class-divided and often labyrinthine structures that define the regional film market. A closer look at economic factors driving aesthetics in the region will help to further explain the basic archipelagic approaches to cinema identified in the last chapter, emphasizing a different but no less important perspective: that of the conventions' emergence in films that were also necessarily products. Without mass consumption and wide circulation, such products and their unique, regional styles would have been overtaken and wiped out by the flood of imported films with which Southeast Asian markets were inundated before and after World War II. This is especially the case with imports from Hollywood, which stationed studio representatives in key cities throughout the region to ensure political and economic conditions remained amenable for the consumption of American movies.

To better explain and comparatively frame the combination of aesthetic, political, economic, and class factors driving Southeast Asian cinemas in the mid-twentieth century, I expand on Miriam Hansen's (1999, 2000, 2012) concept of classical Hollywood and East Asian popular cinemas as supranational "vernacular modernisms." Digging deeper into histories of regional aesthetic practices and their financial roots, I argue that Southeast Asia's unique brand of vernacular modernism differs from Hansen's conception in two key ways. First, the signature approaches of films contravene the broadly accepted idea that motion pictures functioned as a seminal, epistemic break from dominant modes of entertainment and communication that preceded them. Instead, I propose that the aesthetics of regional cinemas are formatively entangled with a series of popular, widely circulating, live vernacular theaters that emerged in parallel with the global spread of motion pictures. Expanding on the previous chapter's analyses, I show that regional cinemas did not fundamentally break from these live forms but grew out of them "horizontally." Most important, filmmakers inherited the broad, mainly lower-class, audiences whose money supported their works from these vernacular theaters—audiences whose habits and tastes played a key role in transforming wildly fragmented, precinematic archipelagic modes of representation into enduring regional film conventions.

Second, while Hansen sees Hollywood as especially influential in the U.S. and abroad owing to its innovation of a new, and broadly accessible, "low" modernist aesthetics, I argue that Hollywood's reformulation by Southeast Asian audiences as a predilection of elites signals critical distinctions in what, and *who*, was able to define mass modernity in the region's decolonizing nations. As my analysis of *Tiga Dara*'s opening suggests, these conditions led to a further, vital development that would distinguish the region's films from the products of popular, vernacular modernist aesthetics in the West and in East and South Asia. In my reading, the complex, sociopolitical and economically based refusal to lend contemporary regional societies a "sealed," natural-looking, and implicitly immutable appearance onscreen created gaps and openings through which the modern was strategically suffused with elements of the regional past. However, the endurance of conventional assumptions about national cinemas and the actual role played by Hollywood in the region has led to ongoing confusion regarding how and why certain local filmmakers chose to engage with its tropes.

In 2016, following the theatrical rerelease of a restored, 4K digital version of *Tiga Dara* in Indonesian theaters, critic Damar Juniarto wrote disparagingly that Ismail's now-classic film, with its trappings of fancy, upper-class cinemagoing, "smelled American" (cinemapoetica.com). For Juniarto, the film played into a particular vision of 1950s Indonesian modernity—one held mainly by urban intellectuals, including some filmmakers and apparently also the otherwise left-leaning president Soekarno. Their ambition, as detailed by Tanete Pong Masak (2016:147), was for the capital city to be transformed into "Djakartawood": a hub on the Asian side of the Pacific for the production of glamorous, up-to-date, and globally viable movies. But why, Juniarto asks, would Usmar Ismail, whose reputation was forged in the pursuit of a supposedly purist style associated with critical nationalism, "make a U-turn" in the direction of what he himself had vehemently sworn off: entertainment-oriented fare that many found to reek of Hollywood? While progressive reviewers in the 1950s generally lauded Westernized aesthetics, Ismail's and others' legendary, retrospectively simplified "nationalist" stance is the one most often championed by critics in Jakarta today—a group who generally frowns on the Djakartawood fantasies of their forebears.

As noted above, in comparison to the films reviewed in the previous chapter, *Tiga Dara* is indeed surprisingly lacking in irony in its appropriation of more typically Hollywoodian techniques and flourishes, as in its opening song and dance. In my assessment, however, the assumption that Ismail had simply sold out and turned to classical Hollywood as an inevitable model for his own work risks misreading the complex regional and local media flows and markets in which filmmakers at the time were forced to swim or sink.[1] A closer look at *Tiga Dara* reveals much about the material conditions, and often extreme economic pressures, shaping Indonesian and other regional films during turbulent periods of decolonization and national development. *Tiga Dara*'s conception and style were indeed driven by market concerns, something, as we will see, that Ismail himself deeply lamented. Yet, while taking in and carefully analyzing the American odor emanating from *Tiga Dara*'s initial scenes, we may also detect a whiff of something more diffuse, heterogeneous, or, depending on one's perspective, "unclear." To my nose, the aroma evokes what Miriam Hansen calls vernacular modernism, while also potentially stimulating the attentive critic to sniff past the term's limitations. For Hansen, associating popular cinemas with vernacular modernisms conceives of movies not simply as ideologically suspect profit machines but also as vital engines and archives through which the vicissitudes, ruptures, and emergent aesthetics of modernity are collected, displayed, and negotiated.

In Hansen's approach, cinema's most crucial function is a reflexive one. She positions motion pictures as central vehicles and receptors for a varied field of popular discourses and media that, when assembled together onscreen, "allow . . . viewers to confront the constitutive ambivalence of modernity" (1999:71). When combined with other forms of design, urban planning, and entertainment that emerged around and in parallel with cinema, popular films act as key constituents of an accessible, low-modernist aesthetics: what Hansen terms "a sensory-reflexive horizon" (2000:13) and what Zhang Zhen, building on Hansen's work, calls an aesthetic "episteme" (2006:2). Conceived as such, vernacular modernism has the potential to resonate across class and racial borders and beyond the boundaries of nationality that are so often applied to films by default. Especially in light of the potential for "prevailing social and sexual arrangements" to be challenged (Hansen 1999:68) and for "traditional binarisms" to be "at once invoked and undermined"

(Hansen 2000:16), vernacular modernism would seem to at least begin to get at how a film like *Tiga Dara* functioned as a dynamic cultural commodity in Southeast Asia. At the same time, however, the question of whether the film's "Hollywood smell" is what drives its modern perspective on shifting social and sexual habits and cultural identities inevitably draws attention to the epistemological horizon of Hansen's inquiry. Is *Tiga Dara* simply another iteration of vernacular modernism as Hansen defines it, or is it something that might work to expand the basic parameters of the term? As I will show, a close examination of the film's fraught relation to Hollywood is crucial in answering this question.

"Whether we like it or not," Hansen writes, "American movies of the classical period offered something like the first global vernacular" (2000:12). Hollywood in the mid-twentieth century was "an incarnation of *the modern*" (2000:11, emphasis in original), emerging and circulating along with the newest industrial modes of production and part and parcel of the Westernized visions of global mass culture associated with them. Positioned at the very heart of what was new and current (and aggressively marketed in- and outside the U.S.), Hollywood's vernacular modernist movies went more or less everywhere, implying and embedding a sense of inevitability and universality to aesthetics that derived from a very specific place and time. But for Hansen, the key to Hollywood's power in this regard was precisely that it *did not* dictate a rigid or precise idea of what the experience of modernity should be. Rather, films were often fundamentally altered through diverse modes of exhibition and reception in- and outside of North America, as Hollywood came to mean "different things to different people and publics" (2000:12). From this perspective, Hollywood became the "first global vernacular" because it started by treating the U.S. as a diverse, fragmented assembly and not a homogeneous, "hermetically sealed" nation or idea. Its films addressed the U.S. almost like (from the perspective of this study) an archipelago such as the "Malay World" that includes and surrounds much of Southeast Asia or even the world itself, with its various continents, countries, and regions divided and connected by huge expanses of water.

Contrasting with the formal homogeneity associated with Hollywood films, this more fragmented view of the U.S. and the world around it is positioned by Hansen as a fundamental reason for the long-standing success of American movies against their "national-popular rival[s]" elsewhere in the world (1999:68). The question this raises for the study at hand is whether a film like *Tiga Dara* would be preemptively unseated in local markets by virtue of its supposed faithfulness to the specificities of Indonesian experience in which it is assumed to be grounded. To better answer this, I will attempt to follow Hansen's own invective to stay close to the "actual processes of transfer and translation, circulation, and reception" (2012:607) that shape film industries and their domestic and transnational positionings. Over time, this approach pointed Hansen away from the perception of Hollywood's role in the world as unprecedented and exceptional, revealing other, similarly functioning aesthetic epistemes across the Pacific in interwar Shanghai (2000) and Tokyo (2012). Both of these film industries likewise emerged from rapidly developing nations. They produced and circulated movies with themes and undercurrents that flowed, not unlike what we have seen in Southeast Asia so far, "in directions oblique to dominant imperial-nationalist ideology." As such, Hansen argues, the products of both industries showcased "the conflicting potentials of modernity, rather than a unitary national discourse" (2012:617). In this sense, Chinese and Japanese films of the time also remained open to formal experimentation, ambiguity, and parody.

In some sense like Hollywood, but also very different, for Hansen, these films embodied the ways in which culturally and geographically specific aesthetic formations emerge and begin to circulate within and beyond national boundaries. Based on the historical details that came to distinguish the aesthetic features and circulatory patterns of these non-Western vernacular modernisms, the concept itself began to shift in Hansen's view, coming to appear almost sovereign in its own right. Increasingly detached from Hollywood as its basic model, vernacular modernism was now like a living organism (or perhaps a proto-artificially intelligent one), "capable of generating new lines of inquiry" and "revising itself in view of the empirical formations it explores" (2012:607). As the empirical features of other regions arose to lead the way in Hansen's studies, the status of Hollywood as a singular manifestation of *the* modern was no longer sustainable. Instead, it emerged as one of several media hubs—including Europe, the Soviet Union, and Japan—that broke global pathways by placing their particular assemblages of low-modernist culture and aesthetics into circulation within and beyond national and regional boundaries.

I take up vernacular modernism in this evolving sense, as an idea that demands continual revision according to the actual processes and specificities of the locale and historical period to which it is applied. I propose that engaging Hansen's concept through the development and circulation of Southeast Asian cinemas will generate questions and ideas that further deform and open vernacular modernism, expanding the ways in which she and others have understood and used it thus far. As I will show, what most profoundly distinguishes Southeast Asia's particular, circulatory brand of vernacular modernism is that, while it drives and shapes the region's cinemas, it is neither born of nor centered on motion pictures. Instead, I argue that regional vernacular modernisms complicate ideas of mass media as necessarily driven by the currents of global technological advance. As such, Southeast Asian films not only multiply and shift the location of "the modern" across the Pacific but disrupt the sense of chronology and time broadly associated with modernity.

As we will see, particular yet highly mobile and adaptable regional aesthetic trends pulled movies "back" into a mediascape and public sphere defined by embedded modes of live interaction and improvisation. Within this sphere,

I position a regionally circulating brand of live vernacular *theaters* as the most salient force shaping a nascent, modern visuality that included cinemas in its purview. I position these particular structural-economic and aesthetic conditions as facilitating a low-modernist aesthetics that was still more volatile and heterogeneous than those of Hollywood or the East Asian mainstream at the time. Not only were films fundamentally open to interpretation, but their formal and temporal structures performatively mimicked their fragmenting ways of addressing region, nations, and world, as well as past, present, and future simultaneously. As such, the region's strong aesthetic currents caught and spun otherwise predictable transpacific and global flows off course, landing them in a realm where live performance and media interactivity were still (or, depending on how we look at it, *already*) queen.

VERNACULAR MODERNIST THEATERS

Malay-, Tagalog-, and Thai-language vernacular theaters like *bangsawan, stambul, sarsuela*, and *likay* emerged in the late nineteenth and early twentieth centuries, making an immense impact on the region's popular mediascapes in parallel with the birth and global spread of motion pictures.[2] Similar to early cinema, these theaters combined local aesthetic trends and technologies—some emergent, some more established—with those circulating around the world with increasing speed and frequency. Unlike Western cinema's general pattern of homogenization and classicization over the second decade of the twentieth century, however, Southeast Asian vernacular theaters continued to shift and adapt their forms in conversation with the gradual emergence of local film industries. As Dafna Ruppin shows, for example, early touring film exhibitors in the Dutch East Indies (mainly run by Europeans and Indians and mostly showing nonlocal imagery while at times combining film screenings with theater performances) generally used the routes established by vernacular theater companies and circuses (2016:7).

Nadi Tofighian argues that these pathways were also based on the networks of "imperial trade, shipping, and communication" crisscrossing and leading into and out of the region (2013:61). Tofighian sees a flowering of entertainment culture in the late 1800s in Southeast Asia that mirrors similar developments in the West, blending together emergent filmmaking with various other media (2013:46). While in the U.S. and Europe this blending of older and new media would soon be dominated by the emergent mechanics and narratives of Western classical cinema, following Tofighian and Ruppin, I contend that intermedial modes of expression remained a much stronger, more viable force in Southeast Asian entertainment, one that continued into independence and the formation of national cinemas and, in many ways, until the present. From the late nineteenth century to the mid-twentieth, vernacular theaters were generally positioned at the center of these developments and the mixtures of various media they invented and exhibited. To provide a sense of consistency across the otherwise diverse and shifting nature of the aesthetics and styles across numerous troupes' performance locales, common regional techniques such as improvisational *pantun* verse, particular patterns of music and dance vs. narrative, and direct audience address were deployed.

The label of vernacular, a retrospective term used by scholars (like Hansen's application of it to cinemas), relates to these emergent theaters' innovative use of common regional languages such as Malay. Over the previous several centuries, Malay had grown into a widespread lingua franca through its role in facilitating trade between various port cities and economic hubs throughout much of the region. Malay also became a key vehicle for emergent literatures and other forms of communication and exchange, including those used by colonial administration. Like most other aspects of the region, however, Malay was far from homogeneous, with numerous dialects and versions mixing in bits and pieces of other languages circulating in the region such as Hokkien, Javanese, Mandarin, English, Dutch, Thai, Tagalog, and others. Yet most variants were mutually intelligible on a basic level. As Tofighian also notes, new media that adopted regional lingua franca were quickly drawn into the circulatory and trade routes these languages described and arose from, benefiting from the economic opportunities they offered. As Tan Sooi Beng shows, bangsawan, a constantly touring Malay-language vernacular theater that originated in Penang, Malaya, soon established itself as the first popular commercial theater in the Malay Peninsula. Despite drawing on tropes of older, traditional and ritual-based forms, bangsawan was distinguished from them by the need to be economically viable in order to continue. Its often frenzied, heterogeneous development was driven by this need (Tan 1995:602).

Like an actual vernacular tongue that "constructs itself by appropriation" (Sheldon Pollock qtd. in Hansen 2012:609), early iterations of touring theaters like bangsawan drew together an eclectic assembly of transnational and local trends, narratives, and high and low genres and traditions. These were variously braided together to address differences in taste and influences associated with diverse Malay-speaking locales. Continually moving around and between these locales, bangsawan circulated through the region for more than six decades. Its name announced a connection to Malay aristocrats (the meaning of the word *bangsawan* in Malay), who at times served as subject matter for its narratives. Its approaches to style, globalization, and audience address, however, were decidedly populist and greatly influenced P. Ramlee and other Malay filmmakers during Singapore's cinematic golden age in the 1950s and 1960s. Their films, in turn, were some of the most successful in regional markets at the time, pushing others to adopt similar approaches. This is an important reason that I position live, vernacular theaters as crucial forces shaping what I argue to be Southeast Asia's distinct brand of vernacular modernism. But bangsawan was one among many.

As bangsawan was beginning to come into its own as a commercial and aesthetic force in the late nineteenth century, a rival, Malay-language form soon arose under the name *stambul* in Surabaya, East Java. Often called *opera* or *komedie*,[3] *stambul* (or *stamboel* in the old Malay spelling system) the title—foregrounding the form's roots in transnational appropriation—was derived from *Istanbul*, referring to the exotic, loosely Turkish costumes often worn by performers. As in bangsawan, however, the name mainly functioned as an attraction in its own right and often had little or no connection to narrative content. Taking its cue from bangsawan, the first recorded performance of stambul was an improvisational, Malay adaptation of *1001 Nights* in 1891. After a few false starts, stambul quickly became the main regional source of competition for bangsawan troupes (Cohen 2006:49). Working to continually attract audiences, stambul performers began rapidly expanding their repertoires, devouring and combining new "tricks" and established transnational techniques to come up with an adaptable set of attractions. With these, they began touring the Malay-speaking areas of the region, challenging and feeding off of bangsawan.

While what constituted a typical bangsawan performance was equally varied, as Tan explains, an evening's ostensible main attraction would normally be either a long narrative play or several shorter narratives performed one after the other. In between the acts of the longer play or in the time used to reset the stage and costumes after a shorter one ended, "extra turns," sometimes also referred to as "vaudeville turns," were offered. These drew on the influence of touring Western vaudeville groups in the region (Tan 1993:35, 44) and adapted the vaudevillian tactic of presenting a rapid-fire variety of different attractions. In bangsawan these consisted of an almost unlimited variety of other types and forms of entertainment, from music to dance to comedy or at times even circus clowns or a short boxing match (Tan 1993:39–41).

Tan shows that these "turns" often became a greater audience draw than the performed narratives, and troupes went out of their way to provide new and exciting attractions between acts. While drawing on elements of vaudeville, this became a distinctly Southeast Asian style, especially for the time. On the other side of the Pacific, Hollywood studios were redefining American vernacular modernism by eliminating the "anarchic" influence of vaudeville and its former players on films in favor of clearer narratives (Jenkins 1992). Yet even while Hollywood films flooded the region, bangsawan troupes responded to audience tastes as late as the 1930s by featuring special nights where narratives were excised completely in favor of an expanded collection of "turns." It was these fragmented collections that most powerfully resonated as new and contemporary with regional audiences. Singaporean newspapers saw the localized turns as "modelled to suit the modern taste" and appropriate for "all nationalities" (Tan 1993:45). The latter claim reflected the diverse mix of races and places of origin in the region's cosmopolitan port cities where vernacular theaters and Malay lingua francas were most firmly established.

As bangsawan grew in popularity, its far-flung artistic sources and adaptations came to include transnational standards such as Shakespeare, which troupes combined with Arab, Indian, and local Malay and Chinese fare. Tan describes typical bangsawan performers in the 1920s as "constantly [exposing] themselves to new dances and songs of various ethnic origins, learning [them] quickly, developing their stage roles, improvising dialogues, and introducing novelty acts and tricks into their performances. . . . [They] also watched foreign films and theatrical performances constantly, so that they could learn and adapt their dances, songs, novelty acts, and tricks" (1995:611). A newspaper advertisement from the 1920s cited by Tan gives a more specific sense of just how transnational bangsawan was, promoting a show with the "latest English songs and dances," "Grand Russian," Spanish, Hawaiian "Hulla-Hullah," "Oriental," "Genuine Egyptian," "Enchanting Hindustani," "Varied Malayan," Javanese, "Paris Underworld—'The Apache'" among other kinds of music and performance (1989:236).

In the race for the perfect mix to accommodate and inspire local modern sensibilities, Matthew Cohen (2006) shows that stambul was the first major regional form to adapt European proscenium staging, costume styles, painted backdrops, and other emergent aesthetic technologies and special effects. These were then also deployed by bangsawan troupes. But neither form drew on any particular imported style, country, or region (such as Europe or the U.S.) as its main reference or root source. The appeal of both relied on how they translated and re-presented a shifting combination of local, regional, and global elements, throwing homogeneous conceptions of artistic or cultural authenticity out the window, or at least far from the stage. The appropriation of styles, formal elements, and terms like "vaudeville turn" was hence not seen as imitative or derivative in a negative sense. When bangsawan was first performed in the 1870s in Penang, British Malaya, it was even promoted as "tiruan wayang Parsi" (imitation Parsi theater) because it adapted a style performed by Indian migrants, replacing its dialogue and lyrics with Malay *pantun* verse (Tan 1989:231–32). The use of various foreign words and concepts simply added to the attraction of a diverse form of entertainment produced with a geographically, socially, and racially fragmented and cosmopolitan audience in mind.

As "modern" as this was in the regional context in the late nineteenth and early twentieth centuries, it is important to note, especially in Southeast Asia, how these emergent cosmopolitan forms were also marked with strong signs of the past—symbolic and actual elements that rooted them in histories of the *tanah air* (land-water) where they were invented and performed. For example, the use of the name *wayang Parsi* already signaled an adaptation by applying the Malay term for theater: *wayang.* This reflected the deep and continuing influence of regional art forms like shadow play, or *wayang kulit* (as it is called in Malay, Indonesian, and Javanese), as well as the historically embedded narratives and various other theater forms associated with it. These would continue to profoundly inflect the development of modern aesthetics in the region, including those of cinema.

Vernacular theater troupes in Indonesia also often referred to what they did as a form of wayang, while the director would be called a *dalang,* taken from the term for the puppet master in Javanese shadow play (Biran 2008). Even as the localized Parsi roots of bangsawan were gradually overwritten and covered by further layers of appropriated practices, genres, and conventions, many Malayan troupes continued to use names like "Wayang Kassim," or "Kassim's Theater" after the name of the director. The term *wayang*, with its flexible meanings and attachment to screens via shadow play, was also applied to Malaysian cinema. *Nonton wayang* (watching wayang) is still used today as the Malay term for going to the movies.

As bangsawan and stambul expanded into regionally focused Malay-language forms, touring port cities like Surabaya, Batavia (now Jakarta), Medan, and Makassar, they thrived along these bustling trade routes, becoming a vital medium of cultural exchange in the region. As they did so, they changed constantly, but they also held fast to certain, regionally familiar ideas and practices like wayang and also Malay *pantun* verse. The latter was used as a basis for impromptu adaptation and translation of narratives, dialogue, and song. Using this local and regionally grounded approach to globalization and modernity, vernacular theaters developed in parallel with emergent print media like newspapers and regional literatures but exceeded the audience bases of these media. Written materials were also profoundly shaped by the region's networked, transnational-archipelagic imaginaries (Bernards 2015) but were consumed more exclusively by educated elites.

The growth and success of bangsawan and stambul were further buttressed by the near-simultaneous emergence of similar but more geographically and linguistically localized forms such as *ketoprak* (Central Java), *ludruk* (East Java), *lenong* (West Java), *drama gong* (Bali), *likay* (Thailand), *comedia* and *sarsuela* (Philippines), and many others. With slightly more discernible nods to various local and regional traditions, these emergent theatrical styles took up a similarly acquisitive and transnationalized approach to form, genre, and narrative. Indonesian variants such as ketoprak and ludruk offered lower-cost alternatives to touring stambul or bangsawan shows, bringing local adaptations and combinations of *Romeo and Juliet, Wonders of the Deep*, or the regional-legend-based *Djula-Djuli Bintang Tiga* (*Three Star Djula-Djuli*) to appreciative audiences potentially priced out of touring stambul or bangsawan shows.[4] In the Philippines, *comedias* "rehearsed what we might think of as the colonial uncanny" inevitably associated with the trade routes, narratives, and some of the conventions deployed by vernacular theaters. But at the same time, the theaters "furnished a context for domesticating" these new and overdetermined elements as they became "lodged in the vernacular" (Rafael 2005:117).

Among the Javanese subregional variants, ludruk and especially ketoprak followed the paths of Malay-language "operas" in establishing strong reputations that transcended provincial origins. As a result, well-known troupes from Solo, Surabaya, and elsewhere in Java began making frequent tours of other islands, further expanding and diversifying the regional aesthetic circulation established by bangsawan and stambul. From this now multipronged conglomeration grew still more

Malay- and Indonesian-language variants like *sandiwara* and *tonil* (about which more below), producing a distinctive field of emergent vernacular aesthetics that was unstoppable in its circulation around the region from the 1920s to the 1950s and beyond.

As noted above, these developments in Southeast Asia occurred at the same time that classical Hollywood films were establishing themselves elsewhere in the world as "the first global vernacular" and an "incarnation of *the modern*" (Hansen 2000:11–12, emphasis in original). Because of the theaters' popularity and other economic, social, and political factors, the golden age of cinema in Southeast Asia would come a little later. Upstarts like the Filipino Malayan Movies, the region's first native-owned film company founded in 1917 (Tofighian 2013:41), reiterated the salience of linguistic (and variably ethnically conceived) Malayness in much of Southeast Asia. But aside from a handful of films produced in the 1910s and 1920s in Singapore, Bangkok, Manila, and Jakarta (then Batavia), local filmmaking was sparse in most of the region until the 1930s and 1940s. With few movie screens overall and Hollywood films relegated to expensive, elite venues, live, vernacular theaters, not local or foreign films, first came to define an expansive regional aesthetic sphere and network—one that worked precisely to bridge "distinct, highly uneven and unequal formations of modernity" (Hansen 2012:613).

Stambul, bangsawan, ketoprak, and other variants did so by leveling and "lowering" various global and local genres and styles for mass consumption and regional circulation at a time when national borders were still largely in the making. Vernacular theaters also openly reflected and commented on their own processes of appropriation, adaptation, and reconstruction, integrating these elements into narratives and signature styles. As such, they resonate strongly with Hansen's idea of a "sensory-reflexive horizon for the contradictory experience of modernity" (Hansen 2000:13). Yet their almost absurdly dense, globally curated repertoires took things a step further, while catering to and bridging the eclectic tastes of urban, and at times rural, audiences. In many ways, regional vernacular theaters exceeded both the cosmopolitanism and the stark contradictions that Hollywood or other film-centered modernist conglomerations in East Asia and elsewhere injected into the "optical consciousness" (Hansen 2000:12) of their viewers. With the rise and spread of American and Indian cinemas around the same time, narrative and generic tropes exported by film industries in Hollywood, Bombay, Calcutta, and elsewhere were soon included in the expansive purview of Southeast Asian vernacular theaters, where they were brought "back to life" in a way specific to the region.

At a time when local film industries were nascent, subject to heavier colonial regulation, or even nonexistent in much of the region, these emergent commercial theaters occupied a similar function to that expressed by films in much of the West and in South and East Asia. As an added boon, performing arts in many places were of less concern to European authorities than moving pictures, especially because of movies' perceived ability to lend the appearance of objective reality to constructed scenarios (Tan 1989:251). Alternatively, foreign-made films could be seen as overly forthright in revealing the darker sides of Europeans, as if highlighting "the progress of thieves" (Ruppin 2016:22) in ways that might negatively influence perceptions of Westerners' local roles and authority. With less censorship (aside from isolated cases) and little need for expensive imported equipment, vernacular theaters flourished. The potential for transmedial and interclass "promiscuousness" that Hansen sees driving the circulation of vernacular modernist films elsewhere was also amplified in Southeast Asia by the malleability of live performances, which could be adapted and changed on the fly, including by adding short films at intermission, while actors explicitly responded to and "flirted" with viewers.

The broader, more permanent shift from live performance to film happened mainly in the mid-twentieth century, although theater retained a strong influence on film thereafter as well. As much of the region underwent parallel, uniquely rapid timelines of decolonization and nation-formation around the Second World War (see chapter 1), local film production expanded and began to take on more regular industrial structures. In the process, basic sets of conventions and assumptions about what constitutes a proper filmic "world" emerged. As I show in the next section, these regional conceptions of what cinema is and does were generated through the "lowbrow," archipelagic cosmopolitanism produced by the circulation of bangsawan, stambul, and other vernacular theaters. I position the theaters' historically grounded yet globalized interactive live engagements with spectators as a key—perhaps, indeed, *the* key—influence on the development of regional film styles.

PROMISCUOUS VERNACULAR THEATERS, INTERACTIVE MODERNIST FILMS

The enduring social and economic sustainability of the field inscribed by regional vernacular theaters was among the keys to its influence on local-cum-national cinemas. So, too, was the large, multiethnic pool of skilled creative labor that was assembled and trained around it.[5] A majority of the producers, crew, and actors in early Malayan, East Indies, Thai, and Filipino film productions began their careers in vernacular theaters. Foundational 1930s and 1940s Filipino director and actor Gerardo de Leon, for example, came from a family of *sarsuelitas* (performers of *sarsuela* Tagalog theater). De Leon grew up between his family's performances and movie theaters, where he earned extra money playing piano for silent films in the 1920s (*Film in the Philippines*, 1983). The first Filipino feature film, *Dalagang Bukid* (*Country Maiden*, dir. Jose Nepomuceno, 1919), was also based on a popular sarsuela play and used sarsuela performers to sing and play its musical numbers live behind the screen during showings (Lumbera 2011:6). Following the precedent set by *Dalagang Bukid*, numerous Filipino musical films referenced and deployed the tropes of sarsuela from the 1920s until at least the 1960s. Bienvenido Lumbera argues that *komedya* (also spelled *comedia*), another emergent form of vernacular theater in the Philippines, was the source from which "the typical Filipino action film was to develop" (2011:7).

In Malaya, the Indies, and Thailand, when local film production began to ramp up in the 1920s and 1930s, performers and crew likewise shuttled back and forth between live theater and cinema until filmmaking became a more reliable source of income in the 1940s and 1950s. The result was further cross-pollination between local and regional artistic traditions, emergent vernacular performance styles that built on and further developed those traditions, and discourses and practices of cinema that grew more or less directly out of the theaters.[6] The interspersal of films between different scenes or narratives performed by vernacular theater troupes in Indonesia and elsewhere positioned movies as a part of a popular entertainment package still based in live performance.[7] In Thailand, May Ingawanij similarly sees cinema as "a kind of *horizontal* extension—in other words, as the adoption of another 'genre' in a series of proximate entertainment modes whose constituting paradigm they were . . . steeped in" (2012:112, emphasis added). In this sense, like the "birth" of bangsawan as an adapted form of Parsi theater performed in Malaya, the emergence of Thai cinema was positioned not as a broad, aesthetic-epistemic shift. Instead, it was understood as another version of embedded, traditional yet increasingly cosmopolitan forms such as *khon* (mask dance/drama) and vernacular theaters like *likay*. These were modified and combined in various ways as styles and talent migrated "horizontally" from live performance to the emergent local sphere of motion pictures, while theatrical forms continued in parallel, largely unimpeded for several decades.

Echoing this development, lines of influence and exchange between cinemas and vernacular theaters in Malaya can be characterized as horizontal and mutually constitutive, suggesting the region-wide, circulatory nature of what I am calling Southeast Asia's archipelagic and interactive vernacular modernism. As Hassan Muthalib argues, early Malayan films approached their narratives, genre references, and modes of audience address in a purposely disjointed manner that drew explicitly on the kinds of global and local borrowing, adaptation, and combination that vernacular theaters like bangsawan had made into a hallmark of regional modernity. What Muthalib terms "classical" in the context of Malay-language media in the late nineteenth and early twentieth centuries is hence "a motley collection of tear-jerkers, melodrama, horror, comedy and romance" that became "exceedingly popular with the locals" (2013:3).[8] Relations between crews of various nationalities were also, at least ideally and initially, readable in similar horizontal terms: by 1950, as Muthalib shows, locally based "Chinese, Malays, Indians, Filipinos and Indonesians all came together . . . to produce films in the Malay language and targeted at a Malay audience within the Nusantara region" (3). The emergent film industry in Singapore (prior to Singapore's separation from Malaysia in 1965) was thus positioned as the locus of a particular yet constantly traveling "Malay cinema" that brought together not only aesthetics but also people from across the region and far beyond.[9]

Elmo Gonzaga explores the connections between geographic and media-based archipelagoes in Southeast Asia in a related way. He sees the horizontality of various archipelagic modes of exchange as anticipating the emergence of similar patterns in contemporary structures of new media around the world. Drawing on Lev Manovich and others, Gonzaga argues that databases and related "media infrastructures should be seen as having flat surfaces in their inclusion and combination of different modalities without any definitive linear arrangement." Accordingly, this "shapes how knowledge is shared, collaboration is fostered, and difference is managed" (2016:95). As I noted above, Hansen's (1999) view of classical Hollywood as a border-blurring, antihierarchical, low-modernist aesthetic field also positions cinema in terms that prefigure some of the ideals attached to new media and, in Southeast Asia, to old media. But amid the realities of colonialism, nationalism, and the inevitable effects of global economic forces, otherwise horizontally oriented regional, political-, social-, and media-conglomerations were also frequently subjected to vertical stratification, especially around issues of class and ethnicity. As I will show, this led, among other things, to the repositioning of classical Hollywood in a way that is fundamentally at odds with Hansen's view of its function elsewhere.

Especially in Malay-speaking parts of the region (Malaysia, Singapore, Indonesia, Brunei, and parts of Southern Thailand and the Philippines), as the cross-pollination between vernacular theaters and filmmaking intensified, the sphere of live performance went through formative shifts of its own—changes that I argue have left a further, and for this study especially important, mark on regional cinemas. Beginning in the 1920s and increasing in the 1930s and 1940s, a class-based split in audience tastes and, in the references and forms employed by troupes, asserted itself. Popular vernacular theater groups like Orion and Dardanella, for example, began labeling themselves *tonil* (often spelled *tooneel*) to highlight these changes in their approach. This included relying on fixed scripts; drawing more heavily on European forms and international cinema than on local, Asian, or Middle Eastern sources; emphasizing "psychological realism"; and decoupling songs from narratives by positioning the former as filler relegated to breaks between dramatic scenes, while treating such "turns" as less important (Cohen 2006:338). Increasingly, conventions encouraging audience interactivity and the use of temporary stages and impermanent structures (signatures of most vernacular theaters until the 1920s) were seen "as marking a low level of theatrical evolution" (Cohen 2006:375). Along these lines, *tonil* (adopting the Dutch *toneel* or theater) and other emergent, scripted forms like *sandiwara* were progressively distinguished from the spontaneity and potential chaos of stambul and bangsawan, where stories were adapted on the fly by actors with highly developed skills in improvisation.[10]

The fact that with most vernacular theaters, "the public had a direct hand in things," as an Indonesian theater critic put it (quoted in Cohen 2006:375), was becoming a problem for elite intellectuals, politicians, and audiences alike. Indeed, without formalized scripts or written dialogue, lines were often different across various performances of the same show and were frequently changed in response to audience reactions. As an aesthetic schism opened around this approach, it was not only theater critics who sided against it. In the 1930s and 1940s, many Western-educated Malay nationalists joined the chorus of those taking issue with the variability and unpredictability of forms like bangsawan, which strayed from the more "refined" cultural ideals they sought to promote, embed in society, and politicize (Tan 1989:252). In Indonesia, Pané argues that audiences at the time were similarly "split in two, between a small group that lived in a Westernized world" and preferred the new styles of *tonil*, and a much larger, less elite faction that did not (1953:30). As this suggests, despite shifting tastes among the upper classes, and even as nationalist movements gained force around the Second World War, bangsawan, stambul, and localized forms like ketoprak and ludruk retained significant audience bases among the lower classes. These forms thus continued to be performed regularly over the next several decades. In this sense, these vernacular theaters can also be said to have fallen into their own as low-modernist forms that would continue to grow by embedding themselves in regional cinemas.

I propose that these class- and audience-based splits in live performance produced two crucial effects on the film industries establishing themselves in Malaya and Indonesia in the 1940s and 1950s. As crews, actors, and producers migrated from stages to cameras and screens, local films inherited not only the formal approaches and air of direct spectator-interactivity long associated with vernacular theaters. They were also heir to the large, lower-class audiences who had stayed loyal to the wilder, spontaneous forms of stambul, bangsawan, and other vernacular variants. These spectators became the main source of income for Malayan and Indonesian cinemas, while crews adapted and employed the experiences and formal habits associated with vernacular theaters to please them (for this reason, actors and crews who migrated to film from elite *tonil* or *sandiwara* troupes were also brought back "down to earth" to some extent in their conventions and style). The established popularity of many stage actors and actresses also helped production houses and studios to quickly gain access to a larger fan base and served as a platform to launch film careers and build local industries. In this context, the success of a film came to depend on filling the seats in front of the limited number of "C" and "D" screens (some in temporary, theater-like venues without permanent walls or roofs) being constructed for mostly native, nonelite audiences.

This points to a further, still more important, difference from vernacular modernist aesthetics associated with other countries or regions: the stark economic and aesthetic separation of regionally produced films (and their audiences) from Hollywood and other imports. The latter dominated expensive, urban "A" and "B" screens throughout Southeast Asia. Instead of becoming a source of low-modernist aesthetics as it does in Hansen's analysis, then, classical Hollywood is repositioned in Southeast Asia as an elite form of entertainment mainly consumed by a wealthy, literate, and well-educated minority. As Hansen (2000, 2012) shows, beginning in the 1930s, the mainstream films of Hollywood, Shanghai, and Tokyo became more naturalist in their form and approach, mirroring the attraction to scripted, more narrative-driven forms of theater among upper-class viewers in places like Java, Sumatra, and peninsular Malaya.

At the same time, as Jason McGrath argues, a smaller group of leftist filmmakers in prewar Shanghai were making Soviet-influenced films that explicitly mocked classical Hollywood in ways that might be compared to Southeast Asian tactics. These Chinese works, however, were much more focused on attacking the local hegemony of American films specifically. They did so via rapid, potentially disorienting combinations of diverse genres and the purposeful "irresolution" of plots and romantic arcs. In such films, "the spectator is expected to be agitated by unresolved contradictions and nudged . . . to take action in some way or another" (McGrath 2023:110). While these approaches to cinema also reflected the lasting popularity of Chinese theaters and literatures with similarly "jumpy" structures (105), they still largely catered to literate urban spectators who consumed Hollywood and mainstream Chinese films. Owing to the differing preferences of lower-class viewers in Southeast Asia, mainstream shifts toward naturalism, or the specific politicization of typically fragmented regional cinemas as a leftist tactic (about which more below), were effectively prevented from happening on a large scale or, often, at all. In the context of the region's particular vernacular modernism, the idea that "the public had a direct hand in things" and that films were "interactive" and jolting in their form and narrative was still the majority rule, even as stages were overtaken by screens.

Beyond audience preferences, forces of habit made this the case: in the 1950s and early 1960s, Malayan and Indonesian (and as we will see, Thai and Filipino) films were filled with players and crews who had trained, often for decades, to hone their skills at improvisation, formal appropriation, adaptation, and audience provocation. Building on these skills and preferences, Malayan filmmakers frequently attempted to allude to the presence of viewers, even though the "interaction" this produced was not actually live. In director/star P. Ramlee's hit *Pendekar Bujang Lapok* (*The Three Bachelor Warriors*, 1959), for example, "the actors would turn to look at the camera and address the audience," an oft-repeated cinematic flourish with which "Ramlee delighted audiences and brought them into his storytelling" (Muthalib 2013:23–24). According to Hassan Muthalib, Ramlee was also one of the first in Malaya to create a truly successful cinematic adaptation of bangsawan in which "dialogue, mannerism and movements" reflected the influence of vernacular theaters. It was also crucial, however, to do so without the film simply coming across as a recording of a theater performance. Armijn Pané saw a similar, rigid theatricality plaguing Indonesian productions in the 1940s and early 1950s (Muthalib 2013:23; Pané 1953:107). It is the resulting "live," but also palpably cinematic, approach that Muthalib calls the classical style of Malay-language cinema (2013:3). I position this brand of cinematic classicism as another important element in the region's vernacular modernism.

Both within and outside of Malay-speaking areas of Southeast Asia, self-reflexivity, cinematized theatricality, and formalized allusions to audience engagement were standardized throughout the mid-twentieth century as attractions that viewers came to expect. Thai popular films from the 1940s to the 1970s offer the most direct and unique examples of this. As I mentioned in chapter 1, the majority of Thai films at the time were produced on 16 mm film without synchronous sound or intertitles. Sound effects, music, and dialogue were added live during film screenings by teams of "versionists" who adapted vocal techniques from Thai vernacular theaters like *likay* and traditional forms such as *khon* (Ingawanij 2012:109). Building on the approaches of these traditional and vernacular theaters, cinematic dubbers often improvised and directly called out to audiences, going beyond mere formal approximations and making cinema into a live medium with which viewers could *actually* interact. Like others in the region, but even more explicitly, Thai vernacular modernism expressed a dynamic temporality that challenged the idea of cinema (and with it nationhood) as exclusively "modern" and forward-looking. Cameras and projectors were made to function in ways that more closely approximated (or were on a level with) popular theaters and enduring ritual/entertainment forms like traditional dance and shadow play. As elite tastes established their own, more exclusive, aesthetic spheres, it was these "low" and "old" media that cinema needed to level with and become more like in order to attract large local audiences.

Working in concert with dubbers to gauge and engage with spectators, Thai projectionists also frequently "lifted" or removed reels from the middle sections of films if they felt the audience was becoming bored. Narratives were hence pulled apart and reedited on the fly, while the gaps this created were bridged by dubbers' improvised dialogue (Ingawanij 2018:25). Mirroring Malaysia and Indonesia, the Thai approach and its stark difference from Western classical cinemas resulted in a class-based split in Thai viewership. Popular, vernacular theater-derived 16 mm cinema emerged from and was sustained by "the communal viewing conventions of the lower-class and rural upcountry audiences" who were outpriced by, and generally uninterested in, the Hollywood and Chinese films shown in luxuriant Bangkok movie houses (Ainslie 2018:304). With their own brand of low, vernacular cosmopolitanism, 16 mm films were "particularly opposed to the modernity and 'progress'" (314) conveyed by high-budget American films shown in urban venues with which local productions "largely did not compete for revenue or overlap in any way" (Ainslie 2020:178). The feeling was mutual: for Thai and foreign elites, popular 16 mm films and the intermedial, theatrical, and lower-class media ecosystem supporting them were generally dismissed as an embarrassing blight on emergent national aesthetics.

In the Philippines, wealthier viewers with higher levels of formal education similarly cited the theatrical, "backward" nature of popular local films to suggest that their lower-class audiences were culturally and intellectually lacking. For example, Filipino critic Bienvenido Lumbera argues that Tagalog movies influenced by sarsuela theater in the inter- and postwar periods were supported by "a special market consisting mainly of viewers whose low socio-economic status had impaired their ability to fully comprehend the language and the content of Hollywood cinema" (1984:196). These audiences were disparaged by urban elites as *bakya* (clogs), or clog-wearing peasants. In a similar vein, in 1953, Usmar Ismail wondered in writing if "*Bang* Amat and *Mbok* Minah," an imagined Indonesian lower-class husband and wife, "are going to understand me if I create a scene in . . . [a typically American] way" (1983:181). Yet these were the viewers that filmmakers in both places most needed to impress. For Lumbera, this ostensibly embarrassing condition also offered Filipino cineastes a built-in audience base. Although markets remained more challenging in Indonesia, like their Malayan-Singaporean and Thai counterparts at the time, Filipino producers were able to "not only survive . . . [but] flourish . . . with great vitality" (2011:8). I position the "backward" yet economically and aesthetically enabling tendencies of regional movies to formally interact with and "talk back" to their faithful, lower-class viewers as a key element distinguishing the nature of Southeast Asian vernacular modernisms from those developing elsewhere.

In one sense, this sociocultural bifurcation made Southeast Asian films appear regressive vis-à-vis popular cinematic trends in much of the rest of the world. Elsewhere, films were becoming less overtly intermedial while presenting formally "sealed" onscreen spaces that appeared self-functioning and fundamentally separate from those watching them. But from another perspective, regional producers' close attention to audiences' tastes and constant, almost on-the-fly, adjustments to content and style look forward to what was then the distant, unknowable future of global mass media. Building on the work of Gonzaga (2016) and others, I propose that regional film industries and the screen cultures around them in the mid-twentieth century anticipate not only the horizontality and fluidity of digital infrastructures; they also resemble a protomodel for the obsessive attention to algorithms and instantaneous digital feedback that currently drives the approaches of content creators, from independent YouTubers to hegemonic global streaming platforms. The fragmented mixtures of elements and styles on 1950s and 1960s Southeast Asian screens might additionally be seen as approximating the vast searchable "interactive" databases of films and series provided by services like Netflix, Amazon, or Mubi. Comparing these temporally disparate practices and media ecologies showcases a continuity in broad, global thinking and selectivity, as well as in producers' and directors' attempts to placate the varied, "low"-yet-cosmopolitan tastes of the majority of viewers—tastes that are still, and perhaps more than ever, potentially at odds with those of (mainly elite, well-educated) filmmakers themselves.

The influence of vernacular theaters and other determining factors such as the limited numbers of screens for locally made films effectively compelled filmmakers and nascent studios to take a dynamic, populist approach to their work in the 1950s and early 1960s. Just over a decade later, Fernando Solanas, Octavio Getino, and other founders of explicitly oppositional cinema movements in South America would insist that films should be conceived to facilitate a profound connection to mass audiences (Gabriel 1982; Shohat and Stam 2014). While the results in Southeast Asia were often quite distinct from the loftier ideals of Third Cinema, I suggest that regional movies were, from their inception, eminently "by and for the people" (so perhaps Solanas and Getino should have been careful what they wished for). Yet despite the deep entanglement of economic factors with style in the region, there was still a palpably political, "oppositional" effect to film aesthetics and film markets there.

The live theater–derived market conditions and audience makeup in Southeast Asia marginalized Hollywood movies and other Western products, reducing their influence on films consumed by the biggest national and regional audiences. At the same time, unlike many other cinemas in the world, the particularities of the regionally focused market and vernacular aesthetics in Southeast Asia shaped local cinemas in ways that challenged emergent ideas of films as necessarily representative of the national. Like vernacular theaters, films in Southeast Asia presented highly "impure" outlooks that constructed, deconstructed, and then rebuilt emergent nations in particular ways, while embedding regional and transnational fragments and reflecting on doing so. This process anticipated both the formal structures and collectivist political stances later (at times far later) employed by South American and other variants of Third Cinemas.

In the next section, my close reading of *Tiga Dara* provides a case in point that demonstrates what I term the productive "undecidedness" of Southeast Asian vernacular modernisms vis-à-vis the ideals of elite national, regional, and global aesthetic regimes (including explicitly oppositional ones). But this was not necessarily an ideal situation for all parties. As I show, *Tiga Dara* is emblematic of the fact that stylistic choices were in many cases forced on filmmakers by a combination of economic conditions and official political apathy toward local film output. Yet despite the market orientation and ostensible Hollywood "smell" that were lamented by *Tiga Dara*'s own (elite) director, I propose that the film's *de rigueur* use of stylistic bricolage and formal interactivity align with regional cinematic approaches that reflect on and contest the dominance of transnational movie trends, and of the importation of rigidly "modern," national identity along with them. The film's challenges to how modernity should be shown, experienced, or framed draw on the force of certain regional traditions that, as we have seen, are themselves always in the process of change. I begin with an analysis of the specific market forces pushing and pulling *Tiga Dara*, especially its form and narrative, highlighting the ways in which both Hollywood and other regional movies were included or excluded from the social, economic, and aesthetic calculations of such a film.

THE REGIONAL FILM MARKET AS MODERN PRESSURE COOKER

Engagement with Hollywood and other foreign players was one of the main themes taken up in the first book-length study of Indonesian cinema, published in 1953 by Jakarta-based poet, playwright, filmmaker, and scholar Armijn Pané. According to Pané's figures, more than eight hundred Hollywood films were screened annually in Indonesia between 1950 and 1952 (1953:76), making up the majority of foreign-film imports (one thousand to thirteen hundred per year altogether). The total number of cinemas (650 at the time, including open air venues) was tiny for a population of seventy million, and with the influence of American studio representatives posted in most major cities in the region, the hold of Hollywood films on urban, class A and B theaters was virtually absolute. The C and D theaters to which regionally produced films were relegated constituted only 15 percent of the already small total number of screens. This made things difficult and frustrating for local producers, who, despite having the largest potential audiences, had very limited venues through which to attract and exploit them. At the same time, however, the class/screen split enforced a sort of financial and stylistic "freedom" from Hollywood: Indonesian films competed for their tiny market share not with high-budget Western imports but mostly with the Philippine, Indian, and Malayan movies preferred by the lower-class audiences who patronized, and were carefully targeted by, local productions (Pané 1953:75–77; Masak 2016:165–67).

These conditions made indelible marks on films like *Tiga Dara*, which was released at the height of the "Golden Age" of Malay cinema, consisting of films produced in relatively opulent and well-funded studios in Singapore, before its split from Malaysia in 1965. *Tiga Dara* included numerous song-and-dance numbers that evoked not only Hollywood but even more so the work of top-selling Malaysian cineastes like Malay actor-director P. Ramlee or Indian and Filipino expat directors such as S. Ramanathan or Eddy Infante.[11] During this period, Singapore-based Shaw Brothers' and Cathay Keris studios (the former produced Ramlee's films) effectively ruled regional screens, turning out between ten and twenty Malay-language films per year. Owing to the status of Malay as an established regional lingua franca, Malay-language films produced in Singapore could be easily understood by Indonesian audiences. By 1954, a number of Indonesian filmmakers, including Usmar Ismail, were increasingly feeling the effects of such stiff competition on their bottom lines. Armijn Pané went as far as calling for "a way to investigate the reasons these imported [Malayan] films are more interesting, and then follow their strategy, while improving on it" (1953:107).

Adding to the pressure on local producers, urban critics and nationalist intellectuals rarely praised their work, chiding filmmakers for doing what was needed to survive the difficult market conditions: adhering to particular regional aesthetic patterns heavily influenced by vernacular theaters. Producers and directors were often caught between economic pressures to make films a certain way and the opinions of reviewers, who most filmmakers otherwise saw as their intellectual peers. Usmar Ismail's *Lewat Djam Malam* (*After the Curfew*, 1954), for example, flirted more faithfully than most with Hollywood and European approaches. The result is often compared to film noir, and critics found in the film's unusual generic homogeneity the "seeds of development for real film art" (Situmorang 1955a:9–10). Based on its lauding by elite reviewers, *Lewat Djam Malam* took top honors at the first Indonesian Film Festival (FFI) in 1955. Afterward, it was one of the "lucky" few that found its way to screens amid an increasingly difficult box-office situation that included an unprecedented backlog of Indian movies. Yet once in theaters, the film's self-consciously global style trapped it in a small, upper-class niche of the lower-class market conditions it ultimately depended on as a regional production. Even with newly imposed limits on Malayan imports, *Lewat Djam Malam* performed poorly on C and D screens and began a slide toward bankruptcy for Ismail's production house, Perfini.[12]

Because of the failure of Ismail's "idealism" in his attempts to subvert, or at least stretch, the aesthetic standards shaped by the regional market, Jakarta critic Salim Said asserts that the success of *Tiga Dara* was imperative in order to save Perfini from closing its doors for good (1991:57). In 1953, Ismail's film *Krisis* (*Crisis*) had succeeded in exploiting a controversial rule instituted by Jakarta's mayor stipulating that all A and B cinemas in the capital would have to screen at least one Indonesian film every three months (Masak 2016:174). *Krisis* was one of the only local films to garner any interest from elite viewers, while most others fell flat. Even then, local representatives for American studios had fought bitterly to end *Krisis*'s A-screen run earlier than planned in order to make way for their own Hollywood products, at one point resulting in a physical confrontation with Ismail (Masak 2016:175). In light of the extremely limited appeal of local films in elite venues and the political economic forces that further limited their chances of success, trying to duplicate the rare, crossover success of *Krisis* represented a significant risk. For Ismail, however, market conditions in the mid-1950s left few options other than to stake the future of Perfini on *Tiga Dara* beating the odds once again and wooing both its core C and D viewers *and* local elites. Ismail had been proud of *Krisis*, but as his friend and fellow Perfini director D. Djajakusuma tells it, the higher levels of pressure and aesthetic calculation involved in *Tiga Dara* meant that "Usmar was quite ashamed of the movie. . . . How difficult it was for him to accept that he had been forced to make such a film" (quoted in Said 1991:57).

In the end, despite Ismail's disgust at what he considered a low-grade entertainment movie, the effort and stress paid off, and *Tiga Dara* duplicated or exceeded the success of *Krisis*, playing screens from A to D throughout Jakarta and in lower-class venues in other cities. Aside from the complaints of contemporary critics like Juniarto, both the market and history have been kind to the film, which is considered a classic and has been licensed by Netflix and Bioskop.com, an Indonesian streaming service. In hindsight, considerable thought and skill are evident in the picture, which gave upper-class viewers a Hollywood fix that rivaled the technical standards of Tinseltown or, at the very least, those of Singapore. At the same time, *Tiga Dara* comments on, and performatively mocks, itself for putting on Hollywood airs, giving regular viewers of regional films precisely the kind of self-referential satire they were accustomed to. In doing so, it brings to the fore the playful, self-reflexive structures of appropriation and display inherited from the emergent-cum-traditional-cum-cosmopolitan approaches of vernacular theaters, eclipsing the "clearly modern" odors of naturalism and rigid formal consistency most broadly associated with Hollywood's global influence.

This is the case even, and in fact especially, in *Tiga Dara*'s glamorous opening number. Hansen's vernacular modernist precept of watching while "participating" in the broader cultural patterns presented onscreen is amplified and literalized by the scene's regional emphasis on liveness and theatricality. This in turn inflects the sisters' abovementioned plan to *nonton*—or watch a movie on a fancy, Djakarta-wood screen—as part of the celebration of Nunung's twenty-ninth birthday. As the women form a Tinseltown dance-line and break into exuberant song, their male friend Herman (Bambang Hermanto) begins to move and shake along with them, acting as if he will follow the women out of the kitchen and into the private areas of the home. Here already, the specter of Western-style shifts in gender relations is called up only to be performatively exorcised. The exorcism is carried out through the agency of local values that seep in through intentional cracks in the film's formal bricolage of styles and references. Finding himself at the tradition-laden boundaries of the home's public spaces (its kitchen and parlor), Herman comes to his senses and stops abruptly, incurring stern glances from father and grandma for even entertaining thoughts of passing into the restricted, feminized sphere within. The gag is filled with winking, self-aware humor, but audiences are clearly expected to sympathize with the view that certain restraints on access to gendered spaces should remain in place.

Simultaneously, however, a measure of flexibility is shown toward the mechanics of emergent modes of viewing to which even the most persistent human taboos do not necessarily apply. Where Herman must stop, the softly clicking phantom in the room—the motion picture camera—continues unimpeded. Taking the viewing public into ostensibly uncharted territory, it implicitly offers up something "foreign": what one would expect to see on an elite urban movie screen, framed here as a special attraction within an Indonesian film. Flowing past the home's

FIGURE 8. Nenny pulls Nana out from behind a wooden divider as if reminding her she needs to undress in front of the camera (*left*). Nana unzips the back of her dress just before the camera "tastefully" pans away to a table where the dress will be placed (*right*).

various customary barriers, the camera follows the girls into the back, ogling obediently as they prepare to shed their house dresses for a trip to the city (fig. 8), a portrait of Marylin Monroe hung suggestively on the wall behind them. But instead of positioning the audience as voyeurs who can enjoy the illicit view without being called out for it, camera and actors collaborate to turn the scene into a spectacle that highlights the fact and the process of giving such emergent pleasures to viewers.

As Nana (Mieke Widjaja), the middle sister, is about to change her clothes behind a movable divider at the back of the room, she is stopped by Nenny (Indriati Iskak), the youngest sister. Gesturing theatrically in the direction of the lens, Nenny acknowledges the mechanical wraith capturing the scene, along with the audience and its presumed desire to see what is normally hidden. Not missing a beat, Nana advances toward the camera, flashing a practiced smile and catching the light perfectly as she unzips, while turning her back so as not to show *too* much. As if taking the hint, the camera tilts down to a table where Nana will place her clothes momentarily, avoiding the potential for any actually explicit imagery. Across a series of jump cuts, the table is filled, suggestively but tastefully, with the girls' discarded dresses and undergarments. What is "revealed" in the end is mainly that the work of cinema is premised on an intricate dance of hiding and showing, in this case driven by estimations of the shifting cultural, political traits and desires of the expanded group of regional viewers with whom *Tiga Dara* seeks to interact. The scene reads as a self-reflexive interaction between actors and camera—human and mechanistic elements of the cinematic apparatus—that acknowledges the presence of the audience, while gesturing toward its particular attributes. At the same time, those attributes are implicitly presented as subject to negotiation.

Engaging the broader contexts of Indonesian and regional cinemas at the time, the screen functions as a cracked mirror for audiences to see themselves in, reflecting the actual splits that divide them: if the opening scene prepares us to go to the movies in grand, idealistic style, a later one takes us there in something closer to the reality faced by the majority of viewers. While Herman is a university student of above-average means, when he invites Nenny, the youngest sister, to watch a film at the same, A-class theater, he is shown carefully counting the money in his pocket before ferrying her to the venue on the back of his bicycle (the scene is filmed at the Metropole, an actual elite theater and the site of *Krisis*'s earlier success and Usmar Ismail's fistfight with a local Hollywood agent in defense of his film's right to continue screening there). When it turns out scalpers have raised prices even higher, Herman balks and is forced to settle for separate seats for Nenny and himself. *Tiga Dara*, while catering to the rich, "Djakartawood" crowd that it hopes to woo, simultaneously implies that A-list establishments like the Metropole are elitist and beyond the reach of most Indonesians, even upwardly mobile ones like Herman. While including American bits and flourishes as attractions to expand its audience, Hollywood's local positioning as the figurehead of an elite, *high*-modernist aesthetics is reflected on in a negative light by *Tiga Dara*. Ismail's "national" film is hence premised on a self-reflexive engagement with a region-wide problem.

Despite the bad taste it left in the writer-director's mouth, Hollywood makes impressive entrances throughout *Tiga Dara*. But as soon as it appears, it is, as in the scene of the girls' un/dressing above, doubled back on and translated in ways that privilege the vernacular habits and tastes of lower-class viewers. American flourishes are framed as foreign, high-modern aesthetics in a way that would allow elites to gloat while the masses in the movie theater across town could enjoy a good laugh at their expense. The film as a whole is also divided into different sections that appear specifically addressed to different audiences. The film's three glamorous opening numbers are followed by a further three in which national/regional modernity is given a different feel, produced by distinct sets of visual, aural, and cultural references.

The first of these numbers consists of a youthful *tamasya*, or outing (in this case to the countryside), made into a fantasy song-and-dance sequence for which the main reference appears to be Indian popular cinema. At the time of *Tiga Dara*'s release, aside from Malayan musicals, Indian song-and-dance films were the most pressing competition for local movies. As noted above, this was due especially to importers flooding local screens with hundreds of Indian titles they had stockpiled prior to the planned imposition of an annual limit (Masak 2016:197). While the *tamasya* scene clearly recalls the typical Hindi-language fare of the time, it also appears intentionally ludicrous and over-the-top, in line with the regional low-modernist practice of films reflecting and commenting on their own aesthetic borrowings.

Along with the visuals, the music captures the transnational *masala* or "mixed" spirit of much of Bollywood's signature music, but it distinguishes itself by showcasing genres popular in Southeast Asia in the 1950s and 1960s. Flute, Spanish-sounding acoustic guitar (played by Nana, the middle sister), and a hand drum are displayed as the diegetic sources of the scene's song, to which nondiegetic woodwinds and strings are added. For Andrew Weintraub, conglomerations of varied sounds and musical textures like this build on the region's historical position as a hub for global exchange, tying "together youth cultures in Asia and beyond" (including East Asian, Arabic, Portuguese, Hawaiian, and others in a mix rivaling vernacular theaters) while reveling in stylistic and cultural impurity (2022:2). *Tiga Dara*'s next two numbers take viewers deeper into this regional soundscape, featuring back-to-back house parties filled with similarly nonaligned, populist transnationalism. While the energy is equally exuberant, the style is less openly absurd in these more realistic scenes where the music is played within the film's diegetic world. Unlike the Bollywood picnic above, visuals, sound, and mise-en-scène mimic what one might see at an actual social gathering at the time.

One scene showcases rumba- and cha-cha-infused music and dancing typical of the 1950s global craze for Latin rhythms, which had been adapted by groups in Indonesia and regionally since the 1930s (Weintraub 2022:2). The other party features Sumatran and Malayan adaptations of Arab, Egyptian, and other Middle Eastern popular musics (this style is locally referred to as *gambus*—a genre that, along with *keroncong*, also led the way to regional Latinization in the 1930s). The musicians are surrounded by young men and women in Muslim-accented garb, adding religious overtones to the party, while the music and dancing highlight distinctions between Indonesian and Malayan adaptations of Islamic culture. In the typical Middle Eastern variants that regional films localize, popular music is generally kept separate from religion. Both scenes also evoke popular tropes from Malayan films like Ramlee's *Penarik Beca* (*Trishaw Puller*, 1956), *Semerah Padi* (*As Red as Rice*, 1956), or *Bujang Lapok* (*Overage Bachelors*, 1957).

The difference in formal structure and key references between *Tiga Dara*'s first three numbers and its second three blankets the film's initially expensive, Hollywood smell with a typically regional, archipelagic bouquet of borrowing, adaptation, and self-referentiality. If we include the music, the list of global and local sources is virtually countless. I argue, however, that the inclusion of clearly distinguished "high" and "local" sections (the latter of which are stylistically "low" despite featuring middle-class scenarios) in a single film reveals the particular structure of the regional market for cinema at the time. The structure further points to the unique role of Hollywood as a marker of rarefied elite, rather than base vernacular, culture. Even if Ismail had wanted to completely smooth over the film's many distinct stylistic approaches corresponding to the stark socioeconomic and aesthetic stratification of its target audiences, it would have been difficult, if not impossible, to do so. Despite its perception in hindsight as a symptom of misguided Djakartawood idealism, *Tiga Dara* is a long stretch from the kind of "transparent," formally homogeneous narrative vehicle that became the hallmark of other vernacular modernist traditions like Hollywood or the naturalist screen-modernisms of interwar Shanghai or Tokyo.

APPARENT ANOMALIES AND
DUALIST COSMOPOLITANISM

It is important to note that although the above patterns are well-established and can be easily identified throughout much of the region, they are not absolute. In Thailand, for example, despite the dominance of 16 mm films shot without sound and hence reliant on dubbers or versionists for exhibition, a few filmmakers—following a more globally familiar cinematic path—pushed hard to make "quality," synch-sound cinema shot exclusively on 35 mm film. One such work, Rattana Pestonji's 1954 *Santi-Vina* (fig. 9), won awards at that year's Asia-Pacific Film Festival in Tokyo with its consistent, steady approach to genre and style and its more or less "sealed," noninteractive onscreen spaces. Mary Ainslie calls Pestonji the "sole Thai auteur" active during the Cold War (2020:172). The noirish crime drama *Prae dum* (*Black Silk*), another one of Pestonji's seven feature films (made between 1951 and 1964), also screened at the Berlin International festival in 1961.

The Philippines, with four established film studios in the 1950s, was perhaps most successful in producing cineastes whose work was recognized in regional festivals and markets and also in the West. Actor, director, and producer Manuel Conde, for example, screened his 1950 biopic *Genghis Khan* in competition at the 1952 Venice Film Festival. But even then, like the Indonesian company Perfini, Conde's Manuel Conde Pictures, founded in 1947, mainly turned out films that centered on a now-familiar "ingenious potpourri of Western and local mythologies and pop culture" (Francia 2002:347) preferred by local viewers. Conde is thus perhaps best remembered for his *Juan Tamad* series (1947–63) based on the eponymous legendary folk figure, who is famous for his laziness. Like other intergeneric action-comedy-dramas in the region, the series also succeeded in "giving birth to the popularity of political satire" in the Philippines by showcasing the "absurdity" seen as inherent in national politics at the time (Cruz 2011:385).

Prominent Indonesian writer-director Bachtiar Siagian can perhaps be seen as more thoroughly bucking regional vernacular modernist trends by making many of his films in a style that was much more self-consciously Hollywoodian.[13] Currently, the only complete copy of a Siagian film available—the 1962 romantic tragedy *Violetta*—is the Indonesian movie that, in my reading, most closely resembles the consistent, continuous form, narrative, and themes associated with classical Hollywood. *Violetta* and other Siagian films were also quite popular, resulting in a long-standing rivalry with Usmar Ismail. In light of this rivalry, Siagian appears as a rare example of American vernacular modernism exerting an influence in Southeast Asia that is closer to how Hansen (1999, 2000) sees it functioning elsewhere in the world. But even such unusual engagements with Western cinema are

FIGURE 9. A still from Rattana Pestonji's 35 mm classic *Santi-Vina*.
Courtesy of the Thai Film Archive.

surrounded by seeming paradoxes that stem from localized reinterpretations of
the geopolitics of movies.

Despite the more authentic American scents emanating from his work, for
example, Siagian was championed by the staunchly anti-Western Indonesian
Communist Party (PKI), which also led the charge to ban Hollywood imports
in the early 1960s.[14] In a 1957 essay in the magazine *Purnama*, Siagian, who first
encountered film theory in a translated copy of Vsevolod Pudovkin's *Film Art*
(Siagian and Yusuf 2013), further displayed his leftist credentials: he used the
Marxist principles of thesis, antithesis, and synthesis associated with Soviet
montage figures like Pudovkin and Sergei Eisenstein to explain how cinema
functions at a basic level (Siagian 1957:9–10). On one hand, such notable exceptions to the forces that I have shown to govern most Southeast Asian cinemas
are tempting to frame as mere anomalies. But on the other hand, they constitute
further evidence of the transnational nature of regional and national filmmaking
and the fact that, in line with the tastes of upper-class critics and audiences,
there were and are spaces for expression of more Western and globally inflected
aesthetics alongside localized ones.

During Singapore's golden age in the 1950s and early 1960s, for example, big
studios like Cathay Keris also often had "sister" operations locally and in Hong
Kong that produced a separate set of films in Cantonese, Mandarin, and Hokkien
for the large subsection of local Chinese-speaking audiences. The same producers
responsible for the typically fragmented interactive regional vernacular modernist Malay films thus also produced works like the Cantonese-language *Ye Lin Ye*
(*Moon over Malaya*, dir. Kim Chun and Yuen Chor, 1957), which appear to more
closely follow the protonaturalist patterns of East Asian vernacular modernisms

as Hansen formulates them. This explicit splitting of form and content along ethnic lines also stands as a regional anomaly that reflects the policies and planning specific to British colonialism in Malaya and Singapore. But it can also be read as constituting a variation in local responses to the same fragmented cosmopolitan tastes and diverse, multiracial, and polylingual populations that have defined the region for hundreds of years, and not solely owing to the influence of Western imperialism. The split in this case also builds on the specific patterns defining vernacular theaters in Singapore and elsewhere in Malaya, where popular Chinese operas competed with Malay forms like bangsawan, with each at times also borrowing conventions and stories from each other (Tan 1993).

For Rosalind Galt, the ethnic divisions specific to Malayan Singapore also created potentially productive combinations: a "polyglot mix" that was "one of the few places where Indian, Chinese, and Malay people worked together" so closely in the region (2021:42). This is quite similar to what Jakarta-based novelist and filmmaker Armijn Pané saw as a key basis of the ideal "heterogeneous psyches" that he sought to further develop as an ideal foundation for nationalism (Pané 1953:87). Reflecting on the inspirations for his film *Antara Bumi dan Langit* (*Between the Earth and the Sky*, 1950), Pané wrote that he combined American and British approaches to cinema; Russian literary flourishes; and German and Indonesian musical styles, including ones typical of regional vernacular theaters. Yet for Pané, the diversity of his film was not simply a matter of aesthetic fragmentation. He also explicitly promoted his film as a "collaboration among many different nationalities" (1953:87) with roles both behind and in front of the camera.

Along with local Chinese and Dutch workers, this interethnic collaboration included a codirector and cinematographer known as Dr. Huyung. Originally a Korean citizen, Huyung was inducted into the Japanese army during World War II; he deployed to Indonesia, where he chose to stay after the war, becoming known as a founding national filmmaker and film educator. In front of the camera, Pané also prominently positioned Grace, an "Indo" or mixed Indonesian and European woman, as lead actress. As with other elements of the nation, he saw calling attention to the plight of mixed-race citizens as promoting a healthy "dualism" (Pané 1953:87). Pané also hoped that the open display of difference and formalized incongruity in *Antara Bumi dan Langit* would garner the film's appreciation beyond the borders of Indonesia. Yet rather than sending films to America or Europe, he envisioned an alternative circulation that expanded on the regional market for most Southeast Asian films, including "India, the Philippines, Malaya and Egypt"—countries he perceived as having "already introduced their own films to Indonesia" in a way that would potentially facilitate mutual exchange (Pané 1953:88–89).

I position racial diversity as both an especially important and a historically volatile aspect of the region's specific brand of vernacular modernism. From a much earlier time, before the advent of local productions, cinema exhibition is argued by Tofighian as an emergent site of mixing among different groups, one with the potential to "disrupt . . . [colonial] racial divisions and creat[e] . . . more inclusive social spaces" (2013:61). But as we have seen, related spaces such as those created by vernacular theaters were eventually stratified and turned into bastions of supposed aesthetic and cultural backwardness. Similar conflicts arose around the region's cinemas in the era of decolonization. Like the real tensions driving the different ingredients in the fragmentary, globally heterogeneous combinations of style and references in *Tiga Dara*, the ethnically diverse makeup of films behind and on the screen at times caused bitter conflicts. As Pané found out soon after the release of *Antara Bumi dan Langit*, for example, its inclusion of Indonesia's first onscreen kiss, highlighting what he called the "foreign customs" (85) of the film's mixed-race female protagonist, did not go over well. As a result, the film had to be recut, excising the kiss, and was rereleased under the title *Frieda*, the main character's name.

Despite Pané's well-meaning, if perhaps poorly calculated, idealism, tensions over racial difference and colonial legacies seen as advantaging certain "foreign" groups over others were common in Indonesia as elsewhere in the region. Thomas Barker points out that in a 1951 newspaper article, writer-director, poet, and essayist Asrul Sani, a close collaborator and friend of Usmar Ismail's, specifically singled out ethnically Chinese producers for attack over perceptions that they favored "entertainment" over "nationalist" films (Barker 2019:31; Sani 1997:302). But in this case, the problem aired by Sani and others at the time was arguably more about the nature of national cinema and its economic support systems and did not question the fact of Chinese-Indonesians in the film industry itself; along with Indonesians of Indian descent, they have continued to play an important role in local filmmaking and exhibition.

In Malaysian Singapore, however, the foundational racial divisions, and associated tensions, led to a disastrous impasse. The increasingly ethnonationalist stance of Malay intellectuals and politicians led to the broad replacement of Indian and Chinese filmmakers with Malay ones and to gradual trends toward more homogeneous, "realist" films. Furthermore, racial divisions also caused the permanent splitting of Malaysia and Singapore into separate nations defined along explicitly ethnic lines in 1965.[15] As I take up in more detail in the next chapter, the unprecedented postcolonial national split caused Singapore's once regionally dominant film industry to suddenly go "blind," as production came to a near standstill in both nations for the next fifteen years.

In my analysis, the rapid dissolution of Malaysia and Singapore after only eight years of independence from British rule highlights both the strength and the fragility that coexist in the extreme fragmentation and theatrical self-reflexivity that define regional vernacular modernisms. In some sense, the sudden demise of Singapore-Malayan cinema that brought its golden age to an end can be related to the growing ethnonationalist repression of the typically diverse, archipelagic forms, approaches, and narratives that local and regional audiences demanded. In chapter 3, I explore the ways in which the conventions of regional films constitute a particular kind of force—one that, like the ideals and challenges of racial diversity, is imbued with the potential to unify but also to break apart or destroy another crucial aspect of a region's collective national modernities: the politics of gender. More specifically, I closely read the cinematic representation of gender and power via what I term the "matrifocal gaze."

3

Archipelagic Modernism
and Traditions of Gender

The Matrifocal Gaze and the "Undecided" Modern Girl

To begin this chapter, I briefly return to Usmar Ismail's troubled but successful film *Tiga Dara*. As I showed in the previous chapter, *Tiga Dara* represents an especially varied aesthetic-economic compromise aimed at bridging the gap between lower-class audiences and elite ones who preferred Hollywood and other foreign fare. The film, as I argued, uses its typically cosmopolitan, purposely "unnatural" mixture of traditional, modern, regional, and global flourishes to woo a wider range of spectators. But as I show below, it also addresses an issue, perhaps among the most pivotal in the conception of regional modernities, that links the allegedly private domain of the household to the public sphere. At stake, I contend, is the historically established "domestic" power of women and its potential to shape national and regional societies in particular ways. As I will explain in the following sections, this power, and the female figures who are shown to wield it, becomes the source of a key regional cinematic trope that I term the "matrifocal gaze." Comparing *Tiga Dara* with films from elsewhere in the region and with the gender politics of Indian cinema, I highlight the uniqueness of Southeast Asian approaches to the "universality" of patriarchy in modern societies. Building on the splits and contests between different groups that I show to be centered in regional movies, I also focus on growing divisions over the ethnicity of local modernity, particularly in Malay films that foreshadow the bitter split between Malaysia and Singapore in 1965.

In line with ongoing debates over shifting gender roles in the 1950s, *Tiga Dara*'s plot is driven, and alternately stalled, by the effort to marry off the "aging" twenty-nine-year-old Nunung, the eldest of three sisters in an upper-middle class family

FIGURE 10. In both of these shot–reverse shot sequences from *Tiga Dara*, young women are placed in positions of implicit power through the use of formal techniques. In the top pair of stills, Nunung stands to converse with her father, who is seated and wears a typical worried-yet-firm expression and body language. In the bottom pair, the middle sister, Nana (Mieke Wijaya), is briefly given a more extreme sense of formal authority (through pointing the camera up at her in the over-the-shoulder shot with her grandmother [*right*]), also around the issue of making her own decisions regarding marriage. The choice of lens and framing magnify her image, making her appear almost "larger than life" in confronting the traditional authority of her elders.

during early postindependence in Jakarta (fig. 10). Women her age should already be married with children, her grandmother laments. Nunung's personal lack is therefore a potential source of (public) shame to herself and to those closest to her. Belying her family's distress, however, Nunung generally exudes confidence and appears unconcerned with her marital status. After the death of her mother several years earlier, as the firstborn female, Nunung has inherited a key position of authority in the domestic affairs of the house. Despite the concerns of other family members with preventing her from becoming a *perawan tua* (old maid), she is hence also accorded a fair amount of leverage to determine her own fate, romantic and otherwise.

From the beginning, the film's blocking, camerawork, and editing collude with this power, investing Nunung and often her sisters with a palpable visual authority. In her conversations with her father, for example, we consistently look up at Nunung and down on him. This further materializes the sense of Nunung's inherited responsibility, power, and duty. Although her influence is limited in scope, it is implied that Nunung may want to savor and hone her role as would-be matriarch before moving into an unfamiliar domestic situation—one where her authority would potentially be reduced as a newcomer if she were to move in with her husband's family. In her current home, Nunung is able to wield tradition with one hand while denying or modulating it with the other, using her unspoken, but constantly shown, agency to put off marrying, which paradoxically extends her role as a surrogate "mother." Doing so involves negotiating the youthful impulsiveness of her sisters, the staid traditionality of her grandmother, and the unambitious reticence of her father. The ability to engage with these varied combinations of ages and interests gives Nunung an ambiguous yet dynamic status. This in turn imbues the household she runs, and the film in which it is a central component, with a multifarious sense of time and progression. While others are put off by the challenges she faces, Nunung works with increasing consciousness to shape the future around her in a way that might better suit her own needs and those of her younger siblings—although they don't seem to realize it yet.

Outside the family's home, the city appears far less pensive, full of actors racing to fulfill the ever-expanding hopes and ideals of independence, while barely pausing to lick the social, economic, and spiritual wounds inflicted by savage years of Japanese occupation and nationalist struggle (1942–49). In the face of this inevitable flow, Nunung is neither "now"—like the city itself and her irreverent, yet eager-to-marry younger sisters—or "then"—like her staid, bureaucrat father. Her aging grandmother also clearly represents a kind of "pastness." But as I have shown in the context of regional vernacular modernist films, the past—be it in the form of conventions, media technologies, or, as in this case, a character—is very much alive and never static. In her own way, the old woman is positioned as a more experienced connoisseur of the heterogeneous time that Nunung is learning to perceive and wield. The grandmother's practiced manipulation of the girls and their father in the service of her own goals and visions of an apposite future reveals an embedded domestic power that, like Nunung's, reaches beyond the home. For Nunung, whose mother's absence has in some sense made her a protégé of her grandmother, this "traditional" power is a tool with which to expand her contemporary role as a woman. As Ekky Imanjaya has also noted, in various ways, the film's structure and narrative raise "issues regarding women's rights and social status" (Imanjaya 2021:100). The air of light family melodrama and romantic comedy that *Tiga Dara* appears at first to be selling is belied by its entanglement in a deadly serious contest (fig. 11).

The questions raised by the film connect the capital city to small islands of domestic influence within, and implicitly outside, its borders. As its typically fragmented form, heterogeneous time, and deceptively amusing narrative reveal, the

FIGURE 11. A number of shots in *Tiga Dara* appear to suggest a "transfer" of power to Nunung from her grandmother. The two women look meaningfully into each other's eyes with the elder woman placed slightly higher but almost on the same level.

"private" politics of the home are surreptitiously shaping the public sphere such that the very foundations—and the outcome—of modernity are at stake. Here, traditions relating to gender and power are given spaces—created by films' combinations of archipelagic form and particular regional narratives—where they receive special consideration as principles aimed for inclusion in local formulations of modernity. In a related yet converse way, with the institution of more formalized realism and less self-reflexivity in East Asian vernacular modernisms, Miriam Hansen sees a different pattern emerge in the increasing appearances of the "modern girl" who is positioned to challenge "traditional" gender binaries. For Hansen, the function of the modern girl is mainly to highlight the traps and paradoxes of modern life. These consist in the "socioeconomic conditions and ideological fixations that make [female] characters fail" (2012:616). In contrast to regional films' tendency to call attention to themselves as constructions, modern girls are shown to fail in Shanghai and Tokyo films that increasingly seek to mimic or "copy" a certain view of reality in their use of Western classical conventions, especially in their mainstream iterations. One important effect of this, Hansen argues, is that movies work to naturalize or give the appearance of inevitability to certain consequences understood to accompany the global rise of a particular kind of industrial capitalist society.[1]

In my analysis, what emerges most profoundly in the open-ended form and narratives of Southeast Asian cinemas is how tradition, particularly historical ideas of women's agency, informs and challenges global patterns in which

Western gender ideals—along with their significant cultural baggage—are positioned as an inescapable modern paradigm. Such Western ideals have circulated to places like Indonesia, Malaysia, and Thailand, as well as to East Asia. But the idea that they could easily or uncomplicatedly take root there assumes the existence of particular modern family structures, and relations between men and women within them, that are often quite distinct from those in Southeast Asia. At the center of *Tiga Dara*, for example, Nunung's status as neither a typical "modern girl" nor a woman held back by the "inexorable chains of the past" resonates with the kinds of figures rising to the fore across various regional media at the time, including literature, theater, film, and visual arts. Nunung's lack of temporal fixity according to global modern standards is precisely what I suggest imbues her with a dynamic aura, an aspect that captivates those around her in particular ways. In this context, Nunung's modern "undecidedness" offers an opportunity to influence the circumstances and timing of her position as a woman in developing independent Indonesia.

We might look at the foundational connection of regional popular cinemas to live vernacular theaters in a similar way. Due to a complex combination of historical and class-based divisions in taste, market conditions, and embedded aesthetic attitudes, regional filmmakers refuse, or at times are discouraged from, clearly differentiating between live performance and film, and therefore between past and present, local and transnational, live and mediatized. In this context, and especially with movies inheriting and sharing their central place as engines of regional modernity with theaters, the idea and experience of modernity itself is made pointedly "undecided." Yes, Hollywood and other forms of imported, Western modernist aesthetics or political structures have inevitably penetrated the consciousness of emergent nations throughout the region. But strong cultural, political, economic, and epistemological undercurrents receive and reposition such elements in ways that prevent them from becoming modern in the way that Hansen calls "an incarnation of *the modern*" (2000:11). As we have seen, the lack of clarity about what is modern conveys stigma for some, but for others it carries productive, potentially radical, possibilities.

One key to this radical potential in comparison to other global cinemas is borne out in distinction to Hansen's positioning of the "modern girl" figure on interwar East Asian screens as a critique of what she terms traditional gender binaries. For Hansen, the critique and the girl are still fated to tragically fail in their progressive mission, poetically pointing to the paradoxes inherent in global capitalism as they do. In the post–World War II period we are discussing in Southeast Asia, both Chinese and Japanese films abruptly broke with established patterns of gender representation. In the latter case, this change was especially abrupt, comparable to a "180-degree transformation" (Saito 2014:336). After Japan's loss to the Allied forces and subsequent occupation by the United

States (1945–52), filmmakers under heavy American censorship began turning out "idea films" aligned with American directives to democratize now demilitarized Japan. As Ayako Saito shows, these films were filled with ostensibly liberated, independent "female characters as oracles of democracy" (330). Such figures were also heavily overdetermined by the political situation. At the same time, onscreen Japanese men were "denounced [and] culturally and visually castrated" (329). Yet soon after the occupation was over, Saito argues, filmmakers appeared to overcompensate via the emergent *ero-guro* (erotic-grotesque) genre in which the female body was reappropriated, heavily sexualized, and symbolically reconquered by the otherwise defeated and defiled authority of Japanese patriarchy (350).

After the declaration of the People's Republic of China in 1949—in some sense mirroring the Japanese idea film but in a very different, overtly triumphant political context—films were filled with "strong women figures who were characteristic of Chinese revolutionary representation" (McGrath 2023:238). For Jason McGrath, these figures were not generally positioned as objects of a directly eroticized look; rather, like male characters, onscreen women were constructed as politicized models of comportment. Their "socialist realist gaze," peering into the distant, glorious revolutionary communist future, could be emulated by audience members. In concert with this development, themes of romanticized love were heavily deemphasized, again departing from China's cinematic past. Spectator interest and pleasure were instead generated, McGrath writes, by the "*replacement* of private libidinal desire with the appeal of a revolutionary sublime, to which Communist film protagonists directed their longing" (2023:177, emphasis in original).

In both Chinese and Japanese postwar cinemas, then, women on the screen undergo radical shifts in related-yet-distinct ways, in line with the alternating political currents of triumph and loss, respectively. The changes in both places (and subsequent change *back* in Japan) are claimed in relation to what are generally understood as local histories of patriarchal dominance. As I have shown in previous chapters, Southeast Asian nations also underwent extremely radical transformations during and after World War II, changes that are continually reflected on and returned in the work of emergent national filmmakers. But what would happen if, as in much of the region, traditional structures of gender and power were matrifocal, which describes a high level of structurally embedded female influence in societies that may otherwise be labeled patriarchal?[2] And what if this is precisely what the formal gaps and undecidedly modern images in regional films allow to seep through, inflecting the "modern girl," imbuing her with a different mission, fate, and path of transformation?

In *Tiga Dara*, Nunung appears to relish the position of woman of the house that she inherited after her mother's passing. Her desire to put off marriage despite her "advancing" age will allow her to occupy the position for a bit longer as she watches over the developments in her family while shuttling back and forth between her home and the bustling capital city surrounding it. Despite occasional difficulties in dealing with heavy traffic, Nunung is shown to negotiate urban landscapes with the self-assurance of someone who occupies a stable place in society—a position that also appears anchored by her status in the family home. This confidence, in turn, imbues Nunung with a certain magnetism; as she wanders Jakarta's streets singing in one of the film's musical numbers, young (and also not-so-young) men constantly bump into or approach her, with several immediately asking for her hand, imploring her to "*pilihlah aku*" or "pick me." As she politely but firmly turns them down or erects lyrical hurdles in their processes of wooing her, the film implies even more strongly that the difficulties in getting Nunung married are a matter of her own choice.

THE MATRIFOCAL HOME VS. THE MODERN BOY

To deepen the sense of the role of tradition (and power) in Nunung's position as an "undecided" modern girl who is also quite sure of herself, I turn to the Malaysian P. Ramlee's classic *Ibu Mertuaku* (*My Mother-in-Law*, 1962). Ramlee's film will provide an apt, comparative formulation of the home-based power of Malay women in Malaysia around the same time. It will also provide a clearer demonstration of the real tensions embedded in contests over gender and power in the region at the time. Ahmad Fuad Rahmat argues that the narrative and formal elements of *Ibu Mertuaku* collude to "position . . . [matrifocality] as an active force of culture making that pervades the taken-for-granted expansion of the modern public sphere" (2020:97). Through its exposition of the politics of domestic space in particular, Ramlee's film highlights the continuing relevance of an enduring, supranational Malay matrifocality that flows beneath the otherwise patriarchal surface of contemporary Malaysian society. In the context of *Ibu Mertuaku*, the matrifocal appears as if it will "eventually . . . dictate the terms of Malay modernity itself" (Rahmat 2020:97).

Like *Tiga Dara*, *Ibu Mertuaku* positions local pop music—combining Latin, Western, Arab, Malay, and other elements—as a central indicator of the times. The opening credits roll over the image of a saxophone and then cut to a radio announcer who exclaims, "*Inilah radio Singapura!*" (This is radio Singapore!). A song begins under a sequence of medium close-ups of hands playing a transnational array of instruments (bongos, stand-up bass, accordion, piano, drum set, and maracas), ending on a medium shot of the band leader, P. Ramlee's character Kassim Selamat (fig. 12), coming in on tenor saxophone. He appears as the quintessential regional modern man: guiding his band with deft hand gestures and other cues, he looks in command of the very texture and sound of the now as it is simultaneously produced and broadcast to thousands of radio sets throughout Malaysia and beyond. In front of one such set in Singapore, a young woman named Sabariah (Sarimah) literally swoons, running her hands over the speaker in an exaggerated manner as if vicariously stroking Kassim's face, then rolling

FIGURE 12. P. Ramlee as the band leader Kassim Selamat in the film
Ibu Mertuaku, which he also directed and cowrote. His closed eyes
foreshadow the blindness with which he is stricken later in the film.

on her bed with an enraptured look. The consciously exaggerated emotions
and facial expressions add melodrama while calling attention to themselves as
comically overdone, signaling Ramlee's mastery of regional modes of vernacular
theatrical cinema.

What the film, and its exaggerated form, are saying about gender is also purposely over-the-top and similarly subject to shifts in meaning. For the moment,
Kassim looks to be the master of Sabariah's desires for all that is new and contemporary (and masculine) in the region. But Sabariah, the daughter of a wealthy
widow, Nyonya Mansoor (Mak Dara), soon awakens from her trance and picks
up the phone. In the radio studio, Selamat is surprised but takes her call. It is
now he who swoons as Sabariah tells him his "mellifluous saxophone moves her
heart," after which she asks him to meet her at a Jazz club that very night. Although
taken aback, Kassim's excitement gets the better of him, and he agrees. As Sabariah
strums his heartstrings over the telephone, it already seems that Kassim is not the
only one able to wield a powerful influence via electrified modern soundwaves.
In line with the "real" picture of gender and power that the film now begins to
build, the only person Sabariah can't seem to control is her mother, Nyonya Mansoor. The crass-talking, cigarette-smoking Mansoor is presented as an autocrat in
a Malay *sarong* and *kebaya* who lords her authority over family and home.

After a few comedic plot twists through which Sabariah and Kassim fall in love,
Mansoor stands firmly in the way of their marriage. For her, Kassim's status as
a modern, globally styled "freelance" icon is unclear. In the context of Malaya,
despite his fame and trappings of wealth, Kassim lacks a stable job and a proper
socioeconomic foundation; and Mansoor has already lined up a Malay doctor who
has just returned from medical school in the U.K. to marry Sabariah. The result is
a battle of wills between an equally hardheaded mother and daughter. Cognizant,

it seems, that she will inherit her mother's power, Sabariah finally puts her foot down, playing at subverting the established power of her mother. For Mansoor, however, this is no game, and the result is an elaborate, almost shocking, show of a matriarch undiminished by "acquiescing" to the demands of her daughter and next-in-command.

When Kassim answers Nyonya Mansoor's order to appear at her door, pulling up in a fancy Cadillac with his whole band in tow, she is not impressed. Descending from the house's elevated private quarters on the second floor, she pulls Kassim by the arm into the foyer, where guests are assembled, leaving his band confused outside. Using what appears to be considerable physical strength to back up her cultural authority, she pushes him to the floor and orders him to marry her daughter that very moment. Shouting a command to the male imam she has preemptively called in to perform the ceremony, she returns to her bedroom, where she counts out a pile of money. When the ritual is complete, she returns to the living room, throws the money and a suitcase of clothes at the newlyweds, disowns her daughter, and commands them to leave the house immediately. Although this showcases the "success" of Sabariah and Kassim realizing their modernizing desires by choosing their own marriage partners, unlike Nunung, Sabariah has now been disengaged from the lineage of power and money that flows to her from her mother; the scene's violence and negative tone foretell a disastrous outcome. From here on out, the film shifts from comedy to tragedy.

As it turns out, Sabariah has her own special rules for her new family unit with Kassim: he must no longer perform onstage, lest he attract the gazes of other women or further reduce the chances of reconciling with the matriarch Mansoor. Lacking savings or other qualifications, he takes a job in construction, and with the couple's lavish lifestyle, they quickly fall into poverty. When Sabariah is about to give birth to their first child, she relents and begs her mother's forgiveness, returning to the comfort of her family home without Kassim. When he calls, Nyonya Mansoor informs him, falsely, that Sabariah has died in childbirth. Over the next months, Kassim literally cries himself blind. Sabariah, however, thinks Kassim has abandoned her and agrees to marry the doctor her mother originally chose, who raises the child together with her. Kassim is temporarily saved by another, culturally and financially enabled mother and daughter who feel sorry for him, take him into their home, and sponsor his return to the stage. But when they find a doctor to cure his blindness, it turns out to be Sabariah's husband. Regaining his vision, Kassim sees how he has been manipulated by Nyonya Mansoor, resulting in him losing his wife and only son. Kassim is so stricken by what he is witness to that he blinds himself again with a knife and wanders off to a future in which his only certainty appears to be tragedy.

Here, unlike the politically fated falls and constructed "liberations" of onscreen women we have seen in China and Japan, the emergent figure who must invariably and poetically fail is not the modern girl but the "modern boy," represented by Ramlee's Kassim Selamat. In the end, although Malaysia in the early 1960s is ostensibly capitalist and patriarchal, his status as modern, individualistic, and male in a more typically global sense seems to unmoor and weaken him. The women he encounters, in contrast, use their traditionally sourced strength to adapt to changes around them and rule the day. As Rahmat also asserts, they do so without appearing behind the times or as static or idealized remnants of a vanished past. Nyonya Mansoor is certainly anything but a figure of nostalgia. She is presented as mean-spirited and manipulative yet not quite evil because her power is culturally justified. Her influence deftly bridges the private and the public, the past and the present, and, with her house and base of operations in Singapore, the rural/traditional and the urban.

As Timothy Barnard writes of *Ibu Mertuaku* and other, similarly themed Malaysian films, the city, shown to be filled with "foreign" materialism and individualism alongside powerful "traditional" figures like Mansoor, "created such ambivalence that it was often glorified as a place of possibility" (Barnard 2005:437). At the same time, urban centers like Singapore, Jakarta, and Bangkok, standing in for regional modernity, inspired hopelessness in those who could not abide by their seeming contradictions. Invoking a similar dichotomy, the kindhearted mother-daughter duo that saves Kassim and restarts his career midway through the film appears to represent the potential for good contained in the same female power with which Mansoor is invested (tellingly, they live in a rural, *kampung* area that is implied to be a seat of more virtuous Malay values). Furthermore, neither Mansoor nor any other woman in the film are made to appear thoroughly traditional in the sense of being behind the times. From outfits to speech and mannerisms to lifestyles, women in Ramlee's film, including those in villages, constitute a mixture of local, regional, and global elements. Like Nunung in *Tiga Dara*, whose sense of style is similar, if slightly more refined, they appear at home in Malaysia's rapidly expanding urban settings, as well as in the countryside.

As in much of the rest of Southeast Asia, in peninsular Malaysia and in Java, where *Ibu Mertuaku* and *Tiga Dara* are respectively set, research over the past several decades indicates a level of gender parity that differs from that in the West. As such, like the approaches of regional cinemas, regional gender roles also distinguish themselves from traditional structures in East and South Asia.[3] This parity can be attributed to a complex and changing array of factors, but women's strong financial positions within families and local market structures are a key consideration. In many areas across the region, purse strings, along with important financial decisions, are traditionally held and taken by wives and mothers. As Gloria Poedjosoedarmo writes of Javanese villages in the 1970s, for example, "economics is almost exclusively the domain of women. . . . In addition to marketing their own produce, at all levels of society women are involved in buying and selling for profit" (1983:7–8). While major shifts in the structures of urban economies and national-level socioeconomic policies from the 1950s onward challenged women's economic positions, films like *Ibu Mertuaku* stress that the socially and financially grounded power of wives and mothers was far from diminished.

Because of their integration with and control over local markets in many parts of Southeast Asia, women also became de facto "mediators in the transcultural exchanges" that determined early stages of globalization in the region (Andaya 2007:8); many were effectively trained as modern "capitalists" through their experiences with foreign traders (including Western ones). Such experiences and the emergent status they conveyed often eluded men, especially in lower-economic strata. This also speaks to the patterns and associated abilities of women to adapt their traditional standing to engage with the kinds of changes brought on by globalization and various forms of modernization. As Barbara Andaya argues, "the market environment allowed even a 'low-status' woman to acquire a reputation for commercial shrewdness and organizational skills" (2007:124), potentially raising her socioeconomic standing and that of her family. Something similar would appear to be the case with Nyonya Mansoor, whose crass habits and rough manner of communication bespeak more humble origins than her opulent surrounds imply. Certainly, her shrewdness with domestic finances is portrayed as enabling her to extend her agency into political and economic circles far outside the home.

As Wazir Jahan Karim explains it, the "informal" spaces where women's engagements with society are sanctioned are "so visible and important that . . . most political and religious activities are enacted within this . . . sphere" (1995:19). In comparison to *Tiga Dara*'s deceptively playful, entertaining take, the situation presented in *Ibu Mertuaku* stands as a more pointed example of the endurance of these quasi-informal regional patterns. Even as it begins to signal a degree of masculine doubt, Ramlee's film helps to concretize the expansive influence of female domestic power that I argue is also behind Nunung's reluctance to marry "on time" in *Tiga Dara*. Unlike Sabariah, the death of Nunung's mother has turned her into a special kind of matriarch: she is given access to the power afforded by wifehood and motherhood without the stress and strain involved in marriage and child-rearing. Similar to Nyonya Mansoor's attitude toward Kassim's youthful career as a pop musician, Nunung finds the parties to which her sisters drag her in hopes of meeting men to be beneath the maturity and dignity that comes with her assumed position. "They all think I'm their auntie," she complains. While on one level self-deprecating, her comments also imply that her authority is real enough to make youthful partiers, who in fact aren't far from Nunung's age, uncomfortable in her presence.

Belying her motherly gravitas, however, Nunung *is* still young and is a far more multifaceted and sympathetic figure than Nyonya Mansoor.[4] In a scene where her grandmother arranges a party to show her off for her father's office mates, who are supposedly eligible bachelors, Nunung allows a different side of herself to shine. She does so not in the interest of finding a husband (the party's secret purpose, which has been kept from Nunung) but as the home's hostess and would-be matriarch. At the guests' request, Nunung sits down at the piano, where she displays her own ability to mix and match global and local sounds and rhythms. Using the keys to accompany a vocal melody that recalls *keroncong*, a hybrid adaptation of Portuguese *fado* that typically accompanied stambul performances, her playing and singing entrances her onlookers. In classical regional vernacular modernist form, the music's fluid style also brings to mind Malay-ized vocal jazz records by contemporary groups like the Medan, Sumartra-based Orkes Tropicana. The result, while somewhat more mature-sounding than the youthful songs at some of Nunung's sisters' parties, shows Nunung's gift for entertaining, rivaling the modern-boy tactics of P. Ramlee. But unlike Kassim in *Ibu Mertuaku*, Nunung is not easily seduced, and she performs with a confidence, poise, and class grounded in the established agency of the home. As the scene shows, she deftly turns the domestic space into something quintessentially regional-modern: a temporally and culturally dynamic stage with herself at its center.

The patterns of gazing triggered by Nunung's performance also bear closely on the film's formal bricolage and exposition of breaks and continuities in regional structures of gender and power. Building on previous scenes, the party showcases how the organization of domestic space in particular enables the women's voyeuristic evaluation of their male guests. While Nunung's performance draws the stares of guests and camera alike, this "male gaze" is elicited mainly as a distraction that facilitates a more dominant, semicovert female look. As in many of Ismail's other films and those of his contemporaries, here, he carefully underscores the gazes of central female characters. A related pattern of "reversing" the male gaze is identified by David Hanan in three later Indonesian films released between 1969–1982 (2017:253–276). Anticipating these patterns, in *Tiga Dara*, the house, while decorated in a somewhat generic modern style, reveals its "traditionality" in that it seems built specifically for women's eyes. A curtain, for example, can be drawn to separate the public space for guests from private areas. This provides Nunung's sisters and grandmother a perfect vantage point from which to single out and closely scrutinize each man as he, in turn, watches Nunung at the piano, unaware that he himself is being watched. When the grandmother is handed her glasses, however, what comes into focus are similarly bespectacled men of around her own age. "God forgive us!" she exclaims. "They're all toothless . . . with one foot in the grave!" To comedic effect and much to the women's dismay, there are no eligible bachelors in sight (fig. 13).

For her part, Nunung appears unaffected by her guests' lack of eligibility: regardless of age, their presence has allowed her to assume a more public facet of her role as "mother"—that of domestic/public entertainer and master of the typical "matrifocal home." As in Malay society, and unlike most Western family dwellings, Rahmat writes, the matrifocal home "has not been privatized and culturally isolated" (2020:86) and remains profoundly interconnected with the workings of society at large. Anticipating *Ibu Mertuaku*, in *Tiga Dara* women are the gatekeepers of the hybrid public/private family home. This begins with their control

FIGURE 13. Nunung sings for a group of appreciative elderly male guests (*top left*) while her grandmother and sisters peek out at the scene. The men watch Nunung, but the emphasis is on the evaluative gaze that the women turn on them, one that soon becomes mocking and satirical.

over who enters and exits and continues with their charge of mobility within the house. From the opening scene, where the "invisible hand" of tradition prevents Herman from following the girls out of the parlor (see chapter 2), to the party scene described above, *Tiga Dara* has likewise underscored that "movement across domestic space is most enjoyed and expressed by women rather than men" (Rahmat 2020:97). The film's camera angles, blocking, dialogue, and story also continually show Nunung's father as the most passive character—a man whose narrative interventions and even physicality (the latter mainly due to camera angles) are visibly diminished by the women surrounding him.

In *Ibu Mertuaku*, the contrast in men's and women's engagement with the matrifocal home, and with society at large through the home, is starker still. Male elders are excised completely from the film's world, and Kassim, while initially penetrating family spaces via the radio, is soon punished for his transgressions. After his deceptively empowered opening scenes, he is consistently positioned outside of, or in tension with, female structures of authority (including the physical forms of houses they occupy) that so profoundly inflect the modern. For Rahmat, this leaves Kassim in a state of "homelessness to be contrasted against the matrifocal 'home' where his identity is both unsettled and questioned and, thus, decided"

(94). Those who command domestic spaces increasingly act on and alienate Kassim, ultimately governing his fate in society at large; thus, the feminized home transcends its ostensibly private status "to become the space where history in the final instance is determined" (94). Like the girls' father in *Tiga Dara*, even the young doctor who takes Kassim's place is shown passively carrying out the plans of Nyonya Mansoor, his power authorized by his moving into a domestic space dominated by its female inhabitants.

VISUALITY, DUALITY, AND BLINDNESS

One important question that is raised by both *Tiga Dara* and *Ibu Mertuaku* is how to *show* this complex web of gender relations that shapes regional modernity but contradicts "constitutive" global modern patterns of behavior. To further complicate things, Western modes of seeing via overdetermined masculine gazes are at times also held up as ideals by Southeast Asians. The associated problem of visuality—of representation of what is experientially real but difficult for some to see and thus to accept or believe—transcends the arena of cinema. Scholars of Southeast Asia, particularly those who study gender and agency, find themselves grappling with the power of suggestion expressed by grand narratives regarding the nature of global modernity. For Malaysian scholar Wazir Jahan Karim, "part of the problem . . . is that [Western] social scientists tend to see male dominance in religious and political life as 'traditional' and 'customary'" (1995:27), leading to theories that minimize by default the influence of women's domestic or "private" activities. The assumed alliance of tradition and male authority leads to the view that Western-style modernity, with its neopatriarchal values and emergent feminist perspectives premised on countering them, can function to disrupt the kinds of "traditional binarisms" around gender that Miriam Hansen and others see in East Asian films—albeit often in ways that are beset by modernity's "paradoxes" and are hence destined to fail (Hansen 2000:16).

Indeed, there is much evidence to indicate that this is the case in the West and far beyond, providing more fuel for the fire of scholarly assumptions. The stark differences that define much of Southeast Asia, furthermore, are not simply a limited effect of processes of decolonization and national development that happened half a century ago. In her recent *Gender in Southeast Asia*, Mina Roces echoes earlier takes like Karim's, arguing that "Southeast Asian concepts of power empower women in ways that are not possible in Western societies" (2022:2). Along with all the other problems addressed by regional filmmakers in the 1950s and 1960s, the issue of how to make visible a modern regime of gender and power that from various "universal" perspectives appears impossible emerges as especially pressing. Across the films I review in this chapter, and many other films as well, the question of how to show, and also to *see*, these ostensibly untenable power relations becomes a major source of formal and dramatic tension. I argue that representing

FIGURE 14. Toto's first encounter with the modernized and formally elevated "matrifocal home."

this tension, while not always resolving it, relies on the fragmented aesthetics and split metaphors innovated by vernacular theaters and inherited by cinemas. The gaps and cracks made visible between scenes and along the seams of different genres and stylistic approaches that films patch together reveal the modern in a specific way: like history, it appears always already in process and subject to negotiation or even to backtracking or spontaneous revision.

The trials and tribulations of Nunung's eventual love interest, Toto (Rendra Karno), underscore the same difficulties in showing and seeing modern female spheres of authority. Like Kassim Selamat in *Ibu Mertuaku*, Toto resembles a quintessentially modern man, with his expensive collared shirt and slacks and his shiny Vespa scooter, a symbol of emergent mobility then unaffordable to most. The potential problems of such "free" movement and visuality are foregrounded at Toto's first meeting with Nunung, when he accidently runs her down on a crosswalk in the center of Jakarta. While not seriously hurt, Nunung is furious and refuses his repeated apologies and offers to ferry her home, choosing a lowly pedicab instead. When relating to her grandmother and sisters what has happened, Nunung describes Toto as a "man who doesn't have eyes, he thinks he's the only one on the road!" Just then, as if to underscore his apparent problems with visuality, he appears on the street below her house, a confused look on his face, along with black sunglasses similar to those Kassim dons after losing his sight (fig. 14). He briefly removes the glasses as he looks up to see Nunung helped into the house by the other women.

Here, the steep, grand-looking set of stairs leading from street to house, which sits along a row of homes on a small ridge, is used to visualize a shift in power dynamics that has occurred between the city center and Nunung's place of residence (which is still in Jakarta but not in its bustling downtown). On the city street, they are on the same level, and when Toto's scooter knocks her down, he ends up looming over her. In front of her house, however, the stairs are placed in the foreground in a way that splits the image, creating a much clearer power differential between the modern man on the street and the matrifocal home and its inhabitants towering above him. Even in the city, Nunung's fiery, feminine self-confidence after a physical knockdown seems to catch Toto's eye, and he follows her home. But now, removing his glasses and glimpsing the steep climb he must negotiate to reach her, he quickly puts them back on and makes a U-turn toward the bustling metropolis.

In line with the arguments of Karim and others, this scene suggests at least two visions of contemporary gender relations: a primarily "public" one in which men ostensibly hold greater sway, and another, less formally institutionalized, domestic or "private" one that is nonetheless positioned as at least equally influential and at times more so. Seemingly very aware of the "informal" influence she has assumed as a would-be matriarch, Nunung does not hesitate to exercise it on Toto. She accuses him of focusing on the speed and flow of the overtly masculine/public sphere such that he loses sight of what is more important: the other forces that collude to drive society forward and, when appropriate, to pull culture "back" into the domains of feminine power that continue to shape modern experience. In addition to blocking and camera angles that position one character above another, this power differential is repeatedly symbolized by the elevation of Nunung's house vis-à-vis the street, where Toto is more at home. He is frequently shown waiting at the bottom of the stairs or riding his gleaming scooter back and forth on the pavement below, while visually dwarfed by the rows of steps and residences positioned in the background. Even when Toto later succeeds in climbing the steps, he is initially relegated to the jungle-like garden outside—framed by palm trees, bushes, and flowers—before he can approach the more civilized spaces of the home.

Similarly, in *Ibu Mertuaku*, Rahmat argues that the elevation of Nyonya Mansoor's house recalls the "culture vs. nature" divide historically displayed by traditional Malay homes on stilts (Rosalind Galt [2021] underscores this argument by showing that nature and jungles are established by numerous Southeast Asian films as a sphere of undomesticated, but also feminine, power that surrounds the home). This divide is mapped by the film onto Mansoor's more modern matrifocal dwelling by focusing on the stairs, producing "the effect of elevating the status of [the home's female] masters" (Rahmat 2020:103, 106).[5] As settings, locations, and other elements of mise-en-scène signal in both films, we are not in Kansas. Toto's dogged pursuit of Nunung in *Tiga Dara*, as with the other men she encounters in the city, is thus inspired by her visual/symbolic elevation and "undecided" shuttling between past and present, tradition and modernity, and matriarch and marriageable girl. To win her heart, or even just come up the stairs to try, Toto must constantly negotiate with the women of the house, their ordering gazes lowered at him.

Toto's hard-won "triumph" hence relies on the realization that he must realign (or in fact, split) his expectations and what he sees or doesn't see from his position as an elite modern man. In essence, he must both submit to and learn to *see through* what I call the "matrifocal gaze," which I position as a central, structuring principle of both films. Although Toto wins Nunung's affection in the final scene, unlike a typical Hollywood ending where everything is resolved and clear, no plans for a wedding—the lack of which is the central problem introduced at the beginning—are announced or even hinted at. *Tiga Dara* thus sides with Nunung's agency and control over her own destiny, while pushing viewers to see this as part and parcel of modern life in Indonesia and elsewhere in the region. Kassim in *Ibu Mertuaku* is far less fortunate than Toto because he fails to adapt to this dynamic view and the mode of seeing it implies. When he catches a clearer glimpse of the "other" power that determines his masculine agency, he is blinded by tears. Like Toto, he hides his lack of ability to see and to negotiate the complexities of regional modernity behind dark glasses. But when modern medicine gives him a second hard look at the reality surrounding him, he shuts out the inexorably feminized view for good through self-inflicted violence.

This points to an important divergence between *Tiga Dara* and *Ibu Mertuaku*, which I relate to the specific, national political situations in which each film is embedded. In *Tiga Dara*, Toto's eventual acquiescence to the matrifocal gaze signifies a greater ability to accommodate the inherent paradoxes of modernization. But as I showed in chapter 1, the undecidedness and contradictions of local modernities were amplified throughout the region by unusually rapid processes of decolonization and nationalization around the time of the Second World War. This process had especially profound effects in starkly ethnically and culturally stratified Malaya, which negotiated independence from Britain relatively late, in 1957. After officially joining with Singapore as independent Malaysia in 1963, the two sides quickly split up into separate nations in 1965. Embedded in this process and the increasingly politicized debates over cinema that it engendered, in *Ibu Mertuaku*, Malay matrifocality appears darker and more rigid in comparison to how it is shown in *Tiga Dara*. Especially given Kassim's self-blinding in response to the urban female authority he sees, the film moves the issue of modern gender and power beyond mere undecidedness and closer to irreconcilability.

For Barnard (2005), this corresponds with a shift in the attitude of many popular Malay movies during the period from the 1950s until the mid-1960s. This shift is especially clear in the large, regionally unusual number of films involving the theme of blindness. As tensions rose between Malay and ethnic Chinese nationalists in Chinese-majority Singapore in the early 1960s, groups of mostly male, foreign-educated Malay elites stepped in to "decide" the form and content of local modernity once and for all. They envisioned a new, more clearly patriarchal, society that mixed Islam with progressive European values but would be founded on a (very) selective reenvisioning of Malay traditions. Films, it was hoped, could help lead the way in disseminating this hurriedly reengineered national culture to the masses. At the Third Malay Language Conference in Singapore in 1956, Malay actor, director, and producer S. Roomai Noor "made a passionate plea for [ethnic]

Malays to gain control over the content of Malay films so that they would reflect the cultural values and proper language of Malays" (Barnard and van der Putten 2008:144). Ethnically diverse, politically contested Singapore was particularly important not only as a cultural and economic hub but also as a center of film production with the power to help, or potentially hurt, the Malay nationalist cause.

In light of this, new censorship laws especially targeted popular, pre-Islamic Malay cultural concepts like female spirits who were invested with what amounted to superpowers. These ubiquitous ghosts, not wholly unlike mortal women who combined traditions and modernity to powerful effect, were increasingly seen "as a dangerous remnant of forbidden beliefs and a threat to hegemonic order" (Galt 2021:197). Beginning in the late 1950s, local and expat Indian, Filipino, and Chinese crew members were largely replaced by Malays, many of whom were more sympathetic to nationalist concerns over race and gender. In line with mounting tension around these processes, the metaphor of blindness, first taken up in the early 1950s, begins to shift (Barnard 2005:434). Blindness changes from a more hopeful, curable uncertainty about the future to outright suspicion of the possibilities attached to modernity and to what were perceived as negative changes in traditional values around modernity and urbanization.

Men like Kassim Selamat are accordingly offered modern cures for blindness only to realize that "the world that accompanied this technology was one that was unbearable" (Barnard 2005:452). Tellingly, the one female character who makes the same transition (Daeng Sofia as Annie in the 1965 film *Sayang si Buta* [*Pity the Blind One*, dir. Omar Rojik]) is delighted by what she sees and transforms herself from an innocent blind village girl into a powerful urban woman. As portrayed by the film, however, she also becomes manipulative and immoral. Beyond the pattern of progressively negative views of modernity in which Barnard positions the film, this shows the most direct connection between gender and the cinematic expression of the fears of contemporary Malay nationalists. Kassim Selamat, with everything lost at the end of *Ibu Mertuaku*, reclaims his blindness in a horrific act of self-mutilation. With much to gain from modernity, Annie in *Sayang si Buta* does nothing of the sort, but the film once again closes around mutilation as she is conveniently reblinded by "fate" in the form of an accident that puts out both of her eyes.

Although Annie now comes to "see" and repent the folly of her modern ways, I argue that the film—produced three years after *Ibu Mertuaku*, at the height of tensions that led to the split between Malaysia and Singapore—has symbolically closed off the avenue for women, whether as bearers of tradition, progressive figures, or some combination thereof, to decide the outcome of modernity. Amid boiling debates over ethnic and gendered aspects of Malay nationality and its representation, *Sayang si Buta* effectively blinds the matrifocal gaze. Especially when compared to other films about blindness made just a few years earlier, it does so without offering a viable alternative, patriarchal or otherwise. This suggests a broader impasse in seeing and negotiating the formative schisms of regional modernity, be they gendered, temporal, ethnic, or, more likely, all three. These images of visual irreconcilability experienced by Malays onscreen also allegorized the dissolution of interethnic relations in Malaysia. Malay nationalists, the film suggests, could not "see" their way past the modern powers of either women or the Chinese Malaysians who formed a majority in Singapore.

This juxtaposition of gender and ethnopolitics signaled the emergence of an anomaly in the region's cinemas, as well as among the political, economic, and cultural ecosystems in which they were embedded. The particular, vernacular modernist "glue" with which other Southeast Asian nations were held together onscreen and off—ethnic and political splits, undecided matrifocality and all—had ceased to stick in Singapore. In this context, Malaysia can be seen as a test case for the limits of archipelagic representation. *Sayang si Buta* was in fact one of the last films ever made by the Singapore studios responsible for Malaysia's dominant position among the region's archipelago of film production and circulation. Not coincidentally, its release in 1965 corresponded with Malaysia and Singapore's final, unmendable geopolitical split into separate nations along clear ethnic lines.[6]

As I mentioned in chapter 2, the ethnopolitical "mutilation" of Malaysia and Singapore also imposed a long period of cinematic blindness. With the departure of Malay audiences and talent from Singapore, its major studios (Shaw Brothers Malay Films and Cathay Keris) quickly ceased production. Filmmaking in the city-state did not begin to recover until the 1990s. In post-1965 Malaysia, things were almost as bleak: while viewership expanded and filmmaking was not completely halted, the industry in Kuala Lumpur imported 95 percent of its films from abroad until the early 1980s. With local production at a tiny fraction of Singaporean golden-age levels, Indonesian-made films were positioned as "substitute" Malay fare (Frymus 2022:66). This helped set the stage, I suggest, for the eventual return of the matrifocal gaze in Malaysia.

THE MATRIFOCAL GAZE AS GLOBAL ANOMALY?

Notably, the factors and pressures leading to the separation of Malaysia and Singapore and the severe drop in film production that followed did not at the same time accomplish elite Malay (or Chinese) projects of moving toward more stable, singular modes of self-representation. Formerly "disobedient" national cinemas did not reform; they simply stopped making films for a while. With moribund or nearly catatonic industries, the fates of both nations' cinemas, and especially Malaysia's, speak to the particular, historically embedded strength of the region's brand of vernacular modernism: a seeming global anomaly that structures looking in ways that denaturalize homogeneous, patriarchal modern visual regimes. Departing from this, for Singapore and Malaysia, resulted in a temporary cinematic eclipse.

Perhaps the closest points of comparison for the matrifocal gaze in popular Western cinemas would thus be other anomalies like the 1968 French *Barbarella* (dir. Roger Vadim), in which a female protagonist's pleasure drives the narrative and "the male look finds no surrogate" (Young 2018:40).[7] In fact, the film's closest approximation of masculine heroics is found in a male angel who is also blind. Yet *Barbarella* is set in a distant, mostly utopian, future where human reproduction is mechanized and families have ceased to exist. Its radically lowbrow aesthetics and vision of gender parity are still a far cry from Southeast Asian efforts to locate a feminized visual regime in the historical endurance of traditional, matrifocal family structures. But what of modern girls and boys, or women and men, in still other global-vernacular modernist traditions, such as Indian popular cinemas, that are similarly "anomalous" vis-à-vis the self-enclosed, naturalist structures of classical Western narrative films? Might we find a more productive point of comparison in the politics of gender and modern visuality there?

As Ravi Vasudevan shows, popular Hindi "social" films of the 1950s also engaged globalization via fragmented transnational appropriations and recombinations of form and reference—conventions similar to those I have linked to the matrifocal gaze in Southeast Asia. If we look backward in time to the formation of vernacular modernist aesthetics in the late nineteenth and early twentieth centuries, the similarities only increase. As we saw in chapter 2, Hindi (and other Indian) films also developed "horizontally" through contact and convergence with older, live forms of entertainment. In this case, as Vasudevan and others show, the Parsi-language vernacular theaters that toured India in the late nineteenth and early twentieth centuries played an especially key role. This reveals an even more specific link to Southeast Asia, because *wayang Parsi*, as Parsi theater was called there, also came to Malaya via Indian migrant workers in the nineteenth century. After establishing itself in Penang, it became a key inspiration and source for Malayan and Indonesian vernacular theaters like stambul and bangsawan—forms that, as we have seen, exerted a profound influence on the regional cinematic conventions that followed them.

In India, Parsi theater's diverse and loudly displayed global and local mix of sources and references likewise anticipated and informed "the geographical reach of Hindi cinema and its hybrid structure" (Vasudevan 1989:30). The genre-bending, "omnibus 'musical tragi-comedy' form" (Vasudevan 1989:30) deployed by Parsi and other traveling theaters was also inherited by early Indian filmmakers, who used it to transform Hindi movies into a non-Western global institution and "nodal point of the . . . 1960s" (Sunya 2022:15). In the context of my analysis, this common, formative relation to live theatrical forms of vernacular modernism helps to explain the various similarities in Indian and Southeast Asian cinematic conventions and attitudes toward globalization. But does the open nature of Hindi film aesthetics, which more often resolve narrative and formal tensions in the end, also allow visual and narrative spaces for dynamic female characters to emerge?

Vasudevan argues that in blockbuster Hindi "social films," Indian women onscreen were often positioned as figures who "set limits to the image of modernity" (1993:65). This is especially true of "the mother's iconic presence," which exerts a "gravitational pull . . . over the very process of narration" (1993:67). As in my analysis of *Tiga Dara, Ibu Mertuaku,* and other regional films, the result is a particular, emergent mode of representation where it is "difficult to separate out 'traditional' from 'modern' address" (Vasudevan 1993:65). This initially sounds promising. A brief analysis of the Hindi film *Deedar* (*Vision,* dir. Nitin Bose, 1951) will help to highlight what is similar in the positioning of central female characters in Hindi and Southeast Asian popular films in the 1950s. Yet it will also point to deeper issues that I argue make gender representation very different—perhaps ultimately incompatible—across South and Southeast Asian cinemas. As its title suggests, *Deedar* points to a further thematic parallel between Indian and Malaysian films, this time in cinematic representations of vision and blindness around issues of gender.

The plot of *Deedar* contains a number of striking similarities with P. Ramlee's *Ibu Mertuaku* specifically. Like Ramlee's Kassim Selamat, the protagonist of *Deedar,* Shamu (Dilip Kumar), is in love with a young woman, Mala (Nargis), whose family disapproves of him and aims to keep them apart. The class differences in this case are starker, as Shamu is the son of a lower-caste servant who lives with Mala's family, and his illicit affection for her is the reason that they are separated early in the film. As in *Ibu Mertuaku,* Shamu is sad during the separation and becomes blind, although the official cause in this case is a storm. Shamu also eventually comes to work as a singer, and through his music, he makes the acquaintance of a young, idealistic eye doctor (Ashok Kumar). Impressed with Shamu's spirit, the doctor offers to cure Shamu and restore his sight. In one of the film's closer anticipations of the narrative written for *Ibu Mertuaku* a decade later, when Shamu regains his vision, he suddenly sees that the object of his heart's desire, the now adult Mala, is engaged to the doctor who cured his blindness.

This point of convergence between the films is striking but leads us to the most significant distinctions: the doctor in this case appears to be a true blue socialist-modernist. He agrees that his love for Mala does not rise to the level of Shamu's "worship" of her and insists that Shamu marry Mala in his stead. An even more telling contrast with Ramlee's film is that the matrifocal figure of Nyonya Mansoor is here replaced with a patriarch—the stern figure of Mala's father (Murad). Mala's mother is largely absent, and it is the father whose closely calculated manipulations derail the impending intercaste marriage. The result, as the reader may already have guessed, is that like Kassim Selamat, grief-stricken Shamu puts out his own eyes, this time with the doctor's fancy fountain pen. Barnard's conclusion that modern cures for blindness in Malaysian films reveal that "the world that accompanied this technology was one that was unbearable" (2005:452) could also be applied here. But even while *Ibu Mertuaku* was, in a certain way, gesturing

FIGURE 15. The actress Nargis as Mala is positioned above the action throughout much of *Deedar*. The result is an aloof, rather than grounded and active, female character.

negatively toward the more staunchly patriarchal (and ethnonationalist) ideals embedded in the oncoming split between Singapore and Malaysia, in *Deedar*, the result of blindness is basically the reverse.

Contrasting sharply with the active, romantic Sabariah, Mala, Shamu's love interest, has from the beginning remained mostly in the background and clueless as to Shamu's feelings for her. She has no inkling of, or role in, the dramatic goings-on among the three male characters—Shamu, her father, and the doctor—which the film shows to have determined *her* fate. Curiously, at the end, Mala is shown descending a lavish staircase in a setting that closely resembles Nyonya Mansoor's matrifocal home. But Mala's positioning "above" other characters seems mainly an expression of her pervasive aloofness toward her own and others' interests and fates (fig. 15). She is only vaguely disturbed when she hears that Shamu, her child-hood friend, has suddenly put out his own eyes and left for good. Her wrinkled brow soon shifts to a dutiful smile at the now unimpeded prospect of her own "proper" marriage to the young doctor. Here, she is again positioned towering over her wealthy fiancé in a way that recalls the Southeast Asian matrifocal gaze. But in this case, I contend that Mala's visible elevation mainly indicates a symbolic pedestal that confers little practical agency.

Vasudevan concurs. In a separate article dealing with the same set of 1950s social films, he complicates the idea of women's cinematic images "setting the limits" of modern national identity. They do so, he argues, mainly as part of an iconic rela-tion to an idealized, desexualized, and heavily overdetermined "pure" mother- or goddess-like figure—one whose ostensibly elevated status is most often "inscribed as a figure subordinated to a narcissistic male structure of desire" (1989:36). The other side of this female archetype is constituted by women whom proper society is defined against: those attached to "the world of vamp and villain, counter pointed to the realm of morality and romantic love" (Vasudevan 1993:66). In this context, the presence of a more subversive "good" woman such as Nargis's rebellious lawyer in Raj Kapoor's famous *Awaara* (*The Vagabond*, 1951), or of the actress Padmini's dialectical combination of wholesomeness, intelligence, and active (armed) rebellion in *Jis Desh Mein Ganga Behti Hai* (*The Land Through Which the Ganga Flows*, Karmakar, 1960) can be said to be anomalies in the broader conventions of Hindi social films.

Even in the independently produced, explicitly radical work of Bengali writer-director Satyajit Ray, the traditional feminine power embedded in the figure of the *nabeena*, or "new woman" (echoing Hansen's star-crossed "modern girl"), is treated in a way that resonates more closely with *Barbarella* than it does with Southeast Asian variants: as something that can only be expressed in a distant future. As Keya Ganguly argues, in Ray's films from the 1960s to the 1980s, the *nabeena*, while frequently a central element, is represented in traumatic terms as "not yet conceivable in the world except as catastrophic, disastrous, or monstrous" (2010:44). In relation to historical trauma and to Malaysia, specifically, India does share the same former colonizer (England) and bears a further, catastrophic similarity in its process of nation formation around independence in 1947, a decade before Malaysia's. British India, too, was quickly and violently broken apart into two new nations, India and Pakistan, over a perceived inability to acknowledge and accommodate embedded differences between opposing groups, in this case Hindus and Muslims.

In India, however, postpartition nationalist pressures on cinema did not result in decades of cinematic vacuum as they did in Malaysia and Singapore. I have also argued that despite Malaysian cinema's eventual move toward more rigid, "realistic" patriarchal cinematic conventions, it remained, until the end, mainly under the sway of the matrifocal, however negatively defined. Recall that even wayward, modern Annie in *Sayang si Buta* is punished by fate and not a man's decision, while it is the actions of men who directly determine the lives of Shamu and Mala in *Deedar*. Malaysian cinema would become what I position as an anomaly within a larger anomaly: Southeast Asia's vernacular modernist traditions, to which the approach of Malaysia's films would eventually return. The relation of an event like the splitting of a newly minted nation, therefore, however momentous, appears insufficient as a singular determinant of the nature of domestic or regional representation.

HISTORIES MADE BY WOMEN AND MEN

If we look backward past independence and pay closer attention to the nature of live vernacular theaters in the nineteenth and early twentieth centuries—media that I position as critical influences on the development of Southeast Asian and Indian cinemas—a key distinction reveals itself. The difference, I suggest, anticipates the gap in gender representation between the two. In Indian Parsi theaters, unlike forms such as bangsawan and stambul in Malaysia and Indonesia, female characters were almost exclusively played by men. As Kathryn Hansen (1999) shows, this policy drew on the conservative mores of British Elizabethan theater, where women were allowed as spectators but not onstage, giving rise to a tradition of female-impersonating male actors.

In India, Hansen argues, the ubiquitous staging of men masquerading as women was "productive of new ways of looking at the female form" and potentially "enlarged the performative possibilities of . . . imagining and viewing women" (1999:128). But with its basis in colonial values, cross-dressing became a funnel for conservative patriarchy, reinforcing cultural ideals in which women stayed at home and did not appear in public (women in the audience were often placed in a separate seating area and were accompanied to the theater by male chaperones). Unlike the case in much of Southeast Asia, this more rigid positioning broadly limited the ability of Indian women to use the powers of motherhood, economic control over the home, or market savvy to influence social and political spheres outside of the home. The convention of theatrical female impersonation also continued to express a formative influence on how women were imagined and viewed when they did take to the stage in greater numbers in the 1920s.[8] Owing to the horizontal transfer of India's burgeoning, exuberant "culture of the visible" (Vasudevan 1989:31) from stage to screen, these emergent female performers and their inherited, "man-made" characteristics quickly became a central attraction in Indian films.

For Kathryn Hansen, men who played women in Parsi theaters set the stage and "structured the space into which female performers were to insert themselves, effecting the transition from stigmatized older practices to the newly consolidated Indian woman of the nationalists" (1999:127–28). This space, belying the potentially fluid, hybrid nature of male masquerade performances and of Indian vernacular theaters more broadly, was one in which public images of women were now made to exude "bourgeois respectability." The capacity to suffer, often at the hands of patriarchal society, was also singled out as a central, modern feminine virtue (129). Hansen argues that this version of femininity, which was originally something that men "did better" than women, became a "visual template that enabled recognition of [women's] 'spiritual' essence" (140). In this context, one can glimpse the roots of the Hindi cinematic gaze where, in films like *Deedar*, women are visually revered markers of national identity but at the same time appear to lack a certain substance or interiority.

In stark contrast, as Tan Sooi Beng shows, women bangsawan actresses touring Malaysia, Indonesia, and elsewhere in the region in the 1920s and 1930s were increasingly acknowledged, not only in their roles as public performers but for their contributions to the financial stability and success of the troupes they worked with. Alongside men, the broad recognition of female members as stars began to expand conceptions of women's power being relegated to domestic or "informal" spheres as "women were afforded the unprecedented opportunity for [new kinds of] self-expression in public" (Tan 1995:603). Tan suggests that the socioeconomic, emotional bonds of the bangsawan community itself also offered an important platform for women's empowerment outside of the family. Even as women's long-standing ability to end unhappy marriages, for example, was threatened by the modernization processes of traditional societies like the West Sumatran Minangkabau, in bangsawan, troupe-communities began to facilitate new opportunities for "women themselves . . . to initiate a divorce or separation" (Tan 1995:613).[9] This reduced considerably the risk of serious social or economic consequences for women seeking to end their marriages.

As these changes were taking place, women who starred and sang in vernacular theater productions were also increasingly contracted by regional and transnational record companies (this mirrored similar patterns of intermedial expression and marketing in India, although with different results in terms of gender politics). Because their work was advertised and their lives reported on in newspapers and other emergent print media, these women's greater visibility in the public sphere made them into household names (Tan 1995:603). In the following decades, films would pick up and expand not only the form but the gender politics built by the vernacular modernism of regional theaters, funneling both, I argue, into matrifocal gazes built around female characters. On the screen, as we have seen, filmmakers and actors would further publicize and reflect on the blurring of women's traditional, "informal" power and its influence on official and institutional levels of finance, politics, and culture.

It is important to the regional scope of this study to show that the transfer of live, theatrical modes of female cultural influence horizontally to emergent filmmaking practices was not limited to the Malay/Indonesian-speaking areas I have addressed so far. As May Ingawanij shows, for example, beginning in earnest in the 1940s and 1950s, Thai cinematic versioning, or live dubbing, similarly became "a terrain of artistic practice available to women who, at that time, could not access institutional artistic training, and who were neither born into an economically privileged household nor an artistic lineage" (2018:28). Combining vernacular theaters and cinema in the most literal way, Thai film versioning provided new opportunities for female performers to expand established "informal" influence into emergent public spheres and to travel extensively and interact with viewers.

In the Philippines, vernacular theaters drew large crowds who consumed similar conglomerations of foreign and local conventions that were translated and positioned as a particular kind of emergent attraction—one with locally and regionally specific characteristics. Such gatherings constituted both a complex new aesthetics and novel ways for Filipinos to imagine themselves as a fragmented yet materializing public—a burgeoning society that, for Vicente Rafael, was likewise assembled "*not* in the name of the father" (2005:118, emphasis added). Vernacular theaters "constituted disparate individuals into audiences of sorts not wholly within clerical or state control" (2005:119). While the Spanish Catholic church and colonial governance at the time both emphasized absolute patriarchy as a basis for any

Philippine nation to come, live vernacular modernist aesthetics were already conceiving of a different kind of authority.

Even in the more overt deployment of machismo in many of the Filipino films that grew out of live vernacular forms like *comedias* and *sarsuelas*, I contend that the sense of a public founded *not* in the name of the father remained deeply embedded. In cineaste Lamberto Avellana's *Anak Dalita* (*Child of Sorrow*, 1956), for example, the female protagonist, Tita (Rosa Rosal), is an agent of heterogeneous temporality and divided symbolic authority par excellence. Recalling *Tiga Dara* and *Ibu Mertuaku* (and, in a different way, *Deedar*), the setting of *Anak Dalita* features a prominent set of stairs, in this case ascending to the ruins of a cathedral that was damaged when American troops killed thousands of Japanese soldiers trapped there at the end of World War II. Like Toto and Kassim in *Tiga Dara* and *Ibu Mertuaku*, the male protagonist, Vic (Tony Santos), ascends the stairs only after he submits to the authority of Tita, who has been positioned via camera angles, blocking, and editing among the female "heads" of the squatter's village built amid the wreckage. In the plural symbolic order assumed by *Anak Dalita*, Tita's strong personality, outspokenness, and work ethic are normalized, even if she may at times bow her head in symbolic offering to Vic's needy, war-torn masculinity.

Ironically, it took much longer for women's representation behind the camera to begin to catch up with the images of them as agents in fictional films. But this is not to say that there were no women writing or directing films in the early years of Southeast Asian national cinemas. Sazkia Noor Anggraini, Rahayu Harjanthi, and Tito Imanda (2021) compiled data on men's and women's roles behind the scenes in Indonesian filmmaking, for example, beginning in the early twentieth century. Although there were no women producers or directors before the 1950s, during that decade, 3 percent of producers were female, and for the remainder of the century, at least 10 and often almost 20 percent of producers were women (2021:21). During the 1950s, 6 percent of directors were women (although that figure shrunk to 2 percent for several decades thereafter), as with screenwriters (Anggraini, Harjanthi, and Imanda:29, 32), whose numbers also continued to grow. As I take up in chapter 6, after the fall of President Soeharto in 1998, the percentages of women working in key positions in the film industry rose sharply and has been more or less consistent since.

I have yet to find such comprehensive data on women's historical participation in other Southeast Asian cinemas. But like most others in the film industry at the time, many of the women directing and producing in Indonesia in the 1950s came from backgrounds in vernacular theaters that toured Malay-speaking areas of the region, including Singapore and elsewhere in Malaya. Early Indonesian female directors Sofia W. D. and Roostijaty, for example, took this route, beginning as actresses on stages and then screens while also working behind the scenes. Chitra Dewi, the star of *Tiga Dara* and many other films, also became a producer, started her own film company, and directed three films in the early 1970s (Kurnia 2014:42). Others such as Maria Menado, an Indonesian-born woman discovered by Singaporean studios when she entered a beauty pageant there, played in her first film at age nineteen in 1951 and subsequently built a strong career both in front of and behind the camera. After her first film, she quickly became a star, later taking on the infamous role of the monstrous feminine *pontianak* in 1957—another early, multifarious patriarchy-challenging character that Rosalind Galt calls "a feminist embodiment of active female protagonists, combined with an anticolonial commitment to representing a heroic vision of Malay culture on-screen" (2021:55). Menado was also tough with male studio bosses, getting very publicly fired for a conscious breach of contract in 1958. Undeterred, she left Singapore to work on Indian and Indonesian films, and she returned to start Maria Menado Productions in 1961. This made her Singapore/Malaysia's first female producer and led to a further string of successful films (Galt 2021:55–57).

In postwar Thailand, at least four women, one of whom was also a cinematographer, directed films in the 1950s, followed by numerous others in the 1970s and 1980s.[10] In the Philippines, likewise building on long-standing patterns of female participation in public arts, women like Brigida Perez Villanueva and Carmen Concha began directing films in the early 1930s (Yeatter 2007:29). But what Bryan L. Yeatter argues made a far bigger impact on Filipino cinema overall was the lasting "studio matriarchies" that began forming the same decade. Most notably, Dona Narcisa Buencamino de Leon, a successful businesswoman, founded the legendary LVN studios with two partners, another woman and a man, eventually becoming known as "The Grand Old Lady of Philippine Movies" (Yeatter 2007:29). In the 1950s, Dolores H. Vera rose to become the one "with the final say in studio matters" at Sampaguita Pictures, another major early producer. At both LVN and Sampaguita, the female heads largely determined what kinds of narratives were made into films and by whom, including in the case of matrifocal *Anak Dalita*, which was produced by LVN. Vera and de Leon were also far from the only Filipina studio matriarchs. For Yeatter, because of what he terms the "patriarchal nature of Asian societies," "the uninitiated might be surprised to observe the preponderance of women listed as producers in the credits of Filipino films" (Yeatter 2007:29–30).

Others, for example, like Grace Swestin, have asked why so relatively *few* women worked in film in Indonesia despite having "women in decision-making positions in other fields for a considerably long time"—including a supreme court judge fifteen years before Sandra Day O'Connor in the U.S. (2009:109). The answer appears to involve a certain amount of misperception around the actual numbers of women historically involved in the region's filmmaking, an issue driven by a further problem. As Umi Lestari et al. (2022) argue, archivists, especially in Indonesia, have long prioritized the films of the so-called "fathers" of national cinemas and their male colleagues for preservation and restoration. Lestari, together with three other scholars and archivists is also trying to address this disparity and have promoted and worked to secure funds for the now near-complete restoration of *Dr. Samsi* (1952), the second film directed by Ratna Asmara (1913–68), an Indonesian actress and producer who was also the country's first female director.

Like many of the women discussed in Tan's study of gender roles in bangsawan, Asmara, a native of the matrilineal Minang society in West Sumatra, got her start in show business when she left home with two female siblings in 1928 (at age fifteen) to become the *tauke* (manager) of a traveling vernacular theater company, Suhara Opera (Anisah 2022:143). After touring around Java for a few years and taking up acting as well as management for the troupe, she met and married Andjar Asmara, the stage name of Abisin Abbas, a theater actor, writer, and director. Adopting his nom de plume, Ratna became business partners with Andjar, joining her theater company with the one he worked for at the time, Dardanella, which was well known and toured regionally and internationally. Their first film work, an adaptation of Andjar's play *Dr. Samsi*, was produced by Coy Films in Calcutta in 1937. Afterward, they started their own theater company, while working on movies with The New Java Industrial Film, a production company owned by Chinese Indonesian entrepreneur The Teng Chun. Like most others around them, the Asmaras moved back and forth between theater and cinema work until a more stable film industry began in the 1950s (Anisah 2022:143).

After the Japanese occupation (1942–45) and the national revolution against the Dutch (1945–49), Ratna was given the chance to direct her first film, *Sedap Malam* (*Sweetness of the Night*, 1951) for Jakarta producer Djamaluddin Malik's Persari studios. Subsequently, she and Andjar founded Asmara Film, for which she directed two more films, including a further remake of *Dr. Samsi* (1952). After divorcing Andjar in 1953, she started her own Ratna Film, directing two further movies before being sent by the Indonesian government to study at the Centro Sperimentale di Cinematografia in Italy in 1954. Thereafter, she accompanied her second husband, a diplomat, on his missions outside Indonesia and ceased working as a filmmaker (Anisah 2022:143).

Based on *Dr. Samsi*, the only remaining film of Ratna Asmara's that has not been lost and is in a condition that makes restoration possible, Julia Pratiwi (2022) takes up the question of how a woman's representation of the experience of women onscreen might differ from those directed by men. Pratiwi secured a prerestoration digitization of the film, which centers on a mother reconnecting with her son born out of wedlock and then "adopted" by his wealthy father, who, together with his wife, raises the boy after their own child dies. In conveying the separation and reunion of son and biological mother in particular, Pratiwi argues that the film's camera angles and editing construct a *bahasa keibuan*, or filmic "language of motherhood" (2022:121). This is in line with the changes Ratna Asmara made to Andjar's theater script, shifting the perspective from that of Dr. Samsi (M. Said), the child's biological father, to Sukaesih (played by Asmara herself), the biological mother he has never known. In comparison to what I have termed the matrifocal gaze, here, the cinematic language of motherhood, while clearly empathizing with women onscreen, appears to underscore victimization rather than agency.

Sukaesih, a poor woman who lost her child to a rich lover who then abandoned her, is later falsely accused of a murder. In a twist of fate, the young lawyer who will defend her turns out to be her son, Sugiat (Kamaludin). In Pratiwi's breakdown of the scene where they are reunited, "Sugiat is always positioned in front, to the left and right sides, and behind Sukaesih" as if to show that "her son will protect her . . . from anything." In this context, Pratiwi argues, Sugiat is positioned heroically as the one who enables "his mother to speak again" (Pratiwi 2022:123) after her long silencing at the hands of other powerful men. At the end of the film, furthermore, despite Sukaesih's clear longing to reveal to Sugiat that she is his mother, she chooses to silence herself on this matter, leaving the constructed status quo of Dr. Samsi's family intact.

Asmara's 1951 directorial debut, *Sedap Malam*, shows a similar focus on women constrained by the power of men. Based on its narrative (a copy of the film has yet to be located), Lestari argues that Asmara's intervention into the gender politics of the time was based on highlighting the "traumatic aspects of World War II and their effects on the bodies and lives of women" (Lestari 2022:37). *Sedap Malam* takes up a topic that had quickly become taboo after the Japanese occupation of Southeast Asia: women who had been forced to work as *jugun ianfu* (comfort girls) for the Japanese military. While many other films by men at the time had prominent sex-worker characters (the ex-*jugun ianfu* in *Sedap Malam* also ends up working as a prostitute after the war), for Lestari, men presented such women as "enigmas" while in Ratna Asmara's hands they were victims (Lestari 2022:37).

Without being able to see either of the above films, it is difficult to get a more detailed sense of how they compare to the "matrifocal gaze" that I have identified in a number of regional films made by men around the same time—a trope that I argue to signify a complex feminine agency that shows women engaging, at times successfully, with the power wielded by men and its potential to silence or victimize. I very much sympathize with Lestari's and her colleagues' critique of the gendered politics of archiving and applaud their efforts to resurrect at least one of the results of Ratna Asmara's pioneering work. Perhaps when the restored version of *Dr. Samsi* is completed, and when it is hopefully followed by access to more of the films of other Indonesian and Southeast Asian women directors, this discussion can be continued.

For the moment, I suggest that regional films made by both women and men demonstrate a strong, common interest in exploring the roles of women (and men), and the politics of gender more broadly, in the modernization processes of many historically matrifocal societies. The attitudes expressed by such works, and the fact of numerous women holding important positions behind the scenes in theater and film (and also outside of the entertainment industry), arguably constitutes a platform—one from which stronger positions can be consciously built and issues of gender can continue to be addressed. I pursue this idea further in the coming chapters, which focus on a set of very different, more overtly masculine, regimes of visuality and authority that would soon beset the entire region. In chapter 4, I focus especially on the active role of another actress-producer-company owner, Suzzanna, in resisting these forces through a long series of populist cinematic critiques.

In the context of the present chapter, I propose that the result of regional cinemas' broader focus on gender was still a globally rare, (and oft-contested), cautiously net-positive positioning of women as constitutive actors shaping modernity on national and regional levels. In cinema, the quintessentially modern medium of the time, women's positions onscreen, and at times behind the camera, were structurally reinforced and projected by the looks of female characters. The situation depicted in films, however, is emphatically not a utopian view in which continuities and shifts in women's empowerment are presented as an easy solution to the myriad problems faced by the region's young nations. Even while the work of numerous filmmakers implicitly or explicitly sustains and bolsters feminine influence, the question of elite, masculine- and high-modernist challenges continues to loom. In this context, the relative ease with which a film like *Tiga Dara*, or *Asrama Dara* (*Girls' Dormitory*, dir. Usmar Ismail, 1958) after it, shows women's influence accepted in the public sphere would soon take on the appearance of a high point in a longer process of push and pull.

Produced in a period of relative political calm before a series of storms engulfed much of the region, both films end on a tentatively upbeat note. Even so, the potential for a typically global/modern, naturalist aesthetics and patriarchal symbolic order (and conversely a particular kind of women's movement based on opposition to such an order) is undermined in a way that certain elite nationalists or religious modernists might well deem "unresolved." As I discuss in chapter 4, less than a decade later, in 1965, this situation would suddenly and radically shift. Mirroring the forces responsible for the split and cinematic "blinding" of Singapore and Malaysia the same year but expressing them in a different way, elite, patriarchal nationalists elsewhere in the region would take the problem of clarifying modern authority into their own hands. While film production generally continued, the mid-1960s saw the emergence of numerous Southeast Asian "strong men" who would use military violence to take and sustain power, while reframing public and private spheres around the symbolic order of a stern national Father.

Screen women, however, like their real counterparts, were not so easily tamed. Women behind the camera, while still limited in numbers, kept up their contributions to gendered discourses on- and offscreen as well. But things were becoming increasingly difficult. As we will see, the increased symbolic and actual marginalization of women that followed the ascent of several Western-aligned dictator "fathers" had a paradoxical effect on regional aesthetics: it threw widespread ideas of parity and partnership between genders out of balance. At the same time, however, it led filmmakers to double their efforts in seeking out and exploring the roles of women expelled from their traditional bases of authority in the spheres of family and home. These realms were, in any case, never the sole bases of women's power. Female shamans or other spiritually potent women have long constituted another formidable sphere of authority throughout the region, one that relies far less (at times not at all) on marriage or other officially recognized relationships to men.

A host of feminine spirits and monsters are frequent interlocutors of these transcendent figures and are themselves often understood as agents who act from a place of strength still farther outside the spheres of male authority. In chapters 4, and 5 we will witness the rise of a virtual army of "outsider" women and superhero-like female ghosts, including urban prostitutes who fight in ways that parallel female shamans, demons, and ghosts. I position the result as a regional response to what were ultimately unsuccessful attempts to institute "real" modern patriarchal regimes.

4

———

Signatures of the Invisible

Southeast Asian Patriarchs and the Feminization of Resistance

THE MATRIFOCAL, THE *BOMBA*,
AND THEIR URBAN AFTERLIVES

Serbis (*Service*, dir. Brilliante Mendoza, 2008): In 2008, a mother in her late thirties ceaselessly walks up and down sets of stairs that connect screens, seats, and projection booths in what was once a majestic, A-class movie theater in Angeles City, the Philippines. Its walls are now full of graffiti, and its art-deco flourishes are dirty and in need of repair. The woman's entire extended family lives in converted offices inside the building, under the watchful eye of her own mother, the matriarch and big boss of a dwindling business that once included three bustling movie houses owned and managed by their group of relatives. But now, as digital technologies and mall-based multiplexes shift screen cultures and economies the world over, they barely scrape by with the semi-illicit profits from a single dilapidated venue. As a teenaged niece gets ready to accompany the matriarch to court for her divorce from the movie house's philandering former patriarch, the camera catches the niece naked, drying herself with a towel and preening in front of a mirror. As she applies copious amounts of lipstick, she strikes stereotypically sexualized poses and whispers "I love you" to her own image, seeming to imagine herself facing the eyes of a lover. The shot travels from her face to her midsection and breasts, where it repeatedly, exploitatively returns and hovers, raising questions about whether a Western-style male gaze has finally invaded Southeast Asian, or at least Filipino, cinema.

That the shots of the niece look sharply up at her, however, begins to suggest a possible ruse, which is confirmed when the scene cuts to reveal the source of the camera's look: a boy of around eight years old, who is quickly outed and chased

116

off by the object of his snooping regard. Frequently featured throughout the film, the boy's curious, bespectacled peeking is directed at everyone and everything in the theater, including the seventy-something matriarch as she, too, towels off after a bath. At one point the boy shows up wearing garish lipstick that he seems to have applied himself, suggesting an engagement with the space and its inhabitants that is not controlling or strictly masculine but based on appropriating and trying out what it sees. As we soon realize, this is what the niece was also practicing in front of the mirror—positioning herself in the kinds of poses and states of undress that are regularly presented in the mix of local, East Asian, and Western softcore pornographic fare that has become the theater's specialty. Further complicating the gender politics of the theater, the mainly heterosexually oriented fare on its screens is consumed almost exclusively by homosexual male spectators who "imitate" but likewise transform the acts onscreen. They do so together with male and transgender companions who offer an intimate corporeal *serbis* (service) in the darkened seating areas for a relatively small fee.

Although fictionalized, *Serbis* is driven by an impulse to document aesthetic practices that emerged in the dark corners of aging Southeast Asian movie palaces following the region-wide economic collapses and reforms of the 1990s. Elmo Gonzaga sees this and other Mendoza films as also engaged in selling "slum voyeurism," an aspect he argues to overshadow "the libidinal experiences that transpire in the movie theater" (2017:119). Images of the goings on in the seating areas in front of the screen are nonetheless striking and plentiful. Perhaps these especially stood out to me given the nature of my own investigations of historical patterns involving interactions between regional viewers and films. In 2012 and 2013, I conducted ethnographic research on similar procedures at the once majestic Rex Theater, built to serve Dutch colonial patrons in Pasar Senen, Jakarta (then Batavia) in the 1920s. Following independence, the Rex was among the capital's elite venues exclusively presenting Hollywood fare and shunning locally produced works. Likely also due to competition from mall-based multiplexes beginning in the late 1980s, the Rex was subsequently split into two interconnecting venues with multiple screens. By the time of my research in 2012, it closely mirrored the venue in *Serbis*: a dusty, run-down shadow of its former self relegated to attracting patrons through allowing companions (in this case both male and female) to wait outside the ticket booth and offer extra services inside the theater for an additional fee.

What especially interested me in both *Serbis* and the Senen Grand and Mulia Agung theaters, as the Jakarta venues were called in 2012, was how they allowed viewers and would-be ethnographers to engage with more or less functional remnants of otherwise-vanished cinematic histories—physical traces that might soon be lost to urban renewal campaigns that see them as embarrassing blight. Entering a space like the Grand, if one looks past the tabloid aspects of semi-illicit sex acts, the ritualistic acts of spectators responding to and reshaping the movements of figures and events on the screen before them exude an uncanny resonance with my own and others' research. I see in them echoes of the interactive attitudes and forms of regional cinemas discussed in the previous chapters. Filmmakers in the 1950s and 1960s adapted the open, improvisatory, onstage worlds of vernacular theaters, using formal techniques to reach out "through" the screen, as if eliciting actual exchanges from spectators. As their live performing antecedents had also done, local cineastes expanded these approaches, opening diegetic spaces—the story worlds of their films—to engage, engulf, and comment on the globalization of modernity happening on both sides of the screen. In concert with audiences, films also appropriated and ironically deformed the transnational genres and trends that markets imposed on nascent national aesthetics, displaying and consuming them as localized modern attractions. In this chapter, I refer to filmic elements that appear to reach out through the screen toward spectators as "transdiegetic."

Documented in *Serbis* and revealed by my observations of the Grand are more recent exchanges between working-class spectators and transnationally circulating images that suggest some of the same basic assumptions about cinema. Diegetic spaces are understood as always already open to live interactions or formal approximations of these. This is especially the case in the reflexive, ritualistic queering of the conventions of various sex-saturated, transnational B movies through the performance of "service." I position the cinematic habits of these spectators as tenuous and potentially generative bridges to the region's vanished cinematic pasts, when such open, exuberant engagements with films, while not involving audience sex acts, were likewise regarded by elites as primitive, lowbrow aesthetic blight (this general elite aversion was briefly complicated by attraction to sex-oriented local films in the 1970s, as I show below). Most important for the purposes of this chapter, the combination of "degenerate" aesthetic innovation and economic survivalism via prostitution forms an even stronger link with one of the region's most legendary cinematic golden ages: the early 1970s, a period when sharp increases in film production and unprecedented expansion of audience bases occurred in Indonesia, the Philippines, and Thailand.[1] As I will show, sex, and particularly sex workers onscreen, were positioned as both populist attractions and as an emergent, transdiegetic and transgender system of spectator identification. This altered formal arrangement became a signature trope of many of the highest grossing and most discussed works of the era—one that crucially also functioned as a "safe" method of delivery for urgent political messages to large, diverse groups of citizens.

Films deploying this system in Indonesia later came to be identified as a distinct genre defined by its central focus on characters who fall into prostitution. I argue that this "prostitution genre" was in fact a regional phenomenon triggered by seemingly coincidental political developments across Indonesia, Thailand, and the Philippines, and especially by the worsening conditions this caused for poor and politically marginalized citizens. Beginning in the mid-1960s (soon after the 1959 onset of Lee Kuan Yew's thirty-one-year grip on power in Singapore), all three nations were beset by the rise of hypermasculine, U.S.-aligned dictators who came to power, or held on to it for decades, through violence, intimidation, and obsessive censorship of counternarratives or direct critiques of the state. Films foregrounding sex were hence ironically able to get into theaters with minimal cuts.[2] This opened the doors for what, following Ernesto Laclau (2005), I call a gray area of contamination—in this case, an ethically complex situation in which the convergence of prostitution and the political onscreen positioned sex workers as ideologically unveiled seers. This builds on, but also departs from, the more strictly negative aspects of mass politics in Laclau's view. As I show, these "unlikely" emergent female figures were invested with the potential to regain a modicum of the ability to act that was purloined by the rise of dictatorial authority. In the same symbolic stroke, the new, exclusively masculine agency promoted by the three emergent states was implied to be dysfunctional and false.

On the screen, men with increasingly rigid, singular visions of how to look and act—evoking the tragic cinematic "modern boys" of the 1950s and 1960s but with even less ability to self-reflect—were shown to be outclassed by the agency of fallen women whose fates they inevitably fail to alter. As these women move from traditional bases of female authority like village markets and matrifocal homes, I show how feminine symbolic power "follows" them as they resettle in urban locales such as brothels, slums, or, in some cases, prisons. These onscreen shifts point to actual crises of agency and moral and political identities triggered by dictatorial rule. The result of filmmakers' interventions was movies that were populist, sex-saturated, and unclear in their alignment with any particular party or oppositional group. At the same time, however, I argue that the prostitution genre produced powerful, inverted reflections of the absurd, mass-media-saturated symbols, tactics, and campaigns of the three dictators, especially Soeharto (Indonesia) and Marcos (the Philippines). Spectators of all genders were formally aligned against these leaders' authority and with the genre's signature figures: politically and economically marginalized women who have been forced to sell their ideals and bodies to survive the rise of a new national Father.

Combining local and transnational perspectives, I position films like the Indonesian *Bernafas Dalam Lumpur* (*Breathing in Mud*, dir. Tourino Djunaidy, 1970), the Philippine *Maynila sa mga Kuko ng Liwanag* (*Manila in the Claws of Light*, dir. Lino Brocka, 1975), and the Thai *Theptida Rong Ram* (*Hotel Angel*, dir. Chatrichalerm Yukol, 1974) as beacons of the ambiguous, paradoxical geopolitical alignments that brought Southeast Asian dictators to power and kept them in office, often, as I have mentioned, for several decades. In particular, the rise of these super-patriarchs ironically reflects the efforts of the U.S. and other Western nations to spread democratic values, aiming to block a leftward fall of Southeast Asian "dominoes" into the hands of Soviet or Chinese communism. Following these currents, I extend the aesthetic and political gray areas of the prostitution genre to the larger, constantly swirling zone of blue-gray defined by the Pacific Ocean—among the most crucial theaters through which the Cold War and its global contradictions were played out and amplified. In this context, I position films as regional responses to (and localized scrambling of) West-to-East geopolitical messages that often begin as seemingly altruistic, symbolically ambiguous cultural imperatives ostensibly selling democracy and free trade. The transpacific journeys of these imperatives raise the specters of violence and exploitation that such Cold War interventions inevitably beget, revealing the horrific realities of corruption, intimidation, and wanton killing directly or indirectly sponsored by Western powers—as documented by and through the lives of the region's onscreen prostitutes.

NEW DICTATORS, YOUNG ACTIVISTS, AND SEX ON THE SCREEN

To better explain the gritty populism inflecting (and, for some, infecting) the genre I position as the most politicized mode of regional 1970s cinema, it is necessary to backtrack briefly to the 1960s and the rise of the Filipino *bomba* and what became known as "pocket bedroom literature" in Indonesia. Most crucially, both genres contributed to a supranational cinematic trend that, for the first time, began to attract elite viewers to the work of Filipino, Indonesian, and Thai cineastes in significant numbers. On the surface, the shift may appear unlikely because it was triggered by a further "lowering" of what elites already derided as lowbrow form and content in locally produced movies. But as filmmakers began adding more sex to their list of attractions, many elites seemed to forget their snobbery, fixing their collective gazes at increasingly steamy regional fare. Looking a bit further into the phenomenon in the Philippines, where it first appeared, many of the politically active "elites" of the mid-1960s and early 1970s were also curious young students seeking new ideas and experiences on movie screens, some of which they began to mimic and internalize. Their shifting viewing habits were among the earliest signs of a regional trend where audiences of diverse socioeconomic and educational backgrounds were drawn (although not always to the same screens at the same time) to populist fare that used explicit sex and violence as base attractions. At the same time, such imagery and themes were increasingly politicized by filmmakers and through popular and critical reception.

Numerous historical factors were involved. The Filipino studio system that thrived in the 1940s and 1950s began to decline in the 1960s amid labor-management issues and increased competition from foreign films. Since many of the exports from East Asia and the West also now came in the form of "B movies" flaunting action, spies, guns, and sex, independent local producers quickly began exploiting a change in the censorship policy that allowed for an "adults only" rating. Under the new law, filmmakers churned out "such curiosities as

Filipino cowboys, Filipino samurai and kung fu masters, Filipino James Bonds, and, most notorious of them all, the *bomba* queen" (Lumbera 1984:202–3). The rise of "funny" Filipino screen-cowboys that satirized Western-global genre tropes mirrored earlier developments in Indonesia, Malaysia, Thailand, and elsewhere as detailed in my first chapter. The simultaneous emergence of Filipino bomba films, which earned a reputation for being more sexually explicit than foreign fare, is generally understood to have caused the biggest political ripples. It was the explosion of the "hitherto repressed sexuality of Philippine films" (Espiritu 2017:86) that began attracting the apparently suppressed desires of middle- and upper-class youth and young professionals—crowds who until then had steadfastly sworn off local, Tagalog-language films in favor of Hollywood and other fancy foreign fare.

As exhibitors responded to this sudden shift in taste and market trends, for the first time, local films began to be shown in A-class theaters in Manila and other urban areas, while consistently outselling their international competition. Even censors approved, opining that Filipino cinema was finally maturing. As Talitha Espiritu sees it, "the litmus test of the cinema's purported coming of age was not so much the films as the audience drawn to them" (2017:87). The "cheap" adult content and thematically realistic portrayals of the underbelly of city life innovated by bomba filmmakers had suddenly become widely acceptable and even fashionable. As Espiritu and Bienvenido Lumbera (1984) also show, the coincidence of the bomba with political trends of the 1960s and 1970s was a key factor in the emergence of the more socially critical—but still prurient, melodramatic, and hence populist—wave of films led by a group of young, self-styled auteurs including Lino Brocka, Mike de Leon, Ishmael Bernal, Marylou Diaz-Abaya, and others who came of age during the bomba-saturated late-1960s.

Many of the college students becoming increasingly politicized in the years leading up to martial law and dictatorship in the early 1970s were critical of the government's connections to the imperialist West, especially the U.S., with its history of colonization of the Philippines. As curious, young, burgeoning activists, many of them were attracted not only to onscreen sex but also now to the strong historical association of locally produced, Tagalog-language films with the lower classes—an especially key concern in the political debates of the time. As Espiritu argues, "the *bomba*'s status as . . . a native-language cinema . . . influenced its . . . patronage by radical youth." Familiarity with such films became a mark of affiliation for groups of young nationalists who took "the *bomba* as a touchstone for the 'masses'" (2017:104). In addition to the alignment of youth activism and onscreen sex, the early 1970s saw rapid increases in political violence and mass demonstrations, often led by the newly radicalized, bomba-fied students. Ferdinand Marcos, who was elected president in 1965, was increasingly targeted owing to irregularities around his reelection in 1970. In response to the combination of student protests and media attacks against him in the early 1970s, he used martial law to install himself as a dictator until 1986, inadvertently setting the stage for a perfect storm of sociopolitical cross-pollination (or contamination) on urban and rural screens that had already become dominated by explicit local views. In this context, as I show below, filmmakers like Brocka adapted and deployed the tropes of the bomba as a critique of Marcos and his self-legitimizing media campaigns.

Along with some important differences, especially economic ones, overall trends in cinematic markets and in the local effects of the Cold War elsewhere in the region produced similar patterns. In Thailand and Indonesia, audiences and screens for local films likewise expanded significantly in parallel with a greater proliferation of sexualized imagery and themes.[3] As in the Philippines, these came to function both as key attractions and as engagements with rapid political, economic, and social shifts occurring with the rise of military dictators in the transition from the 1960s to the 1970s. In Thailand, the economic situation undergirding the changes in local screen cultures and markets was unique: government support for local productions using 35 mm film and synchronous sound was an important factor driving greater public interest in local cinema. An unfortunate side effect of this was the end of the 16 mm, live-dubbed era that most elites had seen as embarrassing and backward (Sungsri 2004:146).

In the mid-1970s, the institution of greater vertical integration in the film industry (precisely what had dissolved in the Philippines through the 1960s) also helped the works of local filmmakers get to more and "better" screens. As I will show, these economic shifts in Thailand coincided with a regionally familiar rise in sexualized and indirectly politicized imagery in films. This trend began in in the later years of military strongman Thanom Kittikachorn's rule (1963–73), continuing through the periods of unrest and repeated military coups that followed it. As elsewhere in the region, the state's instability or narrow focus on strictly "political" matters in the mid-1970s at times worked in favor of Thai filmmakers, increasing their ability to get certain kinds of messages, including critical ones, to diverse domestic viewers. At times, as in the Philippines, government intervention was very helpful to filmmakers. For example, after levying an extreme hike in taxes on imported films, resulting in a boycott by Hollywood and other foreign exporters, Thai productions not only competed better but came to dominate all classes of screens for the next several years (Chaiworaporn 2001:147; Sungsri 2004:146–47).

In Indonesia, cinema production took a sharp downturn in the mid to late 1960s during and after the mass violence that brought general Soeharto to power through a drawn-out coup in 1965–66. Similar to the flowering of bomba on Filipino screens, however, a bustling trend in sex-centered pulp novels swept national literary markets. As the fortunes of producers shifted in the early 1970s, many of these novels also became the sources for a new wave of films. The narratives and visuals of these films typically focused on the expansion of Jakarta's seamy underbelly following Soeharto's power grab. Ali Shahab, one of the most prolific of the emergent pulp authors in the 1960s, followed the flow of literary works to local screens, becoming increasingly involved in the production of cinematic adaptations of his own novels. By the early 1970s, he had established himself as a writer-director and explained that he frequently used prurient topics as a "layer of sugar for the bitter pill" of political realism and critique that he aimed to deliver to the broadest possible audiences (quoted in Yngvesson 2014:56).

Often centering on the lives of bar hostesses and prostitutes, these novels-cum-movies echoed developments in the Philippines, while also building on the work of earlier nationalist artists in the 1940s and 1950s. During and after World War II and the struggle for Indonesian independence that followed it (1945–49), many painters, poets, and novelists in the capital focused on the lives and experiences of prostitutes as symbolic stand-ins for "the masses" (Yngvesson 2014; Yngvesson 2016). In some sense, this anticipated Filipino students' attraction to bomba films as tokens of the culture of "the people" a few decades later. Like the bomba, prostitution films in Indonesia helped create a positive shift in the economics of cinema at the time. Among the various categories of films produced in the early Soeharto years, the attention-grabbing posters, imagery, and themes of the prostitution genre had an especially outsized effect on the market, helping trigger a golden age of increased production in the 1970s and 1980s similar to those in Thailand and the Philippines.

Along with other populist fare such as family melodramas, narratives focused on the lives of sex workers began to shift the position of historically themed films as the most frequent recipients of awards at the Indonesian Film Festival (FFI) and praise from critics more broadly. At the same time, the local market's preference for comedies was expanded as more diverse groups of spectators gravitated toward the new attractions and perspectives proffered by Indonesian movies (Sen 1993:207). If curious young intellectuals (or curious older critics) were drawn to the prurient "layer of sugar" with which many films were laced, they were also inevitably faced with the corresponding "pills." As I explain further in the next section, popular films in Indonesia, like those in Thailand and the Philippines, quickly began pointing out emergent realities filled with bitterness and suffering, especially for women. Their fictionalized narratives, while avoiding direct critiques of those in office, documented a steep rise in moral degradation and dehumanization following the forced installation of a new and hypermasculine form of authoritarianism—in this case under Soeharto as national dictator-cum-father.

NEW ORDER, NEW INSTRUMENTS

As debates and splits between leftist and other parties heated up along Cold War–defined lines in the early 1960s in Indonesia, artists, especially filmmakers, became increasingly polarized. In many cases, growing ideological divides forced avowedly nonaligned, politically "independent" cineastes to join with a particular party or camp in order to defend themselves from the attacks of another party or camp, which often played out in the press. Usmar Ismail, Asrul Sani, and other core members of his production house, Perfini, often expressed political views that did not easily align with those of any one party, especially in their films. Instead of keeping them "safe," however, their nonaligned stances increasingly exposed them to scathing and very public attacks from the left (including the Communist Party, or PKI), which accused them of proffering "counter-revolutionary" aesthetics. The debates over what constituted a proper nationalist political perspective came to an abrupt and terrifying stop in 1965–66, however, as the rise of Soeharto decimated and silenced the left on a massive scale: five hundred thousand to one million were killed and tens of thousands more imprisoned for the next fifteen years. The Indonesian Communist Party (PKI), then the largest in the world after Russia and China and often the loudest voice in local disputes, was suddenly outlawed. Anyone believed to be directly or indirectly associated with the PKI was targeted for prosecution or far worse. As military and paramilitary forces scoured and terrorized the nation from capital city to remote villages on outlying islands in search of the new "enemy," no one, from party leaders to rank and file to friends and family, was spared.[4]

Due to their rocky relationship with the left in the early 1960s, one might assume, as many have,[5] that Ismail, Sani, and their closest collaborators supported Soeharto's violent coup d'état, if not necessarily the extrajudicial killings. In the late 1960s, Ismail indeed wrote bitterly of the left's attacks on himself and others in the media. But other writings and the few additional films he produced before his untimely death in 1970 show that his attitude toward the rise of the New Order itself was typically critical. His perspective on Soeharto in many ways mirrored his habit of highlighting corruption, collusion, and political infighting in films made under Soekarno (Ismail 1983). Asrul Sani, an accomplished essayist and poet as well as director and script writer for screen and stage, was more critical still. Reading across the articles and statements he composed in 1966 and 1967 reveals a profoundly negative view of Indonesia's sudden lurch to the right at the hands of military factions that were cozy with the United States. To blame the "black years" of the early to mid-1960s on the influence of the PKI, the left, or any one group, he wrote, is to "scratch one's head, even while one knows very well that the itch is coming from one's knee" (1997:672).[6]

In Sani's view, the rise of the PKI and its subsequent decimation by Soeharto were symptoms of a broader problem, one that paralleled but exceeded the effects of the Cold War: a global trend of "extreme secularization that simultaneously assigns a religious value to democracy, nationalism, or socialism as replacements for religion" (Sani 1997:6). With the rise of an emboldened religion of the state under Soeharto (a problem Sani also associated with Soekarno), Sani argued Indonesia had for the first time become truly saturated with "humanity's first-ever universal culture" (666)—one of Western-style consumerism and mass media, and of "tourism, vacations, empty time, the press, comic strips, film, radio, television, etc." (665).[7] As Indonesia became inundated with this broad cultural attitude under

Soeharto's leadership, Sani argued the new government had begun to conceive of the nation as something "fake" or entirely "without roots" that could potentially be reconstructed from the ground up. This would allow for the state to maximize broad political, cultural and economic control (665).

In light of these radical negative shifts, Sani argued that artists and intellectuals now lacked the proper "instruments" to "provide a clear picture of the state of affairs surrounding them" (665). Nonetheless, he concluded, it was all the more crucial for artists and critical thinkers to speak out, despite the greater dangers of doing so under a military dictatorship. As he noted, "we need to position ourselves within this new cultural milieu and to do so we must be brave and honest in order to project our thoughts into the future" (668). Many other filmmakers and artists appeared to agree. As soon as the dust of mass violence had cleared in the late 1960s, those left standing got down to business, probing the current state of affairs in hopes of acquiring the proper "instruments" to critically engage the shifts in Indonesia's cultural politics and symbolic order. A brief period of government film funding (1968–71) inadvertently emboldened their efforts, before being unceremoniously withdrawn.

Among the first of six projects selected to be produced was Nya Abbas Akup's *Matt Dower* (1969), which David Hanan calls "a bizarre and grotesque . . . allegory of the power struggle between Suharto and Sukarno . . . and in particular the increasing political repression and abuse of human rights" carried out by Soeharto (2009:14). When state censors saw the finished version of *Matt Dower* and seemed to finally understand its implications, the film's release was purposely delayed and curtailed. Despite being a showcase of arts funding from the new government and being among the first Indonesian films to be shot in color, the distribution of *Matt Dower* was limited to smaller cities where it was shown in grainy, black-and-white prints (Hanan 2009:27).

Released the same year and funded by the same government program, Asrul Sani's *Apa Jang Kau Tjari, Palupi? (What Are You Looking for, Palupi?*, 1969) shares *Matt Dower*'s theme of Soekarnoist excesses that only increase after Soeharto's coup (fig. 16). But Sani's film was set in the present and was therefore perhaps more cautious about how its critiques were framed and expressed. On close reading of the film, what emerges is an unsparing deconstruction and rejection of the New Order. Yet *Palupi*'s politics are mainly under the surface, and it appears to have so thoroughly confused Soeharto's newly anointed Department of Information that nothing was done to hamper its release. Building on the complex regional marketing strategies of the 1950s and early 1960s, in *Palupi* Sani worked to bring together a diverse array of views that were seemingly, as in Usmar Ismail's 1956 *Tiga Dara*, aimed at different classes of viewers (see chapters 2 and 3). Yet in this case, in a film paid for by the same government that he would use it to criticize, Sani was presented with an opportunity to minimize the market-influenced aesthetics and attractions of previous decades. With *Palupi*,

FIGURE 16. An image from the title sequence of *Apa Jang Kau Tjari, Palupi?*, now considered one of Asrul Sani's greatest works. The sequence is composed of a series of stills of Farida Faisol (then Farida Sjuman), the actress and Soviet-educated ballerina who played Palupi, set to an orchestral score with operatic female vocals. Palupi's frequent asides and looks into the camera are among the film's most striking techniques, expanding the conventions of local cinema from the 1950s and early 1960s in a way that aimed to address the drastic changes in Indonesian life, politics, and media following the rise of Soeharto. The feminine cinematic perspective that this began to more fully formulate builds on the "matrifocal gaze" and was followed by many of the popular Indonesian films of the early and mid-1970s.

Sani's first production under the New Order, he began the process of developing new modes of critique capable of addressing the radical shifts under way in Indonesia and elsewhere in the region.

In my analysis, the film therefore appears more carefully designed to deliver a coded message than to sell tickets. While reminiscent of some of his earlier efforts, Sani's experimentations in *Palupi* address elite viewers in a way that refuses to cater to their well-known attraction to Hollywood fare. In its attention-catching, if somewhat convoluted, manner, *Palupi* builds on Sani's warnings about the rise of the New Order in writing two years earlier. Like his written work, the film is brimming with intellectualized moments and references, such as when a character wanders through a park clutching a copy of *Cahiers du Cinéma*, the famous French film journal. But these instances of apparent "high" modernism, the kind of lofty ideas and aesthetics that Andreas Huyssen and others position as typically "patri-archal . . . and masculinist" (Huyssen 1986:60), perhaps hewed too close to the cultural politics of Soeharto as self-proclaimed, dictatorial national *bapak* (father). In *Palupi*, such elite intellectual tactics are generally implied to be the detritus of a bygone era and are treated as problems rather than potential solutions. The film's modernist flourishes are hence countered with a flood of typically "low," populist-style attractions such as cheap jokes and unprecedented levels of nudity, the latter one of the few things that was, in fact, excised by censors in the end.

Palupi (Farida Faisol), the film's central figure, is a housewife unhappily married to Haidar (Ismed M. Noor), an idealistic artist—a politically progressive screenwriter and director of experimental theater who struggles financially. Both appear to have lost their sense of self and direction in life, a psychic condition that is implicitly timed with the change in regimes. The difference in their responses also reflects the high/low, masculine/feminine contrasts of the film's aesthetics and themes. While Haidar buries himself ever more deeply in radical art, Palupi embarks on a mythical pursuit of the glamour and fulfillment she is certain awaits her in the sphere of mainstream movies. This sets her up for a fall into what is left of the 1950s "Djakartawood" dream factory, now presented as a dump decimated by years of neglect and political violence in the 1960s, crumbling anew under the false ideals of the current regime. The film's various quasi-explicit attractions and potential distractions notwithstanding, I propose that Sani's decision to focus on a woman's experience of the early Soeharto years innovated a potential way out of the trap of "masculine" high modernism (or perhaps reinvented it, updating it as a weapon against a dictator). It also anticipated one of the most widespread cinematic modes of critique under Soeharto—one that would soon be adapted and further developed by other, likeminded filmmakers. In *Palupi*, this instrument-in-process guides viewers not only to look *at* the women on the screen but to follow them in paying attention to the gendered nature of the ideological shifts instituted by the New Order, something that female characters are especially well positioned to discover.

If a new aesthetic instrument can be said to have arisen from the ashes of Djakartawood at the end of the film, I submit that it is not in the impotent, masculine-intellectual purview of Haidar. Nor is it in the sleazy, greedy looks of the men who exploit Palupi for pleasure and profit. The sexualized imagery that the film does provide is overtaken by an explicitly feminized view: what Palupi sees as she struggles to become a perfect symbol of New Order womanhood, a process that pulls her down through the filthy worlds of entertainment and business in the nation's capital. Unlike the clearer, satirical jabs of Nya Abbas Akup's *Matt Dower*, Sani's critique is hidden in the most "unlikely" of places, in the purview of a woman who does not identify as an intellectual and appears eminently uninterested in politics (this also distinguishes her from many of the central matrifocal characters in the films of the 1950s and 1960s). Through Palupi's eyes, audiences may experience the ruinous truths that finally rip her emergent, Soehartoist naivete to shreds. In line with the film's overall aesthetics, the spectacle of her fall at times waxes hyperbolic, as when Palupi, finally discarded by both the film industry and the wealthy lover her brief stardom afforded her, is hauled off from an elite nightclub in a garbage truck. The point, however, is clear enough: to attempt to embody or become an ideal image of the national/mass cultural character sold by the state as a new "religion" is to be made into a fungible, disposable product. In the end, Palupi's journey of self-realization as an elite, outwardly independent, new woman of the New Order has effectively transformed her into a prostitute.

Palupi's dizzying view is constructed across the gaps between the film we are watching and the various films within it (in which she stars and that we are often

FIGURE 17. Seated in a movie theater and bringing to mind Indonesia's monochrome cinematic past under Soekarno, Palupi stares intently in the direction of the camera (*top*), as if looking out at the audience. The reverse angle (bottom), however, shows what she is "really" looking at in the top still—an image of herself embedded in the diegetic version of New Order Jakarta, in what is implied to be a mainstream "commodity" movie of which she is the star. The latter film, however, is not finished, and in the discussions of the director, producer, and art director, one of whom is visible behind Palupi in the top still, it is suggested that they will either scrap the project or fix it by making it about Palupi's "real" life. The finished version of the "bad" film on the bottom, then, is implied to be the film that viewers of Palupi are watching: the story of Palupi's rise and fall.

also shown), signaling familiar local-cum-regional problems of visuality and fragmentation that the emergent regime and its cineastes imbue with new twists and turns. As we observe Palupi at the center of the screen in front of us, she is often shown intently staring at herself on another screen, as she struggles to embody some empty "Eastern" feminine ideal. Unmoored from material-historical sources of power like the matrifocal home and focused on the process of becoming something that is in fact nothing, Palupi's look and sense of self are increasingly alienated (fig. 17).

FIGURE 18. As the walls of a set come down, leaving only emptiness surrounding her, Palupi appears distressed. A hard cut then shows her at an elite party, which is at first implied to be another constructed scene in which Palupi is acting but is in fact full of "real" Jakartan movers and shakers who are just as fake.

While we watch her watching herself, she turns to look out at viewers, acknowledging their copresence in theaters and symbolically linking the spaces they inhabit to hers: a capital city largely depicted as a series of dispensable movie sets (fig. 18). Her look positions audiences to see New Order Jakarta—theirs and hers—as an approximation of how the city was characterized in Sani's writing two years earlier: "as if they were now facing something that is made up and doesn't have roots" (1997:665). This reading is underscored as the sets that constitute the city onscreen are continually torn down and replaced in front of our eyes. Sutured via Palupi's "apolitical" perspective into a world of backdrops that keep crumbling into blackness, spectators are given no way out of Sani's, in fact, deeply politicized (and feminized) view of Jakarta—a city he believes Soeharto's New Order is turning into the setting of a tawdry movie. Cheap imagery hence constantly overlays and interrupts the "real" *Palupi*, threatening to overtake whatever substance or credibility the film may have left.

While it is clearly too late for Palupi to save herself, I argue that the point of the film is not to save Palupi but to *become* Palupi, as viewers are formally and emotionally invited to do. As they tumble into her stifling, constructed reality, one from which there is finally no escape, audiences are exposed to a view that reveals the new political and symbolic orders as false constructions. At the same time, they are all too real and mortally dangerous. Sidelining the more "legitimate" interventions of male characters, Palupi—a woman falling through the cracks of Soeharto-ist ideology—emerges as the new instrument deployed to undermine the regime of universalist patriarchy that has been unceremoniously imposed on Indonesia. Sani's views are translated and safely harbored in Palupi's feminized gaze—a secret weapon with the potential for critical realization and dissemination, if not yet for inspiring direct action. To support this new instrument, Sani and his film would need to fall from grace along with *Palupi*, sliding and leading viewers into the low-brow, red-tinted, corruption-fueled, rock-and-roll "hell" where she finally lands. Others would soon follow.

CINEMATIC CRITIQUE
AND THE "PROSTITUTION GENRE"

If Sani had discovered a new screen-instrument to criticize the New Order, he had yet to perfect it as a weapon of mass ideological unveiling. Economically, *Palupi* stumbled on its release, its fate contributing to the canceling of the government program that funded it. Unlike Usmar Ismail's winning combination of regional populism and faux-Hollywood glitter in *Tiga Dara*, Sani's mix of lofty intellectualism and transnational B-movie tropes fared much poorer at the box office. It did win first prize at the 1970 Asian Film Festival, held in Taiwan, but audiences and critics back home were unusually unified in their lack of appreciation for *Palupi*, which seemed to go either over or under viewers' heads. After "searching" throughout its 127-minute running time, one critic came to the conclusion that the film was "one quarter Jean-Luc Godard, one quarter Turino Djunaedy [an Indonesian director, actor, and producer known for combining action and sex], and the rest is I don't know what" (*Pedoman* 1970). Despite the film's one nude scene being censored, Sani was also criticized by some (and salaciously reported on by others) for deigning to add such potentially inflammatory imagery in the first place (Sjarief 1970; *Pedoman* 1970).

Hindsight has been kinder to *Palupi*, which was among twenty-nine films chosen for restoration in 2012 by Sinematek, the Indonesian film archive, and is remembered by many contemporary filmmakers as an inspirational classic (when I selected it to screen at the *Arkipel* festival in Jakarta in 2013, it attracted a full house at the local Goethe Institute and sparked a lively discussion). Even in the months directly following its disappointing commercial release, other filmmakers appeared to take careful note of Sani's rendering of the seamier aspects of life in Jakarta. Two of the most influential films of the early Soeharto years, Usmar Ismail's *Ananda* (1971) and Tourino Djunaedy's *Bernafas Dalam Lumpur* (*Breathing in Mud*, 1970), built on Sani's combination of titillating imagery with a pervasive, underlying air of prostitution, literalizing the latter while restrategizing the former. Palupi's fall from privilege is reimagined by Ismail and Djunaedy through the experiences of lower-class women whose star-crossed fates bring them to sex work or other, related fields. Both *Ananda* and *Bernafas* also featured numerous scenes in which women are scantily clad but not nude, thus minimizing what would be excised by the censorship board.

For Ismail, *Ananda* represented a departure from his depictions of women in the 1950s and early 1960s in films like *Enam Djam di Djodja* (*Six Hours in Yogya*, 1951) and the aforementioned *Tiga Dara* and *Asrama Dara*. In those films, women were positioned as important sources of revolutionary fervor or as key actors and sources of historical grounding during difficult processes of postindependence development and modernization. *Ananda*, by contrast, can be seen as building on certain elements of the noirish 1954 *Lewat Djam Malam*, which had also been penned by Sani. Although *Ananda* is female-centered, as in *Lewat Djam Malam*, the sense of hope, tempered idealism, or humor infusing many of Ismail's other earlier works takes a darker turn.

Perhaps not coincidentally, this plunge into darkness follows Ismail's personal downfalls during the extreme political and economic shifts of the 1960s. Although like Sani, Ismail came through the killings and arrests of 1965–66 politically unscathed, the film market tanked, and Perfini, Ismail's production company, was in and out of bankruptcy throughout the 1960s. Ismail took a four-year hiatus from production (1965–69), trying his hand in the fields of banking and finance, embedding himself ever more deeply in structures of capital and state authority that he had long endeavored to criticize. Although reportedly in good health, in early 1971, shortly after completing postproduction on *Ananda*, Ismail unexpectedly died at age forty-nine.

Along a similarly downward path, *Ananda* follows its eponymous central character (Lenny Marlina) through a lengthy cycle of losses and negative realizations about the changed world in which she exists. As in Sani's *Palupi*, these events are triggered by Ananda's continual exploitation at the hands of others. As Krishna Sen (1993) points out, however, the fact that Ananda is from a lower-class background further emphasizes the sense of her victimization. Indeed, unlike Palupi, Ananda's fall does not merely lead to the realization that the new regime's patriarchal ideals are false. Without money or a group of wealthy men who take interest in her career, Ananda's tumble places her in constant danger. For Ekky Imanjaya, "Usmar's critical attitude toward the (supposedly) modern New Order, which was still very young and defined by materialistic values can be felt throughout" the film (Imanjaya 2021:36). Abandoned by an uncaring family and preyed on sexually by men, Ananda soon takes up with a gang of criminals who introduce her to the degenerate worlds of nightclub singing and actual prostitution—political-economic spheres into which Ismail, who also tried his hand as a club owner when times were tough in the late 1960s (2021:29), had himself fallen, albeit in a different way.

Drawing on feminist film theory as an analytical lens, Sen is generally critical of the representation of women tendered by the flood of early 1970s prostitution-centered films, including *Ananda* and *Bernafas Dalam Lumpur*. "The prostitution films," she argues, "directly use the female body to sell the product (the film), while at the same time condemning that body" (1994:145). Yet, as one of the few critics to have taken the genre seriously, Sen recognizes a glimmer of radical potential in its unwavering focus on marginalized women. A woman, she writes, whose "sexuality is aroused outside of the sphere of monogamy . . . signifies a crisis for the symbolic world," potentially "transform[ing] her body into a weapon against which men have no defense" (1994:144–45). But like Miriam Hansen's (2000, 2012) argument that norm-challenging "modern girls" in interwar Chinese and Japanese cinemas are destined to tragically fail, here, Sen argues, "death is inevitable in a moral order which cannot tolerate an unattached woman who is sexually active" (145). For Sen, the potentially weaponizable flame of sexuality outside monogamy in New Order Jakarta is snuffed before it can burn anything of consequence.

While this would seem to foreclose on the genre's radical potential, others, like Alicia Izharuddin (2017) and Soh Byungkuk (2007), have argued that Sen's findings are "too simplistic and narrow" (Byungkuk 2007:77) in their assessment of sexualized women on 1970s Indonesian screens. On closer inspection, in fact, Sen's argument, like Hansen's, unfolds over multiple engagements with the same material. Taken together, her readings allow for more of a "gray area" of symbolic flexibility to emerge, mirroring the political and moral ambiguity I see as carefully built into the films. It is precisely this sense of complexity, and at times slipperiness, that most interests me about the prostitution genre as a response to the New Order's sudden, forced installation of Soeharto as an omnipresent national "father." In this vein, an earlier (1993) essay by Sen on melodrama in Indonesian cinema anticipates the overall conclusion of her classic *Indonesian Cinema: Framing the New Order*. Yet at the same time, the essay identifies a further space of radical potential, focusing on a pattern of gazing and audience identification that complicates the symbolic function of the central figure of the falling/fallen woman. This forms a bridge to my reading of *Palupi*, while underscoring a similar, morally ambiguous capacity for political critique in prostitution films like *Ananda*.

In both cases, as David Hanan (2017:246) also notes, Sen's analysis evokes Laura Mulvey's classic (1975) identification of a controlling male gaze operative in Hollywood films. The gazes of male viewers, as Mulvey argues, align with the active, masculine looks of men onscreen. Camera angles, editing, and overdetermined acting function as formal prompts for spectators to identify with these powerful male characters, while the looks and agency of onscreen women are suppressed.

For Mulvey, the classical Hollywood system therefore imbues female figures with a passive, "to-be-looked-at-ness"—a complex state of being that encourages audiences to look at women on the screen, aligning their view with male characters in a controlling, "masculine" way while discouraging spectators' imaginary association with screen-women ([1975] 1999:837). In Sen's reading of *Ananda*, she applies a similar understanding of how cinema can assign or deny power along gendered lines, arguing that Ananda, the central female figure, is "*acted upon . . . to be the way she is, rather than *acting*, to create herself and her circumstances*" (Sen 1993:208, emphasis in original).

While this assessment of Ananda's role in the film rings true, Sen also makes an important, if unacknowledged, departure from Mulvey's theory. On the surface, Ananda is certainly passive and eminently "to-be-looked-at." But as in my reading of Palupi, her positioning vis-à-vis the gazes of spectators—what one might call her *to-be-identified-with-ness* (my term)—complicates and calls attention to the limitations in Mulvey's exclusive focus on how films objectify women. Among other things, even in the context of America, Mulvey avoids grappling with numerous Hollywood "women's films" in which female characters have been argued to "appropriate the gaze" (Doane 1987:5). Despite registering a certain level of "strain, if not caricature" (Doane 1987:37) in doing so, women are positioned as protagonists or as subjects driving a film's narrative. Mary Anne Doane sees the tension readable in such films as signaling their own status as "pathologies"— albeit extremely common ones—in an otherwise conventionally masculine system of representation (36). A certain connection can therefore be made with the female-centered, Indonesian prostitution genre and its laser focus on sex work and sex workers as "pathologies" triggered by the installation of a new, hyperpatriarchal system of order. As I will show, however, the differences in what this means both politically and in relation to mainstream regional cinematic conventions is quite stark.

As Sen acknowledges, the central gaze around which the prostitution genre is structured—the look with which viewers are formally aligned—is, in fact, that of the *prostitute*. The effect is anything but heroic or typically masculine. Instead, for male and female audience members, "the world is seen from the point of view of the victim. The pleasure of this perspective is one of passive individual identification with the victim, in the recognition of one's own circumstantial inability to act" (Sen 1993:208). The abject status of the prostitute thus symbolically mirrors the experiences of *all* viewers living with the pervasive effects of Soeharto's rule, regardless of their gender. No one onscreen is presented as active in the classical sense. As I established in the previous chapters, regional films are embedded in a system of representation in which women are often positioned as powerfully wielding a matrifocal cinematic gaze. While ideal heroic agency à la Hollywood is much rarer overall, women are presented as active, narrative-driving figures at least as frequently as men, and men are often also presented as stuck or unable to negotiate the emergent conditions of local modernity. In some ways, the prostitution genre departs from this and can be seen as evoking a masculine discourse of power—one of fallen women and individualist male saviors—closer to that of Western classical traditions. But this is mainly a ruse; in doing so, the genre also takes pains to show that such "new" discourses of authority are also difficult or impossible to implement in the context of Indonesia under Soeharto. Even the ostensible agents of evil driving the victimization of others are unclear as to their power to act as individuals: "villainy is not . . . concentrated in any character or any institution but rather dispersed though everyone, including the victim herself and every social institution" (Sen 1993:209).

Reading across the productive ambiguities in Sen's analysis, I suggest that the power of marginalized, sexually active women to trigger a crisis of moral and symbolic orders in 1970s Jakarta is hardly diminished if one such figure happens to die (in fact, many did not, nor were most co-opted or "saved" through marriage). Rather, I argue that the emergent focus on prostitutes ultimately circles back to the idea of the matrifocal gaze, even if such a structure may have been temporarily dismantled in the early years of the New Order. This works to challenge the perception of both men as ideal actors and of fallen women as simple victims. The dynamic and vital perspectives with which many screen prostitutes become imbued are linked to their falls into the depths of Soehartoist exploitation and depend on what is revealed to them in the process. Like Palupi, for example, as Ananda appears to plunge further and further from the fleeting possibilities of agency and unrealistic ideals of womanhood surrounding her, her perspective—what, where, and how she sees—is opened in both terrifying and potentially empowering ways. In the context of the film, her "defiled" yet profoundly expanded vision functions as a tool or instrument facilitating her own, and by extension Ismail's, engagement with the new and often seemingly insurmountable challenges of the times.

The embeddedness of this fallen/expanded vision as a repeated, generic convention that audiences are aligned with points to the broader emergence of a transdiegetic—and trans*gender*—system of audiovisual attachment.[8] Responding to the rise of Soeharto and various associated political economic shifts, the system reshapes the relationship between audiences and figures on the screen. Reaching "behind" the screen as well, such transdiegetic looks entangle filmmakers in their relay of gazes and imaginary identifications. The seamy, populist figure of the prostitute offers cineastes the chance to connect with broader audiences on a wider variety of screens, challenging the historical, class-based limitations of regional cinematic apparatuses and reimagining public spheres of the 1970s. Removed from what regime change signaled as the only "respectable" location for agency—active men—filmmakers' aesthetics of protest are hidden in a seemingly unlikely vehicle: a deceptively passive subversive who smuggles critique past censors while simultaneously using her "cheap" wiles to attract variously gendered and classed recipients of the message she carries.

THE PROSTITUTE AS SEER
AND MELODRAMATIC AMPLIFIER

As in many of the early 1970s prostitute films, in Tourino Djunaedy's *Bernafas Dalam Lumpur* (*Breathing in Mud*, 1970), a complex series of negative sociopolitical effects is impressed upon and conveyed by the gaze and body of Mila (Suzzanna), the central female character. At first, these effects are framed as seeming coincidences, but they soon reveal the sketchy outlines of a hidden, yet pervasive system of exploitation, dehumanization, and masculinization—the machine set to work beneath the otherwise bustling, rapidly developing surface of Jakarta. Many of the key points and moments that lead to this sensory-political mapping are compiled in a long flashback sequence around the film's midpoint. In a tearful hotel-bed confession, Mila explains to Budi (Rachmat Kartolo), the film's deceptively virtuous, powerful man and Mila's wealthy client, how she was transformed from rural farmer's wife to urban prostitute in a matter of days. The sequence consists of Mila remembering and interpreting a series of events that cause radical shifts in her life and worldview. Since arriving in Jakarta, she has been wantonly, and at first seemingly randomly, victimized by men, including multiple rapes occurring in the space of twenty-four hours. The acts are so ubiquitous, their perpetrators—from a variety of different socioeconomic backgrounds—so unrelenting, that hearing Mila's explanation (while being shown renderings of her memories as extended flashbacks), one is indeed left with a collective or systemic, rather than an individualized, sense of their cause.

The problem, rooted in class differences and shifting perceptions of political status after the recent historical violence in Indonesia, is clearly amplified by gender. A poor village woman who enters the city looking for her missing husband—an extremely common tale after the mass killings and arrests of suspected communists in 1965–66—signals a figure that has fallen outside the rigid norms set by the newly arisen state. As was the case with thousands of other women who suddenly found themselves identified with the "wrong" (i.e., left) side of the political spectrum, Mila is instantly categorized by the men and women she encounters in the city as a *lonte* (whore) who must be dealt with severely. Doing so invokes a shift in public attitudes in line with the government's fabricated media reports of communist women castrating and killing army generals, while purportedly singing and dancing naked around their bodies. In their extensive efforts to "prove" these accusations, the military disproportionately targeted women, including numerous sex workers who were imprisoned and tortured, then forced to sign statements claiming they were leaders of Gerwani, a progressive, PKI-linked women's organization that most of them had never heard of. The statements also claimed Gerwani had planned and carried out the sexualized killings of the generals (Wieringa 2002:291, 296–98; Roosa 2020:71–77).

As Saskia Wieringa shows, the targeting of women who seemed to fit, however vaguely, the emergent profile of a depraved "communist whore" was thereafter both practiced by the military and justified for the public using blatantly false yet widely accepted media reports that conflated progressive gender politics with prostitution: "instead of being loyal wives and good mothers . . . [politically progressive women] were becoming politically active and morally loose, unleashing their frightful sexual powers in indecent ways and committing unspeakable atrocities. Therefore, the public was made to understand, it was justifiable to erase communism and especially Gerwani and so cleanse society and restore order" (Wieringa 2002:301). John Roosa also shows that newspapers, following the military's lead, not only sexualized and demonized the left but implicitly and explicitly justified attacks on and murders of those accused of supporting the PKI. Statements were printed to the effect that communists no longer "had the right to live in Indonesia" (Roosa 2020:71).

On the one hand, *Bernafas Dalam Lumpur* plays it safe by not mentioning communism or making any other direct references to state or military policies and practices. On the other hand, what happens to Mila is eerily similar to the treatment of actual, marginalized women who were ubiquitously portrayed in media and society as "loose," "suspicious," or worse following the rise of Soeharto. In this context, what happens in the film is clearly a political pattern and not an accident or mere case of bad luck experienced by Mila. Strategically engaging with the politics of the time, *Bernafas* highlights the grave injustices caused by the state's violence and gendered, self-legitimizing discourse, while building a sense of Mila's strength of character and initially unshakable moral compass when facing such attacks. Whatever abject new category her attackers may have placed her in, she is not easily subjugated or acted on, and she fights rapists and accusers tooth, nail, and discourse, returning their looks and harsh, stereotyping words in kind.

When Mila finally bumps into her husband, she discovers he has left her to join the darkly advancing world of the city, at the side of another woman who owns a busy food stall and will support him. After this most life-shattering shock, she appears at last to give in to the overwhelming nature of the situation in which she finds herself. Taking in what is happening to her, a look of distanced realization spreads over Mila's countenance, betraying a need to separate the shredded remains of her former self—the farmer's wife who was grounded and empowered by home and socioeconomic standing—from the Soehartoist scene at hand. The camera, lingering as the subjectivity drains from her expression, begins to waver and sway, as if appropriating Mila's altered perception and transferring it to the viewer. As she starts to wander randomly, the image aligns itself with her gaze, offering a lengthy opportunity for viewers to inhabit her perspective (fig. 19). Here, however, the resulting "POV" shot

FIGURE 19. *Bernafas Dalam Lumpur:* As the awareness appears to drain from Mila's face (top), the camera begins to sway, as if approximating her "unconscious" view (bottom), floating off-kilter down the middle of Jakarta's busy streets. Like most of the films of its era, *Bernafas* was shot and exhibited in the cinemascope widescreen format. To my knowledge, no film prints remain, although there are numerous cropped and poorly transferred video copies available online.

expresses something closer to the lack of a defined, subjective point of view. What is conveyed is the cumulative shock of Mila's first close encounters with the toxic combination of policies and attitudes introduced by the New Order— something likely to be most powerfully experienced in the nation's capital and by a woman.

Her view seems to unmoor itself from the ground as the camera drifts impassively through the chaotic midst of the city's heavily trafficked streets, accompanied only by the nondiegetic sounds of the meandering, looping, synthesized soul jazz score—a common ingredient, along with heavy rock, of popular aural modernisms throughout the region in the 1970s. Finally, as the camera switches back to a view of Mila, she collapses in a pile of garbage beside a litter-strewn canal, recalling the fate of Palupi after being chewed up and spit out by the same capital city the year before. But Mila's fall occurs much earlier in the course of *Bernafas*'s narrative—rather than a final blow, it is implied to be something closer to a beginning.

One way to understand the rapid transition through which Mila at first appears to surrender control of her body and mind to the circumstances around her is what Gilles Deleuze (1989) calls the "crisis of the action image"—a convention that he also sees as a break from the typical functions associated with Western classical films.[9] For Deleuze, this crisis frequently occurs when a character's discovery of some unbearable truth forecloses the character's ability to formulate an effective response or choose an action that will bring about change. As the term suggests, the result is not just characterological but involves structural/ideological shifts in the film or films built around the figures in crisis. Changes in visuality, especially in relation to what characters see, are crucial. For example, Deleuze positions long, plodding shots or sequences tracking characters through the minutiae of their daily routines as clues that the hegemony of the action image (which he associates with classical Hollywood) is waning and that we are entering the "cinema of the seer and no longer of the agent" (1989:2).

Characters whom circumstances have made into seers effectively lose much of their conscious motor control and are relegated to long moments of contemplation. Often, like Mila, they simply wander off while mutely yet intensely looking around. As Deleuze puts it, they "cannot or will not react, so great is their need to 'see' properly what there is in the situation" (128). However, for Deleuze, the trauma and loss of agency that becoming a seer entails also offer a strange sort of compensation, however delimited—one that opens a more conscious link between characters onscreen and spectators watching them. In being stripped of whatever agency they may have once imagined they had, the seer has "gained in an ability to see what he has lost in action or reaction: he SEES so that the viewer's problem becomes 'What is there to see in the image?' (and not now 'What are we going to see in the next image?')" (272, capitalization in original). Stuck scanning the situation around them and unable to advance, the seer may feel as if the flow of time has slowed or come to a stop—a further, potentially traumatic, experience that also offers an opportunity to take a deeper, critical look at their surrounds.

In *Bernafas Dalam Lumpur*, the process of Mila's shift from potential agent to "seer" likewise imbues her with a new perspective and awareness of what recent political shifts have wrought on society. The thing she sees most clearly, and this is arguably what *Bernafas* poses as a problem for viewers to see along with her, is that the initially shocking indictments constantly thrown at her in Jakarta are in fact new "truths" that have become unavoidable. As the film also implies, this is especially the case for poor women like Mila who can become socially and politically marginalized, literally in the blink of an eye. What her accusers say about her has thus begun to reveal the weight of her own future. Yet I argue there is an important distinction, or caveat, in the way Mila is positioned as a seer in *Bernafas Dalam Lumpur* and Deleuze's analysis of wandering characters who "see differently" in new waves of mostly Western films beginning in the 1940s with Italian neorealism.

For Jacques Lacan, an important influence on Deleuze's writing, the kinds of social, physical, and especially symbolic traumas experienced by seers would normally lead to a "dissociation of the subject's personality" (Lacan [1966] 2002:66)—hence a period of mute inactivity. Indeed, after her "encounter with the real"—in this case with the actual conditions determining citizens' lives under the New Order—Mila undergoes numerous dissociations and splits in her identity and sense of self. But as we see over the months of her life presented in *Bernafas*, the break with a coherent, singular, subjective point of view that defines the seer, while clearly a great psychological burden, is positioned far closer to normative planes of experience for Mila and others like her. Historically, this "super" capacity to process stress and trauma is especially present in female characters, whose ability to keep their heads across radical cultural and political shifts is well-established in previous generations of films in the region, as well as in academic literature. Indeed, unlike the cinematic seers highlighted by Deleuze, and despite the disproportionate targeting of Mila because of her gender, she is relegated to wander mutely for only a short while following the moment she and the film around her begin to see differently.

At the end of the walking sequence, another fateful "coincidence" occurs, as Mila collapses at the feet of Rais (Farouk Afero), a sharply dressed pimp who has just finished relieving himself in a polluted urban canal. He tries unsuccessfully to revive her but then, taking a closer look, exclaims: "Cantik Juga, Perempuan Nih!" (Hey, we've got a pretty one, here!). As Mila later recounts, it was Rais who "saved me from dying of hunger. It was also he who pressed me into the mud," offering, as the film's title suggests, a way to continue to breathe and move and see by becoming precisely what Mila's accusers claimed she was: a prostitute. Now showing a gradual acceptance of her fate by "choosing" it and asserting a modicum of symbolic control over the process, Mila changes her name from Soepinah to the more urbanized Soemila (Mila for short)—perhaps more fitting for a Jakartan sex worker. Later, at the behest of Budi, her wealthy client and would-be savior, she adopts yet another moniker: the more bourgeois sounding Yanti. Instead of sticking to one, new identity as if erasing the past, however, she uses different names depending on context. In doing so, she acknowledges the splits and dissociations she has been forced to undergo, rather than suppressing them. Her multiple names insist on the importance of remembering what has happened and on Mila's ability to adapt to and express these experiences with her wits still about her.[10]

As indicated above, the off-kilter visuals that are triggered by Mila's sudden realization and transition are part of a flashback. Following her acceptance of Rais's offer to become a sex worker, Mila sees ever more clearly what is happening in New Order Jakarta. But she is no longer frozen by shock and is now able to describe what she has seen and what has happened to her. As she relates to Budi the string of seemingly random experiences that brought her to where she is now, she is composed but allows her tears to flow, the feeling of which is abetted by nondiegetic violins. Here, film and seer conspire to show something to, and elicit emotional reactions from, characters and spectators simultaneously. Mila's "to-be-looked-at-ness" certainly contributes to the effect. But while Mila's looks attract attention from those on- and offscreen—she is young and quite pretty, also making her a top earner for Rais—I propose their primary function is to funnel others' gazes into *her* look, constructing her more politically oriented "to-be-identified-with-ness." In this sense, Mila's gaze builds on the function of Palupi's to align viewers with her fall into abjection but further debases and literalizes what viewers are positioned to experience or vicariously become.

As a specific visual "package," I argue that Mila's looks and gaze are positioned as a cinematic instrument that pierces diegetic space, reaching out and fusing the onscreen with the historical and the real. As I will explain below, her gaze also functions to align other characters with her plight and to transfer what she has seen into their bodies and minds, mirroring the way she is formally positioned to offer her views and experiences to the audience. The continuing horrors Mila sees are not fictive allusions but are linked, albeit without naming names, to the workings of the actual current regime. "For the eye of the seer as of the soothsayer," Deleuze writes, "it is the 'literalness' of the perceptible world which constitutes it like a book" (1989:22). Indeed, at this early stage (*Bernafas* is among the first entries in the emergent regional prostitution genre), what Mila sees and conveys is a black and tragic truth about a collective future that radiates from her own. Produced as she is by a particular convergence of cinematic and actual histories, Mila is positioned to highlight and further this information in specific ways. As the film suggests or implies at numerous junctures, Mila's status is no longer mutable, and she can therefore not hope to be rescued in any traditional or modern/positivist sense.

As this understanding gradually soaks in, a further, constitutive-gendered split emerges in the two main views conveyed and offered by the film to spectators: those of Mila and Budi. On hearing Mila's pitiful tale, Budi's eyes are opened to the injustice of her situation but not yet to their structural causes. In response, he can only vow to marry her and become a surrogate father for her child. From Mila's perspective, everything she has seen so far has convinced her that an outcome like this is impossible; the current political system is effectively designed to prevent its citizens from helping or changing the fates of those whom it has positioned as enemy or dehumanized other. Yet part of Mila still harbors romantic ideological fantasies—that a privileged man like Budi could use the masculine power promised to him by the New Order to pull her out of the "mud" where she is stuck. For this reason, Budi's good intentions paradoxically present the biggest challenge to Mila's ability to keep herself together, to keep breathing, and to keep thinking of ways, however limited, in which she might act to help herself and others. Mila the vulnerable, displaced villager is irresistibly drawn to Budi's seemingly sensible reassurances, while the emergent seer and soothsayer she has become is terrified of what might actually happen if an "agent" like Budi should try to intervene.

This tension between a hope that springs eternal and an absolutely hopeless political reality lends an especially poignant, melodramatic force to Mila's death at the end of the film (the result of a fateful combination of the stress of Budi's interventions and drugs, alcohol, and violence at the hands of Rais). In the final scene, as Budi, Mila's mother (Sofia W. D.), Mila's daughter (Kiki Maria), and a fellow prostitute (Sri Harto) hold vigil over her now-unconscious form, a doctor pronounces her dead, confirming everyone's worst fears. On the surface, Mila's demise would seem to justify Sen's argument that prostitutes, as a "crisis for the symbolic world" of New Order ideology (and Western classical action images), must ultimately be eliminated. But in my reading, if Mila is to function as a new critical "instrument" and source of audience identification, then death, however inevitable, cannot simply silence or make her disappear without a trace.

The film, I argue, therefore innovates a method of embedding what Mila has seen and felt into the conscious bodies and minds of those who remain behind. It does so in this case by translating her split, dissociated-yet-coherent identity and history into a profoundly moving sound: at the moment Mila's death is announced, it is as if something invisible emerges from her body and makes itself felt throughout the room. What emerges is amplified and translated by her grief-stricken mother, who utters Mila's original name uncontrollably: "Soepinahhhhh!" As if altered to accommodate Mila's multiple transformations, the appellation becomes a bloodcurdling scream that somehow encapsulates both the strength and the injustice of Mila's life and death. Melding melodrama with horror in its unbearably raw, tear-filled timbre, the vocalizations continue unabated for an unusually long time—around a minute and fifteen seconds.

As they do, Mila's mother joins her on the bed, continuing to shriek and sob while clutching her daughter's lifeless body. The reactions of the others, relegated to stand, watch, and listen, are then shown, one by one, in close-up. Observing them absorb the sight of Mila's body and sound of her mother's scream as it fills the room, viewers are formally aligned with the perspectives of each character, pushed into the same process of engagement with injustice, exploitation, and co-optation running especially rampant since the rise of the New Order. Through the combination of visuals and sound, a parallel process is set up between what is happening to characters and what potentially occurs in spectators' bodies when they are exposed to emotional, melodramatic moments or scenes in movies. As Linda Williams argues, in such instances, viewers become "caught up in an almost involuntary mimicry of the emotion or sensation of the body on the screen" (Williams 1991:4)—not wholly unlike the discussion of *latah*, the supposedly Southeast Asia–specific "culture bound syndrome" we encountered in chapter 1. While Williams's analysis is based on the context of Western melodramas as "weepies" catering primarily to female spectators, films like *Bernafas* aimed their conglomerations of sex, violence, and extreme politicized weepiness at spectators of all genders and with an array of different class associations. Building on strategies innovated by *Palupi*, the mimicry elicited here further thickens the connection between diegesis and reality, leaving audiences with an emotional message that is unambiguous in how it encapsulates contemporary experience but that in its translated form—as a scream—is unlikely to be censored.

The sequence ends with a close-up of Mila facing straight into the camera, as seen from the perspective of Budi leaning over her. Her eyes, previously the source of her powers as a seer and of her identification with viewers, are closed for good. The shot ends with Budi's hands placing a shroud over Mila's face, which fills the frame and hence effectively veils his own look at her and that of viewers. With Mila's death, the false patriarchal idealism of Budi's male gaze—a smaller, but key part of the perspective given to the audience throughout the film in counterpoint to Mila's perspective—has likewise been laid to rest. What is left for him is no longer visual but aural and embodied: the impression made by the sound that coalesces Mila's altered gaze and the tragedy of its extinction. These are combined with the now undeniable realization that Budi's own power to see and act were illusions that could only cause further destruction. As this all sinks in, the "cheap" melodramatic strings on the soundtrack unashamedly deploy another form of highly emotionalized audio aimed at further amplifying characters' and viewers' mimicry of Budi's complex sensations in reaction to Mila's death.

Along with diegetic women and men and female members of the audience, male spectators who may well have come to the theater to see scantily clad sex workers are invited to divide their looks and imagine their alliances expanding beyond those authorized by the new regime. Although they may choose to do something else, the film has forcefully directed its diverse spectators to gaze upon, identify with, and finally *mimic* the politicized melodramatic acts and heightened emotions on the screen. Through these emotions, the audience is linked to a marginalized, unattached woman who is unsilenceable, even in death. And this is not the end: as Linda Williams also argues, the power of cinematic melodrama as a "utopian component . . . of cultural problem solving" (1991:12) comes not only from its solicitation of audience members' mimicry of characters' bodily and emotional states but from its related function as a catalyst for introspection. If millions of viewers are moved to cry, she writes, it is "not just because the characters do, but at the precise moment when desire is finally recognized as futile" (11). In this case,

I argue that the sense of futility around a certain formulation of desire further signals the dysfunction of the newly installed, "classical" patriarchal political system in which it has been embedded. Viewers are thus urged to closely scrutinize the ways in which the New Order state has restructured and narrowed their ability to understand agency, desire, and modern identity.

Unlike *Palupi*'s headier, stranger mix of intellectualism and populist tropes, the more openly lowbrow approach of *Bernafas Dalam Lumpur* made it a huge hit and financial success. This set a precedent for further efforts in the emergent genre that I position as sparked by the rise of the New Order. If *Bernafas* also succeeded as a political instrument aimed at a specific historical context, I would argue it did so precisely because of the "gray areas" it opens between gendered objectification, exploitation, and the emergent and paradoxically empowering modes of visuality it associates with them. Add to this the film's implicit politicization of prostitution and its push for audiences to identify with sex workers—figures at the top of the state's expansive list of enemies of the people. While the number of female directors overall decreased in Indonesia between the 1950s and the 1970s (Anggraini, Harjanthi, and Imanda 2021), actresses like Suzzanna, who was also a producer and production company owner, also actively contributed not only to their roles but to the subject matter and political aspects of films they starred in. Two years after *Bernafas*, Suzzanna's company, Tidar Jaya, produced the hit *Bumi Makin Panas* (*The Earth Is Getting Hotter*, dir. Ali Shahab, 1973), in which she also starred as a central prostitute figure. Director Shahab credits Suzzanna with developing the character and pushing for more and more extreme, shocking, and consciously politicized scenarios for her to inhabit, beyond what Shahab himself had imagined (Yngvesson 2014:70).

In *Bernafas*, Sofia W. D., who plays Mila's mother and was also a director at the time, offers a particularly indelible political, melodramatic contribution in her final vocal performance. Suzzanna's iconic and subtly "gray" interpretation of Mila, a character notably different from the novel the film is based on (by Zainal Abdi, released around the same time), was arguably the key to both the film's popularity and its ability to communicate a subversive feeling-message to a wide variety of viewers. Like Mila (and Usmar Ismail, Asrul Sani, and most other artists and intellectuals), very few Indonesians could claim to have come through the political transition of the mid-1960s both alive and mud-free. In *Bernafas Dalam Lumpur*, Mila's transdiegetic and transgender symbolization of an entire society that has become "dirty" nudges audiences to acknowledge the complex, thorny nature of their own positionalities. On one level, as a victim who exudes to-be-identified-with-ness, Mila works to unify the expanded groups of spectators assembled by the prostitution genre. Following Ernesto Laclau's analysis of populist politics and aesthetics, I propose that the specter of a common political enemy, in the form of a looming, amorphous "institutionalized 'other'" (2005:117), is sketched, however roughly, in the visuals and screams that collect and disseminate Mila's experiences. But at the same time, Mila's inexorable fall into the mud of Jakarta's red-light districts has led her to *become one with* the institutionalized villainy that is also, as Sen reminds us, "dispersed through everyone . . . and every social institution" (1993:209). *Bernafas Dalam Lumpur* encapsulates this sense of inexorability and suppressed political and moral heterogeneity in Mila's mother's scream, which then refuses to be suppressed, making itself *"present as that which is absent"* (Laclau 2005:117, emphasis in original).

Yet in a society that has lived closer to certain inherent schisms than Lacanians such as Laclau might believe possible without dissociation or psychosis, the scream can also be read as a call to remember what has been *made* absent in front of the eyes of millions. In this case, I propose that *Bernafas Dalam Lumpur*'s portrayal of the life and struggles of a woman who is more or less forced into prostitution by the rise of the New Order begins the crucial work of identifying and reconstructing the collective archipelagic imagination and political subjectivities that were smothered and co-opted through mass violence and military-authoritarian terror. The film's popularity and financial success helped to embed its emergent instruments of critique, laying the ground for the rise of the prostitution genre. As we will see, filmmakers elsewhere in the region often found themselves, at least at first, with a greater variety of potential avenues of protest to choose from. Yet perhaps because the basic conditions of authority grew much more similar around the region (especially in Thailand and the Philippines), the terms of engagement for an emergent set of popular yet deeply politicized films were conceived along lines analogous to those in Indonesia.

DICTATORS, POLITICIZED PROSTITUTES, AND URBAN MUD IN THE PHILIPPINES

Around the same time that audiences in Indonesia were aligned with Mila's abject-yet-magnetic gaze in *Bernafas Dalam Lumpur*, another hypermasculine, U.S.-aligned dictator was asserting control in another Southeast Asian metropolis: Manila. Ferdinand Marcos did not come to power in a drawn-out coup d'état as Soeharto did, but his election in 1965 and reelection in 1969 were similarly characterized by the standardization of "gold, goons and guns" as tools of political dominance and by huge upticks in political violence and murder (Espiritu 2017:90). Unlike Indonesia, where hundreds of thousands of would-be activists were killed or jailed indefinitely during the mass killings of 1965 and 1966, in the Philippines, many young students became increasingly radicalized, emboldened by a democratic system that ostensibly allowed for direct opposition to elected leaders. But as public disenchantment with Marcos grew, student political activism culminated in the First Quarter Storm, a series of large-scale demonstrations and uprisings against the president in Manila in early 1970. This development tipped the already volatile mixture of violence, underhanded political tactics, and ostensible democracy decidedly toward the former two. The government began to follow patterns established under authoritarian regimes elsewhere in the region. During the Storm, protests were met with progressively harsher responses from the military, ending in the deaths of several young demonstrators.

When Marcos was targeted by the media and other politicians for his role in the killings, his response showed a further rightward shift, claiming the demonstrators were communist insurgents—a classic, red-scare tactic that could have been taken from Soeharto's Cold War–inspired playbook. When threats to his leadership continued, Marcos hurriedly diagnosed the Philippines as a nation in political and moral crisis and sought increasing control of the media, including stricter film censorship. Both the discourse of crisis and suppression of information mirrored similar moves by the New Order in Indonesia to close or simplify gaps and contradictions that previously healthier societies had generally accommodated. The sudden requirement that scripts be vetted and approved by censors before film production could start, for example, basically duplicated a central tenet of Soeharto's Department of Information. Many politicians and bolder sections of the media in the Philippines, however, refused to be browbeaten into submission.

Similar to what happened in Indonesia in the mid-1960s, a volatile political climate perceived as threatening to the interests of the right led Marcos to risk taking a bold step to shore up his authority. With the Cold War as a broader backdrop, in 1972, he declared a state of emergency and on September 23 quickly instituted martial law, much as Soeharto had done during the period of killings in Indonesia. Although no mass extermination was committed in the Philippines at the time, Marcos was emboldened to act with far greater impunity, and he put mechanisms in place to keep himself in power far beyond term limits (martial law itself was officially lifted in 1981). Through these and other means, Marcos succeeded in holding on to the presidency into the mid-1980s, or twenty-one years in total.

Under Marcos's watchful eye and iron fist, Manila became the rapidly modernizing but slum-filled core of what Marcos termed the "New Society." It resembled an only slightly distorted mirror-image of mud-oozing, skyscraper-filled Jakarta—the center of operations for Soeharto's New Order. As in Indonesia, dictatorship in the Philippines had a combination of predictable and unexpected effects. In both places, it inadvertently helped foster a "golden age" of cinema in which the number of films produced each year rose dramatically. Increased production was supported by ever more socioeconomically diverse groups of spectators who rallied around negative views of the changes brought about by the two emergent, strong-man leaders. In the Philippines, this uptick in production also inspired the rise of new genres built around a complexly politicized and overtly "lowbrow" combination of aesthetics, characters, themes, and attractions. As Rolando Tolentino (2012) argues, the controversial, populist subversions of bomba films from the 1960s became a key element of many filmmakers' attempts to intervene in contemporary politics. Finding creative ways to get such imagery past censors, young filmmakers worked to invert the official imagery of the state while referencing and amplifying Marcos's own sordid and highly publicized instances of amorality.

As was the case in Indonesia, in the Filipino iteration of this populist-political approach, a tangible connection between diegetic worlds and the actual feelings and experiences of viewers was paramount. José B. Capino (2020) refers to these films as "martial law melodramas." Lino Brocka, one of the brightest stars among the new directors, wrote that filmmakers should endeavor to play to their intended audiences "by gathering experience that is not alien to the majority of Filipinos at a particular time . . . and by giving back this now crystallized experience to them in films they would enjoy and be moved to take as their own" (quoted in Diaz 2021:322). Echoing my reading of Indonesian variants, for Capino, such films "challenge the notion that [only] certain [overtly politicized, independently produced] modes . . . or . . . genre formations . . . are uniquely suitable to cinema politics" (2020:xiv). Tolentino puts a sharper point on this idea, arguing that in the popular films of Brocka and others at the time, melodramatically amplified "affect . . . simulated the abjection and incorporation of national bodies in the dictatorship" (2012:120–21).

Filmmakers also took cues from their political targets, making thinly veiled mockeries of official media campaigns where the physical forms of Ferdinand and Imelda Marcos were constantly mediatized and "rendered [to showcase] the gendered robustness of [the] then-young leaders" (Tolentino 2012:119). Positioning themselves as ideal models for the formation of new citizens, the Marcoses worked to create "a kind of synecdochic personification in the masses of their bodies" (Tolentino 2012:131). This was accomplished, for example, through designing specialized costumes aimed to project attractive, hardworking, heroic, and ultimately cinematic visualizations of masculine dictatorial power. Owing to the strength of the more recent culture of public protest in the Philippines, 1970s cineastes were bolder in their deployment of onscreen figures that closely mimicked actual leaders, especially the president. The latter's shrewd media tactics provided ubiquitous images and concepts that could be altered and rendered visibly lacking, revealing the falseness and hypocrisy inherent in the Marcos's self-construction, while highlighting the overall decay of Filipino society, especially among the poor.

Young filmmakers like Brocka, many of whom came from student-activist backgrounds, began making "serious" art films as critiques of state repression while mixing in "cheap" melodramatic and other techniques that lower-class audiences were known to respond to. Such techniques included the added benefit of framing thinly veiled versions of public figures in an even more unflattering light. Toward the beginning of the early Brocka film *Tinimbang ka Ngunit Kulang* (*Weighed but Found Wanting*, 1974), for example, a corrupt, womanizing political official (Eddie Garcia) is prominently made to look like a version of Marcos, at first seemingly in a complementary way: after being shown shirtless and muscular, he dons Marcos's typical *barong* shirt-jacket, the picture of an aging-but-still-virile man of about the president's age (and with the same macho haircut). In another scene, the man,

Cesar, is positioned directly across from an actual portrait of Marcos hung on the wall at a party while he introduces his son, Junior (Christopher de Leon), to the men gathered around. Here the picture is less flattering. One of the men jokes that the son will be "just like him"—strong, handsome, and, as everyone knows, a rabid philanderer—while another quips, "A carbon copy. The source is deadly."

Even while skewering Marcos, however, the film holds out hope for the next generation. After formative encounters with several victimized yet self-possessed social outcasts, the privileged Junior learns to see the world anew via the marginalized points of view of his new companions. Held up against the leper and the madwoman whom Junior takes as his adoptive "parents," his own, Marcosian father and mother are ultimately, as the film's title suggests, "weighed but found wanting." Around this theme, Brocka hammers his points home with extreme images like a bloody fetus that is intercut in flashes with the horrified face of the woman who has just been forced (by Cesar, her former lover) to abort it. As Espiritu argues, this signals another key feature in the rise of a particularly styled, "oppositional aesthetic: the mobilization of the splice-and-shock methods of the *bomba* film and the resuscitation of the *bomba*'s 'illegal' tropes" (2017:110). Like Brocka, in *Kisapmata* (*In the Blink of an Eye*, 1981), Mike de Leon deploys shocking, explicit violence to underline the broader stakes of the Marcos's imposition of ever-more rigid forms of patriarchy and the fates of families and citizens positioned under fathers modeled on the president. In a related way, *Moral* (1982), helmed by Marylou Diaz-Abaya, one of the relatively few female directors working at the time, shows the spontaneous emergence of alternate feminine and queer support groups triggered by the extreme and widespread dysfunction of the middle-class nuclear family under Marcosian patriarchy.

While onscreen "Marcoses" and splice-and-shock tactics are both important elements of the politically subversive tropes of Filipino films in the 1970s, I will focus on the common regional elements of these movies that also more clearly engage with the transnational spheres that intersect the region. I argue that the broader mission of these films is primarily accomplished through a thorny, potentially disillusioned, but bracing return to the historically powerful positions of women—as they were positioned in the films of the 1950s and 1960s. In the Philippines, I propose that this is grounded by a post-bomba female gaze that political economic shifts have disconnected from its matrifocal grounding in marriage and the home.

In ways related to what we have seen in Indonesia, the complex, populist view of the "victim" generated through these historical figures emerges as among the most important instruments of critique deployed by Filipino cineastes in the 1970s and 1980s. The year after *Tinimbang*, for example, Brocka made one of his best-known works, *Maynila sa mga Kuko ng Liwanag* (*Manila in the Claws of Light*), a film that begins with a male perspective but leads to a reality only visible through the eyes of a fallen woman. Released in 1975 but set in 1970 with the First Quarter

Storm as a backdrop, *Maynila*'s narrative of abjection would likely also have been familiar to audiences in urban areas of Indonesia or Thailand at the time. It presents a series of events uncannily resonant with those shown in *Bernafas Dalam Lumpur*, structured around a combination of shocking, explicit imagery and tear-jerking melodramatics. The basic similarities, as well as the key differences, of the looks and figures developed and deployed by Brocka will help develop a broader, more diverse sense of what I position as a regional "prostitution genre."

Like Mila's husband in *Bernafas*, who goes to Jakarta and finds himself with little choice but to remarry or starve, Ligaya (Hilda Koronel), a poor young woman from the Filipino provinces, disappears without a trace after accepting an offer of a better life in Manila. Julio (Bembol Roco), her lovestruck boyfriend, follows and is quickly and mercilessly swallowed by the nether regions of the metropolis—precisely what he later discovers has happened to Ligaya. Like Budi in *Bernafas*, Julio fancies himself Ligaya's savior. Unlike the wealthy Budi, however, Julio lacks the means to keep himself afloat while doing so. His first job in the corrupt, under-regulated construction industry that is busy erecting Marcos's signature, modern cityscape (often described as a result of his "edifice complex") nearly kills Julio. After being laid off, he is intermittently employed and often half-starved as he chases the object of his desire around the city like a dazed amateur detective.

Echoing Mila's "coincidental" meeting with a pimp just as she collapses by a canal, Julio's first homeless night in a park fatefully connects him to Bobby (Jojo Abella). Like Rais with Mila, Bobby, a stylishly dressed man around the same age as Julio, seems attracted to him but "wants" him for more complex reasons, including pity. Bobby takes Julio in and feeds him. As soon as he's regained some strength, Julio is introduced to the world of male prostitution—the source of Bobby's well-furnished apartment and relatively lavish lifestyle. With no cash and little hope, despite his feelings of disgust, Julio decides to give it a try. He does not last as long in sex work as Mila or Ligaya (the latter also had far less choice in the matter), but the brief stint becomes an important step in Julio's journey of discovery. What little agency he scrapes together to survive and continue his mission is shown to come from selling himself in Manila's clubs and informal brothels. At the same time, unlike Ligaya, Julio is unable to "see" that he will not be able to extricate himself or, more importantly, Ligaya from the urban muck in which they are both learning to breathe. In scenes eerily evocative of Hitchcock's *Rear Window* (1954), Julio insistently returns to a corner on Misericordia Street, where he suspects Ligaya is being kept. Loitering there, his eyes bore into the second-story window, behind which he imagines a scene of injustice. But unlike Hitchcock's classic construction of an active "masculine" look (which is intriguingly also adopted by a woman), here, the glass is opaque, revealing nothing except for, once, a fleeting silhouette.[11] Julio's eyes are thus simultaneously fixed on a prize and unfocused because their target is invisible. At these moments, a close-up or medium shot of his stare will cut to a reverse shot of the blank window, its exterior covered by bars.

FIGURE 20. In *Maynila sa mga Kuko ng Liwanag*, Julio (Bembol Roco) stares endlessly at a blank window where he believes Ligaya to be kept, while also looking into the lens. Courtesy of Simon Santos/Video48.

At a key juncture in Julio's static journey on Misericordia Street, a sequence dissolves repetitively from the window to him on the street corner looking intently at it (fig. 20), altering the time of day as it does. This sequence suggests he's been frozen there for at least twelve hours, possibly more, and that, as in *Bernafas Dalam Lumpur*, *Maynila* has ushered us into "the cinema of the seer and no longer of the agent" (Deleuze 1989:2). But if the question, as Deleuze put it, is "what is there to see in the image" and not what comes next, the answer, at least in Julio's case, is nothing; he cannot assemble visible evidence to back up his suspicions. Perhaps in this case at least, the truth would be too unsettling. But still, seeing "nothing" will not stop Julio from standing and staring, often looking directly into the lens as he does, as if calling viewers to join him on his lonely corner. In this case, as time seems to slow, it begins to move nostalgically backward along with Julio's thoughts: the reverse shot of the empty window is exchanged with memories of Julio's life in the provinces, a bygone time and place from which he could see and touch Ligaya, the object of his affection. His work as a fisherman also gave him hope of starting a family with her. These psychically imposed images are presented as a powerful motivator for Julio to continue his search, however misguidedly. Even in different parts of the city, Julio's look will suddenly become distant and unfocused, as if possessed by the visions that transform the unforgiving urban landscape before him into a wistful rural beach. As the film repeatedly implies, Julio imagines himself living in a more equitable past that the urbanizing and demoralizing currents leading to the New Society have swept away.

Near the end of the film, when Julio finally does catch a glimpse of Ligaya, the image is again intercut with a shot of her in the provinces, making it unclear if he's simply imagining her in front of him. It is really her, however, and when Julio follows her into a church and sits beside her, Ligaya is frozen by the sudden appearance of a "ghost" from her past—unlike Julio, Ligaya has seemingly survived by convincing herself the past is gone, even if not completely forgotten. Echoing the experience of Mila in *Bernafas Dalam Lumpur*, Ligaya's joy at encountering her ostensible rescuer is belied by doubt and mortal terror, driven by what she has been exposed to and learned to see going on around her. Yet a last, remaining shred of hope in the power of love seems to keep Ligaya from fleeing. Like Mila with Budi, Ligaya reunites with Julio in a seedy hotel where she tearfully recounts her fall into the sex industry or, in this case, something closer to sex slavery in unmarked brothels. As "luck" would have it, she explains, her voice full of irony, a wealthy client took a liking to her and keeps her as an unofficial second wife. It is this man, Ah Tek (Tommy Yap), who holds her locked behind the opaque, second-story window that has been the object of Julio's nostalgic gaze. While Julio's suspicions about her status and whereabouts are confirmed, by always looking into the past, he has not suspected the arrival of a four-month-old baby the man has fathered with Ligaya.

Like Mila, Ligaya seems better able to absorb and process what she has seen and experienced than her male counterpart, while keeping her wits together, breathing, and slowly moving forward. Ligaya "acts" in a limited yet unambiguous way, including by recounting what she has experienced. Yet the recipient of the seer's report is in both cases the man who is dead set on a rescue mission but cannot quite get his eyes or mind around the actual causes and stakes of what has happened. Here as well then, Ligaya's narration of her urban fall, a logical-tactical "mistake" in the diegetic context of the film, is ultimately aimed at viewers. Even within the confines of the diegesis, Ligaya, or at least what has become the dominant part of her, seems to grasp the danger of engaging Julio's desire and masculine ideological instincts: as she describes to him the appalling series of deceptions and inhuman treatment that have been heaped on her since leaving the provinces, his gaze is steadily fixed on her, but hers is pointedly turned away (fig. 21). As she recounts her "rescue" from a small locked room by Ah Tek, who paid for her release, she gets up from the bed where she and Julio are lying together and faces the wall, away from the eyes of both Julio and spectators. As she lights a cigarette, her characterization of Ah Tek as a "fool" whose affection for her has cost him so much signals a nascent sense of agency, or at least street smarts. It is implied that learning to use such emotionally manipulative tactics was the only way for Ligaya to extract herself from the brothel where she was first imprisoned, finding her way to a second, slightly more human, captivity.

FIGURE 21. Ligaya recounts her downfall and victimization to Julio in a movie theater and cheap hotel where they are able to meet while she is supposedly in church, one of the only venues her captor allows her to go to alone. As she tells Julio what has happened, Ligaya keeps her gaze averted.

When Ligaya turns to a mirror a little further along in her tale, she casts her eyes downward, as if unable even to face herself. But in fact, as the inclusion of both her image and its reflection also imply, Ligaya is of two minds, both of which are present in her interaction with Julio. One side of her still longs to return home to her family and to Julio, while the other despises this false romanticism of happiness and individual "rights." When her story is finished, it is the old Ligaya who tearfully whispers, "Help me," and she allows Julio to embrace and comfort her while she sobs in a melodramatic mode. Yet she still does not meet his gaze and seems to come to her senses as soon as he starts making plans. She won't leave her baby, she tells Julio, and trying to escape with it will almost certainly bring about her death at the hands of her dreaded benefactor. As her words imply, the risks outweigh the benefits, and there is nothing to be done. If anything, the long session with Julio appears to have had a therapeutic function for Ligaya, allowing her to unburden and explain herself to her former lover, then return to what has become her "normal" life—the existence and identity she has painstakingly constructed in Manila's sordid urban mud.

Even as the two sides of Ligaya fall into closer alignment, Julio looks and looks but cannot seem to see what is implied to viewers. It is as if he has only heard Ligaya's brief and quickly rescinded call for help. What he glimpses now is almost precisely what appeared to him in his months of staring at the barred window: the former Ligaya whom he must save but who does not exist in Marcos's New Society any more than do the conditions of possibility for Julio's anachronistic romanticism. Julio's own experiences as a Manila gigolo seem to have taught him little: instead of having his eyes opened, he has become more and more frozen, frantically staring around him but seeing only the absent past. Driven by desperation, he extracts a reluctant nod from Ligaya; she will consider meeting him that night at a market near Misericordia, from whence he claims they will make their escape back to the provinces. This is, of course, a fatal error on the part of Ligaya, whose status as a seer has already revealed to her the outcome. While what happens is not shown to us, we later find out that Ligaya has been killed by Ah Tek, meaning she must have tried to follow Julio's plan of escape. When Julio realizes what has happened, like Budi confronted with Mila's dead body, he must finally face the reality that has been staring at him since he arrived in Manila. But the shock of his "encounter with the real" is too great and he loses his mind, blinded by masculine rage and lust for revenge.

Brocka uses this moment as a complex, transdiegetic metaphor for the (lost) ideal of political activism. On the way to kill Ligaya's murderer, Julio passes through a parade of what looks like hundreds of student demonstrators, marching in the 1970 First Quarter Storm—one of the events most commonly linked to Marcos's institution of martial law. In a way that is far more direct than any Indonesian prostitute films of the time, this also implies to viewers the political nature of the "real" cause of Julio's and Ligaya's fall into abjection and near-slavery. Triumphantly, the protestors wave banners and urge the gathering crowds to "have no fear!!" and "join the struggle" against Marcos and his U.S.-aligned "bureaucratic capitalism." Yet like Julio's deluded gaze, this, too, is a vision of activism associated with a state of affairs that has already radically shifted and may no longer be possible, taking place three years before the production and release of *Maynila sa mga Kuko ng Liwanag* and shortly before the changes instituted by Marcos leading to martial law in 1972. While the scene may have spoken volumes to Filipino spectators at the time, Julio barely seems to notice the protestors. Pushing and weaving through their lines as quickly as possible, he makes his way toward his own, individual rebellion against injustice.

The scene of collective activism with a fixed historical outcome, however, foreshadows Julio's fate. As audiences already knew, the students would succeed in making a statement but would soon be chased down by soldiers opening fire without mercy. Julio's mission is also initially accomplished. He eliminates Ah Tek—one small agent of the increasing moral decay fostered by state policies—in a horror-styled orgy of stabbing and blood. But even before the police can catch him, Julio is chased and killed by yet another form of "activism": a mob spontaneously forms in response to Ah Tek's family's calls for help, chasing and cornering Julio in an alley. Similar to *Bernafas Dalam Lumpur*, in *Maynila*, the injustice of marginalized lives wantonly ruined and needlessly sacrificed is expressed in a final, horrific scream, this time a man's. As the crowd sets on him, however, Julio's cries are silent, presented symbolically through a final, abject close-up on his mouth.

FIGURE 22. Julio's dying scream dissolving into a frozen, anachronous memory of Ligaya back in the village where they were lovers.

Like the sound of Mila's mother's extended wail at the end of *Bernafas*, this image is drawn out and functions to encapsulate the "unspeakable," yet (the films insist) cinematically representable, horrors and limitations experienced by both relatively empowered and disempowered citizens under the thumb of dictatorship. Each scream—visual in *Maynila* and aural in *Bernafas*—conveys extreme emotions aimed at triggering a gut reaction in spectators, filled with feeling-based criticism of the kind that could be put onscreen in the early years of Soeharto's Department of Information or Philippine martial law. Both also evoke emergent paradoxes in which active, masculine visual regimes are promoted and simultaneously undermined by new national Fathers. While Budi's once-cocky, privileged male gaze at Mila is "veiled" and thus effectively snuffed, the image of Julio's final, impotent scream is frozen into a still, symbolizing his death. It then presciently dissolves into a last image of Ligaya on the rural beach at sunset—also frozen, suggesting that the dream of such an idealist view has vanished along with Julio's nostalgic, backward-facing looks (fig. 22).

For Tolentino, *Maynila* ultimately works to visualize the ubiquitous, systemic, yet "hidden" function and presence of sex work in Marcos's New Society. Prostitutes like Ligaya and Julio, he writes, "were integral to the . . . nation, made to attract foreign capital and to stir up the informal or underground economy on the one hand, and to be rendered invisible as marginal bodies deemed contrapuntal to the official nation on the other hand" (2012:123). In Indonesia, sex workers had once been more publicly recognized for vital roles they played in nationalist projects throughout the periods of anticolonial struggle. Prostitutes working as spies and weapons smugglers against Dutch and British armies in the 1940s were officially lauded by Soekarno, while their slogans and calls adorned nationalist posters (see chapter 1), and their likenesses and stories appeared ubiquitously in the imagery and narratives produced by the artists of the foundational *Angkatan 45*, or "1945 Generation" (Yngvesson 2014). Mirroring the Philippines, however, it was only under the New Order—when sex workers' quasi-legal structural and economic roles in society increased while official regimes of morality and visuality suppressed recognition of their contributions—that prostitutes came to colonize national movie screens en masse.

As I have established thus far, an important reason for this phenomenon is the prostitute's function as a symbol of the structural realities of life under 1970s Southeast Asian dictatorships. A still more crucial reason, I suggest, is the multifarious ways in which screen prostitutes are shown to *see*. The horrific revelations and perspectives to which those who fall into such positions of social, political, and economic compromise also gain access are passed on to viewers, urging them to challenge the ways in which citizens are prompted to look and act under the New Order and the New Society. In comparison to works prior to the institution of dictatorships, many of the 1970s films featuring prostitutes in Indonesia and the Philippines are therefore more closely focused on capital cities or the governments installed there. Among other things, this has led critics to frame filmmakers' interventions in terms of the development of new patterns and approaches in national, rather than regional, cinemas.[12]

Without denying the implicit and explicit logic of nationalism in these films, I will continue to look at them through the lens of particular genres emerging across the region and what I position as not-so-coincidental correlations between them. In this context, the increased presence of sex workers and other marginalized women on movie screens in Thailand at almost precisely the same time as in Indonesia and the Philippines demands further scrutiny. Intriguingly, however, the first such Thai effort implicitly marks the *fall* of a national Father. In my reading, this is an important caveat, implying that, like citizens, the dictator is himself less an actor and more a reaction to or symbol of broader global shifts to which the region is being pressed to respond. As I will show, in diegetic Bangkok, the prostitute is similarly positioned to address conditions of visuality and power that exceed the purview of both dictatorship and explicit, phallocentric modes of resistance in the form of public protests. In this case, however, the sex worker's emergent ability to embody and negotiate the visual and psychic splits of the 1970s is implied to be rooted in her rural past.

PROTEST, PROSTITUTION,
AND "FLEXIBLE MEMBERS" IN BANGKOK

Like *Bernafas* and *Maynila*, the Thai film *Theptida Rong Ram* (*Hotel Angel*, dir. Chatrichalerm Yukol, 1974) uses the experiences of a central prostitute figure as an indirect, and at times almost direct, critique of urban Thailand under U.S.-aligned military dictator Thanom Kittikachorn (r. 1963–73). In this case, however, between the film's production and its release, Thanom was deposed as a result of mass student-led demonstrations and replaced with a democratically elected regime, albeit a short-lived one. *Theptida Rong Ram* hence came on the heels of a rare political triumph against a regional strongman and features the closest thing to a "happy" ending (about which more below) that I have seen so far among Southeast Asian prostitute movies of the time. Many elements of the film's overall political strategy recall those of *Bernafas* and *Maynila*. It projects a populist condemnation aimed to fill the bodies and minds of audiences with seemingly unending injustice, violence, and rape, while offering moving demonstrations of the emotional reactions and shifts resulting from such acts. Despite the coincidence of *Theptida* with political triumph, this strategy is combined with a deep uneasiness about what the actions of "the masses," once triggered, may actually reap.

Theptida's visual engagement with antigovernment protestors, which anticipates Brocka's use of such imagery in *Maynila* a year later, was an even more direct result of the time and place in which the film was made. The massive student-led demonstrations against Thanom in October 1973 literally enveloped the production of *Theptida Rong Ram*, pushing their way through the streets near one of the film's locations. Things came to a head when government forces suddenly attacked the students on October 14, 1973. Mirroring the grim outcome of the First Quarter Storm in Manila, by evening, soldiers had killed seventy-seven protestors and injured eight hundred more. Yet in this case, the extreme show of force inspired more young Thais to join the demonstrations, and as the number of protestors grew to around five hundred thousand, the king announced that Thanom's government had stepped down. The presence of the protests in the film was not scripted but came about owing to the coincidence of proximity between fictionalized and actual political reality (fig. 23). As protestors passed by during the filming of *Theptida Rong Ram*, director Chatrichalerm spontaneously ran outside to capture the melee with his 35 mm movie camera, with no way of knowing what the outcome of the demonstrations would be (Chaiworaporn 2001:146).

The dramatic images shot by Chatrichalerm show thousands of students gathered in the city with bullhorns, flags, and paintings of Thai royalty, targeted by water cannons and surrounded by burning cars. Some look directly into the camera with a mixture of suspicion and unease, as if foreshadowing the sacrifice of many protestors' lives and emphasizing this over the tenuous victory that may not have come without it. The way the footage is integrated into the film further amplifies this sense of apprehension. In a style reminiscent of Soviet montage, the protest footage is intercut with *Theptida*'s darkest moment: a graphic sequence in which a young girl is beaten so severely by a group of pimps that she runs up several flights of stairs and jumps to her death from the roof of the hotel where she is being held. In the context of the film, the girl's unflinching stance against the men forcing her into prostitution is juxtaposed with the literally "suicidal" activist tactics of the young protestors facing soldiers with live ammunition.

FIGURE 23. A scene from the First Quarter Storm demonstrations against Marcos staged for *Maynila sa mga Kuko ng Liwanag* (*top*) and actual footage of protests against Thanom Kittikachorn in Bangkok that was spliced into *Theptida Rong Ram* (*bottom*).

The unfortunate results suggest a presciently negative perspective on the part of Chatrichalerm—one that, when *Theptida Rong Ram* is positioned as part of a regional genre, as it is here, appears to look beyond the limited triumphs occurring in the context of the national. While in reality, the students' sacrifices were rewarded with the fall of Thanom, in the film, the pimps faced by the girl go on about their business after she ends her own life in protest. In my reading, Chatrichalerm's innovative juxtaposition of documentary footage with realistic staged scenes (based on months of research in Bangkok brothels; Richardson 2016) suggests that like any pimp, any particular dictator is constituted by a convergence of forces far outside their own control as individuals: an authoritarian "father" who falls could simply be replaced with another, like-minded thug. Indeed, Thanom's return from exile in 1976 triggered further protests and mass killings, after which the army once again seized power, leading to "the absolute resurgence of dictatorial government" (Chaiworaporn 2001:145).

In comparison to *Bernafas* and *Maynila*, what stands out about *Theptida* is how it develops the perspective of its central character—placed in the eye of stormy, phallic clashes among dictators, pimps, and protestors—into a more detailed formulation of the limited agency potentially built by sex workers. This juxtaposition forms, in turn, a starker contrast to the film's negative depiction and interpretation of the ideals of collective political activism or individualistic heroic interventions. The process begins with a now-familiar scenario, as the main character, a young woman named Malee (Viyada Umarin), is tricked into moving from her rural village to Bangkok, where she is coerced into working as a prostitute. Her early experiences in the city are no less harrowing than those of Mila or Ligaya (or Julio) and are presented by Chatrichalerm with shockingly explicit realism. But in this case, the film focuses more closely on the process through which Malee slowly comes to accept and adapt to her fate and how she is able to use part of the money she saves to help her family build a new house in the farming village where she grew up (Mila and Ligaya also use what they earn to help their families, but this aspect is only mentioned in passing by both *Bernafas* and *Maynila*).

This is shown in a formally innovative sequence that also represents one of the few uses of humor in *Theptida Rong Ram*'s otherwise stark atmosphere. Shots jumping from early to later stages in the construction of the new home are intercut with scenes of Malee in her hotel room, moving equally rapidly through a series of johns, each of whom provides an absurd or obviously overdone show of masculinity. The succession of images is underpinned by the kind of "country" or folk music popular in the provinces, contrasting with the use of Thai and Western rock in other scenes set in Bangkok. The sequence ends with a graphic match of Malee opening her bra for a customer, juxtaposed with her father opening the doors to the completed home. As the house is finished, Malee also sends a poster-size photograph of herself, which her father frames and mounts on the wall by the front door (it seems that, like dictators, prostitutes also erect edifices to the regimes of development, however large or small, that they sponsor).

Malee, it appears, can imagine herself a revered, active figure, at least in the eyes of her family and perhaps also her pimps. Yet what she becomes over the course of the film is emphatically not a source of rigid, dictatorial vision or power. Like the young woman whose tragic fate is intercut with the October protests, Malee's journey begins when she is misled by an agent posing as a boyfriend who will help her find a good job in Bangkok. Shortly after they arrive in the capital, he disappears, leaving her to work off the "debts" concocted by the hotel/brothel where they spent the night. As with most newcomers, and like Mila and Ligaya, Malee is shown to have a hard head and a strong moral compass. Becoming a prostitute is not an acceptable outcome of the situation, and Malee's first reaction is disbelief and rebellion. When she attempts to escape, however, she is beaten. As the process repeats, she becomes increasingly shocked and dazed by the new and horrifying truth that she is forced to see: the "universal" morals she grew up with back in the village do not operate in the urban mud where she has found herself stuck.

Gathering her wits about her, Malee makes a quick calculation and decides to acquiesce and bide her time, while looking for ways, however small or seemingly insignificant, to begin to turn the situation around. Willfully suppressing her gut reaction to revolt, she begins to perform the opposite, exuding a sense of softness and pliability. Soon, Malee's attitude and looks make her a top earner, and with her "debts" paid off, she keeps much of what clients pay for her services and begins saving and sending money home to her family. She also begins to see that her strategic sacrifices have gained her a modicum of power, which she starts to act on. When another newcomer arrives and is beaten even more severely for resisting, Malee stands up and intervenes, while the pimps, who have begun to trust her, step back. In a gentle, almost motherly tone, Malee convinces the young woman that she is sympathetic to her plight but that for the moment, there is no hope of escape. Complying with her captors sooner than later will save her from distress, injury, or far worse. Over time, the head pimp, Tone (Sorapong Chatree), begins to see Malee as something closer to a partner, treating her with increasing respect and even tenderness, while the rest of the staff follow suit. The gains are small but tangible.

After a few months in Bangkok, Malee has adapted to, if not fully adopted, the new morals and modes of comportment she has encountered in the brothel, while learning to deploy them differently. On an individual level, as the film implies, she has weathered what is effectively a sudden epistemic shift—one that I read as an allegory of the broader changes occurring in Thailand and other Southeast Asian nations. Almost every country in the region is being pushed to make itself fall, like a "domino," on one or the other side of the global political fault lines associated with the Cold War. It is important, therefore, that Malee is shown to have come through the shifts imposed on her without completely losing herself. I argue that the stronger position assigned by the film to the rural and the traditional functions as a key source of Malee's ability to endure. *Theptida Rong Ram*'s imagining of the countryside as an active counterpoint to the urban lairs of pimps and dictators is also what most profoundly sets it apart from other regional efforts like *Bernafas* and *Maynila*.

Beginning with its opening images, for example, *Theptida* foregrounds and returns to particular aspects of the area in Northern Thailand where Malee grew up. The title sequence is made up almost entirely of expansive shots of rural landscapes where trees, grasses, and clouds move gently in the wind, drifting or bending but never breaking under the constant forces of nature. Chatrichalerm repeatedly comes back to these scenes, rendering the rural not as a silent, vanished nostalgia but a vibrant locale that reacts in particular ways to developments in the far-off capital. On one hand, this recurring focus on rural prettiness functions as a source of visual relief from otherwise stark imagery and themes. On the other hand, it is a strategy that underscores and contextualizes the symbolic and actual powers with which the film invests its central female character.

Research on healing practices in Isan, Northeastern Thailand, for example, points to a basic emphasis on flexibility that is both physical and psychological. Devon Hinton, a medical anthropologist, shows that healing ceremonies there consist of "multimodal presentations" that mix actual flexibility exercises with metaphors of suppleness (2012:151). The latter are produced by aesthetic techniques blending lyrical imagery with music played live on instruments made of flexible natural materials like bamboo. Through song and dance, participants are urged to move as plants in the wind and imagine themselves as pliable and therefore less likely to snap or break under pressure (152). For Hinton, the central message is to "bend according to the various forces, consider all the possible options, survey the multiple patterns that may be played, and respond flexibly to the forces of the moment'" (153). He argues that healers' techniques and concepts function by embedding cognitive flexibility and social adaptability through reemphasizing two common cultural "master codes": the inevitability of encountering "shifting patterns" that challenge one's situated perspective (which could include epistemic shifts) and the injunction to embody the properties of a "longitudinal flexible member" (151).

From a psychoanalytic perspective, the idea of a flexible longitudinal member as a basic symbolic model is striking in its contrast to the concept of the phallus as the "rigid designator" (Žižek 1989:97) of masculine authority. As in the posturing of the dictators who used mass violence, false ideological claims, and dubiously amassed funds to put themselves in power throughout much of Southeast Asia in the 1960s and 1970s, the phallus as the "basic" or "pure" signifier of order and authority must seem rigid and immutable. Appearing in this way functions to mask the arbitrary, historically specific nature of men's positioning by default as the heads of families, churches, mosques, and states—and of these particular men's claims to absolute power. As a strategy of resistance to the emergence of an especially virulent, phallocentric patriarchy, Malee's soft voice and movements, performance of agreeability with clients and pimps, and ability to hold out until her situation changes are deceptively meek. In light of the film's ending, where Malee walks away from the brothel and camera carrying a fashion-school diploma she has also paid for with her work, the strategies that got her to that point can be seen as expressing the concept of a "longitudinal flexible member"—one that, over time, highlights the inevitability that a rigid, phallic approach to power will break and be cut short.

FIGURE 24. Malee framed by plants bending in the wind (and hard but flexible bamboo) in the opening of *Theptida Rong Ram.*

The first full shot we see of Malee in her village likewise emphasizes this rural/traditional/natural flexibility, positioning her in the shadow of a livestock pen while all around her, brightly lit, swaying cattails and green leaves fill the foreground and background, as if enveloping her in their calm kinesis (fig. 24). Throughout the film, Malee continues to perform and embody flexibility, even, and especially, when she is trapped in the hard, masculine world of urban hotel-brothels and their pimps (some of the pimps are women, but they fortify their claims to authority in a similarly rigid and violent manner). As she patiently faces veritable armies of these miniature dictators and their minions and johns, Malee remains at the center of the film's imagery and narrative, performing compliance but always meeting the gazes of those who command her—and the looks of those who watch and identify with her from the other side of the porous screen where she is on display. Because her mode of "flexible activism" outlasts the ability of any one pimp to stay in power, and often to stay alive, Malee eventually accomplishes what the would-be heroes in *Maynila* and *Bernafas Dalam Lumpur* cannot: extracting herself from the ever-more pervasive urban mud into which she had "coincidentally" fallen. Another key difference is that by the end of *Theptida Rong Ram*'s narrative, the numerous male characters who have attempted to save or impose their romantic ideals on Malee have all been sidelined and are hence not positioned to unwittingly cause her demise.

In this sense, Malee, in her role at the center of the film, enables its function as a "multimodal metaphor," much like what is deployed in treating those with physical and psychological ailments: a model of comportment and much-needed source of healing for citizen-victims facing the arbitrary, rigid, and violence-begotten rule of a military dictator. In a broader, regional sense, ending up as an unattached, sexually active, and increasingly critically minded woman, Malee embodies the flexibility shown to underpin the symbolic order that ultimately prevails—or at least endures where others snap—in *Theptida*'s brutal onscreen world. Exposing and juxtaposing this pliant, strong figure to the punches and kicks of pimps and to images of actual Thais attacked by the forces of a real dictator further muddies the distinction between diegetic and actual, building on the populist politics of other regional prostitution films. The logic driving *Theptida Rong Ram*'s various montage sequences and visual comparisons implies that Thanom's inflexible response to the demonstrations is precisely what has made it impossible for him to endure. At the same time, radical leftist imperatives of meeting state violence with armed insurgency are tacitly questioned and compared to the rigid tactics of government authorities.

PROSTITUTES, CONJUGAL DICTATORS, AND THE RETURN OF FEMININE ACTORS

As the above analyses suggest, the near-simultaneous emergence of Malee, Mila, Ligaya, and other marginalized, sexually active screen women is no mere coincidence or convergence of market forces around gendered imagery. Taken together, these populist figures point to the advent of complicated models of resistance and the political necessity of the "gray areas" infecting screens across the region via its new prostitution genres—just as strongmen were forcing their way into the highest offices of the affected nations. I argue that sexualized figures who merged and blurred conceptions of activity and passivity, tradition and modernity, firm and flexible modes of comportment, and masculine and feminine symbolic power provided important, regional spaces of convergence that were, like the figures underpinning them, pointedly multimodal.

In line with previous waves of films in the region, the global cinematic impact of such figures and the genres they spawned in the 1970s was also "gray" and difficult to categorize, leading to comparatively minimal recognition outside the region, with a few prominent exceptions. For example, the formal "shocks" (as in splice-and-shock) delivered by Brocka and other emergent Filipino auteurs such as Mike de Leon and Ishmael Bernal across numerous films are particularly resonant with oppositional techniques innovated by pioneers of Soviet montage such as Sergei Eisenstein and Dziga Vertov. In *Kisapmata* (*In the Blink of an Eye*, 1981), de Leon also references later Soviet cinema like Andrei Tarkovsky's *Zerkalo* (*The Mirror*, 1975) with a slow-motion, black-and-white dream sequence of a house flooded by water, contrasted with other natural elements like wind and fire—a Tarkovskian signature. In this sense, many Filipino populist and political films of the 1970s show a clearer interest in the tropes of established art and oppositional cinemas elsewhere in the world. They also received more attention at international festivals than many of their regional counterparts, although a few Thai films also made waves outside the region.

For Espiritu (2017), however, two important factors still distinguish the work of Brocka, Bernal, de Leon, Diaz-Abaya, and others from recognized oppositional movements like Third Cinema: the lack of a manifesto or clear stylistic coherence and the inspiration provided by the wave of lowbrow bombas that preceded them. As the latter aspect establishes, one thing that *does* tie the works of 1970s Filipino auteurs together is a frequent focus on sex and "fallen" women. In this context, more than as global auteurs, I position Brocka, Bernal, de Leon, and Diaz-Abaya as part of a Southeast Asian populist movement triggered by similar political and aesthetic patterns emerging around the same time across the region. Especially in films focusing on prostitutes, common conventional patterns also emerge. Thai films like *Theptida Rong Ram* and *Theptida Bar 21* (*The Angel of Bar 21*, dir. Euthana Mukdasanit, 1978) are full of montage-like splice-and-shock moments such as those Espiritu identifies in Brocka's *Tinimbang*, as well as explicit violence and sex (although little actual nudity), heartrending melodrama, and globally unusual formal experimentations. For example, *Theptida Bar 21*, a garish musical, includes numerous scenes in which characters break into sarcastically joyful song in Bangkok brothels, slums, and amid stinking garbage dumps. Indonesian films like *Bernafas Dalam Lumpur* and *Bumi Makin Panas* (especially the latter) similarly reveled in blood, sex, swoons, and Soviet montage–like techniques aimed to stun and appall. While not a prostitute film per se, Soviet-educated director Sjumandjaja's *Atheis Kafir* (*Atheist*, 1974) went as far as quoting (applying key imagery and shots to a different setting) Sergei Eisenstein's famous "Odessa steps" sequence from *Battleship Potemkin* (1925).

One question this raises across all three locales is, even with filmmakers' general avoidance of direct references to, or critiques of, actual political figures or institutions, how were such shocking, scathing images and themes (and gender politics clearly at odds with dominant symbolic regimes) consistently able to make their way past censors? Most prostitution films presented a moral landscape made up almost entirely of "degraded" citizens who thwarted and invalidated the official, ubiquitously disseminated ideals of New Societies and New Orders in almost every conceivable way. Looking into the reasons for this further deconstructs the myths of Southeast Asian dictators as having quickly and successfully installed "modern" masculine symbolic orders that were actually functional. Doing so, I propose, points to still another key gray area at the very center of "masculine" state power.

In the Philippines, for example, Tolentino and others argue that filmmakers' ability to pass such challenging narratives and images through Marcos's strict crackdowns on "indecent" cinematic fare relied on a critical and very public division of his authority: especially after the institution of martial law and himself as unelected national Father, Marcos shared power with his wife, Imelda Marcos, in what came to be understood as a "conjugal dictatorship"—a collaboration in which "Ferdinand mainstreamed Imelda in the political life of the New Society" (Tolentino 2012:117). The dictator's wife was not simply a symbolic presence but was made governor of Metro Manila, minister of human settlements, and patroness of the arts. It was thus Imelda who was tasked with carrying out many of the key social and aesthetic reforms that she and her husband envisioned for the New Society.

A major goal of the Marcoses' planned transformation was to visibly align the Philippines, and especially its capital city/region Metro Manila, with global standards (and Western anticommunist politics). Imelda sought to project an up-to-date, progressive image, especially with cultural products like cinema that could be consumed and appreciated abroad, as well as at home. Filmmakers like Brocka saw an opening in this emergent aesthetico-political need and played their cards skillfully to become producers of the New Society's global image. They shaped their films in ways that were calculated to appeal to global festivals, but, as noted above, without losing sight of the bombafied tastes and harrowing experiences of the Filipino masses under a corrupt and exploitative conjugal-masculine regime. As Espiritu writes, this produced internationally popular yet "unflattering allegories of the martial-law cultural state." Filmmakers like Brocka were able to toe this delicate line, she argues, because Imelda felt she needed them: "without them, her 'national art' could not have garnered the international attention that she desired for the New Cinema" (2017:113). Even as self-styled and at times open critics of Marcos and his repressive martial law, Brocka, Bernal, Ismael, and many of their contemporaries benefited greatly from Imelda's promotion of them as a "modernist vanguard."

Allowing the flaunting of boldly critical, uncensored imagery on movie screens, while potentially tarnishing the image of the New Society, was not only seen as a demonstration of national artistic talent. As Joel David argues, it was simultaneously calculated to counter international (especially Western) criticisms of the Marcoses' institution of martial law, "act[ing] as . . . [a] showcase of cultural democracy" (2008:10). As a result, films like *Tinimbang* or *Kisapmata* passed through censors mainly unscathed. At the same time, Brocka, Bernal, and others openly demonstrated against censorship and other political concerns, with Brocka even jailed once for his activism (Tolentino 2012:120). Like their Indonesian counterparts, these emergent, simultaneously self- and state-styled Filipino auteurs saw the possibility of political activism and personal and economic profit through multiple modes of "selling themselves" and their work. Marketed by Imelda (and themselves) as national and international artists, their reputations at home and abroad benefited, opening further opportunities for expression. Yet with no limits on Hollywood and other imports domestically, these "art" film enthusiasts still needed to market their work to both the so-called *bakya* masses and local intellectuals in order to survive economically—a financial aspect of their films that aligned with their commitment to engage with Filipino politics.

With onscreen sex now an established mode of selling both tickets and democracy, Brocka and others focused more closely on the critical potential invested in the figure of the prostitute, engendering a thorny symbolic mimicry of their beloved, reviled patroness, Imelda. The typical life-circumstances of sex workers allowed filmmakers to make not so carefully veiled references to aspects of the first lady's background—especially those that she most fervently worked to cover up with regimens of personal image building and overspending that rivaled her megalomaniacal architectural transformations of slum-filled Manila. Despite her current status as among the world's richest and most powerful women, as Tolentino puts it, like many of the central female characters in the New Cinema, Imelda was "born into poverty, illegitimate, provincial, female, lacking educational support, but . . . beautiful." As the first lady "used her feminine qualities for maximum political results" (2012:132), she simultaneously created an alternate aesthetic space, however tainted or impure, for the broad dissemination of critical images at odds with the basic, moralist tenements of Ferdinand's and her own conjugal cultural regime as a whole.

Raden Ayu Siti Hartina, Soeharto's wife, also known as *Ibu* (Madame) Tien, was neither from a poor family nor a glamorous former model like Imelda Marcos, but she had a similarly outsized role in the New Order's program of cultural reconstruction beginning in the 1970s. Taman Mini—the massive, upbeat, theme-park "version" of Indonesia that opened in Jakarta in 1975—was the brainchild of Ibu Tien, who was reportedly inspired by a visit to Disneyland a few years previously (Roberts 2000:162). Beginning in the 1980s, she also commissioned an international team to produce a series of IMAX films collectively known as *Indonesia Indah* (*Beautiful Indonesia*, 1984–91). The films were then shown year-round in a specially constructed theater in the park, shaped like a golden snail drawn from local legends. Park and films together formed a typically heavy-handed, Ibu Tien–style cultural bundle that was used for diplomacy as well as domestic and international tourism.

In addition to her central role in the repackaging and globalization of Indonesian culture, Ibu Tien also made complicated interventions in Indonesian gender politics. Banding together with the conservative women's organization Dharma Wanita, for example, she pushed through a 1983 rule banning civil servants from engaging in polygamy. The rule was an addendum to the 1974 marriage law that already limited the legal possibilities and options for polygamous marriages, including requiring the explicit consent of a man's present wife or wives before he can marry again. As Sonja van Wichelen argues, from the outset of the New Order, the Soehartos set out to promote (and, I would argue, embody and symbolize) a modern ideal of "the conjugal couple and nuclear family" in ways that pointedly brought together "Javanese fatherism, nationalism, and monogamous heteronormativity." For van Wichelen, these were bundled and shifted in ways that "resembled western constructions of family . . . and masculinity" (2007:231–32), as if bolstering the Soehartoist imposition of a symbolic order with the father/phallus as its cornerstone.

Soh Byungkuk concurs, arguing that Ibu Tien's marriage law, like Filipino New Cinema, was also "a success in progressing and modernizing Indonesia and making it a more important actor on the world stage" (2007:80). In my reading, however, the very public role of Ibu Tien in asserting an ideal "Western" family while at the same time *limiting* the absolute power of men in both mainstream Western and Islamic visions of gender and power opens another gray area where the contestation of masculine authority takes place, albeit not in the typical terms of Western/global feminist critique. Such contestation is based, I argue, on the reassertion not only of Javanese ideas of fatherism but of traditions of matrifocality and strong mothers that balance and at times overrule the power of fathers and kings. While Ibu Tien did not, to my knowledge, contribute directly to censors' leniency around sex and prostitution in films, I suggest that as a symbolic figure in her own right, she worked to open a space in which the political interventions of the prostitution genre *made cultural sense*. Not unlike the first lady's reclamations of motherly power in the public sphere, films about sex workers can be seen as rapid, almost reflexive responses to the New Order's promotion of exclusively masculine symbolic power: a modern, Western ideal that is anathema to the complex and enduring histories of gender politics in Indonesia and much of Southeast Asia.

As a genre produced by and responding to particular historical shifts in Indonesia and elsewhere in the region, however, prostitute films shifted the bases of female power outside of the traditional matrifocal home. In particular, these traditions were shown to endure as they followed women into demoralized spaces like brothels and urban slums, producing a distorted mirror image of the Soehartos' safe, "wholesome" (yet in fact violent, murderous, and alienating) version of gender and cultural politics. In films responding to the symbolic regimes of dictators, the central characters are almost inevitably economically and socially marginalized women from the provinces, who come to inhabit the distinctive "mud" of Southeast Asian urban slums. Doing so, they carry with them the cultural memory of female social, political, and economic power associated with various traditional societies. Gradually, and to the extent that it is possible, they apply these ideas and practices to their lives in constantly expanding capital cities. These women's "backward" rural thinking conceives of activity and passivity in ways that undermine and interrogate the dysfunctional masculine/direct symbolic ideals applied by Marcos, Soeharto, Kittikachorn, and their ilk. Lacking other choices, persistence, unflappability, and psychological flexibility become tools for these emergent seers to bide their time and formulate what they have seen and learned as something approaching acts.

If audience members of all sexes, genders, and classes are called out and positioned to identify with the (generally female) "victims" onscreen, they are also pushed to feel and mimic these women's rage, their mode of seeing and "unlikely" potential for power, and the possibility of solidarity in the dirty, crowded spaces where marginalized women, both onscreen and off, survive. The prostitution genre invites audiences to inhabit the illicit, subversive views from the other side of the narratives of New Order and New Society. In so doing, the simplified Western discourse of Cold War politics circulating fluidly around the Pacific to Indonesia, Thailand, and the Philippines is reformulated as a more complex and less pure struggle evolving and deforming itself on local and regional playing fields. The emotional, melodramatic, and heavily mediatized gray areas of populist contamination wielded by 1970s dictators were not the kind of thing foreseen by Western and Soviet "domino theories" of Southeast Asia.

As in Laclau's understanding of the problem of mainstream politics versus actual, messy populism, these distant theories envision and map the region and its nations as clearly readable, homogeneous "unicities" under the control of deceptively friendly dictators like Soeharto, alias the "smiling general." Such assumptions are reflexively and brusquely challenged and "grayed out" by the symbolic and actual excess brought to the fore in the work of regional cineastes. This is especially the case, as I have argued, in the emergence of prostitution genres in Indonesia, the Philippines, and Thailand—allegedly the three staunchest allies of the anticommunist West. The patterns innovated by the films in this chapter, furthermore, are continued and expanded in later efforts such as the above-mentioned *Theptida Bar 21*, the Indonesian hit *Bumi Makin Panas* (also starring and produced by Suzzanna), and Brocka's legendary *Insiang* (1976), among many others.

As Laclau writes, "I see this grey area of contamination not as some kind of marginal political phenomenon, but as the very essence of the political" (2005:222). Indeed, these filmmakers took as their raw material precisely the emergent and convoluted terms of power, agency, identity, citizenship, and social and political abjection set during the rise of so many would-be national fathers. In particular, regional cineastes focused on the various symbolic and economic "needs" for prostitutes produced by the emergent patriarchal-developmentalist regimes. Their films highlighted the resultant inclusion and equally pointed disavowals of the growing presence of sex workers in urban landscapes—a process that strikes at the heart of how these dictators understood and carried out "the political." Yet in this regional formulation of political reality, unpalatable truths that Lacan, Deleuze, Laclau, and others relegate to unconscious, unseen, or unrepresentable areas of experience are introduced into the visible spheres of Southeast Asian societies living under conjugal dictatorships—regimes flaunting thin veneers of masculinity and democracy that filmmakers dispensed with. Underneath official surfaces of respectability and representability, I contend, they located their attacks in areas where gender and power are not so easily divested of their historical dimensions. Although for Laclau, these spaces are necessarily "grey" and ill-defined, in the films analyzed in this chapter they are invested with vibrant color and psychic depth.

It is precisely these aspects of regional-global politics that generally exceed the scope of potential outcomes imagined by the United States or other overly concerned observers of the region. At the same time, the filmic collaborations of Brocka and Koronel, Djunaedy and Suzzanna, and Chatrichalerm and Umarin complicate theories of gazing and spectatorship where cinematic expressions of feminine agency are understood to symptomatically register "a certain convolution and instability" (Doane 1987:36). For Mary Anne Doane, this instability is inseparable from the broad positioning of masculinity in Western societies as "a pure, unified, and self-sufficient position" that is the foundation of language and hence "the very process of looking in the cinema" (Doane 1987:8, 36). Conversely, I suggest that what appears "pathological" in the grand scheme of Hollywood was recognized by regional cineastes as the most salient basis for a transdiegetic and transgender screen activism that would complicate the regional masculinization of authority. Doing so resonated with a broad cross-section of local viewers to whom, as I have shown in this and previous chapters, identities, gazes, and bases of authority are more openly divided between differently gendered symbols and actors.

As we will see in chapter 5, outside of and surrounding the urban environs of prostitutes, slum dwellers, and high-ranking politicians, regional dictators' sudden, synchronous implantation of masculine symbolic orders took on a different tenor. I argue that in rural locales, masculine power and violence, while prevalent, is understood as always already embedded in an enduring, dualistic structure of authority influenced by the earlier spread of Hinduism in the region, combined with local, animist practices and beliefs. This structure showcases and balances masculine and feminine signifiers or "poles," while allowing for spectrums of gendered expression that occupy the spaces in between. As I will show, especially in Java, this dualist symbolic order is ideologically reinforced by ongoing rituals. Not unlike the situation in *Serbis* and in the aging classic Jakarta movie theaters with which this chapter began, the rituals feature men and women who perform agency by mimicking yet twisting and modifying the characters and roles of local legends and histories.

I position such practices as working together with one of the most long-standing regional cinematic genres, the mystical horror film, producing a dynamic, symbolic-material package that sustains both movies and rituals. While politics are officially decided in cities like Jakarta, Bangkok, Manila, Singapore, and Kuala Lumpur, I argue that the pervasive nature of rural rituals and films ruled by female spirits constitutes a formidable aesthetic and political force that engages and works to keep the homogenizing, masculinizing trends of transnational modernity and monotheistic world religions alike in check. Chapter 5 will focus in particular on the explosion of such films in the 1970s and 1980s but will refer to multiple periods before and after in which they have played equally important roles.

5

Monstrous Feminine Superheroes

The Order of the Other and Regional Screens

The day after the 2023 iteration of the Association for Southeast Asian Cinemas Conference in Los Baños, Laguna, the Philippines, I joined a tour of historical sites and other attractions in the area. Just outside of Metro Manila, Laguna is a mainly rural province located along the southern shores of Laguna de Bay, the country's largest lake. Among centuries-old churches and murals, my interest was drawn by the studio and gallery of a well-known wood carver, Luisito Ac-ac, in the town of Pila. We were given a tour of his gallery by his oldest child, a transgender woman who offered two names, Paul and Lucy, and identified herself as LGBTQ. During the tour, she extolled the quality and passion that characterized her father's work, while also explaining that he considered the human form to be invested with a holy spirit. He rendered details of bodies, including genitals, she explained, in particularly vivid detail.

Many of the sculptures in the gallery expressed a sense of rapture, with eyes that consistently looked as if they were in a trance, high, or overwhelmed with some strong sensation, recalling politicized scenes of melodrama from numerous regional films. In this case, the settings around the carved figures depicted churches or other elements of Catholic events or rituals, implying a spiritual source for the figures' visible elation. Yet despite the descriptions given by Lucy/ Paul, the figures were mostly clothed. As I continued admiring the works, a colleague tapped me on the shoulder and pointed toward an enclosed space within the gallery with its own lockable door, the contents of which were not visible from without. I had just been explaining to her how I had begun to see many areas of Southeast Asia in terms of a symbolic order with two basic signifiers rather than the single phallic one around which psychoanalysis understands gender, power, and communication to be arranged. Referring to the contents of the special room, my colleague said: "I think I understand what you were talking about now."

As I entered, immediately to the left of the door were two figures that looked to have been carved from small tree stumps or large branches. Both consisted of exposed sections of human bodies from the thighs to the midriff, focusing the viewer's gaze on the uncovered genitals, which were indeed rendered in great detail. One of the figures was male (not erect) while the other was female. The rest of the room was filled with pairs of male and female statues with the same, rapturous eyes. In this case, however, there were no obvious allusions to religion, and the couples were all engaging in sexual acts in various poses, none of which appeared to suggest the dominance of one partner or another.

As implied by the structure of the space, the separate door, which could presumably be locked to keep certain groups of guests from seeing its contents, there was a "pornographic" aspect to the figures it displayed. Yet this did not appear to be its primary attraction. In light of my discussions with my colleague, I began to see the room, among other things, as a symbolic map. That it was hidden in plain sight in the midst of so many references to the importance of Catholicism seemed to convey a further message. Complicating the more straightforwardly Christianized outside spaces, the interior room and its gendered stumps can be read as commenting on the local status of a religion imported from Europe. Catholicism especially influenced Lacan and others in their formulation of "the" symbolic order—constructed around the phallic lineage of father, son, and holy ghost, and with the Name of the Father in particular as a cornerstone of masculine authority. Here, a father and his plurally gendered child produced and displayed a holiness imbued with the living ghosts of older spiritual beliefs and symbolic orders. Without looking for it, I seemed to have stumbled onto an aesthetic representation of *two* basic signifiers of authority: masculine and feminine or, in the South Asian, Hindu-derived terms that one still often encounters around Southeast Asia, *yoni* and *lingam* (the latter is usually spelled *lingga/linggam* in Indonesia).[1]

Thereafter on the tour, it was difficult to stop seeing further signs of plural or divided symbolic power, often with an emphasis on the female side. For example, after the wood carver, our guides took us to a fifteenth-century church in the same town, which happened to be having a display of its voluminous collection of statues of the Virgin Mary. This meant that the space was dominated, approximately one hundred to one, by representations of female spiritual power. The wall of a tourist trinket shop nearby displayed a large mural that appeared to document the arrival of Catholicism in Laguna, one of the first places in the Philippines to be visited by European missionaries. The mural showed churches and priests in robes emerging around the shores of the lake. Hovering over the water in the middle, however, was a huge female figure with a fish in her lap (fig. 25). The shop owners explained that

FIGURE 25. Author's photograph of Mariang Makiling in a tourist shop in Laguna, the Philippines. She appears to be positioned to mediate between diverse interests, epistemes, and symbolic regimes that are shown descending on Laguna de Bay.

this was Mariang Makiling, the guardian spirit of the lake and nearby mountain, Mt. Makiling (Mariang is a localized version of Maria, to which the name of the deity was changed sometime after the arrival of the Spanish). Mariang Makiling, I was told, negotiates between different groups on opposing banks of Laguna de Bay. From the content and layout of the mural, it seemed she also played a role in encountering the arrival of forces from across much bigger, saltier bodies of water. Especially given the fact that Makiling also appears in classic Filipino films in various forms and guises (Lumbera 1989:8), I was struck by the formal and contextual resemblances between Mariang Makiling and Kanjeng Ratu Kidul, the Javanese spirit-queen of the South Sea. Ratu Kidul is similarly positioned as a powerful political negotiator and teacher who resides at the local edge of an important, connective body of water. Her appearance, powers, and identity are traced by scholars to earlier, Hindu-derived goddesses like Kali and Dewi Sri.

As I will show, figures like Ratu Kidul and Mariang Makiling are often also situated as "national icons," while at the same time working to deconstruct the geographic and temporal/historical sanctity of Southeast Asian nations. As Ratu Kidul's modern iconic status indicates, her influence in Java and throughout much of Indonesia is sustained through both ongoing rituals and popular mass media (films, novels, paintings, and digital imagery and text) in which the queen figures as a central theme or character. I position such firmly rooted feminine icons as key examples of the endurance of a plural conception of power, issuing from basic signifiers that are female and male rather than from a single one that is masculine (or feminine). Throughout this chapter, I argue that Southeast Asia and much of its mass media are influenced, often profoundly, by this enduring, dualistic symbolic order—an underlying conception of power that, like the matrifocal in chapter 3, informs and modifies the function of societies generally understood as national patriarchies. Using examples from films, visual art, rituals, and other contexts, I show how this articulation of order guides the distribution of symbolic and actual power between two distinct, gendered poles. Yet this does not mean that power is always produced in or by a clear binary. Like Ratu Kidul, who at times appears as a man, many local and regional figures and metaphors that have been crucial in negotiating and localizing the arrival of outside powers and symbols have the ability to shift from one gender to another or to express both at once.

As Ben Murtagh (2013) argues, a lionizing of the potential power unlocked by sexual in-betweenness and nonbinary gender identities can also be seen in Indonesian films focusing on male-to-female transgender characters, often known locally as *waria* (a conjunction of the words *wanita* and *pria*, or man and woman). Following Tom Boellstorff's (2005) ethnographic research on waria, Murtagh shows how media produced during the New Order (1966–98) played on widespread (although not universal) understandings of local transwomen having special abilities. Their lack of adherence to one or the other gendered pole, and the resultant ability to *wield* attributes of both, was often seen as a source of great power or even physical strength. A scene in which a waria is "dewigged" and stripped of a key feminine attribute—her long, fake hair—thus paradoxically empowers and encourages the "victim." For Murtagh, "not only does she reveal her male body, but so too she affirms her *wadamness* [another local term for transgender women] . . . as the real men run for their lives" (2013:29). Aspects of such films, Murtagh acknowledges, can also be aimed at mocking waria, laughing at their propensity to "destabilize and trouble dominant Indonesian notions of gender" associated with Soehartoist masculinity. But in the end, he argues, it is often the waria characters who triumph and have the last laugh at the expense of heteronormative ones (Murtagh 2013:34).

The ability to switch between or combine the basic gendered poles is likewise at times a source of comedic moments but is also framed as a particularly valuable "superpower" by numerous legends, narratives, and traditions that continue to develop in concert with mass media throughout much of the region. Building on the previous chapter's analysis of onscreen prostitutes, I propose that this is the case even, and often especially, under sociopolitical or economic pressure to impose a more focused, singular or "modern" symbolic state of affairs. Even broad, concerted efforts to implement rigid patriarchal rule, including the rise of hypermasculine dictators accompanied by mass violence, have inevitably triggered responses, representations, and acts that reflexively refuse such rigid, singular authority. This was the case in the Philippines under Ferdinand Marcos Senior. It now appears to be continuing, however "quietly," under the thumb of his son, Bongbong, whose authority builds on the return of a rigid, masculine symbolic regime imposed by the president that preceded him, Rodrigo Duterte.

Throughout this chapter, I support my analyses with recent ethnographic observations that show the continuation of patterns I identify in older regional films. The films themselves will be drawn from various periods, focusing especially on the late 1970s and 1980s, as well as the 1950s and 1960s, when "supernatural horror" or "mystical" films were especially popular across much of the region. These genres are deeply entangled with ever-present problems of gender and power that extend from the twentieth century into the present. At stake is the status of the traditional feminine power that the last chapter showed to have been displaced from matrifocal homes broken and restructured by the rise of the region's national father-dictators in the 1960s and 1970s. I argue that supernatural horror films—especially those featuring politically empowered female spirits such as Ratu Kidul, the queen of the South Sea—map a path for sexually active, socially unattached women to wage their struggle with unruly patriarchs using faculties based outside the more conventional empowering grounds of marriage, home, and heteronormative femininity. In the process, they also use romance, desire, intelligence, and force to recruit and educate men as partners to fight alongside them.

As I will show, the mystical horror genre is grounded in the agency of numerous legends and spirits that are common to, or have related political economic and cultural bases throughout, much of the region. Unlike the prostitution genre, the potential demise of central human actors leads to a different kind of power as access is gained to the world of spirits—a place that is always intermingled with the human realm but that more easily dispenses with its physical and symbolic limitations. It is this volatile combination of spiritual and actual, seen and unseen, and typically masculine and feminine traits that the mystical horror genre works to articulate and materialize in the context of contemporary national and regional politics. The result, as I will show, is a popular transdiegetic cinema that builds on, but critically expands, the work the prostitution genre. Collectively, films construct a reality-infused fictional sphere that brings together screen-based and other art forms with rituals. Cinema thus remains in direct conversation with active networks of inter- and subreligious spiritual philosophies, value systems, and political practices. It is in these mediatized yet actual, interactive reality-expressions that ideas of power as a "plural unity" composed of shifting combinations of masculinity and femininity are at once hidden and inescapable. These combinations are also simultaneously local, regional, national, radical, and profoundly institutionalized. To better illustrate these connections, I begin at the scene of one such interconnected ritual before turning to the analysis of films and other related media in the following section. In so doing, I hope to provide a thicker sense of the cultural-historical milieu that I argue underpins supernatural films.

BARED ROCKS IN PARANGKUSUMO

It is an auspicious day in 2013 owing to the conjunction of Friday, generally the fifth day on the Gregorian calendar, and *Kliwon*, the last of the five days that make up the Javanese calendar in its current version, which dates to 1633. Occurring every thirty-five days, Friday *Kliwon*, or *Jumat Kliwon*, is among the most popular days in this part of Java to hold rituals (Friday *Pon*, the third Javanese day, as well as Tuesday *Kliwon* or *Pon* are also commonly slated for ritual events). Like many of the attractions that the first two chapters show to be embedded in regional popular media, timing rituals with points of coincidence between different calendrical systems underscores the importance placed on the interaction of distinct epistemological spheres, including those of humans and spirits.

Not far from a central area featuring two largish rocks embedded in the ground and surrounded by a low wall (fig. 26), a man looks at me with an odd, rapturous glint in his eye. He appears to be in his fifties.[2] Speaking quickly and excitedly, he explains that he lives in a small nearby city. We are standing just north of the beach in Parangkusumo, a gateway to the palace of Ratu Kidul, the Javanese spirit queen of the South Sea, located on the southern coast of Java about twelve and a half miles south of the city of Yogyakarta. To get there, the man explains, he took a bus that runs on a special timetable for ritual days, arriving around sunset and scheduled to return after dawn. He has a wife and two children and has been regularly going to rituals like this for several years. He is also a frequent attendee at similar events at Gunung Kemukus in Sragen, Central Java. He always goes to these rituals alone, without his family.

"It's only fifty thousand here [roughly five U.S. dollars at the time]."

"Ah, I see."

"That's cheap!" he exclaims, referring to the average price charged by sex workers who frequent this and other ritual events. He looks me straight in the eye as he talks, but then quickly glances down at his feet. "I'm sorry if I'm being impolite and talking about things that are naughty [*nakal*]."

Just then, the *gamelan* (metallophone) orchestra that had been setting up in front of the large, wood-framed screen erected before us starts to play, causing the man to look away. The music signals the introductory section of a shadow play (*wayang kulit*) performance that will begin its narrative, a section chosen from the Javanese adaptation of the Mahabharata story cycle, in thirty minutes or so. For many, the puppet show will be one of the night's central attractions. As my interlocutor has indicated, however, his interest lies elsewhere. "I'll talk to you later, okay?" he says, and makes off in the direction of the beach. Underneath the peaked roof of the *pendopo* where I am standing, men and women in formal attire are already seating themselves in the chairs provided for invited guests, behind the *gamelan*. In their look and manner, the invited guests strike a contrast with most of those standing on the perimeter and beyond. In the darkened ritual areas, crowds of teens and college students, mothers, and children, old men in Javanese *lurik* jackets and young ones with sarongs wrapped around their shoulders mix with the *peci* hats and *hijabs* worn by those who look to have just completed their evening *Isya* prayers at the nearby mosque.

Roughly twenty meters to the west, a walkway connects beach, mosque, and the main ritual space with the two rocks in the center. The area around the rocks consists in a small, walled-in area for burning incense and spreading flower petals

FIGURE 26. The central ritual area of Parangkusumo, built around the two stones on which the queen and the would-be prince of Mataram once sat, is prepared for evening crowds by late afternoon (*top*). The East *pendopo* pavilion, where the gamelan and shadow play normally take place, is visible on the right side of the frame. To the southwest of the ritual area, in the direction of the beach, the mosque (*bottom*) is positioned adjacent to the crowded walkway where prostitutes wait for clients and where night-market hawkers often claim overflow space, as depicted here. Photographs by author.

and is already crowded with people in formal Javanese *kebaya* tops and *batik* sarongs who have come to seek blessings. Along with chanted prayers in Arabic and Javanese, incense and flowers serve as the media with which attendees pay their respects to Panembahan Senapati (d. 1601), the first ruler of the Mataram dynasty (r. sixteenth century ongoing), a division of which still governs the area around the nearby city of Yogyakarta, which includes Parangkusumo. But ritual attention is especially focused on Ratu Kidul, Senapati's most crucial ally, political adviser, and muse. Their relationship, and that of the queen with all subsequent rulers of Mataram, is said to have begun on the two rocks that adorn the center of the small space. Leading away from the ritual area, the walkway is mostly dark, veiling much of the goings-on there in semiobscurity.

Along the path, directly in front of the mosque, women ranging in age from twenty to forty or so are already lined up, ready to perform a special ritual function, in this case for a fee (the fifty thousand rupiah quoted by the man above). Together with several colleagues, a woman whom I will call Siti stands close to a single row of lights, illuminating herself sufficiently for passersby to take a look. Those who do so, mostly men in small groups, move dreamily, almost as if in slow motion, floating along and turning their heads left and right. Wearing a thick layer of white powder, lipstick, and eye shadow, along with a medium-length skirt and a hooded sweatshirt to protect her from the wind, Siti stares back at them, peering into their faces as they draw close to examine hers. Earlier in the afternoon, she tells me, Siti and her friends chartered a bus with about thirty other women to come to Parangkusumo for the night. They regularly show up at most of the local rituals where popular legend advises participants to copulate in imitation of the divine or otherwise revered figures to whom the ritual sites are dedicated. The rules are understood to stipulate that the ritual sex should take place between partners who are not wed. More male than female participants generally show up to do so, creating the possibility for women to earn money for their participation. Like Siti, many of them are also sex workers outside the rituals.[3]

Often, even locals who may have heard of these sites, but haven't actually been to them on ritual nights, express surprise that such transactions could take place undisturbed directly in front of a mosque. As one of the official *juru kunci* (key masters) who are employed by the palace of the sultan of Yogyakarta to lead ritual prayers told me derisively, women like Siti come to "exploit" the fact that the rituals bring hundreds or thousands of people together in one place, offering numerous potential customers. This appears to be the official palace line on the matter of ritual prostitution, but from what I have observed and read, the reality appears more complex. Ahmad Rafiq, a local scholar who conducted research at Parangkusumo a few years earlier, told me that sex workers come in greater numbers on ritual days mainly to "purify themselves." The potential financial gains, as indicated by the prices quoted by the man above, are minimal compared to most other places where prostitutes work, suggesting a combination of reasons, including nonfinancial ones, for the volume of women who come to offer services at a steep discount on *Jumat Kliwon* or other auspicious times.

The anthropologist Volker Gottowik compares Parangkusumo to other, Central Javanese ritual sites like Gunung Kemukus in Sragen, where historical legends link the "exceptional love" of a powerful, venerated couple to particular locations with storied pasts. At such sites, adding to the idea of purification above, "pilgrims visit . . . and try to re-enact the behaviour of these sacralized lovers . . . to acquire some of the spiritual power they embody" (2018:394). In their capacity as spaces for the practice of ritual sex, Parangkusumo, Gunung Kemukus, and other similar locales take on material patterns that closely mirror the miniaturized symbolic "map" displayed in the inner gallery of Luisito Ac-ac. In this case, instead of carved wood genitals displayed in a special enclosure, it is pairs of rocks or tombs, each attached to a female and male member of a legendary "power couple," as Gottowik calls them, that form the site's symbolic center. Around this dual locus, numerous mortal couples arrange themselves in mimicry of the mythically generative union of partners symbolized by the two objects in the middle (in Parangkusumo and Kemukus, they do so in shacks and short-time hotels surrounding the central ritual areas and provided for this purpose, as well as reportedly in the grass or on the beach).

In the case of Parangkusumo, as chronicled in the Mataram dynasty's official history (*Babad Tanah Jawi*), the legendary power couple is the aforementioned Ratu Kidul and Panembahan Senapati, the prince who, after a few nights spent with the queen in her underwater palace, rose to become the dynasty's first king. Established in the *Babad* and by various other narratives and scholars, Parangkusumo is where Senapati first encountered Ratu Kidul.[4] As Senapati meditated on one of the two rocks mentioned above, his powers of concentration were reportedly such that the sea boiled, disturbing the queen's dominion and hence getting her attention. She emerged from the water to see what was happening, seating herself on the other rock in front of Senapati. After becoming acquainted, the queen's curiosity was further piqued, and Senapati was invited for a history-making, legendary three-day sojourn in the queen's undersea abode.

The couple's physical relations became a conduit for political alliance and for Senapati's education in the art of statecraft. As Nancy Florida writes, Senapati was "taught . . . the knowledge of kingship [and] the secrets of authority over both human and spirit realms" (Florida 1992:23). Afterward, the queen pledged her support for Senapati's campaign to consolidate power in the region under a new dynasty. In return, she stipulated that he and all successive rulers must be wedded to her—but on her own, spiritual terms rather than the more restrictive human, legal ones. Taking mortal wives, in addition to being the spirit queen's king, was therefore not an issue. The current sultan of Yogyakarta, Hamengkubuwono X, a direct descendant of Senapati's, is the first to have stated that he no longer has sexual relations with the queen. But both he and the recent Sunans of Surakarta continue to fulfill a yearly ceremonial requirement where special offerings stipulated in the queen's spiritual contract are brought to the beach at Parangkusumo and cast into the sea.[5]

As my own and others' observations show, the current leaders' reticence to "physically" engage with the queen has done nothing to diminish the crowds of civilians who continue to attend rituals in her honor twice every thirty-five days (Gottowik 2018; Smith and Woodward 2016). For Gottowik, the rulers' attitudes have fostered a greater "democratization" (2018:404) of spiritual power and access to its venerated conduits over the past several decades. Sites like Parangkusumo and Gunung Kemukus receive several thousand visitors each month (the latter up to ten thousand on a given ritual day), producing significant economic boons for the areas around where the rituals take place. This in turn helps foster political will among local leaders to resist constant calls by religious conservatives for such sites to be closed down (Gottowik 2018:396–97). While most such ritual areas now stipulate the use of Islamic prayers in Arabic to ask for the blessings of founding spirits or historical figures associated with them, the ritual processes are generally categorized as *pesugihan*, a local concept taken from the Javanese word *sugih* (rich).

As this suggests, the rituals are believed to carry the potential to enrich participants, in return for which they must provide an offering stipulated by site-based custom or the person officiating the exchange. As in the case of Senapati, what was produced by his interaction with Ratu Kidul was not monetary but political and knowledge-based; nonetheless, it resulted in the enrichment of Senapati's now-legendary career and that of his descendants, who presently remain deeply involved in both political and economic aspects of Yogyakarta and Surakarta, cities with outsized national footprints. My interviews with participants and *juru kunci* (who lead ritual prayers) suggest that what is asked for by nonroyal participants ranges from success in business, to the ability to charm others, to protection from danger for those, like soldiers or *preman* (gangsters), whose work frequently exposes them to violence. What is asked of pilgrims in return can in some cases be quite onerous. In Parangkusumo and Gunung Kemukus, prayers and offerings of flowers and incense are officially stipulated by *juru kunci*, to which long-established beliefs and legends attached to the sites add ritual sex—an aspect that most pilgrims also see as compulsory. While many look forward to it, the ritual involves the sacrifice of the sanctity of monogamous marriage and, as we will see below, of the official conception of modern nationhood.

My interest in Parangkusumo stems from its status as a lively material and practical foundation for the influence and long-standing media presence of Ratu Kidul (and from her similarity to other regional goddesses such as Mariang Makiling). I position such popular feminine spirits as signs of the enduring influence of plural conceptions of symbolic authority adapted from older Hindu and animist ideologies. After learning more about the goings-on there, I conducted ethnographic and film-based research at related sites like Gunung Kemukus (2008–17). In my analysis, these sites offer material demonstrations of how local and regional conceptions of gender and power are reproduced through shifting conglomerations of myths; religious and spiritual beliefs; and historical narratives, figures, and events. Research over the last two decades has often sounded the death knell of these practices at the hands of rising waves of conservatism, particularly among increasingly populous and vocal hardline Islamic groups.[6] The localized, syncretic versions of Muslim and other monotheistic beliefs that are embedded in many ritual sites, and that Robert Hefner praises as "decentered and multifarious in origin" (2011:77), are also argued by Hefner to have been in decline since the 1960s.

In some areas of society (such as the vast increase in Arab-influenced Islamic garb among Indonesians and Malaysians in the last twenty years), there are almost constant signals that appear to indicate this decline to be actual and ever-increasing. But such signs can also be deceptive, and from the vantage point of a crowded ritual night at Parangkusumo or Gunung Kemukus, more recent studies of such rituals have pointed out that precisely *because* of the waves of conservatism, which are undeniable, "the rising tide lifts all boats"—including those in which syncretism floats (Gottowik 2018:395). Gottowik argues that contemporary processes generally labeled Islamization and understood to include steep rises in conservatism and scripturalist doctrine are, in fact, better conceived of as "religionization"—a process that results in an all-round intensification of belief and practice, conservative and otherwise. Looking at current religious shifts in this way, while connecting them to enduring structures of gender and power in films and other modern media, engages with and expands my argument in the previous chapter.

As I showed there, the imposition by masculine dictators of rigidly patriarchal, antipluralist regimes in the 1960s and 1970s was met with a reflexive rise in critical screen representations of female victimization implied to be driven by such regimes. More important, many of the most popular and impactful of such representations also included demonstrations of an embedded female agency that would find ways to adapt and endure, rising to challenge the attacks aimed at it. I argue that similar adaptability is expressed by ritual sites such as Parangkusumo and Gunung Kemukus, which have weathered numerous challenges and waves of change—conservative, radical, scripturalist, patriarchal, and otherwise—over the past several centuries (Parangkusumo, for example, hosted its first legendary power couple in the late 1500s).

Many of the prostitution films of the 1970s feature a strong female response to the imposition of a rigid, singularly patriarchal symbolic order, suggesting a process of "evening out" the gender of power after the scales have been tipped toward masculine authority. These ritual sites and their founding figures continue this work, generally promoting a sense of equilibrium between male and female signifiers and actors, although they, too, often lean toward feminine power. I argue that the rituals operate in ways that reflect and amplify the underlying functions of local and regional films, especially those of the supernatural horror genre, which features deities from many of the rituals at the center of screen-narratives. In Parangkusumo, when certain pilgrims embody fragments of the past by mimicking or venerating the legendary acts of the queen, for example, she connects them with feminine and nonbinary symbols and icons that came to the region before colonialism, before nationalism, and before monotheism, which Gottowik calls "tantric fragments" (2018:403). Similar to how films attract and communicate certain things to viewers, rituals offer a particular sense of agency to pilgrims who participate in them, while working in parallel with films and other media to normalize certain "ancient" ideas about gender in the present.

SUPRANATIONAL ICON

In 1950, just after Indonesia's independence from Dutch rule, Basoeki Abdullah, an internationally established Indonesian artist, produced one of the best-known portraits of Ratu Kidul. Imbued with an updated, "official" look, the queen's image was transported into the presidential palace and mounted on the same walls as portraits Abdullah had done of Soekarno (he would go on to paint Soeharto and Imelda Marcos, among other regional luminaries). But even after entering the highest office in the land during a new and unprecedented phase in Indonesia's history, the queen's appearance was not fixed or contained as an attachment to that office or era; fluid, like the ocean, she would be painted, "photographed," and novelized repeatedly over the next seven decades and beyond.

Since the late 1970s, Ratu Kidul has been the subject of numerous popular films and TV series, the market for which, like the queen herself, appears "eternal" (the latest film I am aware of is the 2019 *Lukisan Ratu Kidul* [*The Painting of Ratu Kidul*], dir. Ginanti Rona). More recently, the actress Cinta Laura, who attended the 2023 Cannes Festival as a L'Oréal brand representative, made much of the fact that her red-carpet gown was inspired by the queen. In concert with her media presence, Ratu Kidul's political career has also continued since the 1950s. A particular highlight was when Soeharto's first elected successor, Abdurrahman Wahid, made a widely publicized pilgrimage to Parangkusumo to ask for the queen's blessing for his candidacy in 1998. In this context, she can be seen as having guided Java, and, by extension, the archipelago that would become Indonesia, from the arrival of European envoys and then colonizers in the sixteenth century through independence, dictatorship under Soeharto, and into the more overtly democratic era of *reformasi* that followed. Owing to events such as Wahid's pilgrimage and to the queen's enduring, ubiquitous media presence following independence, Karen Strassler refers to Ratu Kidul as a "national icon" (2014:100).

In line with the queen's symbolically complicating influence on modern Indonesian society, I understand this iconicity as binding the nation to Ratu Kidul and the accumulations of times, regimes, features, and abilities she has absorbed and represents, more than the reverse. As a national, Javanese subnational, and,

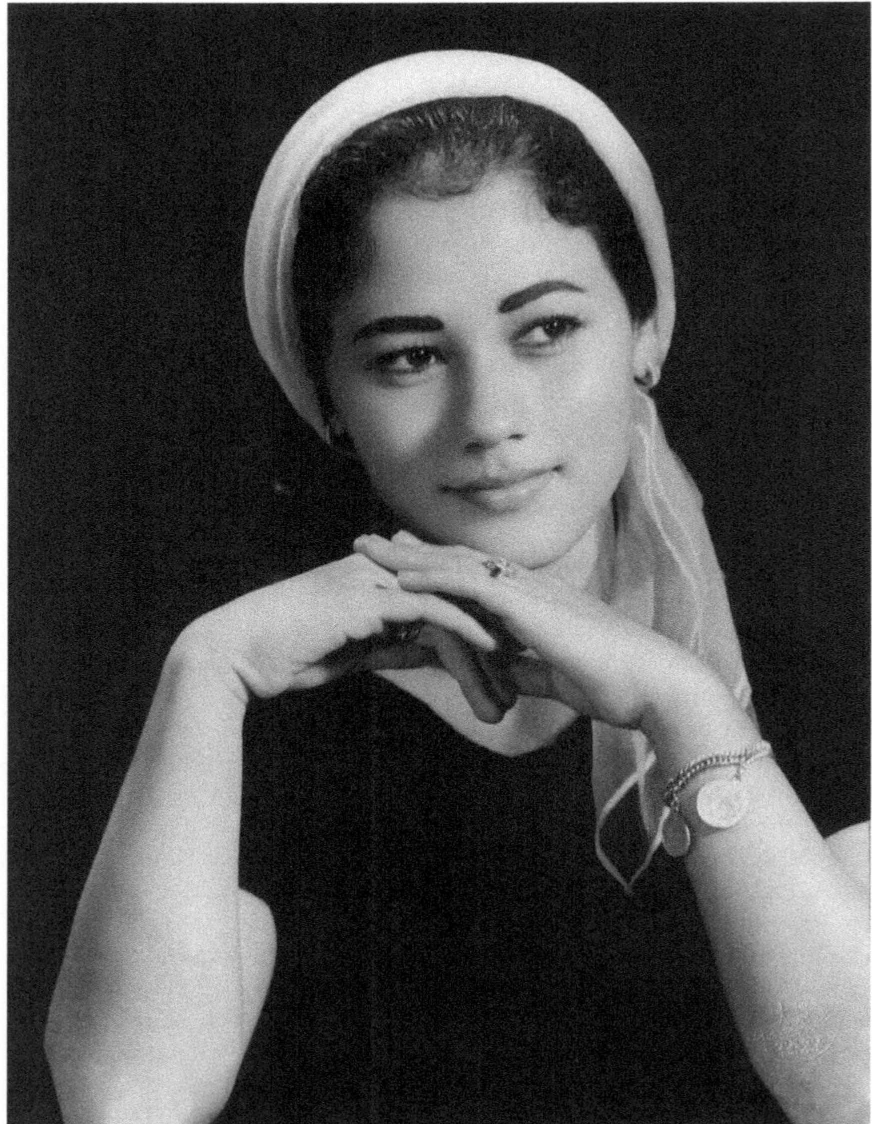

FIGURE 27. The actress Suzzanna in 1963. Courtesy of KAFEIN/Chris Woodrich.

as I will show, supranational cinematic icon, the queen and other related female spirits can also be seen as further developing and transforming the medium of cinema in particular ways that are associated with both regional aesthetic histories and spiritual practices. For example, Ratu Kidul was most famously played by Suzzanna (fig. 27), the actress and production company owner who became known as "*Ratu* Horror Indonesia" (Queen of Indonesian Horror) for her multiple portrayals of Ratu Kidul and other ubiquitous movie ghosts such as the *sundel bolong*. Typical of her deep, creative influence on the characters she played in the early 1970s, Suzzanna's approach to preparation for these roles, especially that of Ratu Kidul, interpreted them not as anachronous legends or mere fiction. Instead, she acted as if she were portraying actual figures in a sort of biopic (albeit a highly dramatized one), while always asking "permission" from the figures themselves.

Suzzanna, who died in 2008, was known to conduct detailed ceremonies in preparation for her film roles portraying historically and culturally established spirits. Doing so articulated thick lines of connection among ritual, representation, and lived experience. Among other things, Suzzanna would conduct a *puasa mutih*, or traditional Javanese "white fast," eating and drinking only rice and water for a few days. She would also make a pilgrimage to a room at an upscale hotel in West Java that since the 1950s has been set aside as a shrine to Ratu Kidul, asking for her blessing to portray either the queen herself or other spirits under her authority (Ariesti 2008).[7] The result, I argue, was films that were imbued not only with a screen-transcending aura of the spiritual but also with the political power associated with figures like the queen of the South Sea. Especially via Suzzanna, whose career was launched by prostitution films like *Bernafas Dalam Lumpur* and *Bumi Makin Panas* (see chapter 4), I propose that the rise of powerful female screen spirits in the late 1970s can be seen as an expansion of the subversive, transdiegetic movie roles of sex workers in the beginning and middle of the same decade. As noted above, the complex connection between sex work, legendary female spirits, and rituals in their honor is well established offscreen as well as on.

Bangunnya Nyi Roro Kidul (*The Awakening of Nyi Roro Kidul*, dir. Sisworo Gautama, 1985) is in my analysis one of the clearest examples of the political and gender-based interventions delivered via the cinematic manifestation of the queen, who serves as the film's central character and ethical-ideological driving force. Like the films of the prostitution genre that preceded them, and reflecting the seedier, "low class" elements of rituals at Parangkusumo, supernatural horror films also deploy generous helpings of melodrama, action, sexual innuendo, and comedy to help ensure a broad viewer base and financial success. To give a detailed sense of how the film positions Ratu Kidul in the context of 1980s Indonesia (around the halfway mark of Soeharto's thirty-year dictatorship), I will summarize various sections:

> It is a Friday *Kliwon* in 1985. The woman (Suzzanna) lies in wait at
> the bottom of the sea, not far from the shore, clad in a *batik* sarong
> and bright green lace *kebaya*. After passing through a storm of
> bubbles and radio static, two scuba divers happen on her motionless
> form and take her for drowned. Earlier they had joked about
> meeting the legendary queen of these waters, whose submerged
> palace is believed to be nearby. One of the men quickly dismissed

her existence as *tahayul*, using the Arabic word to distinguish "superstitions" from beliefs sanctioned by religion, in this case Islam. But if they do find her, he brags, he will take her to bed.

She allows herself to be carried from the water, draped across the arms of another man, as if going through the motions of a valiant rescue despite the fact that she appears to be dead. One of the men leaves to inform the police, while the other two wait at a cabin station in the woods nearby where the motionless woman has been placed on a mattress and partially shrouded with a blanket. Standing up to look around, the man who earlier cried *tahayul* glances down at the woman's supine body, scanning from head to toe with growing interest. Suddenly, the blanket flies off, accompanied by a spooky, nondiegetic synth sound, revealing bare legs where the woman's sarong has fallen open. When he bends to cover her, he peers closely at her face. She is made-up as if for a special occasion, her hair improbably adorned with a wreath of unwilted flowers. As if driven by an unseen force, the man leans in further and plants a kiss on her lips. As he does, her eyes fly open like shutters, meeting his gaze with an empty, robotic stare. He leaps backward, his face a mask of shock.

Slowly, she sits up and turns toward him, but instead of running, he removes his shirt and sits beside her. As he stands and pulls her up with him, a familiar smugness replaces the terror in his eyes. But this, like the man himself, is short-lived. In a flash, he is blinded by bolts of yellowish-white light that issue from the woman's eyes and mouth, striking his face and body and immobilizing him (fig. 28). He can only scream as he and his gaze are charred to a crisp. Leaving his smoking corpse, the woman wanders away through the trees until she comes to a road. Remaining silent, she waits for her real target to appear, her steady look warding off each gawking, goading passerby. Only when a Volvo 240 sedan pulls up with a black-sheathed sword affixed to its grill—signaling its passenger to be a government *pejabat* (civil servant)—does she accept the offer of a lift. As it happens, the bureaucrat is going exactly where she is headed: Jakarta, the capital. She introduces herself as Neneng, a traditional dancer coming from a performance (which explains her costume and makeup). Shortly afterward, the man pats her thigh and promises to help her find work in the capital if she can "help him out" now. Suddenly, the car begins to float, and the bureaucrat meets a fate similar to that of the *tahayul* man. Newspapers record the two mysterious deaths the next day.

FIGURE 28. The queen of the South Sea (Suzzanna) makes short work of the male gaze (*left*) and then does some undercover shopping at a trendy Jakarta mall (*right*).

Not simply a killer, the woman, as we learn, is on a mission. She chooses one of the other divers as her assistant—a polite, handsome university student named Ario (George Rudy), whom she takes a liking to and does not fry. With his logistical help, "Neneng" makes short work of a gang of human traffickers linked to the bureaucrat she has already eliminated. As Ario discovers (and as the audience will have known from the beginning), Neneng is in fact Nyi Roro Kidul, alias Ratu Kidul, the South Sea queen of ancient legend who has awakened, seemingly as a result of steep increases in crimes against women, and is working undercover to fight the perpetrators.

For a spirit from the sixteenth century, Neneng/Ratu Kidul seems perfectly at ease in modern Jakarta. In one, comedically tinged scene, she pulls the stunned Ario onto the dance floor of a downtown club where they have arranged to meet, where she shows off all the latest moves. Predictably, after assisting her to defeat the gang, Ario declares his love but is again taken aback when the queen refuses his offer of matrimony. Despite her status as a spirit queen with superpowers, she explains, her feelings are similar to those of other women. But while she, too, has grown fond of Ario, the paths ordained for them do not lead to matrimony. "Love does not always end in marriage," she assures him, returning his sad, puppy-dog gaze with an experienced, sympathetic look.

For weeks after she vanishes into the sea, he wallows in self-pity, sitting on the beach and staring into the waves. But his friends urge him to return to his studies. Indonesia needs people like him more than ever, they claim, teasing out a sense of nationalist duty from the emotional quandary caused by the sudden end to Ario's exhilarating ride with Neneng/Ratu Kidul. As if on que, the queen appears on a nearby rock with waves crashing around her and calls out to Ario, implying that their connection is not severed and that she'll be watching over the nation's transformation at his hands. Elated, the three friends sprint across the beach toward the queen, accompanied by a 1980s rock song on the soundtrack. The film freezes them in mid stride, superimposing the word *sekian* (that's all) over the still.

Given the fact that Ratu Kidul rubs elbows with kings and presidents and is known to appear when a major political shift or regime change is needed, her ultimate target was likely not the government-connected gang. If we follow the historical-political narratives associated with the queen, her actual goal would likely have been to meet and empower Ario, a young man in whom she saw the potential to carry out a broader, more important, mission: in this case, to fix, or perhaps overthrow, the government under which gangs of sexist men led by civil servants operate with impunity. While the name Soeharto is never mentioned, it is clear enough that the film is critical of his regime. In its version of Indonesia, Ario is implicitly positioned as the next in a long line of leaders, stretching back centuries, whose careers were jump-started or helped along by the queen. Furthermore, if Ario is an invented character who is contextualized historically, the queen appears as "herself": a figure who has granted permission for her portrayal (requested by Suzzanna, as indicated above) and who is not invented for the narrative of this or other films. The specifics of her dialogue and how she appears are variable between various media and times. But she is always identifiable as the same queen who grants the authority of ancient and contemporary kings and who, roughly thirteen years after the release of *Bangunnya Nyi Roro Kidul*, would play an important role in the process of Soeharto's actual fall and replacement by Abdurrahman Wahid (see above).

If the specifics of her storied past and many modern media appearances have made the queen a national icon, the layers of material history and representation that she carries along with her transcend the temporal and spatial borders of both nation and screen. Saturated with the historical attributes of archipelagic representation in Southeast Asia and with the importance of water in connecting diverse groups and places, I argue that the queen of the South Sea constitutes a transdiegetic and also transmedial force—one that interpenetrates and links distinct genres, styles, and modes of expression and the different places and eras associated with them. Her continual manifestations and reentrances serve to reconstruct a plural symbolic order around herself, while drawing in and positioning other, contemporary figures as her stand-ins or partners, doing so across the various technologies and formats of representation, places, and practices she inhabits. At the same time, what she enacts and represents is by design not "pure," symbolically or otherwise. She is neither a virgin nor even necessarily male or female and can be national, local, regional, or transnational (in her capacity of localizing the global spread of both Hinduism and Islam, and her role in local responses to Dutch incursions along Java's southern coast). As in the film above, her awakenings, and those of other female spirits discussed in the following sections, generally occur at times in which particularly virulent strains of patriarchy have taken hold; this is one reason, I propose, for the popularity and constant production of supernatural horror films under Soeharto. Even if a film featured a less exalted spirit than the queen of the South Sea, the increasing number of roles played by Suzzanna leading to her status as the of queen of Indonesian horror created a broader sense of supernatural movies as contests between the masculine agents of the New Order and an iconic feminine force that took different forms at different times.

FEMININE SPIRITS VS. *KIAI* EX MACHINA

Compared to elsewhere in the region, the emergence of supernatural horror as national cinematic staple in Indonesia happened relatively late, with *Beranak Dalam Kubur* (*Giving Birth in the Grave*, dir. Awaludin and Ali Shahab, 1971). A year after her rise to superstardom in the prostitution-themed *Bernafas Dalam Lumpur*, Suzzanna's role as coproducer and star of *Beranak Dalam Kubur* positioned her as both an iconic and a strategic behind-the-scenes link between politically subversive sex workers and the female spirits that would appear in greater numbers toward the end of the decade. *Beranak Dalam Kubur* was the first of twenty or so supernatural films Suzzanna acted in (fig. 29), most of which were released between the late 1970s and the 1990s, when national horror fever was in full swing. Although her later hits were not produced by Suzzanna's company, she was known to use her star power as well as her experience in the business side of the industry to exert an unusual level of creative control.[8]

As in *Bangunnya Nyi Roro Kidul*, spirits and monsters played by Suzzanna and other actresses constituted female vigilantes who intervened on behalf of police, government, or religious authorities, the latter groups usually male and consistently shown to be ineffective. Owing to the movies' enduring popularity and their established connections to politically powerful, noncinematic spiritual discourses and practices, they were not always warmly embraced by those in power. While movie prostitutes initially went under the radars of hyperpolitically attuned censors, the screening of subversive female legends and spirits like Ratu Kidul became a concern of the state and other influential groups. As Katinka van Heeren shows, officials and religious authorities "saw mystical films as an obstacle to Indonesia becoming a modern, pious nation" (2012:142–43). Partly reflecting this concern, new censorship guidelines were created in 1981, and numerous special committees and commissions were convened, such as the commissions for "Film and National Morality," "Film and the Awareness of National Discipline," and "Film in Its Relation to Devotion towards the One and Only God" (van Heeren 2012:139). To address

FIGURE 29. The poster for *Beranak Dalam Kubur* (*Giving Birth in the Grave*), the first horror film starring "Suzzana" (i.e., Suzzanna). Courtesy of KAFEIN.

such concerns, filmmakers often inserted a character who represented a religious authority, usually an Islamic *kiai* (cleric), who "would step in and restore order at the end of the film." It was mainly due to these sorts of conventional capitulations, van Heeren argues, that political sensitivity generated by the presence of "the supernatural was tolerated" in Indonesian popular cinema (143; see also Sen 1994:144).

This was especially the case, I suggest, in the majority of such films that feature "lower"-level spirits lacking the state-recognized status of someone like Ratu Kidul. A pattern does emerge in numerous Soeharto-era horror movies where a kiai or other male religious figure will appear and intervene in the disruptions caused by spirits, resulting in a trope that is often taken in retrospect as an unwritten (and largely self-imposed) rule of New Order cinema. This is in line with the broad perception among scholars and much of the Indonesian public that Soeharto's rule was characterized by a deep and rigidly patriarchal conservatism. It was, but this chapter's use of a supernatural cinematic lens to view the New Order points to other layers that are often obscured by the modernist-developmentalist surface attached to the regime.

As Dhanurendra Pandji (2021) and others point out, for example, many of the military leaders of the New Order, including Soeharto himself, had strong backgrounds in Javanese mysticism. On an official level, *kejawen*, or Javanese spiritual beliefs (often combined with Islam), and other localized belief systems were marginalized by a law that required Indonesian citizens to follow one of five state-recognized religions (Islam, Protestantism, Catholicism, Hinduism, or Buddhism, the last two reformulated with a "One God" figure at their center). But these gestures toward nationalized monotheism also concealed the deeper, enduring affiliation of Java-based authorities like the New Order with typically syncretic local and regional belief systems that alter and undermine the sanctity of purist understandings of Islam, Christianity, and other world religions. As Pandji shows, a key New Order minister, Inspector General of Development Sudjono Hoemardani, was responsible not only for urbanization and modernization but for a massive and expensive reconstruction of a late Majapahit-era (1293–1527) Hindu-Javanese temple, *candi* Cetho, in the mountains above Surakarta in Central Java. Pandji argues that the temple's reconstruction symbolically asserted a cyclical (and typically *kejawen*) rather than a chronological-developmentalist view of history underpinning Soeharto's power (2021:26–27).

In 1983, the New Order government also took over Gunung Kemukus, one of the legend-based ritual sex sites mentioned above, converting it into an official tourist destination. According to interviews I conducted with officials and participants there in 2008, 2009, and 2017, the intent was not to align the site with more clearly monotheist or developmentalist principles but to amplify its original function.[9] The number of pilgrims thus greatly expanded owing to the state's promotion of the site, causing an attendant increase in not only *kejawen*-infused ritual sex but prostitution. These and other examples above reveal a regime that is far more heterogeneous and politically inscrutable (and hence often also more insidious) than it appears on the surface. Underneath its signature promotions of a rigidly singular, masculine view, the New Order state shows a canny facility for keeping various distinct and potentially conflicting groups and discourses in line by carefully balancing and playing them against each other; but in doing so, I argue, it also opens itself to attacks such as those staged by supernatural horror films.

In line with this argument, I contend that the phenomenon of inserting kiai figures in New Order supernatural films as deus ex machina tasked with putting spiritual-political matters back in order is also a more complicated and less decisive convention than it might at first appear. Even in what to my mind is one of the purest examples, the 1980 film *Pengabdi Setan* (*Satan's Slaves*, dir. Sisworo Gautama Putra), the success of the kiai is ultimately undermined by a final twist that strongly hints his order-restoring work may have been reversed. Just as the disruptive spirit seems to have been banished for good, the film's spooky, ghost-attack soundtrack suddenly returns. It is then made to look as if the Javanese, black magic–wielding woman who appeared to have been easily killed by the kiai in the film's penultimate conflict may in fact be alive and well. If the kiai rule is slyly undercut by filmmakers in one of the main examples that demonstrates its validity, what, then, actually transpires in the numerous, less conventionally faithful approaches, and what does this tell us about the politics of the genre as a whole?

In *Sundelbolong* (*Devil Woman*, dir. Sisworo Gautama Putra, 1981), another megahit supernatural horror film, the presence of the male religious figure functions—in typically archipelagic fashion—to call attention to local/regional/ transnational conventions like the kiai ex machina in order to poke fun at them. By initially making a comedic show of acquiescence, the film implicitly contests the legitimacy of the onscreen kiai and also the police. A closer look at the film's exploitation of the complexities, paradoxes, and resultant holes in the surface of New Order authority complicates the ways that gender politics have been understood to be negotiated between male authorities and female ghosts on the screen. The conventional theme of female victimization by the darker aspects of New Order patriarchy, however, is quite clear.

The film's central character, Alisa, again played by Suzzanna, has died under complicated, violent circumstances: she was raped by several men while her newlywed husband (Barry Prima), a ship's captain, was away at sea. After discovering she is pregnant, Alisa despairs that her husband will no longer accept her or the child. Some later assume that she committed suicide, but it is shown fairly directly (although not stated) that she, in fact, dies while trying to give herself an abortion. After her death, Alisa turns into a sundel bolong, a legendary female ghost with a bloody hole in its back. Normally, the hole is covered by waist-length hair and is then suddenly displayed as a tactic to shock victims, who at first take her for a beautiful woman and not a vengeful ghost (fig. 30).

As with many other types of Southeast Asian female ghosts, women generally become a sundel bolong if they die from complications with childbirth, often also involving violence at the hands of men. Particularly in the latter case (and here it is both), a sundel bolong will use her supernatural powers to take revenge on her attackers. Accordingly, when the men who raped Alisa start turning up dead, the police appear to suspect that the causes are supernatural. That this conclusion is at odds with the official, rational perspective of Indonesian police is played up by the film for humor, while also mocking the conventional role of the kiai. After one of the men's deaths, which happens to have taken place in a graveyard, Alisa's husband, Hendarto, meets up with the police chief, the local village headman, and a kiai. The policeman—in spotless uniform, hat, and aviator glasses—approaches the village head with purposeful, official-looking strides:

> *Policeman:* Do you believe that a person's soul can arise from the dead and take revenge?
>
> *Hendarto (interrupting):* Is that what happened to Alisa?
>
> *Policeman:* Sorry, I didn't mean to talk about your wife like that.
>
> *Village head:* This incident is very confusing.
>
> *Kiai:* Unnatural deaths always bring mystery. Especially if they commit suicide. God hates people who commit suicide. We seek refuge with Allah from that.
>
> *Hendarto:* What do you mean?
>
> *Kiai:* We can't be upset. Only in Allah do we take refuge.

FIGURE 30. In *Sundelbolong*, Suzanna's direct look pierces the screen (*top*), connecting the diegesis to the world of spectators, while the hole in her back (*middle*) solicits and engulfs the modern within an "ancient" but expansive diegetic spiritual politics that is always playing underneath the visible and the national.

What is indeed mysterious is whose death they are even talking about: the clearly "unnatural" death of the man whose bloody corpse has just been carted off from the cemetery with a headstone piercing his torso or that of Alisa, whose ghost the policeman seems to suspect is the killer. The kiai might be suggesting that the man has committed suicide and that we should not mourn his death. He could also be hinting that he believes Alisa's death is a suicide and that this may have contributed to her becoming a sundel bolong. While the film performatively gives the appearance of doing its "duty" to insert not one but three official male perspectives on the matter (four if you count the husband), their conversation seems intended to confuse matters rather than to clarify, undermining the authority of the speakers. Part of the problem (and this is where it starts to become funny) is that the officials seem to be "aware" of their roles as authority figures caught between duty and the need to keep up appearances in front of the viewing public on the other side of the screen. They give the impression that they realize the diegetic scenario they are presenting to audiences is far from conforming to an idealized image of an ordered society and that they are using misdirection and their official status as "trustworthy men" to cover it up.

These self-aware attempts to misdirect are emphasized by the scene's formal structure: when the police chief apologizes to Alisa's husband for suggesting his wife is a ghost, he turns and looks directly into the camera, smiling, as if talking to the audience in the role of a friendly officer (fig. 31). Because his first statement to the village head seems much more direct and purposeful, it's almost as if he realizes he is being "watched" and then abruptly changes tack, obfuscating and hiding the supernatural reality from the public (and from Alisa's widower, who might be shocked or offended). Then, when the kiai gives his minispeech about Islam and suicide, during the last line, he, too, turns directly to the camera, while visually separated from the others in a medium close-up. At the end he pauses and smiles, again in a way that suggests he is addressing someone not in the present scene: viewers.[10] The scene then cuts to an informal discussion among a group of women familiar with the case, contrasting official with private speech. The women, facing each other instead of viewers, state very clearly: "Poor Alisa. Why did she become a sundel bolong?"

In the end, it becomes clear to everyone that Alisa has in fact become a sundel bolong. Like Ratu Kidul dealing with patriarchal thugs and government officials (although in that case notably without a kiai present whatsoever), she flies, shoots lasers from her eyes, and throws trees, making relatively quick work of the entire criminal gang who ruined her life. Hendarto, the police, and the kiai arrive just as she is finishing off the gang's leader, strangling him with a metal pipe she has bent with her bare hands. They plead with her to stop, and she loosens her grasp just long enough for the man to admit to his crimes against her in front of everyone and state that he was wrong (cut to reverse shot of police chief nodding

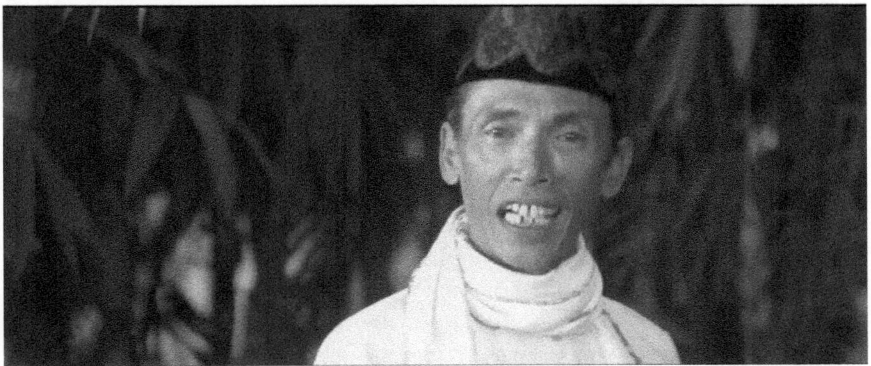

FIGURE 31. A friendly neighborhood policeman and *kiai* give official-sounding (but purposely confusing) "statements" looking directly into the camera, adding a layer of self-reflexive satire in *Sundelbolong*.

to kiai—okay, case closed). But when the man asks for her forgiveness, Alisa the sundel bolong tightens the pipe again and he falls dead. She then apologizes to Hendarto for killing everyone who "ruined our happiness."

He, in turn, pleads with her to go back to the spirit world where she will be at peace. With all the bad guys deceased and their guilt established, Alisa does not need to be forced to leave, something that appears in any case impossible. As she looks at her husband silently, the sounds of a woman crying are heard, although her mouth and face do not move. As if on cue, the kiai, police, and Hendarto raise their arms in prayer. The sundel bolong disappears and Alisa briefly materializes, floating in the air, before turning back into the ghost and then vanishing again. The prayers continue to be audible until the soundtrack brings back the adventure-esque orchestral score used for scenes where the ghost attacks, seeming to imply she could return at some point in the future—something that Hendarto, despite keeping up appearances for the authorities surrounding him, would seemingly enjoy. The familiar word *Sekian* appears on the screen.

THE DIVISIBLE FEMININE SIGNIFIER

As I read the film's ending, the kiai and police in this case did not need to set things back in order because Alisa, with her powers as a sundel bolong, has already done so. Rather than using Islam or the law as a force to control or expel her, the men simply follow her lead, praying for Alisa's safe return to the realm of the dead. The film's gender politics are thus not in line with the trope of a female supernatural disturbance controlled and brought to order by masculine authority, religious or otherwise. More important still, in contradistinction to masculinity, which appears mainly homogeneous in the film (although it can be "good" or "bad"), feminine power is divided into two parts, the active, vengeful, justice-doing sundel bolong and the amorous deceased wife who looks like her old self and rekindles her relationship with her husband (consummated in a love scene), cementing his partnership in her revenge plans. Even before she becomes a ghost, Alisa displays active and passive sides: when first cornered by her attackers, she shows strength and skill in martial arts, fighting off many of them successfully before being outnumbered. Like *Bangunnya Nyi Roro Kidul*, *Sundelbolong* implies that women need to be strong, since the police and court systems are ineffective in stopping or solving rampant crimes, especially by men against women. Indeed, after Alisa's rape, she takes the perpetrators to court, but things go awry when it comes to light that she is a former prostitute, a narrative twist that further implies a conservative, masculine bias in the expression of the law.

Alisa's background in sex work constitutes a further split in her otherwise upstanding character. The film does not present this in a negative light, however, displaying an attitude that I position as a further bridge between the outsider politics of ghosts and sex workers on screen, which together constitute "the most frequent construction[s] of the adult female protagonist outside the scope of monogamy and motherhood" (Sen 1994:144).[11] *Sundelbolong's* formulation of the "double" identity and authority of its female principal also builds on the earlier work of prostitution films—further clarifying, I propose, what those films were "really" getting at. Like them, *Sundelbolong* makes initial gestures in the direction of masculine sovereignty and dominance—a move that is soon outed as a narrative/stylistic feint that purposely misleads. In the end, solving the problems raised in the film will require not only direct "masculine" struggle but feminine interventions from the netherworld of spirits and the undead—acts that take things further in the direction of asserting a dualistic, plurally gendered symbolic order than was possible when prostitutes, with their more limited, mortal powers, were the central figures. Like the spaces of criminals and prostitutes, the sphere of spirits lies officially outside the boundaries of polite, modern society yet in reality is shown to interpenetrate and profoundly influence it. In this context, Alisa's death, while tragic, can also be seen as a cinematic convention that unlocks a potential for justice that cannot be found within the masculinized spheres of police, courts, and law.

Even here, however, the film allows no pure association of any space with masculinity or femininity—the judge who presides over Alisa's case, for example, is a woman, as is Alisa's former pimp, who is the mastermind of the plot against her. Men and women are given roles that alternately adhere to and challenge certain gender stereotypes. This includes the otherwise masculine, male gangster who participates in the attacks on Alisa and Hendarto but inexplicably always has his shoulder-length hair tied in pigtails with white ribbons—potentially marking him as a transgender waria who may also have transcendent powers. But in this case, I suggest that it is ultimately women, and the various shades of active or passive femininity, or at times masculinity, with which they are imbued, that cumulatively express a more viable agency in the elaborate world built by the film—one in which human, spiritual, diegetic, and actual realms are also blurred and closely linked. Viewers are arguably prompted to identify with all types of active characters (mortal and immortal, male and female, but especially women), positioning them, like the figures onscreen, somewhere on a shifting spectrum of possibilities.

In my analysis, despite their connection with spirit beliefs, ritual sites, and the underlying heterogeneity of state authority, films like *Sundelbolong* and *Bangunnya Nyi Roro Kidul* are not suggesting that ghosts will actually appear to reset the distribution of power whenever some overambitious man knocks it out of balance. They do suggest, however, that a certain, collective understanding of gender and agency exists in the public sphere—an understanding that some may relate to "backward," rural areas outside of modern cities but that cannot easily be banished by doubting urbanites. *Sundelbolong* hints at this as well, presenting city-dwelling characters who initially dismiss what they term "village superstition." But like the police and kiai, the characters don't seem to be able to bring themselves to completely discount the power of spirits (or women). Despite making a show of denying ghosts' veracity, when the acts of the sundel bolong can no longer be brushed off as a hoax, the city dwellers quickly enlist the help of a male *dukun* (shaman) to fight her, revealing their basic familiarity with, and belief in, the supernatural. By that point in the film, however, it comes as little surprise that the dukun's power pales in comparison to that of the sundel bolong, and he is quickly killed by the undead Alisa's vengeful manifestation.

What emerge as most powerful, then, are the supernatural forces that, while not foreign to all men, are more closely associated with a multifarious feminine agency—one that ghosts symbolize and underscore but are not, in fact, needed to enact in real life. In this sense, *Sundelbolong* and other films of its genre construct symbolic maps that function similarly to, and draw on the sociomaterial power of, those of ritual sites such as Parangkusumo (and other regional sites, about which more below). Both films and rituals place a heavier weighting on the importance of basic female signifiers over male ones, although the latter are not discounted; indeed, perhaps this is a response to constant pressure by state and societal actors to assert modern patriarchal values. But the ways in which such signifiers manifest or are presented continually works to complicate any equation that would point to a single, basic or "pure" signifier. In my analysis, this is an important reason that the queen or other feminine spirits and legends often display an ability to divide themselves into loosely phallic or *yonic* roles or aspects.

In the case of the queen and Parangkusumo, the site as a whole represents the "female" component of a larger, triangular symbolic structure that connects the South Sea to the "male" volcanic mountain, Merapi, to the north. The palace of the sultan/governor of Yogyakarta, one of the special human representatives the sites continue to authorize, is positioned between them at roughly equal distances from each. But in many narratives (and films), the queen also acts as a whole symbolic foundation in her own right (and Parangkusumo can be seen as a complete symbolic map in its own right, with seats for a man and a woman)—one that functions according to the broader male-female structure, while inflecting it with a more feminine aura. It does so, however, with the assumption, as in *Bangunnya* and in the Mataram dynasty's *Babad* history, that a masculine source of power will eventually enter the picture, imbuing it with a symbolic balance.

Conversely, in Gunung Kemukus, the above ritual site that was made into an official tourist destination by the New Order, pilgrims' performative mimicry of a legendary power couple is focused more closely on the identity of the male member, a rebellious fifteenth-century prince, *Pangeran* Samudro, whose tomb is located on a hilltop there.[12] In a related way, if we expand our category of supernatural films beyond those explicitly labeled horror, we will also find a loosely corresponding genre made up of *laga* (action) films in which male characters with extraordinary powers are generally the central figures. Similar to a ritual site like Kemukus, while readily identifiable as more typically masculine in their overall orientation (the heroes are usually shirtless, muscle-bound men of few words who are skilled in martial arts [fig. 32]), these films also invariably feature powerful female characters. Women are not the central focus yet are often shown to be as powerful as the male heroes and may defeat them repeatedly in fights. In *Si Buta Lawan Jaka Sembung* (*The Warrior and the Blind Swordsman*, dir. Dasri Yacob, 1983), for example, a gang of women under the leadership of a demigoddess named *Dewi* Magi (Sri Gudhi Sintara) offer continual challenges to the status of the male heroes. In fact, the men's lives are only spared in the end because *Dewi* Magi chooses to sacrifice herself. She and her gang are also shown to openly express sexual desire, often more so than the male characters.[13]

The most salient difference between the male-centric supernatural action films and the female-centric supernatural horror films appears to be that the former are normally set in the distant colonial or precolonial past. The latter almost always take place in the modern present.[14] The result is to frame magical or extramonotheistic

FIGURE 32. Poster for the 1983 supernatural action film *Si Buta Lawan Jaka Sembung* (*The Warrior and the Blind Swordsman*). Courtesy of KAFEIN.

spiritual power in men mainly as an "ancient" force associated with legends and mythologized colonial struggles in days of yore. In the bygone settings of these *film laga*, the use of magic by male and female actors alike (disappearing and reappearing, flying, shooting colored beams from limbs or eyes, etc.) does not raise eyebrows or cause shock as it does in modern settings, where such abilities are mainly associated with ghosts and horror. The heroic, magic fighting men in such films will also generally utter a few short phrases in Arabic now and then, establishing the presence of Islam as a component of their anticolonial struggles, but without worrying much over its contemporary status vis-à-vis enduring, pre-Islamic practices and beliefs.[15]

In comparing feminine supernatural horror to *film laga*, I contend that women in the former are positioned as better able to carry over magical, superhuman abilities and deploy them as disturbing, but ultimately much-needed, interventions in the present, especially during the New Order. As noted above, it appears that the somewhat heavier weighting on a dualist feminine power operative in the present is a calculated or reflexive response to the political makeup and needs of Indonesia under Soeharto. Films, like ritual sites, deftly juggle Islam, modern legal authority, prostitution, desire, legendary romance, and the potential for illicit or radical alliances between men and women, humans and ghosts, and at times partners of the same sex or gender. They assert that in most cases, it is a male partner who needs to be coaxed by a spirit to better understand and engage with the world as it "really" is. But the idea that things could be the other way around also continues to circulate in media and spiritual practice.

As in the films of the 1950s and 1960s analyzed in earlier chapters, the particular cinematic perspective that expands on the political economy of rituals is also contested along class lines. Especially in the case of 1980s supernatural horror and *film laga*, locally made films were frowned on as lowbrow embarrassments by elite critics (Imanjaya 2014; Sasono 2014). But like hybrid, and in some sense sordid, "Islamic" rituals that conjure Tantric and other "fragments" of the past through sex and prostitution, supernatural horror and action films were able to create strong economic bases that helped ensure the longevity of their messages. Two of the most iconic stars of these films, the above-mentioned Suzzanna and Barry Prima, were among the highest paid actors in Indonesian cinema at the time. The special effects used in many films, while not precisely in line with the global state of the art, were also often elaborate and visually impressive, as well as expensive. One might think of the imagery created with such effects (including hyperrealistic makeup and explosions, maggots crawling on rotting flesh, and flying heads and entrails, among others) as complex, cinematic "national icons" that connect and build on the similarly ubiquitous—and ambiguous, deconstructive—status of enduring figures like Ratu Kidul.

A REGIONAL PANTHEON OF NATIONAL-POLITICAL PHANTOMS AND SPIRIT DOUBLES

Indonesia is of course far from the only Southeast Asian country in which the transdiegetic, intermedial appearance of the supernatural is effective as a disruptor of modern conceptions such as absolute patriarchy and linear, future-oriented national time. Gazing at mythical-historical supernatural figures that transcend the space and time of the nation, audiences are also positioned to imagine connections across patchy bodies of *tanah air* (land-water) into other regional territories where similar politically, economically, and socially formative apparitions are known to appear. As Rosalind Galt argues, neighboring female spirits like the Malay *pontianak* have since at least the 1950s similarly thrown time "out of joint"

(2021:9) in ways that make nationalist elites uncomfortable or worse. As the various manifestations of the sundel bolong in the film *Sundelbolong* also begin to demonstrate, the experience of spiritual-cinematic disruption is eminently regional.

At certain moments in the narrative, Suzzana's character shifts her appearance in ways that gesture toward both a supernatural and a supranational pantheon. Her most common appearance is still the Indonesia-specific one that fits the general description of a sundel bolong: a deathly pale-faced, yet potentially attractive woman with dark circles around her eyes and long, black hair that covers (and can move to strategically reveal) a bloody, maggot-filled hole in her back. At other times, however, her head turns into a skull that detaches from her body and flies around with its entrails still attached and dragging below. In this form, she more closely resembles the Indonesian and Malay *penanggalan*, the Thai *phi krasue*, the Filipino *manananggal*, and the Cambodian *arb*. All of these are female (although the krasue has a male manifestation) and have heads that leave their lower bodies behind, flying around with guts, lungs, and/or spinal cords in tow (occasionally the organs take on the appearance of tentacles).

Each of these feminine phantoms attack by biting or sucking blood, other bodily fluids, or viscera, often targeting pregnant women and fetuses. A complexly feminist aspect similar to what is described above can also be seen to emerge from this group of characters. For Galt, their obsessive "baby-eating . . . promises to reverse ideas of proper womanhood" (Galt 2026:7). Such ghosts also take revenge or fight for the rights of women victimized by the overextension of patriarchal power and desire, which in most cases is directly or implicitly associated with narrow-minded nationalism. In several other scenes in *Sundelbolong*, the eponymous spirit also hides in the branches of trees above her victims' heads and lets out a high-pitched, demonic laugh that startles and terrifies. This associates her with the known tactics of the *kuntilanak* (Indonesia), *pontianak* (Malaysia), the Thai *phi mae maai* (including the famous *nang* Nak, about which more below) and the Filipino *tianak*: a further set of predatory feminine ghosts whose names resemble each other and whose similar manifestations are likewise triggered by deadly patriarchal violence, especially involving women who are pregnant—focusing on their unique powers of life-giving.

Following the general cultural guidelines attached to the kuntilanak, the pontianak, and related regional forms, one of the male victims in *Sundelbolong* also attempts to tame Alisa's manifestation by inserting a nail into her head (elsewhere it is often placed in the back of the neck). He claims this will turn her into a beautiful, human woman until the nail is removed again, repeating another typical aspect of this particular set of ghosts throughout the region (see, e.g., Galt 2021; Izharuddin 2020). In this case, however, the sundel bolong-cum-kuntilanak scares him so badly that he is unable to insert the (very phallic) nail, and when he tries to run away, he is killed. In scenes like this, *Sundelbolong* works by marshaling regional understandings and representations (cinematic and otherwise) of the supernatural and the spiritual. These are integrated into the film's deconstruction of the New Order's national political identity by reaching beyond imposed borders that do not contain or limit the identities of spirits. In light of films like *Bangunnya Nyi Roro Kidul, Sundelbolong,* and others, I argue that ghosts are positioned alternately as a subnational (Javanese, for example) or supranational (Southeast Asian) "resource" that can be called on to intervene when certain kinds of problems arise on local and national levels.

Galt (2026) sees the function of regional penanggalan-centered films in a similar way, arguing that they "do significant work in creating national cinematic identities," while bringing out "the ideological complexity of the local as a form of cultural meaning" (2–3). Galt's study focuses on a range of examples in which the appearance of penanggalan, krasue, or arb on the screen mark important supranational moments such as the end of the communist Khmer Rouge regime in Cambodia, while also reasserting more localized claims, such as a specifically Balinese identity in Indonesia. Penanggalan films may also intervene, Galt argues, in the national as such, as in movies that focus on the dominant ethnic discourses of Thai history. As we have seen, in their Indonesian evocation of the endurance of older, polytheistic or animist beliefs and practices, regional supernatural films also work to disrupt elite attempts at shoring up and claiming narrowly defined ethnic, national, and religious identities.

As Galt argues elsewhere, the wild popularity of the pontianak as a historically embedded, traditionally Malay onscreen figure also accorded her the status of a national icon, not unlike Ratu Kidul in Indonesia. But because of historical differences in the development of the two nations, the effect of this iconicity was reversed in Malaysia. In Malaysia, the pontianak became a more hotly contested figure, culturally claimed but officially disavowed by both Malaysia and Singapore as each sought to define themselves along racially divided lines toward the end of their joint cinematic golden age in the 1950s and early 1960s (Galt 2021:5). As we saw in chapter 3, the separation of Singapore from Malaysia in 1965 caused decades of cinematic "blindness" as both countries halted or severely reduced film production. Thereafter, the pontianak, whose films had helped to expand local cinemas during the golden age, was positioned as a cursed icon that had previously united and been claimed by both of the estranged neighbors now permanently separated by bitter ethnic divisions. Even when media industries began to recover, such was the negative cultural-political aura of the pontianak and other figures like her that the supernatural was almost completely absent from Malaysian and Singaporean screens until the early twenty-first century. Even now, without the unifying power of the pontianak and the expanded cinematic purview, audiences and industry she helped build in the past, Malay and Chinese-Singaporean cinemas have never quite been the same.

In Thailand, the intermedial and ritual spread of the legend of nang Nak Phra Khanong similarly transformed a *phi mae maai* (a Thai widow ghost most similar to the pontianak) into yet another complex national icon (Knee 2014:220)—one

FIGURE 33. Poster for the 1959 version of the Thai film *Mae Nak Phra Khanong*. Courtesy of the Thai Film Archive.

that has never been banned but that is also understood as a "murderous . . . yet . . . motherly goddess" and an empowering "female archetype" (Wong 2000:124, 129) in the face of Theravada Buddhist–infused Thai patriarchy. The narrative specific to nang Nak (sometimes called *mae* Nak or spelled Naak) is thought to have originated during the reign of King Rama IV (1851–68), although it has also been associated with the previous century (Wong 2000:125). Debuting as one of the first-ever Thai sound films in the 1930s (Guelden 1995:79), the story of *Nang Nak Phra Khanong*, often also called *Mae Nak Phra Khanong*, has been filmed more than twenty times, remade continuously through the 16 mm live-dubbed era (1940–70) and ushered into the streaming present (fig. 33).

Before becoming a film, *Nang Nak* was also performed as *likay*, the early twentieth-century Thai vernacular theater that most heavily influenced the style and form of postwar popular movies (see chapter 2). Similar to how Galt (2021) positions the pontianak in Malaya, then, *Nang Nak* (both as narrative and as ghostly figure) can be said to have played a fundamental role in the formulation of what was to become Thai "classical" cinema. The legend has also been adapted for radio and television and published in written form numerous times, including as a series of comics (Wong 2000:124). Mirroring the ritual sites dedicated to other iconic regional spirits, at the edge of the Wat Mahabute temple complex in Bangkok, on the site of what is believed to be Nak's grave, there is also a well-attended shrine to nang Nak. Pilgrims, including foreign and domestic tourists, pray there for success and luck, offering money, incense, flowers, and other compensation in return.

As in Parangkusumo and Gunung Kemukus in Java, the nang Nak shrine generates significant income for the local community and temple. For Ka F. Wong, the social, economic, and political activities surrounding the site are key factors in how Nak "has . . . transformed herself from a killing corpse to a revered 'deity'" (2000:127). Between the shrine and ongoing media adaptations (the latest of which is a Netflix series entitled *Nak* [dir. Nitivat Cholvanichsiri 2023]), Nak is arguably always both a "killing corpse," whose ever-immanent return, like the pontianak and others, is used by mothers to scare children, and an ancient goddess whose awakenings respond to and broaden the scope of local- and national-level debates and crises. Like the Hindu origins associated with Indonesian icon Ratu Kidul, for Wong, Nak as deity most closely "accords with Durga or Kali, whose sublime manifestations always come with a dark noisome side" (131). Nak is also frequently associated with *Mae* Posop, an ancient rice spirit similar to the Javanese Dewi Sri, and a serpentine fertility goddess known as a *naga*, or dragon (the word and goddess are generally the same in Indonesia and Malaysia), which Wong suggests may be the etymological root of the current moniker Nak/Naak (134).

In this capacity, Nak works to blend official Thai Theravada Buddhist religious practice with older belief systems that continue to circulate throughout the region, troubling the modern, patriarchal values attached to religion by the state. Like the narratives and ritual sites that commemorate Ratu Kidul and other deities and spirits, who are in turn further disseminated by films like *Sundelbolong*, the legend and worship of nang Nak Phra Khanong is also entangled with the idea of an originary "power couple"—the dual figures that I position as basic poles of a broader symbolic order encompassing different sexes, and potentially multiple genders, without excluding one or the other. In this case as well, more contemporary versions of the narrative show the female partner as the one who is better able to embody elements of either side.

Arnika Fuhrmann (2009) also highlights aspects of the nang Nak narrative that suggest an ability to grow, multiply, and intervene based on a formative partnership between ghost and human lover. At the end of most cinematic and other versions of *Nang Nak Phra Khanong*, a heroic and supernaturally gifted monk (the regional parallel, I argue, of the Indonesian kiai ex machina) finally subdues the ghostly Nak, and she agrees to halt her haunting of the village for good. Despite her seeming defeat, for Fuhrmann, the message impressed on Mak, her husband in life and death, and on viewers is not that of acquiescence to official Buddhist patriarchy. Instead, film versions' continual focus on the couple's longing glances conveys a woman's "protest against the ways in which trajectories of desire have been scripted for" her and others like her in nationalist-religious discourse (Fuhrmann 2009:241). As the final images and voice-over in the 1999 iteration make clear, Mak's experiences with Nak are something he will always carry with him, embedded by his undying love for his wife, even after she has died, become a ghost, and vanished into another realm. Through the transmortal agency of his wife, Mak has become a human "vessel" for Nak's spirit and subversive desires.

Because Nak is a deity and spiritual type, however, and not simply the ghost of a dead man's wife, I suggest that Mak's body and soul alone are implied to be insufficient as an archive for all that she represents. Like her real-life shrine grafted permanently onto a mainstream temple, filmic Nak must take on the more rigid and conservative Thai Buddhist institution represented by the powerful monk who subdued her. In a scene highly evocative of the taming of Indonesian and Malay pontianak by hammering a nail into the back of their neck, but with a different outcome, the monk ex machina's assistant uses a hammer and spike to remove a circular fragment from the skull of Nak's now-stilled corpse. Echoing other versions of the narrative where her ghost is trapped by the monk in a ceramic pot, the piece of skull is said to imprison or "contain" Nak. Yet the fragment is not destroyed or disposed of. Instead it is made into a talisman that is worn by the monk. Like Mak, he will carry her with him wherever he goes, becoming her more public vessel or medium of transmission.

For Wong, the skull talisman symbolizes that "Buddhism has recognized the goddess belief," which becomes "rooted in the collective psyche of the Thai people" (2000:135). In the end, Nak's self-sacrificing acquiescence to the demands of the monk deploys Thai Buddhism to do something that it is generally seen as frowning on: internalizing and reproducing a pre-Buddhist, premodern deity with an enduringly radical spiritual, economic, and political influence on modern national identity. Fuhrmann (2016) terms the pleasurable mode of human-spirit contemplation and yearning that makes this possible a subversive, vernacular "Buddhist sexual contemporaneity." It is a space that connects and accommodates beings from different places and times and is not unlike an archipelago, a database, or the "horizontal" convergence of old and new media that I have shown to occur throughout the region's cinematic history. In this case, Fuhrmann connects the term specifically to the conglomeration of media, religion, and spirit beliefs that arose in early twenty-first century Thailand. But I argue that it resonates with earlier periods in modern Thai history from which similarly disruptive versions of *Nang Nak Phra Khanong* and its illicit human-ghost connections emerged.[16]

Looking at the occurrence of this transsexual, -temporal, and -spiritual contemporaneity as not limited to the modern present would seem to better align with its politics of connecting disparate bodies, minds, and epistemologies. Doing so also links Buddhist sexual contemporaneity to other power couplings based on comparable narratives, sites, and practices in other locales throughout the region. As we have seen in numerous films and ritual examples so far, whether in the context of "vernacular, quotidian, and frequently . . . nondoctrinal" Thai Buddhism (Fuhrmann 2016:16), Malay or other animisms, Filipino Catholicisms, or Javanized Islam, different categories of beings are continually represented or embodied as radically, powerfully occupying the same space and time. This amalgam can include ghosts and humans but also possibly illicit male and female or queer couplings. In each context, the result is arguably to open "an idiom of counterfactual possibility" where "counternormative or as yet impossible desires" are willed into being (Fuhrmann 2016:13). To this I would add pre-, post-, or counternational desires and the caveat that whether having a relationship with a ghost is abnormal or "counterfactual" often depends on the specific details of an individual's or group's class and religious alliances (think, for example, of the sultan of Yogyakarta's eternal, culturally sanctioned relationship with Ratu Kidul).

Like other regional supernatural fare, as Thai ghost films bring older practices and spirits of the deceased to life, they often present official patriarchal values as deadly, especially for women. To frustrate the mortal force of masculine power, films thus "write complex plots for female death, desire, and the nature of collective sentiment in this realm" (Fuhrmann 2009:233). The repetition of such complex plots across films makes the deaths of women onscreen into a convention that, as I have noted in the case of Indonesian supernatural film, opens onto other spaces and times where the potential for justice is greater than under a national-patriarchal legal system. In avoiding "real" protections and at times embracing the end of human life, Fuhrmann suggests, supernatural films' interventions into the politics of spirituality and gender in Thailand often contravene more positivist-activist concepts and methods of transnational liberal and feminist thought—an idea that resonates with the messy, melodramatic radicalism of most supernatural horror films and with the complicated conditions under which places like Parangkusumo are run. For each, the conglomeration of economic, social, and spiritual attractions, transactions, and points of reference makes for multifarious experiences and potential interpretations. These include the inevitable, if rarely dominant, "male gaze" deployed by films in certain scenes; they also encompass pilgrims, like the man I described earlier, who seem mostly interested in hiring a prostitute.

Whatever drives attendees to such events, however, I have shown that they are subjected to a spiritual-ideological apparatus that centers on a female symbolic, sociosexual, political, and economic power around which other cultural, historical, and aesthetic fragments—including Tantric ones—revolve. Via her various human stand-ins, the plurally iconic and transdiegetic Ratu Kidul also shuttles between the positions of subject and object and masculine and feminine as she exchanges glances and knowledge with her devotees and potential lovers. On one hand, she demonstrates that one cannot always simply have what one wants and that desire will not be fulfilled as such. On the other hand, her words, acts, and looks impress on humans that they may grow through persistence in their respect and longing (including in the form of ritual worship) for something or someone that may offer what is almost as good: the ability to perceive time and agency—and overdetermined differences like gender—as less subject to the homogenizing limits and conventions traditionally imposed by modernist national patriarchies. I argue that the enduring allure of this skill, and the political perspective embedded in it, is what most profoundly connects the region's feminine cinematic icons.

CANNY REGIONAL GHOSTS, ENDURING ARCHIPELAGIC CINEMAS

I will conclude this chapter by circling back to where I began, returning to the Philippines and to the idea of a dual symbolic order. Filipino cineaste Lambreto Avellana is responsible for what appears to be the region's first supernatural horror film, the 1926 *Manananggal*, titled after the vampiric female spirit of the same name. Like elsewhere in the region, but on a slightly different timeline, a now familiar, enduring pattern of mass media–driven threats to the sanctity of nationalist modernity quickly ensued. This includes not only countless films, but, as Bliss Cua Lim reports (2009), viscera-sucking manananggal that leapt from the ostensibly fictional worlds of screens, literature, and legends to appear in Filipino newspapers in the 1990s. Even more than in the movies, for Lim, the appearance of ghosts in such a modern and ostensibly fact-based medium positioned the phantoms on par with other typical news items like elections, government pronouncements, or power outages (2009:120). The collective sense of "current events" that are otherwise understood (especially when presented via newspapers or television news) to occur simultaneously along the regularized, chronological flow of modern national time was therefore subjected to spectral disruptions emanating from the regional past (Lim 2009:142).

Within the very same mass medium that Benedict Anderson (1983) positioned as the basis of Southeast Asian nations as "imagined communities" experienced in chronological, calendrical "homogeneous empty time," readers were instead confronted with an "unwieldy, occult splitting of the national time, a *heterogeneous meanwhile*" (Lim 2009:126, emphasis in original)—a time-space that I argue recalls Fuhrmann's Buddhist contemporaneity, as well as other related regional concepts. Outside the Philippines, since at least the 1950s, pontianak and *punakawan* (ambiguously gendered servant-gods from the annals of Javanese *wayang*) have also made regular appearances in the pages of weekly and daily national news (see Galt 2021:236; and Hermanu 2010:198). Yet for Lim, even when they are faithfully disturbing national chronologies, variously mediatized (and mostly female) Filipino ghosts are too often positioned in a pattern of push-and-pull between a feminized heterogeneous/spiritual time and a homogeneous national time that Lim sees as masculine. It is not just the occasional entrance of a particular gaze but the medium itself that she conceives as male. This carries the potential to undermine the radical force of heterogeneous time through a nostalgic "fascination with 'old-fashioned' femininity, compensating for the breach of homogeneous time by idealizing patriarchal gender roles" (2009:181–82). The result, Lim argues, is an imbalance in which feminine disturbances are inevitably translated into the dominant masculine frameworks of chronology, simultaneity, and presentness.

For Lim, the basic regularity of clocks, the numbered pages of newspapers and books, and filmic or digital frames into which cinematic movement and time must be divided create an inexorable technical/formal base. Through it, otherwise "immiscible" or unassimilable times, genders, and the figures associated with them flash up, imposing a "glimpse of heterogeneity" (147), only to disappear again at intervals set by masculine chronology. While such figures and times are undeniably "there," they are also, Lim argues, repressed in a manner similar to Freud's understanding of the uncanny: a set of temporally and epistemically dissonant or "primitive" tendencies or "superstitions" that have been "completely and finally" left behind by the rise of modern thinking (110). The implication is that when such fantastic, supernatural elements do appear in the homogeneous flow of the contemporary, if they should *fail* to disappear again, their prolonged presence as real and now signals not only a temporary disruption but a visual-cognitive disorder on the level of psychosis—an inability, among other things, to distinguish what is generally accepted as reality from mere fantasy.

As Lim and others show, there are myriad specific instances of such homogenizing temporal translation and modern, national sublation that occur in the Philippines and within the borders of other Southeast Asian countries. Yet I suggest that if we look at these supernatural, supranational disturbances in *regional* perspective and include the present as part of a historical trajectory encompassing the last several centuries, something else potentially comes to light. We might begin to connect and assemble the heterogeneous dots, moments, and glimpses into something larger, more enduring, and more meaningful—something that overflows and complicates national processes of homogeneous patriarchal translation. Doing so brings what is understood as outside of national, modern, and (masculine) symbolic orders back into an actual public time and space that intersects with and exists in the nation but is not simply suppressed by its chronology or future orientation; it effectively holds the nation "open." As we have repeatedly seen, for example, Southeast Asian supernatural films, along with other media and rituals, work to normalize a view and epistemology that continually perforates and gestures beyond national borders while including, and deploying in the present, supposedly "archaic" symbolic bases for masculine and feminine power.

Constantly repeated across these ubiquitous media and practices, such disruptions to the limited, official time and space of the nation arguably exceed mere glimpses of heterogeneity. When this happens, if the masculine side is often presented as more finite, focused, and perhaps also material, and the feminine is generally more flexible and able to split into or encompass different forms, genders, and times, there may indeed be a sense in which the feminine symbolic functions as an engulfing and potentially threatening or "castrating" force, as it is in psychoanalysis. Yet as I have shown, in myriad Southeast Asian media, rituals, and even official structures of power, the ostensibly monstrous feminine is paired with and understood not as limiting or destroying but as expanding and potentially *empowering* the masculine in a collaborative spirit—while at times pushing or forcing a reticent masculinity to open itself to such possibilities. The feminine is therefore rarely excluded from the symbolic order tout court; it is understood as coterminous and contemporaneous with the masculine.

As Fuhrmann and others insist, filmic and other ghosts venture outside the masculine symbolic as a platform from which to extend desire and reopen time. Positioned as an apparatus of masculine or modern translation, film and other modern ideological mechanisms, including religion, are thus precisely interpreted as tools of feminine agency, drawing viewers into a "heterogeneous meanwhile" more fully outside the symbolic order in its limited, masculine iteration—into a place where feminine "objects" think and act in unexpected ways. Similar tasks are accomplished by the cinematic specters of the queen of the South Sea and other vengeful ghostly paramours around the region. If, on film, such spirits are also necessarily subjected to the endless, regular mechanical progression of frames that produces cinematic time (and I submit that the outcome of this translation is itself up for debate), this is much less clearly the case with the shrines and ritual sites (and openly hidden sections of artist galleries) where pilgrims mimic legendary acts of love between ghosts and humans. For Gottowik, these acts of mimesis constitute "a process of active appropriation and embodiment" in which "the body believes in what it plays at . . . [and] it *enacts* the past, bringing it back to life" (Gottowik 2018:394–95). These rituals and the narratives surrounding them are deeply embedded in contemporary concepts of statecraft and iconographies of national power that obtain around the rituals. This means that the temporal, philosophical, and even geographical sanctity or purity of nations is continually deconstructed even as it is constantly being rebuilt.

Drawing on the various regional examples and analyses in this chapter, I argue that rather than a one-way process of modernization or cinematization, rituals, legends, and associated beliefs function as enduring archipelagic-symbolic bases for both Southeast Asian nations and their supernatural icons, filmic and otherwise. This is not to say that a phallic/masculine symbolic order is simply engulfed or completely overcome. Clearly this is not the case. If the perpetuation of globally circulating masculine, homogeneous time is also inevitable, I propose that films and other media like legends, historiographies, and rituals built around female deities or associated power couples function as tacit forms of ideological training—practices that shape understandings of modern authority as opened to a dualistic, or archipelagically fragmented, symbolic order, to which pilgrims and viewers become reaccustomed.

I propose that the supernatural horror genre, along with most of its prominent screen-piercing, transdiegetic feminine spirits and deities, can be understood to have gradually asserted itself as a key—perhaps, indeed, the most crucial—component of what I have called archipelagic cinemas. Like islands arranged in a body of water, Ratu Kidul, nang Nak, the pontianak, the manananggal, and many others compose a set of distinct ideological loci—and apparatuses of archipelagic epistemologies—that shift and morph and leap between media and times but also share and convey certain basic qualities and lessons. Although they are specific, material icons and believed to manifest in human forms, at the same time (or at different times that converge with the present), they circulate like water in the ocean. As such they alternately separate (as national icons) and join together (as regional spirits) distinct yet related cultural, political, and economic centers. These more permanent geopolitical forms—islands, nations, and subnational regions— are continually shaped by the spiritual-epistemic undercurrents produced by these symbolic agents.

Transcending the limitations of speech and acts carried out by marginalized prostitutes in earlier films, female spirits who are generally understood as *both* subversive *and* national icons communicate in a related but different way: from deep within the heterogeneous tangle of discourses and statecrafts that lies beneath the surface of Southeast Asian countries, tying them together as a region. While nations are still the dominant frames for experience and identity in the contemporary world, it is frequently these networked icons and the epistemological perspectives they produce that act as translators of modern "homogeneous empty time" rather than the other way around. Despite, and in some sense because of, the inexorable continuity of evils associated with modern nationhood, they have proved very difficult to silence.

6

Reclaiming Affect

Freedom, Reform, and Many Historical Returns

In 2016, thirty-six-year-old Indonesian director Anggy Umbara's film *Warkop DKI Reborn: Jangkrik Boss! Part 1* (*Warkop DKI Reborn: Crickets Boss! Part 1*) broke the previous domestic box-office record, set in 2008 by *Laskar Pelangi* (*Rainbow Warriors*, dir. Riri Riza). *Warkop DKI Reborn* attracted 6,858,616 viewers to local movie theaters. As increasing numbers signal, the cinematic past appeared to be fading quickly. Indonesia's film industry was steadily "going mainstream" (Barker 2019) following the fall of President Soeharto in 1998 and the institution of regular elections, term limits, and other important democratic reforms. Further evidence of the Indonesian film industry's mainstreaming was one of the first blockbusters of the post–New Order reform, or *reformasi*, era, *Ada Apa Dengan Cinta?* (*What's Up with Love?*, dir. Soedjarwo, 2002), a teen romance that closely followed a classical Hollywood style. The film's spatial and temporal continuity and narrative clarity arguably set it apart from most works made during the Soekarno and Soeharto eras, attracting enthusiastic viewers from various socioeconomic classes and appearing to draw a stark, stylistic line of demarcation in the development of local and regional cinemas.

Yet as I have shown elsewhere (Yngvesson 2015), the film collectively positioned as the touchstone of the post-Soeharto, Indonesian new wave, the independent and collectively written, directed, and produced *Kuldesak* (*Cul-de-sac*, dir. Nan Achnas, Mira Lesmana, Rizal Mantovani, and Riri Riza, 1998) showed a very different attitude toward the past—one steeped in recognizable tropes of violence, horror, and theatricality. Half of the film's four producer-directors were women, foreshadowing radical shifts to come in the gender of those behind Indonesian cameras. This situation also built, I argue, on the long-standing emphasis on matrifocality, plural symbolic authority, and gender-parity with which I have characterized regional cinemas in previous chapters. Yet despite the progress behind the scenes, in the eyes and hands of *Kuldesak*'s young makers, repetition of darker aspects of Indonesia's history, in which cinema was entangled with personal greed and political corruption, appeared almost inescapable. As Barker also acknowledges, even before the release of *Ada Apa Dengan Cinta?*, other, cheaper, seedier waves were afoot—trends that in my analysis reflected the "dead ends" performatively encountered by *Kuldesak*.

Throughout the 1990s, a combination of government and audience neglect and an upsurge in the popularity of television created a major downturn in Jakarta's film production. Among other things, to go mainstream in the early 2000s therefore meant reestablishing, in many ways from the ground up, a viable industry that could regularly produce and exhibit films. Cheaply made versions of horror movies, the production of which had never quite halted even as budgets plummeted in the 1990s, returned to cinemas almost immediately after the fall of Soeharto. While production values were a far cry from the glory days of the 1970s and 1980s, the continuity of ghosts and demons onscreen, especially many of the female ones highlighted in the last chapter, accounted for approximately one third of the films produced from 1998 to 2010 (Barker 2019:83). Partially propelling and also driven by the new wave, the surge of "lowbrow" horror movies helped generate the funds and minimal levels of viewership that kept the industry running and allowed budding filmmakers room to grow and begin to experiment with other genres and techniques.

Building on these developments, in this concluding chapter, I position the 2016 release of *Warkop DKI Reborn* as an important step in the rise of a different, and more regionally uniform, cinematic "mainstream": one defined by genuine newness yet shot through with the return of certain key conventions and themes, now geared to engage the transpacific waves of democratization and neoliberalism that swept over much of Southeast Asia during and after the Asian Financial Crisis in 1997–98. In Indonesia, the onset of reformasi was often taken as an unprecedented, new, "blank" democratic space in which the problems of the past could be examined, as if from a distance, in an ostensibly more open, direct, and safer manner. But I argue that by the early 2010s, the familiar twists and dead ends that arose again in the post–New Order era became increasingly hard to ignore. As it became clearer that many of these problems were in fact triggered or amplified by the fall of Soeharto and the complex and often unexpected "freedoms" that followed, past and present once again began to converge in the minds, and on the screens, of Indonesians.

One worrisome development that became more radically visible and audible after 2010 was the rising tide of religious conservatism, which mirrors similar, if often quieter, trends elsewhere in the region. But at least as troubling are the parallel ways in which the shadowy forces of supranational, neoliberal corporations operating beneath the surface of democratization steadily shifted landscapes of power, experience, and public symbolism (like rapidly expanding mini-markets and their homogeneous graphic conventions) to their own advantage. These changes became entangled with the gradual, postcrisis development and redefinition of national and regional film industries. Religious conservatism, for example, influenced the emergence of new genres and the return of old ones, while neoliberal economic policies helped drive a sharp increase in the number of screens and in the attendance of middle-class youth, who frequented the spate of fancy, new mall-based multiplexes. What is likely the most crucial (and very much ongoing) development is the nascent yet dominant influence of transnational streaming services that have driven the rise of a new, globalized cinematic mainstream complete with production funds, broad distribution, and, for the moment at least, little or no censorship combined with openness to myriad styles, genres, and conventions.

As in the past, once film industries had recovered from the initial shock of economic crisis and regime change, national and regional aesthetic conventions asserted themselves as powerful receptors and translators for new and foreign ideas, technologies, and trends. As I will show, many of these conventions began to mirror basic historical modes of representation. For example, in response to successive new waves of transnational economic, religious, political, and aesthetic influence after 1998, I argue that Indonesian cineastes and audiences made one of the most important, pervasive historical *returns* of the post-Soeharto era (see below)—a move that mirrors earlier developments in Thailand and roughly parallels those elsewhere in the region. Doing so, however, did not cause a sense of stasis in the industry. Instead, it reinvigorated local cinema (in terms of both audience and critical interest), especially in the genre of supernatural horror, where young filmmakers brought back not only a key female spirit but the "ghost" of the iconic actress known for playing her.

In line with earlier waves and eras in regional cinema, however, the past is not simply imported as was but is selectively appropriated and adapted. In this case, I contend that regional cinematic history returned to engage with two key side effects of democratization and the entrance of new media and digitally networked societies: the rise of religious conservatism and the postmodern "waning of affect" associated with mediatized emotional connections and the perceived dissipation of authentic human experience. This was accomplished, as I will show, by retooling the fragmented symbolic orders and gender politics of older regional films— aspects that I have argued foster "horizontal" connections and convergences of disparate forms and technologies in ways that anticipate the databases and webs of contemporary communication. Whether consciously or not, in the cases I highlight below filmmakers sought out these "modern" historical aspects of Southeast Asian media by going even further back to their origins in live performance. The process of return, however, was indirect and often driven by exasperation or even disgust.

ALL ROADS LEAD TO VERNACULAR THEATERS

In my own experiences talking to both critics and filmmakers in Jakarta a decade after the onset of reformasi, the unending glut of cheaply made horror films often led to a sense of discouragement with the possibilities that the new, "mainstream" industry was capable of generating in the early 2000s. Despite the tantalizing success and smooth, global-cinematic style of films like *Ada Apa Dengan Cinta?*, the market outside of horror was also beset by quirky, raucous comedies shot on emergent high-definition video formats such as the prosumer Panasonic HVX200 camera. Young critics, film scholars, and many filmmakers I spoke with still felt these works failed to live up to the expectations built around processes of national and regional reforms and democratization.

In 2012 and 2013, I conducted several months of research at Sinematek, the privately funded national film archive located in Kuningan, Jakarta. During the 1990s and early 2000s, its employees had endeavored to make their significant collection of historical films more accessible to the public by transferring them to video. But owing to a broad lack of interest and funding at the time, the transfers were mainly done by projecting old movies on a white wall or small, collapsible screen and recording them with an analog video camera. The result was major cropping—often to the point that, when actors were positioned on either side of an original widescreen frame, the square ratio of the transfer imposed in the middle would only reveal the tips of their noses. The prints themselves were frequently not in the best condition, giving an impression that was starkly different from what past viewers experienced watching prints of the films in theaters. Worse still were the pirated videos of classic movies sold in low-resolution VCD (video compact disc) format in shops around Jakarta and other major cities. For contemporary audiences, shifting media formats made older Indonesian films appear cheap and lacking in technical standards instead of them being a rich source of history, entertainment, and potential aesthetic inspiration for aspiring filmmakers. Lack of funding and of better, more affordable means of storage and display meant that Indonesian cinematic history was trapped in a "past" defined by new technologies that were unable to fully contain or express it.

Like elite critics before them, young cineastes now sought to distance themselves from the abject, "low" aesthetics associated with local and regional film histories. After a series of conversations I had in 2012 and 2013 with Sinar Ayu Massie, a thirty-something Jakarta screenwriter, she tellingly handed me a copy of senior film critic J. B. Kristanto's *Nonton Film, Nonton Indonesia* (*Watching Films, Watching Indonesia*, 2004), a compilation of his reviews from the previous thirty years. Within the first few pages, Kristanto repeats a claim he made in the 1980s that "almost ninety-five percent of our films are bad" (2004:4). While in the past such an attitude could be chalked up to the broad, class-based split between elite viewers and critics and the mainly working-class audiences for locally produced films around the region, it was jarring to see how little seemed to have changed so many decades later.

But the early 2000s were also a time of rapid technological change, and outside of film archives (and at times surreptitiously within them), celluloid copies of older films were beginning to be transferred to high-definition video formats at their original aspect ratios. Soon, television stations began playing these better copies of older films to a slowly increasing viewership. At the same time, as mentioned above, the rapid construction of new malls in urban areas increased the number of multiplex screens. A melodramatic, Islam-themed genre that soon became known as *film Islami* began attracting larger numbers of middle-class youth to theaters around 2008. The emergent category and its overt religious and underlying economic themes connected especially well with the steady rise in outward displays of piety among such youth (Weng 2017). The result was at least thirty, usually very successful, religion-centered films over the next decade (Barker 2019:111). By 2016, the film Islami genre and its corresponding youth trends had become well-established, bankable patterns with easily discernible effects on the landscapes of leisure time and what were now becoming more recognizably smooth, glitzy "mainstream" film aesthetics, especially in Indonesia. Developing alongside film Islami in the early years were self-consciously lowbrow, niche viewers who sought out illicit, pirated VCD copies of the mystical horror films of the 1980s and early 1990s. These also began to be shown on television, at first in similarly degraded form.

Combined with the nascent appearance of higher-quality, older films on television, these shifts collectively created a perfect storm that by 2016 had opened a "hole" wide enough for *Warkop DKI Reborn* to stage a proper return to an older set of values, aesthetic forms, and techniques. Doing so, I argue, constituted both a calculated, nostalgic repackaging of a past cinematic success and, more important for my analysis, a disruptive response to what local popular cinema had become—especially in the popularity of film Islami. *Warkop DKI Reborn* was a hit, breaking all previous records (including those of film Islami) by envisioning a more diverse audience that engulfed the heavily middle-class, postreformasi cinematic mainstream and hipster cultists alike in a flood of "bad" old aesthetics. When rendered in high definition, as it turned out, these conventions and tricks appealed to young, outwardly more pious teens in search of something new and perhaps more fun and subversive. Mirroring the golden ages of the 1970s and 1980s, the rebirth of these aesthetics again functioned to touch off what I suggest will be seen in retrospect as a postreformasi golden age.

To do so, *Warkop DKI Reborn* looked backward in time toward a particular target: the common set of theatrical, interactive aesthetic tendencies most deeply embedded in the history of Indonesia's and the region's mass media.

"Warkop DKI" is the name of a theatrical comedy troupe that began performing on radio in the 1970s, quickly moving to sold-out, touring stage shows and then to movies and later television in the 1980s and 1990s. Their path from stages to screens at the time, while especially celebrated, was far from unique. It reflected what I argue was a second wave of entanglement between filmmaking and interactive, deconstructive, and improvisational theatrical forms, beginning in the 1970s. As we saw in chapter 2, the popularity of unscripted regional vernacular theaters like stambul and bangsawan left indelible marks on the audiences, producers, and economies of local films, creating aesthetic circuits that formally, spatially, and economically separated local movies from major global players like Hollywood.

Even as the popularity of these older theaters waned in the 1950s, many troupes continued to tour, and new variations began to emerge, driving the second wave of improvisational, audience-interactive groups in the 1970s. Among the leaders of this movement was the Surakarta-based Srimulat (named after one of the founding actresses, Raden Ayu Srimulat), which began performing in the early 1950s and continued touring, appearing on radio and then television, and selling cassettes of their routines throughout the 1960s, 1970s, and 1980s and then again on television from 1995 to 2003. At the height of their popularity in the 1970s and 1980s, instead of just touring, Srimulat opened franchise troupes that performed similar material under the same name in other cities (Siegel 1986:90–92). For senior Indonesian critic J. B. Kristanto, popular movies of the time were pushed to become a "continuation" and intermedial translation of the tropes and approaches of Srimulat and other related live forms, as filmmakers deployed "the [theatrically based] idioms that most speak to our society and are alive in it" (Kristanto 2004:6). Like spectators of older vernacular theaters, viewers of Srimulat did not seek to distance themselves from the stories and acts unfolding onstage in the way that audiences for classical Western theater expected. As James Siegel puts it, "the spectator of Sri Mulat feels that he must answer what he hears, that the language of the performance is not [formally] closed off from his own language; he does not have *immunity*" (1986:111, emphasis added).

Perhaps because they performed almost exclusively in Javanese, Srimulat did not branch out into films, which at the time were generally in Indonesian, the national language.[1] Yet several other stage-based troupes began to combine similar styles (drawing, like Srimulat, on enduring Java-based vernacular theaters like *ketoprak, ludruk,* or *lenong*) with dialogue in Indonesian, opening the door for them to redefine cinematic comedy in the 1970s, 1980s, and 1990s. One such troupe was the Surabaya-based Surya Group (fig. 34), which collaborated with director Nya Abbas Akup (see chapter 1), often called the "father of Indonesian comedy," on some of his most iconic films.[2] Among numerous others, these included the *Inem Pelayan Sexy* trilogy (*Inem, the Sexy Maid*, 1976–78), a riotous send-up of New Order ideals and discourses of gender, class, and power. It was

FIGURE 34. Promotional still for the live comedy troupe Surya Group, who also played in many of writer-director Nya Abbas Akup's subversive comedy films. Photo taken in the 1970s and gifted to the author by the family of Pak Herry Koko.

into this aesthetic-economic atmosphere that the original Warkop DKI (sometimes known as Warkop Prambors) emerged in the late 1970s. After building a significant following on radio and stages, the three-man troupe produced and starred in an impressive thirty-five feature films between 1980 and 1995.[3] These were most often made up of separate comedic vignettes like the ones performed onstage but tied together with a loose narrative structure. This formula made most of their films into major hits, positioning Warkop among the most influential cinematic stage troupes of all time.

Like regional vernacular theaters and films in the 1950s and 1960s before them, Warkop, Surya Group, and other stage-comedy players such as Benjamin Sueb, who came to cinema in the 1970s, were always already engaged with global and regional circulations. Audiences expected them to humorously puncture the sanctity of the national with the foreign, the emergent, the regional, and the subnational. In the last instance, the Javanese origins of most troupes implicitly underscored the prominence of Java and Javanese people and styles in Indonesia. Yet the mission of such troupes was to satirize and deconstruct everything, including themselves, so at the same time that they traded on and spread Javanese hegemony, they worked to bring out the absurdity of everything Javanese, hence deflating, to some extent, Java's position in Indonesia.

GHOSTS, HOLES, AND *SOTO* REBORN

By explicitly resurrecting the Warkop troupe in 2016, *Warkop DKI Reborn* returns to the regional history of intermedial, stage-screen convergence and to the deconstructive, self-reflexive approaches to cinema and globalization it popularized from the 1950s to the 1990s. In doing so, *Warkop DKI Reborn* refers especially to the earlier Warkop movie *CHIPS* (dir. Iksan Lahardi, 1983), which satirizes the hit U.S. motorcycle-cop TV series *CHiPs* (NBC, 1978–83), poking fun at the absurdly gleaming, heroic masculinity of the American show. At the same time, *CHIPS* characteristically lampoons itself while suggestively highlighting the foibles of the less-polished and often equally bumbling actual Indonesian police (fig. 35). In both the "original" CHIPS and in *Warkop DKI Reborn*, however, the characters are presented as a private security force that only look like police, avoiding the perception of directly targeting actual officials. Doing so would almost certainly result in heavy censorship or bans.

As I will show, the explicit return of vernacular theaters with the rebirth of Warkop in 2016 was important not only because it followed earlier patterns of "backward" convergences between older and newer media. The film's fragmented, archipelagic style was premised on literally opening a hole in its onscreen diegetic world—one that would symbolically (and actually) usher other, even more impactful, elements of the past into the postreformasi present. It was not simply the Warkop characters who emerged as if reborn through this temporal portal; a number of other screen icons from the 1970s and 1980s made hilarious and haunting returns. Most crucial, I argue, was the reappearance of one particular *sundel bolong*, the female ghost with the bloody hole in her back discussed in chapter 5. Perhaps unsurprisingly, it was the one played by the actress Suzzanna in the 1981 hit *Sundelbolong*.

The way she is introduced into *Warkop DKI Reborn*'s modern, postreformasi, comedy-drama diegesis is also telling. Her entrance occurs in part 2, which was released the following year in 2017 and continues the narrative of the first installment. Dono, Kasino, and Indro Warkop, now played by established contemporary stars Abimana Aryasatya, Vino J. Bastian, and Tora Sudiro respectively, have been falsely accused of destroying and burning a fancy Jakarta gallery and the expensive artworks within. Following a series of strange occurrences as they scramble to try to clear their names, the troop finds themselves in Malaysia, where they team up with a woman named Nadia (Nur Fazura).

Chased and caught by a strange transnational criminal gang led by a flying man in a dragonfly (or perhaps a cricket) costume (Babe Cabiita), the reborn Warkop team is told they will be frozen with a special machine that turns people

FIGURE 35. Poster for *Warkop DKI Reborn*, which emphasizes the names of the original Warkop troupe members, played by famous contemporary actors whose names are listed below in smaller type. The film is also loosely based on the original Warkop film *CHIPS*, which sends up the American TV show *CHiPs*. Courtesy of KAFEIN.

into iconic, life-size, relief-style painting-sculptures. Like its theatrical and cinematic predecessors, the film imagines itself in a heterogeneous regional dimension combining Indonesia and Malaysia, which is also humorously shot through with transnational elements. Once frozen as icons, Dono, Kasino, and Indro will join the likes of Elvis, Bob Marley, Michael Jackson, Bruce Lee, and Marylin Monroe, whose motionless bodies already hang on the walls of the gang's lair. Legendary Indonesian figures whose films were, at the time of their release, generally not known or distributed internationally, are winkingly placed on par with major international stars. Riffing on this theme, as the young Indro is about to be transformed into a painting, he is confronted with the older version of himself (played by Indro Warkop, the only surviving original member) climbing out of a TV screen, looking like a portly Rambo with a machine gun. While this mocks Sylvester Stallone's eponymous character from the U.S. *Rambo* franchise, the most important result is that the introduction of the porous television opens a visible hole in the onscreen space of *Warkop DKI Reborn*.

As the bad guys look on in confusion, the Warkop trio, now a quartet with their senior member, escape back into the TV set along with their Malaysian accomplice, Nadia. It is not just old Indro who has been "living" there, however; the TV is home to ghosts and media phantoms from disparate eras. As the group ventures through the various channels, they encounter a number of famous characters who appear to be living inside their old movies. To realize this idea technically, *Warkop DKI Reborn* takes advantage of then-recent transfers of numerous classic Indonesian films to high definition—actual rebirths into the digital present. Scenes are taken from these films, against which the new Warkop crew is placed in reverse shots with matching backgrounds. This makes it seem as if they are facing the classic characters they encounter within the same, heterogeneous media time-space created by "opening" the outdated TV in the digital present. A comedy of errors ensues as Dono, Kasino, the two Indros, and Nadia attempt to communicate with the old characters, whose responses are limited to the lines they spoke in the past. Each change of the TV's channel lands them in a different classic scene.

When the crew suddenly finds themselves in a darkened setting facing a cart selling *sate* (barbecued skewers of meat) and *soto* (a local variety of soup), Kasino innocently quips that they "must have landed in a cooking show." Since the group hasn't eaten in some time, the setup seems ideal, except for the spooky, nondiegetic music, which the characters are also able to hear. As they are about to dig in, the older Indro has a premonition: "don't eat that meat, it belongs to *sun—*" Just then, a woman in white robes with long black hair appears in front of the cart with her back to the camera and issues a one-word command: "sate." Although startled, Dono, Kasino, and Indro are quickly taken in by the woman's beauty and begin arguing over who will serve her, while she repeats her order: "sate." Reverse shots composed of digitized celluloid reveal to the audience that she is the sundel bolong played by Suzanna in 1981, which many would likely have recognized from the opening seconds of the scene. Using the smoothly matched and intercut shots from the older film, Suzanna's ghost is shown rapidly devouring three skewers at once in single bites, continuing until the cart's stock of satay is finished, much to the amazement and dismay of her old and modern onlookers.

"By the way," asks the junior Indro flirtatiously, "what's your name?" The answer, "soto," at first confuses them, until they realize that that will be the woman's response to any further questions. Still seemingly unaware that she is a dangerous monster, they decide to have some fun at her expense. "Name an Italian food," offers Kasino. When the sundel bolong answers "soto" in the same, flat, expressionless tone, they laugh uproariously and begin competing to come up with the most far-flung juxtapositions: "Thomas Alva Edison invented . . . soto; America attacked Hiroshima and Nagasaki by dropping . . . soto; the best contraceptive is . . . soto." Each answer brings even more laughter from the young Warkoppers. When quizzed about the birthplace of Indonesia's then-current president, however, the once-touted political outsider and democratic reformist Joko "Jokowi" Widodo, the otherwise automaton phantom facing the expanded Warkop gang suddenly breaks from her classic script and answers correctly: "Solo" (which conveniently sounds a lot like *soto* and hence smoothly synchronizes with the lip movements of the sundel bolong from 1981).

As the questioners' laughter abruptly stops, Suzzanna's sundel bolong helps herself to a huge pot of boiling soto, which she easily lifts and drains, this time casting a sinister glance in the men's direction in answer to their calls for her to leave some for them. The scene then cuts to the original *Sundelbolong*'s reveal of the soto's broth pouring out from the bloody, maggot-filled hole in the ghost's back as she drinks. Among the TV's spectral movie-residents, it is only Suzzanna's sundel bolong who appears to be able to break out of the looping, diegetic-historical confines of her New Order golden age hit. Like the Warkop characters, she has come to life again in the digital present. But unlike them, she has done so without changing her iconic appearance: she returns, I suggest, not as sundel bolong per se but also as a manifestation of Suzzanna, the queen of supernatural horror, who died in 2008.

Always already an agent of convergence and heterogeneous time, Suzzanna's posthumous reentrance led (or perhaps possessed) *Warkop DKI Reborn*'s director, Anggy Umbara, to create a series of films in which a ghostly, reanimated version of "Suzzanna" is the central figure. I argue that Suzzanna's rebirth, and the trend of higher-budget 1980s-style supernatural horror that it contributed to, was a key, if largely unacknowledged, turning point in Indonesia cinema—one that mirrored similar shifts around the region in the years after the Asian Financial Crisis but, in this case, eventually led to a Guinness world record for the "most horror-focused film industry" in 2023 (Guiness World Records 2023). As I will show, Suzzanna's reentrance coincided with the emergence of a new, but typically backward-looking, approach to the alienating political economic and aesthetic regimes of neoliberal democratization and digital postmodernity.

THE NEOLIBERAL POWER COUPLE

The flood of remakes of 1980s horror that followed Suzanna's return in *Warkop DKI Reborn*, continuing until the present, made room for further experimentation with theatrical-interactive and mediatized spiritual pasts, transforming sundel bolong, *phi krasue, manananggal*, and other regional phantoms into a deceptively new kind of transnational representative. Because of their increasing presence on mainstream global streaming services like Amazon Prime, Disney Hotstar, and Netflix, these spirits would become far more difficult for international audiences and critics to dismiss as "cult" fare with supposedly small (albeit global) niche audiences as they had in the past.[4]

If the post–New Order reawakenings and the digital spread of sundel bolong and other female spirits could at some level have been predicted or "expected" owing to the endurance of structural-ideological mechanisms like syncretic, animist-inspired rituals that support them, the same could be said for the shadowy owner of PT Indomarco Prismatama and dozens of other influential companies shaping contemporary life in Indonesia in countless areas. The huge, related increases in homogeneous, corporate mini-markets can be seen as a symptom of contemporary global patterns—patterns with which I argue rituals and supernatural horror engage in particular ways. Like films and rituals, however, the roots of PT Indomarco's "globalization" of Indonesian business landscapes connect to a much deeper and more localized history and rebirth: that of the Salim Group.

The umbrella for these ventures, known as the Salim Group, was founded in 1972 by Liem Sioe Liong, a Chinese-Indonesian businessman who changed his name to Sudono Salim, and who has been called "Suharto's most important business pillar" (Borsuk and Chng 2014:xii). The post–New Order rebirth of both the Salim Group and sundel bolong signals the strength and adaptability of deeply embedded structures of feeling and of economic, political, and symbolic modes of power, the origins of which precede modernity as such but have come to define it in important ways throughout the region. Owing to the lengthy reign of the New Order, it is perhaps especially inevitable that many of the key players and figures, both onscreen and behind the scenes of governance, would resurface following the fall of the ostensible center, Soeharto.

Recalling how successive rulers of the Javanese Mataram dynasty are framed as part of an enduring "power couple" with the enabling (and potentially disabling) figure of Ratu Kidul, the spirit queen of the South Sea, historians Richard Borsuk and Nancy Chng refer to President Soeharto's relationship with Liem Sioe Liong as that of "a Javanese 'king' and his *cukong*" (2014:1).[5] The latter term typically refers to a wealthy patron (more recently specifying an "outsider" of Chinese descent) who sees benefit in funding the political or creative activities of someone with potential to succeed in order to extend the influence of the *cukong* beyond the realm of finance. The term is frequently applied to wealthy patrons of the arts, including those who provided funding for films in the 1950s and beyond (Biran 2008). When Soeharto forcibly inserted himself in the center of Indonesian politics in 1965–66, he, too, needed a "cukong." He became president of a "country that was both broken and broke" (Borsuk and Chng 2014:xii), having been torn by two major conflicts: the war for independence against the Dutch (1945–49) and the then-recent execution of up to a million Indonesians by the military under Soeharto's own command. Money was needed to sustain and expand both the government's and Soeharto's personal power, and Liem, who had first befriended Soeharto two decades earlier during the nationalist revolution, "stepped up to the plate whenever he was called on, and was able to deliver" (Borsuk and Chng 2014:xii).

Despite Soeharto's cozy relationship with the U.S., and despite the Americans' knowledge of his role in the mass killings and coup against Soekarno, Indonesia's second president was described by the U.S. embassy as a "devious, slow-moving, mystical Javanese" (Borsuk and Chng 2014:7). To become the more dynamic figure later known as "a contradictory mixture of modernizer, single-minded military officer" (Borsuk and Chng 2014:7) and Javanese neomonarch, Soeharto needed a partner who understood his self-positioning better than foreigners, and whose networks of influence extended far beyond the seats of Indonesian political power, snaking around and beneath them. He needed an almost spectral figure who could surreptitiously engage and manipulate the "invisible" hands of the economy to the advantage of the government. The critical role ascribed to the queen of the South Sea of controlling nature and the unseen forces of "spirits" can be read, among other things, as a metaphor for just such a partner, one from whose enabling embrace a leader may never fully extricate him- or herself.

While no spiritual marriage was to occur between Soeharto and Liem, their intimate collaborations and political economic codependency made them "like brothers" (Borsuk and Chng 2014:xiii). This cleared the path for Liem's Salim Group to quickly grow into an early Southeast Asian multinational conglomerate, spreading its tentacles and roots elsewhere in the region and beyond. By the mid 1980s, the Salim Group had influential members such as Soeharto's cousin Sudwikatmono, a film importer-exporter who also founded the dominant Cinema 21 chain of theaters in the 1980s. The group also had at least fifty-four companies under its umbrella, doing business in a number of different areas (Dieleman, 2007:51). Indosiar, one of the first private television networks in Indonesia, was also launched under the Salim Group in 1995 (Sen and Hill 2000:113). As he expanded his businesses, Liem shrewdly lessened the group's direct dependence on the government, while remaining in the inner circle of Soeharto and his powerful family. When Soeharto stepped down in 1998 during the Asian Financial Crisis, the Salim Group similarly experienced a fall, incurring huge debts due to the unexpected currency devaluation caused by the Crisis. With their Jakarta homes under attack during violent clashes between antigovernment demonstrators and police, Liem and his family fled to Singapore to ensure their own safety.

When the dust of regime change cleared, the new democratic government "came under enormous public pressure to dismantle the companies that were previously cronies of Suharto" (Dieleman 2011:213). Shrewdly, Liem's son Anthony, who had been given charge of Indonesian operations, quickly arranged for the effective nationalization of 107 Salim companies, earning praise from former critics. While this also meant additional massive losses for the group, as Marleen Dieleman argues, with two hundred thousand employees, it was simply "too large to fall" (2011:214). Certain other crony businesses of the New Order were decimated during the onset of reformasi. But along with many of Soeharto's children (none of whom he had allowed to directly enter politics), the Salim Group and some of their allies were able to quietly return to their seats of economic power. Because of the crisis and nationalizations, but also because of its successful strategizing and managing of the political economic transition, the group emerged a leaner entity that, according to Dieleman, was "on its way to fully implement[ing] a more market-oriented and less relationship-focused corporate strategy" (2011:214).

Because of its enduring strength and resources—and its ability to restructure itself "democratically"—successive presidents have remained intimately, if somewhat differently, connected to the Salim Group. Its corporate tentacles have continued to stretch across and beyond the seas that connect and surround Indonesia's archipelagic *tanah air* (land water). This kind of relationship is in line with global patterns of neoliberalization that, as a combination of discourse and practice, made especially rapid gains in the region after the "creative destruction" of the Asian Financial Crisis. As David Harvey puts it, "the role of the state" would now be "to create and preserve an institutional framework . . . to guarantee . . . the quality and integrity of money" (2007:2). The ability to do so is linked to the institution of democracy, through which the Indonesian government would now prepare the playing field for private entities like the Salim Group (including newer ones) to take a greater role in national development, while making a show, at least, of less direct interference than in the past. Yet given the Salim Group's and other corporate interests' hand in helping to fund and run the country during the New Order and before, this process would provide a sense of continuity under the surface of reform and change—an endurance of certain historical patterns that would become definitive of Indonesian and regional development in the twenty-first century.

The Salim Group itself has, since its inception in the early 1970s, perhaps wisely remained reticent about speaking to the media or otherwise placing itself in the public eye. Yet the logos of its various businesses, such as the ubiquitous Maspion factories or Indomaret mini-markets, of which there are now around twenty thousand outlets, are literally impossible to miss. Read in connection to the Salim Group rather than as individual entities, these ubiquitous visuals signal rapid shifts in the nation's symbolic and physical landscapes. Yet they testify to the endurance of an understanding of political economic control as divided across a network of visible and concealed actors, even if the latter are hidden in plain sight. The equally rapid spread of Islamic conservatism in the post-Soeharto era appears to reestablish, along religious lines, the New Order principle of singular patriarchal authority. But as during the New Order, this view also ignores or pointedly obscures what is plainly visible if one cares to look: the repeated inability of masculine, Islamic leaders to fully take the reins of the nation or stamp out the myriad, thriving beliefs and practices that for religious conservatives are blasphemous or worse.[6]

In this context, I contend that the rapid return and digital spread of New Order–style supernatural horror in the second and third decades of the twenty-first century makes sense as aesthetic, narrative iterations of the political and structural similarities (and embedded structures of feeling) that connect dictatorial regimes to democratic ones. In familiar and at times critical ways, the return of classic, iconic female ghosts restates the fact of an underlying dualistic symbolic order—one ideally composed of a "power couple" that divides authority among visible, material mortals and shadowy, shifting spiritual-economic actors that not everyone can, or wants to, see. In light of her reanimation and penetrating entrance into the present mediascape via *Warkop DKI Reborn,* I argue that Suzzanna was then positioned to symbolize an "authentic" regional strategy of engagement with the contemporary aesthetic, economic, and religious flows that intersect with Indonesia and other Southeast Asian nations. Having now seemingly inherited the status of supranational icon from the ghostly characters she portrayed, Suzzanna embodies the specific, symbolic continuities that connect the region and its nations to their collective pasts. Such links reveal particular modes of engagement with local democratizations in the context of global neoliberalism and, as we will see below, with the postmodern "waning of affect."

Because she was an actress who wielded significant creative influence and who was also a production company owner in the 1970s, at a time when far fewer women made behind-the-scenes decisions, Suzzanna's life and career helped to pioneer important aspects of the cinematic present—particularly the steady increase in women producers, directors, and writers. These aspects imbue her current status as an icon with a more complex aura. As I will show, Suzzanna's ghostly return resonates emotionally, politically, and economically and "clicks" not only with viewers facing local theatrical screens but also, as discussed in a recent documentary about her, as a particular kind of representative of Indonesia's varied and archipelagic aesthetic history.[7] This function extends to the transnational streaming networks to which many of the old and new films centering on her iconic status have been added and to which diverse local and global media are ever more connected.

As I noted above, the success of *Warkop DKI Reborn* was closely followed by a spate of remakes of New Order horror films, which included director Umbara's theatrical and streaming hits in which an actress effectively plays Suzzanna playing the sundel bolong. The first one, *Suzzanna: Bernafas Dalam Kubur* (*Suzzanna: Buried Alive*, dir. Rocky Suraya and Anggy Umbara, 2018) confronts contemporary, mainstream audiences with a transdiegetic hall of mirrors that, like *Warkop DKI Reborn* before it, brings a historically lowbrow genre to more diverse groups of viewers. In challenging or disregarding the borders between diegetic and actual worlds, *Bernafas Dalam Kubur* also works to provoke and strip audiences of any "immunity"—to use Siegel's term for the interactivity common to local comedy theaters—vis-à-vis the fictional and real political and symbolic orders reaching out at spectators from the screen.

Beginning from its title (which directly translates to "Breathing in the Grave"), the film combines ideas and words from two of Suzzanna's best-known films: *Beranak Dalam Kubur*, one of the earliest New Order "horror" films that is also a gruesome thriller, and the smash *Bernafas Dalam Lumpur*, in which she played a politically marginalized woman who falls into prostitution (see chapter 4). The narrative of the 2018 *Bernafas Dalam Kubur* loosely follows the 1981 *Sundelbolong*, the first film in which Suzzanna played the eponymous female ghost with the hole in her back. To further blur past and present and fiction and reality, the name of the central female in Umbara's version is Suzzanna. She is played by Luna Maya,

FIGURE 36. Luna Maya as the "new" Suzzanna, positioned in front of paintings of herself and also of the deceased actress Suzzanna, whom she is effectively playing.

an actress, singer, and public figure who, like Suzzanna Martha Frederika van Osch (Suzzanna's full name, sometimes also spelled with only one *z*), is of mixed European and Javanese descent.

On the fateful night when Luna Maya's Suzzanna, who has recently found out she is pregnant, will be killed and turned into a sundel bolong, she is shown attending a *layar tancep* (mobile cinema) screening in the commons of the village where she and her husband, Satria (Herjunot Ali), live. The movie being projected at the diegetic screening is *Telaga Angker* (*Haunted Lake*, dir. Sisworo Gautama Putra, 1984), the second film in which Suzzanna van Osch played a sundel bolong. In other scenes, paintings of both Suzzannas are displayed prominently on the walls of the main characters' house, positioned as if looking at each other or at times staring out at viewers. Building on this ghostly iconic-mimetic play of gazes, during the mobile cinema screening of *Telaga Angker*, audiences are confronted with the "new" Suzzanna fearfully watching her doppelganger turned into a sundel bolong on a movie screen, just before she herself is killed during an attempted robbery and likewise becomes one. It really begins to seem that, as I contended above, *Warkop DKI Reborn* has "released" Suzzanna back into the contemporary, porous cinematic atmosphere where she now runs *amok* in the visually and corporeally transformed figure of another actress (fig. 36).

As this also shows, in the onscreen world where a woman attacked by men turns into a powerful, vengeful ghost, people also watch "fictional" accounts of the same thing. Implicitly, then, the audience watching the 2018 film is likewise not immune from such terror (or the potential for justice it represents). They are part of a reality where hauntings are seen to take place—like the characters in front of them, viewers also watch "fictional" female spirits onscreen yet live in a contemporary world where the same spirits actually exist, are claimed by political figures, and are regularly engaged with and honored through rituals. *Bernafas Dalam Kubur* is set in 1989, the year after Suzzanna van Osch's final sundel bolong film, *Malam Satu Suro (Javanese/Islamic New Year's Eve*, dir. Sisworo Gautama Putra) and not in the present. Yet while it brings back numerous narrative, formal, and stylistic flourishes typical of 1980s supernatural fare, I argue that it is also a response to the conditions under which Indonesian audiences found themselves living in 2018.

Gone, for example, are the typical male representatives of ideal New Order authority like police or *kiai* (Islamic leaders). At the same time, however, there are many more scenes of people praying together in mosques, including a long sequence of Suzzanna and her husband, Satria, completing their *shalat subuh* (dawn prayers) toward the beginning of the film. In my reading, these images reflect the far greater emphasis on public displays of piety in post-Soeharto Indonesia, where such displays are no longer officially frowned on. This includes an exponential rise in Muslim women of all generations choosing to wear *hijabs*. While the film does not reimagine the 1980s as characterized by such clear, outward displays of piety, it appears to try to "make up for" this with its frequent scenes in the mosque. Perhaps producers were also reluctant to feature a typical 1980s setup where a kiai faces off with a powerful ghost in the current religious climate (as I show below, a similar scene in a 2017 remake of another classic horror film created a controversy). In this case, *Suzzanna: Bernafas Dalam Kubur* only shows that chanting prayers and verses from the Qur'an bothers the sundel bolong, causing her to cover her ears and scream. Most of her actual battles, however, take place with ordinary people wielding ineffective physical weapons. She is also, mirroring a trope in 1980s horror, faced with a *dukun* (shaman), who deploys spells and incantations in Javanese to at least slightly better effect.

Despite these gestures to the shifts in contemporary religious expression, however, *Suzzanna: Bernafas Dalam Kubur* strategically opens up perceptions of the present, revealing its continuing cross-pollination with older beliefs, ideas, and practices. In doing so, the film implicitly questions the authenticity of contemporary forms and increasingly vivid expressions of piety, perhaps especially targeting trends of demonstrating that one is limiting one's beliefs to a single group, discourse, or source of power. The film does so, in my analysis, using the "good old" tactics of elongating desire, melancholically yet pleasurably stretching romantic longing into a bridge between the spheres of humans and spirits (and audiences and films and nation and region; see chapter 5 for historical variants). The present context of the film's release also offers more fertile ground than in the past for undermining a stable, collectively verifiable sense of good and evil, especially in the construction of character identities.

The original *Sundelbolong*'s basic plot of a newly pregnant woman being killed while her husband is away for several days for work is repeated here, although Satria is in this case the manager of a small factory in a rural area and not a ship's captain. He is in some sense a protagonist, yet this role is destabilized by the fact of the film's formative conflict, which arises from the resentment of poor workers to whom Satria denies a raise. Sympathy is frequently implied for the struggles of such laborers, reflecting poorly on the lavish lifestyle of the boss and his wife. At the same time, the workers' turn to robbery owing to Satria's lack of empathy—resulting in Suzzanna's accidental killing—is presented in negative terms. The conflict with ostensibly clearer sources of evil (and with the presence of clearer, if often ineffective, representatives of state authority) that characterized supernatural films produced under Soeharto's dictatorship is thus shifted. I propose that this shift reflects changes in the postreformasi era in which presidents and other officials are chosen in un- or less-rigged elections. Yet the same politicians abdicate more power to vast, supranational financial networks run by unelected heads of corporations. Causality is therefore muddied to some extent.

As an elite factory employee, but not an untouchable owner, Satria is less of a wealthy agent than a stand-in for members of the growing, more visibly pious, post-Soeharto middle class. As such, he is in some ways treated as an "object" that has uncritically internalized a certain kind of economic thinking and morality that especially benefits those above him. This implies he is in need of true enlightenment, which, of course, will not occur through prayer, religious study, or labor protest but rather at the hands of his wife, the new Suzzanna, once she becomes a sundel bolong. At first, however, the nice, but hardheaded, and deeply religiously and economically indoctrinated, Satria is a difficult and unwilling pupil. Once he realizes he has been tricked—Suzzanna, who has in fact been killed, is now a ghost who is only posing as his mortal wife—he becomes angry, accusing her of dishonesty and violating religious principles. Gesturing furiously at Luna Maya's sundel bolong while repeatedly screaming "you are not Suzzanna," he produces a moment of high drama and, perhaps in this instance at least, unintentional metahumor. Yet by the end, circumstances have turned the tables, and the rebellious workers who killed his wife have used his rigid convictions to trick and manipulate him. He sits blindfolded, metaphorically and actually, in front of the sundel bolong, who has been subdued, pontianak-like, with a spike (in this case a ceremonial *keris* [dagger]) inserted into her head.

It therefore falls on Suzzanna to use the emotional connection he still clearly feels with her to lift Satria's "veil" and open his eyes to the tangled reality at the root of their problems. His unsympathetic treatment of those under his command has caused them to attack and ruin his family and home. The only thing that can possibly save him now is a power and love that has been cast out from his religion and is contained in the blasphemous sundel bolong, who has become the vessel for his murdered wife's soul. It is to her, and no longer to his shadowy, unseen boss—the owner of Satria's and likely numerous other factories—that he must shift his allegiances. At the last minute, Satria follows his heart, although this will not offer him a shining path of redemption. Joining his former wife in battle, he ends up killing one of the workers as the sundel bolong takes on the remaining two and the shaman, after which Satria declares his undying love for the ghost of Suzzanna—indicating he has been indoctrinated into her heterodox, undead spirituality.

Now that her revenge and ideological "work" is done, however, some things must still follow the rules of 1980s horror, and Luna Maya's Suzzanna dutifully utters lines mirroring those of the ghosts played by her doppelganger in the past: "I love you. Our worlds are different. I have to go." As she disappears, he clutches her white robe with the hole in its back, now empty and spattered with the bodily fluids of many victims. Their blood and hers, the film implies, are ultimately on the hands of the old, simplistic, pious Satria: a protagonist who is not a hero, whose unthinking exploitation has driven workers to violence. Appropriately, as he touches his own back, he finds a matching hole, inflicted by the knife of the worker he fought and killed. He sinks to the ground beside the robe, after which we are shown a funeral where two fresh graves are being covered with flowers while neighbors tearfully pray, chanting in Arabic. In a strangely happy, melancholic, and romantic ending sequence, the ghosts of Satria and Suzanna are shown wandering the village together at night, holding hands and enjoying each other's company. Presumably, with their murderers also dead, they will now guard their neighbors against the various complex contemporary forms of evil instead of sowing chaos or taking further revenge.

The film's implicit juxtapositions of the slippery, democratized present with the authoritarian past underscore that even though things have changed and perhaps taken a step "forward," an older understanding of the nature of power is more crucial than ever. This is especially the case in light of the fragmentation of life and agency following reformasi and the institution of neoliberal democracy, where the market, with its ethereal "invisible hands," "serves as an ethic in itself, capable of acting as a guide to all human action" (Paul Treanor, quoted in Harvey 2007:3). Yet in Indonesia, where neoliberalism, like previous global ideas and practices, is also often understood to have been hybridized, we see a continuation of familiar patronage networks such as those established during the New Order and before. Rather than functioning in opposition to market forces and the ethics they produce, however, they are "mutually reinforcing," according to Edward Aspinall, "at least in the effects that they generate for Indonesian political life" (2013:29). For Aspinall, following the fall of Soeharto, the established webs of patronage have themselves fragmented, yet also expanded, as a result of the exit of the "supreme patriarch" (31). Along with the emphasis on "pure" economics and at least the "performance of competition" (30), culturally and historically determined partnerships between patrons and their "clients" have defined the political economic landscape of the early twenty-first century. These clients sell political allegiance in exchange for the funds to carry out lucrative *proyek* (projects) of various sorts.

As Aspinall shows, such patronage, expanded through atomization, effectively "*enables* oligarchy" but, at the same time, potentiates a "greater scope for individual agency" (2013:51, emphasis in original). Patrons, he argues, and especially their "clients," who are now often actors at much lower, more informal levels of society than in the past, have more choices in front of them, as long as they can see and calculate the continuing importance of these political economic "power couples" (my term). *Bernafas Dalam Kubur* appears to concur. In a similar vein, it asserts that both "good" and "bad" mortals act with the help of murky partners who emerge from the networks that envelop and drive the machinations of society and its political economies. Like ghosts, entities such as the Salim Group have consistently sought to remain in the shadows even while successive Indonesian presidents are "married" to their influence and bound by allegedly democratic oaths to support them. But anyone who cares to look knows that they exist. In this context, the reemergence of iconic spirits like Suzzanna's sundel bolong across the screens of multiplexes and phones and televisions signals the divided, heterogeneous nature of both modern democratic time and of the "old" dualistic symbolic order—of "patronage" defined as a partnership between disparate actors who are often human and spectral, or both—that I argue continues to influence Indonesia and the region.

It is necessary, these specters imply, to consciously engage with forces outside of and surrounding the chimeras of modern religious beliefs and simplified concepts of individual agency as accomplished mainly through the performance of democratic elections. History constantly changes but often does so in regionally specific loops: iconic, archipelagic spirit-partners whose appearances also sold movie tickets and helped drive a golden age of local cinema in the 1970s and 1980s (and elsewhere in the region at different times) began returning in huge numbers because they made a new but related kind of sense in the mid-2010s. In the post-Soeharto era, they also sold tickets and collected views and likes while carrying on their mission as unseen political advisers—figures that imply the pervasive presence of others like them who may be far less well-intentioned. As they continue to do so in 2024, the previously ultraclean, democratic outsider president Joko Widodo—once thought of as the humble "hero" that would finally realize the ideals of Indonesia's reformasi—appears to have been the latest recipient of whispers from an unseen source or sources. He has taken a sudden, dynastic turn and now gives the impression that he is using the considerable influence he amassed during his years in public service—and various other questionable means—to ensure his young, inexperienced son will be the next to enter Indonesia's highest office. The onscreen ghosts appearing in ever greater, world-record-breaking numbers thus appear to have an important message and mission regarding the potential return of a "supreme patriarch."

THE THAI NEW WAVE, THE POSTMODERN, AND THE RECLAMATION OF AFFECT

While the particular political restructurings assembled around the Asian Financial Crisis of 1997–1998 differ throughout the region, the "networked" rise of democratic reform and powerful transnational corporations (and increasingly neoliberal understandings of political economic power) was a key issue taken up across many of the emergent, Southeast Asian cinematic "new waves." In Thailand, for example, a 1997 Crisis-related reworking of the national constitution was heralded as the most democratic version yet. IMF and World Bank strategies appeared poised to allow international investors and guarantors to take control of national finance via restructuring plans aimed at combating what was labeled, in familiar terms, a problem of "crony capitalism" that had led to the crash. The gist of the reforms and liberalization strategies was that "Thai capitalism was to be made more like Western capitalism" (Hewison 2005:311). The changes were largely approved by neoliberal, Western-aligned Prime Minister Chuan Leekpai, who came to power the same year as the crisis in 1997. A "short political honeymoon" (Hewison 2005:315) resulted, with initial support from the local business community.

But domestic financial leaders increasingly felt excluded from the deal, and as the economy continued its downward slide despite reforms, anger spread in Thailand against the new government, which was seen as complicit with Western financiers. The latter were perceived (mainly correctly) as seeking to create opportunities for themselves while ineffectively "saving" Thailand. As Rachel Harrison argues, the "distinct shift in Thai opinion vis-à-vis the West" quickly became inspiration for an emergent "new wave" of Thai filmmakers who addressed the shifts "with a certain humour, irony and rich social comment . . . open to the cultural complexities of the moment" (2006:328). Most of these emergent directors who began turning out feature films in 1997 had come from advertising, where they had honed their skills to an extent that separated them from new wave filmmakers elsewhere in the region.

Both technical-aesthetic prowess and humorous social commentary are demonstrated in a commercial directed in 1998 by Wisit Sasanatieng, one of the emergent commercial directors-cum-new wave filmmakers (Thevoideck 2010). Sasanatieng was also the screenwriter for *Antapan Krong Muang* (*Daeng Birley and the Young Gangsters*, dir. Nonzee Nimbutr, 1997).[8] Along with *Fun Bar Karaoke* (dir. Pen Ek Ratanaruang, 1997), *Antapan Krong Muang* is considered one of the first offerings of the Thai new wave. In Sasanatieng's advertisement, a Thai boxer (Chartchai Ngamsan) gets into the ring with an American opponent at a crowded match in what appears to be Bangkok. When the bell rings, before the American can even throw a punch, the Thai contestant delivers a kick to the side of his head that sends the American's mouth guard flying and knocks him out. The local crowd appears both jubilant and aghast, staring after the young boxer, who trots casually out of the ring. The "kicker" comes just afterward, however, as the piece is revealed to be an ad for Wrangler jeans, finishing on a close-up of the Thai boxer's gleaming, satirically winking smile with the classically American cowboy–associated logo (spelled in cursive with a "rope" font that recalls a lasso) superimposed to his left.

The commercial was reportedly also a trial run for the look and lead actor Wisit planned for his upcoming feature *Fa Thalai Jone* (*Tears of the Black Tiger*, 2000) (Thevoideck 2010), another new wave classic that parodies the western/cowboy genre. *Fa Thalai Jone*, like the advertisement and Nonzee's *Antapan Krong Muang*, is set in the 1950s. Not coincidentally, all three look back to the era during which Thailand first came under the influence of the U.S., taking spectators "on a dizzying visual journey down Cold War memory lane" (Harrison 2024:337). Among other things, this "hard nostalgic" tour was positioned as a historically informed engagement with the present state of affairs leading up to and during the Asian Financial Crisis. Despite its status as an advertisement for an American company, the Wrangler piece showcases the new wave's emergent "pitch black humor" (Knee 2003:102), boldly juxtaposing the more dynamic and effective appearance of Thai kickboxing with American boxing (which forbids the use of kicks). In a contest with the West, it implies, Thailand would prevail by doing things its own way. According to Harrison, the early features of the Thai new wave similarly delivered a kick to the international film world, especially in the West. Both *Antapan Krong Muang* and *Fun Bar Karaoke* were also celebrated outside of Thailand in major film festivals, with the latter showing in Berlin. The former played in London to a "packed and rapturous audience at the epicentre" of England's film world (Harrison 2006:323). This touched off a trend in global travels and appreciation for Thai films that for Harrison functioned to showcase "amazing Thailand"—with avant-garde, yet slick, commercial aesthetics comparable to national campaigns to promote tourism—to the rest of the world. Both works also signaled what would be a pattern of young Thai filmmakers exploring the country's political and cinematic pasts (about which more below).

Perhaps not surprisingly, political currents appeared to be running in parallel to cinematic ones. Only a year later, in 1998, the Thai Rak Thai ("Thais Love Thais") Party was founded by Thaksin Shinawatra, a local mogul and former high-ranking police officer, its moniker implicitly opposing itself to the idea that the then-current Thai premiere was in bed with foreigners. Seeing the potential for domestic capital to make a comeback, Thai business leaders quickly got behind the party, which attracted nonelites with the idea of a "social contract" that would financially support regular Thais and help them fund small businesses. A landslide electoral victory soon landed Thaksin as the new prime minister of Thailand in 2001, as he publicly positioned the managed development approaches of Singapore and Malaysia as models for Thailand, emphasizing domestically and regionally focused political economic strategies over Western ones (Hewison 2005:320).

While not doing so in exactly the same ways as Indonesia, Thailand, too, came up with a modified neoliberal reform plan that allowed "domestic capital . . . to seize the state" (Hewison 2005:312) while explicitly pledging support for the less fortunate in society. This led to a second landslide victory in 2005. Yet Thaksin, who Kevin Hewison argues was ultimately the leader of a "government by and for the rich," (320), was soon taking increasingly authoritarian steps to protect himself and ensure the success of various policies, some of which were controversial even with supporters. Thaksin was also accused of massive corruption for helping himself and his businesses to billions of untaxed dollars, and, recalling similar events in previous decades (see chapter 4), he was ousted by popular protests and a military coup in 2006. Although Thaksin fled Thailand in self-imposed exile, his wife, Yingluck, served as prime minister from 2011 to 2014, and his daughter, Paetongtarn Shinawatra, is the current leader, elected in 2024.

It was in this context that the first new wave of young filmmakers like Nonzee, Ratanaruang, and Wisit Sasanatieng began to grapple with the storm of radical changes beginning in 1997. They were followed by slightly younger and still-more-independent-minded filmmakers like Apichatpong Weerasethakul and Anocha Suwichakornpong, who were inspired and emboldened by the first new wave, especially in terms of the paths they opened at global festivals. As was the case in Indonesia, Thailand had gone through a decade of severely reduced cinema production beginning in the late 1980s, and upstarts like Nonzee were bent on revitalizing both the local industry and its typical aesthetic approaches and flourishes, which they saw as outdated. Like their Indonesian counterparts Garin Nugroho (whose interventions began in the early 1990s, making him a sort of founding new wave father figure), Riri Riza, Nan Achnas, Mira Lesmana, and Rizal Mantovani,[9] they did so primarily by looking *back* in time. Earlier trends in lowbrow Thai and regional popular cinemas from the 1950s through the 1970s were mined as the main sources for aesthetic renewal, forming a similar basic set of features through which contemporary, globally circulating trends and ideas could also be interpreted and repositioned.[10]

In some ways anticipating later shifts in Indonesia around 2016, young Bangkok cineastes reframed these older conventions as a new, "higher-quality" cinema aimed to attract larger, more diverse audiences and be appreciated by local elites rather than being looked down on as anachronistic. Many films succeeded in gaining traction on the global festival circuit, which heralded them—with Weerasethakul eventually at the forefront—as part of a new movement in Asian and non-Western art and "slow" cinemas. This has since become a steady trend and multilayered opportunity for emerging Southeast Asian filmmakers who have gained exposure, appreciation, guidance, and, perhaps most crucially, funding, from festivals and related organizations in Europe, Asia and at times the U.S. In line with the arguments of this chapter, the biggest early hit of the Thai new wave was the 1999 *Nang Nak* (dir. Nimbutr 1999), which brought back the historically ubiquitous, eponymous female screen ghost and "national icon" to much local and global fanfare. Along with the 2004 hit *Chattoe: Kot Tit Winyan* (*Shutter: Press to Capture Ghosts*, a.k.a. *Shutter*, dir. Banjong Pisanthanakun and Parkpoom Wong-poom) and other films, *Nang Nak* helped to position Thailand with Japan as an early leader in the global spread of so-called Asian horror—a trend that also heavily influenced reformasi-era horror in Indonesia.

Radiating around the appearance of actual ghosts, the dense, jungle settings of many of Weerasethakul's early films also recall the landscapes most commonly featured in classic and contemporary Thai, Indonesian and Malaysian horror—especially pontianak films, which Rosalind Galt (2021) sees as the basis of what she calls "animism as form," an approach to cinema with its roots in regional aesthetic and spiritual epistemes. Drawn from the imagery of Thai 16 mm films of the 1950s and 1960s (at the time considered the pinnacle of abject backwardness by elite Thai critics), the ubiquitous foliage, red-eyed monkey ghosts, and simple, in-camera effects in Weerasethakul's 2010 *Loong Boonmee Raluek Chat* (*Uncle Boonmee Who Can Remember His Past Lives*), which was shot on 16 mm, were now placed on the highest global pedestal: *Uncle Boonmee* became the first ever Thai film to win the top prize at the Cannes film festival that year. In his acceptance speech, Weerasethakul explicitly positioned his film's victory in the context of Thai history by thanking "all the ghosts and spirits in Thailand that made this possible" (*Bangkok Post*, May 22, 2020).

Weerasethakul himself was born too late to have experienced regular, live-dubbed screenings, but he had watched older, 16 mm films on television growing up (*Bangkok Post*). For his contemporaries, as well, it appeared that the cinematic themes and figures of the past were not only seen as resonating with the contemporary but were inextricably linked to the hybrid local mechanisms and formats on which they had been presented in the past—the conventions and contexts that had embedded them in local cinematic history and lore. To the extent that technology allowed, these formats and forms were imported into contemporary cinema along with the ideas, ghosts, and plural symbolic orders that accompanied them. Toward the beginning of the fragmented and theatrical new wave movie *Hawan Yang Wan Yu* (*Bangkok Loco*, dir. Pornchai Hongrattanaporn, 2004), for example, the contents of a character's mind are magically projected on the wall. His first "memory" is an actual film, taken from an older, likely 16 mm, film version of the story of *nang* Nak. Tellingly, the mind-projection shows the scene where monks are extracting a disc from the skull of the female protagonist's corpse—a disc that, as we saw in chapter 5, will become a "vernacular" talisman and symbol of feminine agency that is embedded and passed down into the future of mainstream patriarchal Theravada Thai Buddhism (and through films like *Nang Nak*, into the future of cinema).

In the context of *Bangkok Loco*, I suggest that the reference to *Nang Nak* also builds on the newer, 1999 version that helped spark the Thai new wave. Like *Nang Nak*, *Bangkok Loco* implies that it, too, will travel backward in time, taking up the conventions and temporality of older Thai and regional cinemas. Like many others at the time, the film is quite direct in its returns and references. It is set in the 1970s, and at one point in the narrative, one of the main characters, Bay (Krissada Terrence), finds himself employed as a live film dubber. This occurs in a spirited scene recalling the classical era of Thai 16 mm itinerant cinema, where a film truck sets up at a temple fair and the dubbers are in full view, constituting as much of an attraction as the film itself. Bay's obvious abilities, furthermore, are shown to be connected to the film's central premise, a fictionalized, Thai Buddhist style of percussion known as the Drums of the Gods. It is this mixture of "ancient" conventions and philosophies that the film positions satirically, but also in earnest and with great detail and flare, as a local source for Thai modernity and contemporary engagements with neoliberal globalization. As such, the God Drum techniques not only empower characters to master film dubbing but also 1970s Thai rock and roll, while inspiring visionary acumen for emergent business practices that will come to dominate the post-Crisis future of the early 2000s.

To master the ultimate, "10th level" of the God Drums, as instructed by an ancient parchment that emerges toward the film's end, requires something similar to the way "power couples" and regional cinematic ghosts express agency: an ability to embody, combine, or switch between masculine and feminine qualities and traits. With its vernacular Buddhist drum philosophy, *Bangkok Loco* humanizes and also further queers these ideas. The film concludes its narrative by investing such transcendent powers not in a ghost but in a mortal female character, Ton (Nountaka Warawanitchanoun), anticipating a pattern in regional supernatural films that followed *Warkop DKI Reborn* (see below). In this case, the combination of male and female traits is literal, and Ton is the recipient of genitals removed from Bay, the male character, which are surgically attached to her body.[11]

As she competes in a final duel with a foreign "Devil Drummer" who happens to be named Ringo Starr, her appearance now flickers between Bay's male body and her female one. The film's satirical intervention into the democratizing neoliberal present is capped with a character who is the spitting image of then–prime minister Thaksin Shinawatra: it is also the old, queer vernacular force of the God Drums, the film suggests, that lifted Thaksin out of a string of business failures. Randomly struck by lightning generated by the polysexual "Buddhism" of Ton's playing, the diegetic Thaksin emerges from the phone booth, holding the flaming receiver, which, like the castrated Bay, has been separated from its "cable." As the typical noise of cellular interference is added to the soundtrack (signaling the heterogeneity of time, since this is the 1970s), the letters *GSM* appear onscreen along with a lightbulb above Thaksin's head. The imagery and sounds poke fun at the actual Thaksin's history of using his own and others' money to fund multiple failed business ventures. He, too, only succeeded years later with Advanced Info Service, a computer rental business that he parlayed into a cellular network. With the help of Thaksin's copious official connections (in line with the expansion of patronage networks), the company then received monopoly rights for twenty years for Thailand's new 900 MHz GSM network.

The shining democratic, increasingly patriarchal-nationalist and business-friendly future following the Asian Financial Crisis is hence linked by *Bangkok Loco* to the prime-minister-to-be's "crazy" partnership with an invisible but densely networked creative force. Doing so also connects the possibility of modern agency to a set of older, queerer Thai vernacular Buddhist conventions and values. The idea of political economic patronage is hence also made to overflow the role of patriarchy or heteronormativity in defining or exploiting it—patronage, or in this case domestic capital, is "democratized" for the neoliberal era in Southeast Asia, but not according to emergent, Western models. Alongside these interventions, and in line with other new wave offerings, the film reclaims the once-disgraced forms and approaches of local and regional cinematic pasts, repackaging and presenting them in ways that appealed to newer and bigger audiences, including global ones. But as the film—anticipating the fall of Thaksin by highlighting his bumbling, corrupt tendencies—also acknowledges, localization alone is not sufficient as a solution. *Bangkok Loco*'s trafficking in the nostalgic cinematic and political discourses of "Thais Love Thais" has raised the specters of gendered violence and corruption and, as we will see, has brought back the "ancient" danger of misinterpretation.

Even as the films of the Thai new wave have transcended localized, lower-class niches by traveling extensively to festivals, they have encountered another, ostensibly "higher" label: the loose global category of art film and the assumptions of critics regarding the applicability of postmodernist interpretation, which has gained currency alongside theories of neoliberalism (Harvey 2007:4). Certainly, films such as *Bangkok Loco* or the works of Weerasethakul or other new wave and independent Thai filmmakers might appear to engage in typically postmodern modes of representation, such as pastiche and the "spatialization" of multiple times in a single image or sequence—something that at first glance appears very similar to the horizonal, archipelagic convergences of distinct media, places, and times I have argued to be a key facet of regional cinemas. But in both cases, intermedial convergence constitutes a conscious engagement not only with history but with particular historical modes of representation that are not understood as either typically modernist or something that follows the failures of modernism. Building on the issue of hybridized, localized neoliberalism, this raises questions about whether the label *postmodernist* is misleading or a poor fit.

As Damian Sutton (2012) and Rachel Harrison (2007) argue, new wave director Wisit Sasanatieng's *Fa Thalai Jone* (*Tears of the Black Tiger*, 2000), which toured a number of prestigious European, Asian, and American festivals, "was firmly pigeonholed as an art-house film, to be viewed, reviewed and interpreted through a framework of irony and camp" (Sutton 2012:41). Yet for Sutton, such interpretations miss the point of work that is, in fact, a "period romp through Thai popular culture, drawing upon real and fictional histories, folk theatre and society" (42). Not unlike *Bangkok Loco, Tears of the Black Tiger* might appear to consist of a "hyperreal" collage of layers of playful but meaningless representation on top of further representations, with nothing material or meaningful at its core. It refers heavily to spaghetti westerns but even more so to Thai 16 mm action films of the 1960s, which most global festival audiences would be unfamiliar with. But Sutton contends that the many swirling referents in *Tears* are material and historical, and "the film is never far from a reminder that modernisation comes with a militarised face" (42). More specifically, it uses warnings about the dangers of Westernization and democratization imposed from without on a society with its own embedded problems of politics, gender, and class as a critique of the state of affairs in post-1998 Thailand.

To do so, Sutton argues, *Tears of the Black Tiger* genuinely, if still winkingly, engages various tropes and regional-global time-spaces instead of simply "pastiching" them (53). As I have shown throughout this book, from the beginning of processes of national development, the heterogeneous modernity of Indonesian, Thai, and other regional cinemas likewise works to avoid the postmodernist traps that Fredric Jameson (1991) and others argue that Western mass media (and non-Western after it) falls into, beginning in the mid-twentieth century. The continuation of regional, archipelagic aesthetics into the postreform present, I argue, does not simply allude to paradoxes, the inevitable failures of modernism, and global democracies that are inseparable from the negative effects of neoliberalism. Rather, as I argued in the case of *Bernafas Dalam Kubur*, regional films work to symbolize, and hence represent, the allegedly unfathomable, ghostly, fragmented, networked realities of domestic and global political economy. Through their shifting-but-recognizable images, representation remains an absurdly scattered, porous, and self-referential endeavor that is also, at its best, resonant with a particular (usually local or regional) set of experiences. Especially with the rise of global streaming services, such films thus communicate things that certain audiences are better positioned to grasp but that others now increasingly look on and wonder about (and at times misinterpret).

In contradistinction, what Jameson terms the postmodern "waning of affect" is signaled by the work of artists like Andy Warhol. Warhol's quirky embrace of commercialization, Jameson argues, highlights and simultaneously furthers the global, mass-market dehumanization of individual subjects, especially in its focus on "stars—like Marilyn Monroe—who are themselves commodified and transformed into their own images" (Jameson 1991:11). This aligns with Harvey's idea that neo-liberal markets function as "guides" for human ethics and behavior, "substituting for all previously held ethical beliefs" (2007:3). But if Southeast Asian media has gone through similar processes, the results are in many cases quite different. The supranational iconicity of Suzzanna or nang Nak, for example, anchors regional filmmakers in older processes of commodification and confrontation with deper-sonalized, spectral images that circulate widely but retain a sense of their own history, place, and purpose (for example, shadow play). In the present, undead, immortalized figures like Suzzanna are made reproducible through digital means but crucially also through sublation with regional deities and myths that have car-ried across numerous historical shifts in media technology. The means of their iconization and commodification therefore do not simply indicate a detached, postmodern present or future with no real past. Nor do they spell the waning of the possibility of affective, emotional investment in films or other media.

Such icons, I argue, point backward and forward at the same time, emanating an accrued historicity and materiality—one paradoxically not unlike the "aura" that Walter Benjamin (1968) insisted was destroyed by cinematic and other emer-gent modes of representation. Watching a supernatural film, like attending a ritual, challenges viewers' "immunity" to the images and worlds on the screen, along with the phantoms and human-spirit partnerships that inhabit them. As in het-erodox local rituals, cinema viewers are positioned as participants and facilitated to identify or mimetically embody an iconic, venerated "power couple" that has, across time and various media, become "democratized" and accessible to ordinary men and women in a regionally specific sense (Gottowik 2018:404). Yet I contend that this occurs without the images (or pilgrim-spectators with them) losing the material bases of their meaning and power, which remain embedded in temples, palaces, and other actual locales. The layers of meaning, referentiality, and experi-ence these intermedial exchanges produce envelop and ground the processes by which commodification occurs in specific local and regional histories. In a similar way, Daromir Rudnyckyj argues that the expansion of spirituality and religiosity in various ways after the fall of Soeharto has led to an increased production of "spiri-tuality as an object of intervention"—one that, as we have seen, can be either pro-gressive or conservative in its intent and effects. "The inculca[tion of] . . . Islamic ethics in combination with western management knowledge" is conceived as a broad-based solution to the problems of linking decisions and culture exclusively to "ahistorical" market forces (Rudnyckyj 2009:132).

In the context of such neoliberal "spiritual economies," instead of announcing the "waning of affect" or the "crisis of historicity," I argue that sundel bolong, nang Nak, the pontianak, and their mediatized spiritual conspirators reanimate the past without a stultifying, detached sense of nostalgia. Such ghosts and deities engage, and potentially indoctrinate, leaders, spectators, and ritual-goers with a complex and at times sorrowful, but also pleasurably deep, historical view. Emotional affect and desire are not made to disappear; they are reinstated via extended relations between humans and various icons and specters. These invest the present with the actual times and places (and practices) associated with ghosts and deities and their past and future existences. Building on my analysis in chapter 5, I compare this to what Arnika Fuhrmann calls a radical "sexual contemporaneity" in the context of Thailand—a convention and mode of relation that is likewise activated across films and vernacular Buddhist rituals. While in some instances, the connection of dissimilar beings and times takes the form of relationships with ghosts, in others, it is produced by complex attachments and modes of illicit desire between particular groups of humans—attractions that are, in the view of mainstream patriarchal Thai Buddhism, "broadly . . . counternormative or as yet impossible" (Fuhrmann 2016:13).

Looking especially at the films of Weerasethakul, Fuhrmann focuses on how alternative, syncretic or vernacular Buddhist concepts are deployed to express and insist on the viability of queer desire and sexuality—something that has also become more directly visible in the era of postcrisis regional reform but bears its own strong connections to the past. Here again, localized, historically embedded concepts are deployed to circumvent certain effects of globalized liberal discourse in terms of how it frames the rights or needs of Thai or regional subjects, especially nonheteronormative ones. For Fuhrmann, new wave Thai cinema, which is also characterized by increasing numbers of female and openly nonheteronormative filmmakers, "deploys Buddhist tropes, stories, and images to move queerness beyond binary notions of liberalism and illiberalism" (2016:10). These localized approaches to representation, she argues, are better adapted to the historical pathways of desire between queer Thai subjects. One reason is that they work to implicitly problematize and deconstruct contemporary global binaries of repression versus the potential "reduction of a Thai queer imaginary to a standard liberal frame of policy-oriented activism" (9). Building on Fuhrmann's work, I argue that despite a complex and variable set of challenges, emerging filmmakers throughout the region have turned to face the neoliberal, postmodern present in distinct but related ways: by reclaiming and adapting the feelings and values associated with "bad," "backward," or "lowbrow" historical forms of representation—locally rooted but regionally networked forms that elite, modernizing, and liberalizing nationalists once sought to do away with for good.

With the rise of more fragmented, yet expanded, spiritual economies and sexual and spectral contemporaneity, the ideas and practices that constitute the regional spheres of business, politics, and "the people" are linked, often via affect, in more concerted, and at times open, ways. In this sense, there now appears to be a potential for greater "agreement," at least on basic conceptual and methodological levels, between these disparate areas and interests. At the same time, films highlighting the interconnection of such distinct spheres using ghosts or queer power couples to realize "as of yet impossible" rights, desires and emotional connections are on the rise, asserting the continued existence of numerous problems and inequities. Such films have also begun to circulate much more globally than in the past, as they have moved from greater festival exposure onto the world's rapidly expanding digital streaming networks. Indonesia has emerged in the last few years as the strongest presence on services like Netflix, Amazon Prime, and Disney Hotstar (among many other locally and regionally based streamers). But the increased global presence of Southeast Asian films in both art-independent and commercial platforms, and the various archipelagic models, symbols, and invectives they deploy in the name of reclaiming (or simply activating or elongating) affect, is a demonstrably regional phenomenon.

REGIONAL INFRASTRUCTURES AND THE EXPANSION OF ARCHIPELAGIC IMAGINATIONS

Outside of Thailand and Indonesia, Gaik Cheng Khoo (2006) sees middle-class independent filmmakers in 1990s and early 2000s Kuala Lumpur using cinema to negotiate problems that are basically similar. Instead of national-patriarchal interpretations of Buddhism, new wave Malaysian cineastes face rigid, top-down interpretations of Islam, often even more so than their Indonesian counterparts. In ways that roughly reflect official Theravada values in Thailand, these Muslim ideals are positioned as the basis for a rationalist-modernist and, especially in Malaysia, ethnonationalist ideology—one that arose in the 1950s and has been increasingly enforced by the government and Malay elites since the 1970s and 1980s. As in Indonesia, "spiritual economies" in Malaysia have become a much more visible force since the early 2000s, but they are more conspicuously driven by religious conservatism, with far fewer prominent movements deploying spiritual inclusivity or localized versions of Islam to balance it out.

As Khoo argues, however, young Malaysian filmmakers in the postreform period have used their work to imagine and push for a more visible presence of local and regional syncretisms. In their films, "modernity facilitates the conscious and unconscious recuperation of *adat*" (Khoo 2006:4), a set of hybrid, often animist-derived, Malay values and customs that predate the arrival of both Islam and Western colonialism in the region. In spite of the fact that conservative nationalists inaccurately tar them as Westernized liberals, Malaysian new wave filmmakers like Yasmin Ahmad, Amir Mohammad, Tan Chui Mui, James Lee, U-Wei Haji Saari, and others strove to avoid a simple recourse to typically empty, postmodern image economies or to neoliberal, globalizing discourses of repression vs. activism. Their approaches reflect thematic and stylistic patterns that are well established in Malaysian history and that I suggest are similar to forms of representation recouped by young regional filmmakers elsewhere in the region around the same time. For Khoo, emergent Malaysian cineastes' strategy of looking backward and "reclaiming *adat*" after the Asian Financial Crisis was similarly accomplished "through a focus on sexuality or a return to forms of the archaic such as magic or traditional healing" (2006:5). As Galt (2021) and others have shown, this also prominently included the return of previously banned female ghosts like the pontianak to Malaysian screens.

As we have seen in Thailand and Indonesia, these ostensibly archaic ideas and practices are deployed to produce and reengage certain kinds of politically charged emotions, insisting on their contemporaneity with local modernity and democratic reform. More so than the globalized processes of reform, these historically and culturally infused images of *adat* are primed to disrupt the rigid, racialized, patriarchal, and heteronormative interpretations of Islam that characterize contemporary Malaysian nationalist political landscapes. Patrick Campos looks at the rise in independent filmmaking in the Philippines around the beginning of the twenty-first century in a related way, arguing that this was when a longer yet historically less-valorized history of regionality would finally come to fruition. For Campos, the post-1998 era thus spelled the "end" of national cinema amidst the increasingly palpable "condition of not being confined within national space" (2016:2–3). As I have argued throughout this book, aesthetic, philosophical, spiritual, or economic confinement to the terms of a single, national identity or territory has been a relative rarity through the history of cinemas in the region. But what I position here as the return of regionalism in the Southeast Asian twenty-first century can arguably be seen, as Campos asserts in the Philippines, as having recently become even more visible—especially in terms of gaining more acceptance from middle classes and certain groups of elites (not to mention viewers outside the region)—via access to more viable modes of local film production and the growth of subnational screen cultures.

The gradual disappearance of different "grades" of movie theaters (A-B and C-D) that once profoundly shaped the economics, aesthetics, and class associations of national-cum-regional cinemas has undoubtedly had a further impact on how regionalism is experienced and expressed. In many areas, locally made films now compete fairly successfully, albeit at times with the help of imposed quotas, for the same multiplex screens through which Hollywood and other imports (increasingly Korean and Japanese, among others) circulate. As the number of malls has drastically increased, so have screens, along with the companies—now also frequently foreign or partly so—that own them. Throughout the 2010s, the combination of an increase in the percentage of local populations who identify as middle class and the ubiquitous mall-ization of commerce and social life in much of urban Southeast Asia has also had indelible effects on filmmaking. These changes, for example, helped bring new and more socioeconomically diverse audiences to local and international films alike. For better or for worse, this has also raised ticket prices while reducing the sense of a specific, regional circuit of popular films that mainly compete with, and are influenced by, each other.

Where regionality and regional-archipelagic aesthetic strategies have arguably reasserted themselves most clearly is in the emergence of an influential circuit of local film festivals. As brought to light by my frequent festival attendance and participation in various capacities over the last fifteen years and the many resultant conversations, such events have been crucial in exposing regional independent filmmakers to each other's work. This in turn drives new approaches to cinema that often proudly announce themselves as Southeast Asian, or a times also Asian, expanding the sense and potential geographic size of regionality. Festivals have also helped create and secure new sources of funding that have allowed many regional cineastes to produce a first or second film in styles that might present a risk in terms of a theatrical release and potential returns on producers' or investors' funds. Yearly fetes such as the Singapore and Jogja-Netpac international festivals have been especially important in opening roads for emerging talents. The latter, for example, has served as the main platform for launching and sustaining a robust, subnational film-producing center in the city of Yogyakarta, roughly a ten-hour drive from the capital, Jakarta. These developments have not occurred in isolation, of course, and as industry informants have revealed, over the last three decades, regional filmmakers have also turned to European, Korean, and Japanese festivals (and increasingly Chinese ones) and funds to help realize ever-more ambitious and expensive independent productions.

Older, more experienced, and established independent filmmakers who started in the 1990s or early 2000s have also begun opening production and postproduction houses and foundations that help younger filmmakers with funding and critical feedback. Thailand's Purin Pictures, for example, founded by new wave filmmaker Aditya Assarat, holds annual calls for proposals to fund writing, production, or postproduction that are open exclusively to Southeast Asian applicants. Purin's postproduction grants are supported in part by White Light Post in Bangkok, founded by Lee Chatametikool, who has served as editor on many of Apichatpong Weerasethakul's best-known films, as well as numerous other Thai and regional productions. White Light and other Bangkok post facilities also provide paying customers in the region with affordable color grading and other services that are reachable via a short flight from most local filmmaking hubs. Malaysia's Astro conglomerate, a satellite and streaming television company that also co-produces films, has been another key player in funding and finding audiences for work produced and set in Indonesia and Thailand, as well as in Malaysia.

As this suggests, what began in the early 2000s with low-budget independent productions that struggled to find and make money has gradually shifted to become a more economically fluid and "mainstream" segment of local industries—one that is also regionally embedded. As I, Patrick Campos, and others have recently argued (see Lovatt and Trice 2021b), while independents based in recognized centers like Jakarta, Bangkok, and Manila have become more established, other loci have quickly emerged along the "margins" of different areas. As Jasmine Nadua Trice argues, "It is possible to trace a map of recent Southeast Asian filmmaking that would lead in and out of film practitioners' homes" (2024:425), microarchipelagic spaces that increasingly double as locations for production, discussion, or screenings of films. In some cases, as Khoo has more recently noted about Malaysian new wave filmmakers, the unique "systemic and structural challenges" and comparatively "weak internal ecosystem" they have faced since their beginnings around the Asian Financial Crisis have in some cases (along with some very notable successes) driven them back to producing via informal, friend-based networks (Khoo 2024:382–83).

In addition to urban iterations, these various loci and the smaller, group-oriented approaches to filmmaking they foster are increasingly based on separate islands altogether from national capitals and their mainstream industries. As such, they constitute a region-wide "assemblage of film communities" driven by technology, savvy political negotiation, and "a particular mindset of collectivity" (Engchuan 2021:225). Cinematic communities have also been facilitated through regional and international festival-funding circuits along with government grants and other private sources. Aside from Yogyakarta, numerous other subnational regions in Indonesia, Thailand, the Philippines, Malaysia, and elsewhere in the region have emerged, many producing films in local, rather than official or national, languages, with subtitles added for national and international audiences who do not speak or necessarily understand the dialogue. Following this trend, in Indonesia over the last decade, increasing numbers of successful mainstream films have used localized variations and dialects of Javanese and other languages (Yngvesson 2021).

Along with the continual adaptation of conventions and styles that I identify with a set of basic regional cinematic features, the emergence of so many new filmmaking "islands" along regional circuits further embeds the sense of a specific, archipelagic aura linking mainstream and smaller-scale contemporary Southeast Asian moviemaking. But perhaps the most crucial, ongoing development in the region, as in the world around it, is the rise of the multinational and local-regional streaming services with their insatiable need for ever-greater amounts of "content." It is too early to say what the broader outcome of this may be, and reports of big streamers underpaying for content, especially in certain Southeast Asian countries, are becoming increasingly common. But the interest taken by transnational producer-streamers like Netflix, Amazon, Disney Hotstar, and HBO in global cinemas, including Southeast Asian ones, has, at least for the moment, served to bolster and consolidate many of the moving parts of contemporary regional filmmaking. While films on Netflix or Amazon are often simply labeled Indonesian, Thai, or Filipino and are not grouped as a region for most international viewers, in my experience, algorithms and suggestions of titles often select across Southeast Asia and can contribute to a sense of an archipelagic group of styles.

Somewhat like a horizontally constructed database, the result also mixes together independent "festival" films with less theatrical traction and popular, higher-budget movies while at times providing funding that has blurred the boundaries between the two. This has worked, I suggest, to reimagine and repopulate the regional cinematic mainstream and the diffuse national ones within it. One key outcome of this digital, semiautomatized reshuffling is that numerous older films, and especially older supernatural horror films like the 1981 *Sundelbolong*, are now vying, in pristine, restored colors, resolution, and original widescreen format, with newer takes on the genre for the eyes and ears of regional, as well as transnational, viewers. Especially given the lesser content restrictions and censorship generally applied to streaming moves in the region—again, at least for the moment—I argue that this has been instrumental in creating a platform for the resurgence of remakes and films set in the past but addressing the present. It has also helped open a space for the return of iconic ghosts and figures such as Suzzanna in the 2016 *Warkop DKI Reborn*.

SETANISM, THE ARCHAIC MOTHER, AND THE LIVING FEMALE "GHOST"

Now that Indonesian and Southeast Asian supernatural films are exposed to a much broader international streaming market (a sphere that less often traffics in ideas like the postmodern waning of affect or categorizes popular regional horror as niche-based "cult" fare), they have become one of the most visible and promoted genres in the new regional cinematic mainstream. In the context of this book, this has allowed for a broader circulation and visibility of films, ghosts, and icons that I associate with the idea of a plural symbolic order. As I have mentioned, the reclaiming of affect and of local approaches to gender politics have, not coincidentally it seems, occurred in parallel with a significant rise in the number of women and openly queer filmmakers working across the region. Over the two decades since the Asian Financial Crisis and various political-economic reforms that followed, Intan Paramaditha also sees the emergence of a more concerted and self-conscious "transnational women's cinema" (2024:79)—one that responds, critically and often with typically searing onscreen violence, to the assumptions of global feminisms premised on a Western point of view.[12] In this, the problem of interpretation more readily continues to rear its head.

Although I am not focusing on films made by women per se, I suggest that the emergent patterns identified by Paramaditha also build on collective local and regional ideas of women's symbolic and actual empowerment—and the need, at times, for women to physically fight with or kill men who have adopted more radical or Western forms of patriarchy. As I have argued, the actress and producer Suzzanna can be understood as both an icon and an active part of the historical processes and infrastructures that contributed to the platform on which this attitude is sustained in the present. In this vein, Paramaditha calls contemporary Indonesian female writer-director Mouly Surya's *Marlina si Pembunuh Dalam Empat Babak* (*Marlina the Murderer in Four Acts*, 2017) a localized "feminist western"—one that also includes many regional horror elements (fig. 37).

FIGURE 37. Marlina (Marsha Timothy, *far right*) traveling with the severed head of her rapist in the "feminist western" *Marlina si Pembunuh Dalam Empat Babak.*

Set on the Eastern Indonesian island of Sumba, but also reflecting basic regional patterns of matrifocality I have identified in Indonesian films of Javanese and Sumatranese origin, the film highlights that women's "strategies of resistance are not made outside but within the domestic space" (Paramaditha 2024:75). It is in "feminine spaces," like kitchens and bedrooms, that the female antihero (Marsha Timothy) "chooses her weapons" and concocts a plan to single-handedly kill a band of men who have come to rob and rape her. The film was celebrated at numerous festivals in Indonesia, regionally, and further abroad (including Cannes). Yet Paramaditha argues that in the more rarefied views of local and international critics, especially male ones, the idea of women's agency expressed through violence, functioned to "foreground their own concerns regarding the proper ways of expressing feminism" (77).

In my analysis, this problem resonates with Fuhrmann's (2016) exposition of recent Thai filmmakers' efforts to complicate globalized notions of policy-oriented activism as ideal responses to the repression of the rights of various minoritarians. The issue of "improper" feminism can also be related to the fact that films like *Marlina* have inherited modes of representing gender, power, and gender-based conflict that are specific to regional cinematic discourses—and to such films performing important updates and modifications to these modes that constitute localized feminist interventions. In *Marlina*, the basic theme of struggle for women's rights expressed through violence is not fundamentally distinct from classical works like *Sundelbolong*. In a familiar way, the eponymous heroine can also be said to act from a platform established in part by regional ideas of matrifocality (she is a mother who, for various reasons, is far more active than her husband) and in part by the trope of a "superpowered" feminine avenger. But whether it dovetails Western feminist-activist discourses or not, the film also makes a key change to the women's revenge convention: its feminine avenger completes her mission of killing her male tormentors while she is still alive (and she does not die afterward; in fact, she helps another woman give birth).

Building on Paramaditha's analysis, I position this aspect of *Marlina*'s regional feminist sensibility in terms of a broader shift in the discourse of supernatural horror. The historically established convention in which a woman must die to unlock both connection to the supernatural and the expanded agency that comes with it appears to be slowly changing, for reasons that I will elaborate below. Looking further into the particulars of this modification of a classical theme, I close this chapter and the book with an analysis of two recent Indonesian supernatural films: Joko Anwar's 2017 "remake" of (in fact a sequel to) the classic 1980 *Pengabdi Setan* (*Satan's Slaves*, dir. Sisworo Gautama Putra—see chapter 4 for an analysis of the original) and *KKN di Desa Penari* (*KKN in the Dancer's Village*, dir. Awi Suryadi, 2022).[13]

Both films, I argue, express a similar critical transformation to that of *Marlina*, colluding with Mouly Surya's regionally inflected feminist tactics. In so doing both films contribute to a shift in regional horror in which a mortal female protagonist does not need to be killed in order to act powerfully within the porous, trans-diegetic onscreen spaces constructed by filmmakers. These central female characters, rather than men, come to form a new kind of "power couple" with spirits who are also generally female. While queerness is often not explicit (especially since the ghost and the young protagonist are sometimes related), the films in question point to new ways of deploying an empowering melancholic, affective link between the sphere of humans and the "archaic" one of spirits. In the context of such partnerships as engaged with economically robust regional variants of neoliberal practice that emphasize spirituality, it is notable that both *Pengabdi Setan* and *KKN* also broke domestic theatrical records while drawing significant crowds to Malaysian and Singaporean multiplexes and screening in North America.

The fact that this renewed spirit-human connection has begun to appear in ever-more mainstream contexts is also crucial, I propose, as a counterbalance to the homogenizing or rationalizing forces of religious conservatism and militarism that have grown in parallel to the institution of greater democratic and neoliberal "freedoms." In the 1980s, ghosts like sundel bolong appeared in response to Soeharto's attempts to display a new and unprecedented masculine Order, peeling back the temporal and epistemic layers of his authority to reveal the heterogeneous, dynamically gendered ground on which his regime stood. As I have suggested, these spirits' return on contemporary, mainstream screens (now public and private) appears to signal the need for a new cinematic "instrument," as cineaste Asrul Sani once termed it, in response to the rise of Soeharto in the 1960s (see chapter 4); such an instrument would now be aimed at the complex issues triggered by populist democratic reform and the more open operation of complex, diffuse political economic alliances after Soeharto's fall. In this case, the instrument or weapon would be especially geared to engage the spread of politicized Islamic conservatism that has arisen in the wake of *reformasi*—another consequence of the rise of diverse, often opposing, spiritual economies during regional processes of reform and democratization. The success of *Warkop DKI Reborn*, which provided the initial platform for the return of Suzzanna—a trigger and initial harbinger of the changes I highlight below—was followed most closely by writer-director Anwar's version of *Pengabdi Setan*. As I have mentioned, the film quickly broke attendance records for Indonesian horror and played theatrically in the region and in the U.S. before finding a longer-term home on Netflix.

While unplanned during the film's production, the release of Anwar's *Pengabdi Setan* closely followed the infamous "212" demonstrations on December 2, 2016, when millions descended on Jakarta to protest then-governor Basuki Tjahaja Purnama's alleged insulting of the Qur'an. Purnama was targeted after publicly defending himself from claims by Islamic leaders that Muslims were forbidden to vote for his reelection on grounds that he is Christian. Although it was revealed that his supposedly blasphemous words were in fact reedited and taken out of context, the demonstrations made enough of an impression that judges and other authorities insisted the governor be jailed and stripped of his post. Not long afterward, and without outwardly disturbing the atmosphere of the conservative triumph, the 2017 *Pengabdi Setan* brought 4.2 million viewers to a narrative in which the strong position of conservative Islam in postreformasi Indonesia was continually challenged by what are presented as older and more powerful discourses and beliefs.

As a sequel to the 1980 version that is set in 1981, the 2017 film took a number of liberties with the original's concepts and themes, expanding its view of what constitutes Javanese/spiritual versus strictly "religious" power. Most controversially, the original's classic trope of a male Islamic leader (a kiai or, in this case, an *ustad*) as a ghost-banishing deus ex machina is turned on its head by Anwar's version. To do so, the thematic role of the *ustad* in the original is expanded, while his image as a pious, selfless, and powerful hero is thoroughly undermined. Similar to the 1980 version, in Anwar's contemporary one, the focus is on a family who is attacked by a "satanic" cult.[14] The fact that the family's members are Muslims who rarely, if ever, pray or go to the mosque is raised in both versions as a reason for their targeting. When the family in the 2017 iteration seeks help to fight the attacks by ghosts and zombies associated with the cult, a kindly ustad (Arswendi Beningswara Nasution) who lives nearby agrees but this time with an implicit caveat: "I can only pray and ask for God's help so that you won't be disturbed again." Despite advising the family to pray more themselves because "all beings are afraid of Allah," his wording foreshadows the fact that there are limits to the power of prayer and to what he can do for the family using his religious authority.

Indeed, when the main character, Rini (Tara Basro), the eldest child and only daughter of the family targeted by the cult, prays, it seems to *attract* malicious spirits rather than repel them as it did in the cinematic past. The ustad's son (Dimas

Aditya), who describes himself as more "open to other theories" than his strictly Islamic father, explains that "there are beings who are stronger than people or *jin* [genies]," as spirits are usually categorized in Islam. These beings' powers, he tells Rini and her brother, can be traced to groups that have been around "since before religion," presumably referring to the global rise of Abrahamic faiths. As the film has now implied, Islam, and presumably other world religions, have no way of meaningfully engaging these older powers. As if to reiterate and further drive home the same point, when the ustad sees ghosts attacking Rini, instead of trying to help, he closes the door to the room where he is standing, seemingly out of fear for his own life. His son, and then he himself, are later killed at the hands of the group who is behind the supernatural disturbances.

The closest thing to a hero in the film is thus Rini, the eldest sibling who fights to protect her family from the attacks alongside her father (Bront Palarae), a much weaker figure. The most influential character besides Rini is Budiman (Egy Fedly), an investigative reporter who has been studying the "cult" and understands the values and regulations that underpin and determine their powers. These customs are based on older Javanese spiritual practices such as *pesugihan*, where one can receive blessings and special powers by making ritual sacrifices to spirits—information that I position as a further intervention into the present-day politics of Islam versus syncretic local beliefs. Armed with this knowledge and led by Rini, most of the family members are able to escape the attacks on their home and flee to a shabby apartment building in Jakarta.

In the end, however, things are still not safe—the attackers and their group are alive (or in some cases undead) and well. As in the 1980 version, the group's local leader is female, and the ghosts and cult members have mainly targeted what the film shows to be the family's main support system: its women. Rini's mother, Mawarni (Ayu Laksmi), a singer and the family's main breadwinner, was for years unable to have children. Like other female victims, her one "weakness" was successfully targeted by the group's specialty—the use of magic to increase fertility. In exchange, however, the mother must give her youngest child to the group when he reaches age seven. Mawarni dies shortly before this happens, falling fully under the control of the group. Returning as a ghost, she endeavors to draw her son away from the other family members and toward the group. But the undead Mawarni must face other, stronger women in order to do so. This includes her own mother, Rini's grandmother (Elly D. Luthan), who was always suspicious of the group and now attempts to intervene but is killed in the process. Yet this is a supernatural film in which death can be empowering. The grandmother's ghost thus returns to fight even harder alongside Rini, the central female figure who does not die but is spiritually empowered through partnership with a female ghost. Together, they successfully defend the family against the ongoing attacks of zombies and other disturbances, keeping them safe at least until the next sequel.

Reactions to the film have been varied, with some claiming it as a further example of an emergent, postreform feminist sensibility. Jakarta-based filmmaker and critic Nosa Normanda argues that the women who become ghosts in *Pengabdi Setan* and other similar films are conceived along the lines of the "archaic mother" in psychoanalysis: the presymbolic, prephallic idea of the mother as all powerful and also (especially important for psychoanalysts) universally threatening. In a more typical global horror scenario, it would be the phallus-wielding man who finally banishes the abject archaic mother to her "properly" repressed place in the unconscious (or, in this case, the world of spirits conceived of as fundamentally separate from that of humans). Yet here, the father is "marginalized, while a sincere woman arises to fight the archaic mother with her intuition and ability to improvise" (Normanda 2021:n.p.). In Normanda's view, this kind of representation has only become possible following the fall of dictator and national patriarch Soeharto in 1998, after which many more women also became active as producers, directors, and writers in the Jakarta-based film industry. He argues that directors like Joko Anwar, who is openly gay, are a product of changes during and after *reformasi* that imbue their work with an awareness of "global trends in political correctness and women's movements" (Normanda:2021).

In this context, Normanda contends that frequent collaborations with like-minded female producers, crew, and actors have "shifted the landscape of Indonesian film to become more representative of women" (2021). In a similar vein, Anton Sutandio argues that in comparison to the 1980 film, "Anwar's version brings a more modern interpretation of Moslem women and equality for women in general," promoting "feminist values" (2019:27). For Sutandio, the film also uses the weak *ustad* figure to satirize the increasing political commodification of religion as a weapon of conservatism in the democratic era. I agree that the newer *Pengabdi Setan* is more direct than most New Order films in its critiques of mainstream, masculine religious authority. Yet I argue that in both this aspect and its foregrounding of dynamic feminine agencies with shifting moral allegiances, the film builds on, rather than distances, the work of its Soeharto-era predecessors, while adding a twist. If the mother's empowerment through the age-old but ongoing practice of *pesugihan* has also made her "archaic," I suggest that the goal of the film is not simply to repress this purported primordiality. In line with Paramaditha's analysis of *Marlina, Pengabdi Setan*'s localized feminist intervention does not consist in changing out the gender of the "hero," who in a typical Western scenario would banish the supposedly archaic mother. Instead, the film works to build "connections and solidarity" (Paramaditha 2024:75) between women, in this case including mortal and spectral ones.

This turns on the ability of female characters—especially Rini and her grandmother—to reconnect and continue working together after the latter has passed away and become a ghost. If that also means that the grandmother, like her spiritually empowered but co-opted daughter, is an "abject" threat to patriarchy, the role of the protagonist and goal of the narrative is not to repress her. As a popular movie released in a heated political moment, connecting the "old" sphere of spirits to contemporary life is interpreted by many as a conscious effort to keep religious conservatives, among other forces, from taking absolute power. As in *Marlina*, and unlike the reborn Suzzanna in *Bernafas Dalam Kubur*, Anwar's innovative narrative trajectory keeps Rini alive. In doing so, it positions her struggles more solidly vis-à-vis the living spheres of real politics surrounding the film. She is not fighting conservative Islam in the film, of course, but her ability to exploit the continuation of pre-Abrahamic matrifocal and supernatural powers through partnership with her ghostly grandmother wages a transdiegetic battle. The overall symbolic role of women and spirits keeps her family mostly safe in the film, while openly undermining the masculine, phallic authority promoted by conservative Islam outside it. As Sutandio also points out, the once-crucial male figure of cinematic spirit-human power couples (here the family's father) leaves the family for an extended period during their time of crisis. When questioned by his daughter, he simply answers, "What do you need me for?" (Sutandio 2019:27).

The spate of high-production-value supernatural films that followed closely in the wake of *Pengabdi Setan*'s success continued its disruptive spiritual tactics, positioning *KKN di Desa Penari* to smash the overall box-office record set by *Warkop DKI Reborn*. *KKN* recorded over ten million theatrical viewers in Indonesia (exceeding *Warkop* by three million), while breaking records for Indonesian films in Malaysia and Singapore and also, like Anwar's *Pengabdi Setan*, screening in theaters in the U.S. In *KKN*, the landscape of power is likewise dominated by mortal and ghostly Javanese women, for whom Islam is shown to be one, often insufficiently powerful, tool among many with which to engage the forces of evil and feminine haunting. Also mirroring *Pengabdi Setan*, the young woman who emerges as the closest thing to a heroine figure, Nur (Tissa Biani), does so because of the help of a discolored and initially frightening, but in-fact kindhearted and powerful, grandmother spirit, *mbah* Dok (Dewi Sri).

Although *KKN* bridges humans and spirits and past and present in a familiar way, I argue that it also employs another innovative "old" tactic that distinguishes it from *Pengabdi Setan*. In line with the prominence of spiritual economies as conceptual and material bases for local and regional political development, it works to reconnect, rather than simply differentiate, Javanese spirituality with Islam—reclaiming the local Abrahamic sphere instead of rejecting it. At the end of the film, for example, it is revealed that Nur was educated through high school in a *pesantren*, or Muslim dormitory school. When she visits the kiai who is the head of her pesantren, she is informed that the elderly master has long known of her connection to mbah Dok. When he tried to get rid of Nur's ancient spirit companion in the past, the kiai explains, the spirit made a bargain with him, promising to guard and take care of Nur. This has now been proven by the fact that Nur has survived the deadly supernatural ordeals she and her friends experienced in the haunted rural "Dancer's Village," where most of the film takes place.

Following their discussion and the kiai's confirmation and expression of approval of her attachment to this powerful spirit-partner, Nur bows and bids him farewell with the typical Muslim *assalamualaikum warahmatullahi wabarakatuh* (peace be upon you). As if the kiai's blessing were not sufficient on its own, as Nur exits the frame, mbah Dok appears behind her. The appearance is accompanied by typically spooky, nondiegetic music, a convention used since the 1970s to imply that disturbance-causing spirits are not actually banished. What is new about the use of the convention in *KKN* is that upon seeing the spirit, and in contradistinction to the established meaning of the soundtrack, the kiai simply smiles at mbah Dok gratefully. As the dissonant sounds get louder and she looks back at him, mbah Dok's otherwise scary countenance is broken by a knowing grin. Islam and Javanese spirits, the scene implies, are actually old friends that need not fight and can do more good in the world by working together.

Such a collaboration, of course, also relies on a particular symbolic foundation. As if to underscore this, the resulting two-shot of the old kiai standing across from Mbah Dok evokes the two pillars of power in which I argue the movie, like many before it, is grounded: a mortal, material masculine figure and a spiritual, yet also material, feminine one whose authority surrounds and envelops that of the kiai. Yet as the film shows, the two sides can also be embodied effectively by an active mortal woman and a dynamic feminine spirit that protects and empowers her. Mbah Dok, like sundel bolong and many other regional spirits, represents a sphere of power that will not be repressed or relegated to the past and that refuses to simply disappear from the religious and rational discourses that don't "believe" in it. The kiai is hence implied to have made a wise choice in opening himself to such a partnership. Doing so has saved the life of a girl he has also mentored in the ways of Islam, while broadening her horizons and empowering her to think and act in an expanded, more historically grounded, way. In this context, I suggest that the film represents an emergent variant of supernatural horror that implies, but does not directly announce, its feminist alliances. In doing so, it imbues the overtly pious, hijab-wearing Nur with the potential to become a dynamic, active figure embedded within regional political, economic, and spiritual spheres.

The portrayal of weak, or strong but "too open-minded," religious figures in films like the new *Pengabdi Setan* and *KKN* has at times raised the hackles of religious authorities. But contemporary filmmakers have generally shown themselves to be shrewd and well-versed in the political complexities of spiritual-religious representation, and very few recent films in the horror genre have been considered for an outright ban. When films break box-office records, furthermore, it becomes much more difficult for conservative forces to rally the masses to bring them down, especially after the movies themselves have brought many millions of viewers to multiplexes. Like the ongoing *kejawen* or syncretic Javanese-Islamic rituals discussed in the previous chapter, these films are sustained by the strong economic base that they help to generate. Corruption, stagnation, and various forms of discrimination continue to afflict the region, often in extremely worrisome ways. But for the moment, these spectral economic tactics enable young filmmakers to keep disseminating ideological counterbalances to the spread of monotheistic patriarchies and the strictly financially based neoliberal ethics of modern power. These, like colonial and imperial forces before them, always arrive via the watery, transpacific pathways that are guarded by spirits like the queen of the South Sea.

NOTES

PROLOGUE

1. In a similar vein, Philippa Lovatt explores how cinematic sound and associated "regimes of listening" in contemporary Southeast Asia describe and inscribe an archipelagic imagination, pointing to "how under-the-radar frequencies disrupt regimes of listening associated with empire and the nation-state" (2021:177).

2. As Armes puts it, "the national film industries of most of the countries of East and Southeast Asia are virtually unknown in the West, so only the barest sketch can be offered here" (1987:135). Armes's summary of Southeast Asian cinema histories is indeed a bare sketch and in the end offers nothing to support his prominent positioning and application of Vatsyayan's ideas about Southeast Asian and Indian arts to the study of cinema. Instead, in seeming opposition to Vatsyayan, Armes mainly reports on what he sees as instances of American cinematic influence in various places and times in Southeast Asia. Adding to the confusion, local films that for Armes do *not* seem to imitate the West are generally dismissed as functioning "on a very primitive level" (149). I look further at Shohat's and Stam's work in chapter 1.

3. See, e.g., Driskell (2022); Khoo, Barker, and Ainslie (2020); Lim and Yamamoto (2012); Ingawanij and McKay (2012); and Baumgärtel (2012). The only comparative, single-author monograph among these recent studies is Sim (2020). While there are certain connections to this work, the selection of films is highly idiosyncratic, and comparisons are rarely made between films of different Southeast Asian nations that were produced in the same era. This makes for a difficult time establishing the kinds of regional patterns that my own book explores. Gonzaga (2024) is probably the work that is closest in scope and methodology to what I engage in here. Although it engages with only two Southeast Asian cities, Manila and Singapore, its focus on the convergence of different media and how markets affect, among other things, cinematic exhibition and audience expectations over the course of several decades makes it a companion and late inspiration for this work.

249

4. See Lovatt and Trice (2021b); the special section comprising authors Lovatt and Trice (2021a); Campos (2021); Lovatt (2021); Chulphongsathorn (2021); Trice (2021); and Yngvesson (2021).

5. See, e.g., Andaya (2007); Galt (2021); Karim (1995); King and Wilder (2003); Ong and Peletz (1995); Poedjosoedarmo (1983); Roces (2022); and Wieringa (1997).

6. See, e.g., Soedjatmoko, Resink, and Kahin (1965). Of particular interest are Soedjatmoko (1965) and C. C. Berg (1965).

7. The film premiered at the Documentary Film Festival in Yogyakarta and the Malaysian International Film Festival and played in regional and global festivals, as well as at academic events and conferences. It opened online with a thirty-day run on Mubi.

1. "CULTURE BOUND" AESTHETICS AND ARCHIPELAGIC FORM

1. Usmar Ismail is considered one of the founders of native filmmaking in Indonesia and is often referred to as the "father" of Indonesian cinema. He was also an accomplished essayist, reporter, translator, and maker of theater. He worked prolifically from the late 1940s until his early death in 1970 at the age of forty nine, writing, directing, and producing numerous popular films in various genres, mostly through his own production company, Perfini. He also occasionally worked in Malaysia under a pseudonym, highlighting the fluid, supranational exchanges that I argue define regional cinemas.

2. As Umi Lestari (2020) suggests, the mise-en-scène in *Lewat Djam Malam*, especially the clippings pasted on Laila's walls, was likely inspired by similar arrangements in previous films such as *Terimalah Laguku* (*Please Accept My Song*, dir. Djadoeg Djajakusuma, 1952), *Enam Djam di Jogja* (*Six Hours in Djogja*, dir. Usmar Ismail, 1951), and *Embun* (*Dewdrop*, dir. Djadoeg Djajakusuma, 1952). All of these were produced by Usmar Ismail's company, Perfini, and featured Basoeki Resobowo as art director. In Lestari's reading, the use of newspapers glued onto walls in those films signified the lack of other, more costly decorations, conjuring the typically poor living conditions of the "little people" or lower classes at the time (2020:334). Chalid Arifin, the art director of *Lewat Djam Malam*, had previously worked as Resobowo's assistant. For Lestari, in *Lewat Djam Malam* as in Arifin's previous work with Resobowo, newspapers pasted on walls not only signify lower-class spaces but also indicate the kind of decorations often used in real and cinematic spaces where prostitutes conducted their business (336). While this is certainly the case, what I argue distinguishes *Lewat Djam Malam* from those earlier works is the sense of choice conveyed by numerous scenes in which Laila is shown selecting particularly meaningful images with which to adorn her walls. By contrast, in *Terimalah Laguku*, for example, the walls of certain rooms are simply covered with entire sheets of newspaper from floor to ceiling, without giving the sense that any curation of content or choice of particular symbols has occurred.

3. Indonesia, or the Dutch East Indies as it was often called under colonial rule, was only made an official colony of the Netherlands in the early nineteenth century. But a high level of Dutch influence was established earlier, after the Dutch East India Corporation (VOC) began making trade inroads in the early seventeenth century (following Portuguese and British trade-based incursions into the "spice islands"), gradually using a combination of economic, political, and military means to increase its control over the production of

the spices its business was premised on extracting and exporting to Europe. Only when competition from other European corporations and unstable prices bankrupted the VOC in 1799 did the Netherlands' government step in to officialize the relationship as a colonial one. This met with staunch resistance and several years of war, especially on Java, which was then as now politically and economically important to the archipelago around it. By 1830, Dutch colonial power was fully established. For further information on modern Indonesian history and independence, see Ricklefs (2008b); Reid (2011); and Purwanto et al. (2023).

4. Akup (1932–91) grew up in Malang, East Java. He was hired by Usmar Ismail's Perfini company as an assistant director in 1952. Following the success of his first feature, *Heboh* (*Sensational*), in 1954, and further stints as unit manager and production coordinator on films directed by Ismail, he was given the opportunity to write and direct *Djuara 1960* (1960 Champion, 1956) and *Tiga Buronan*. Both films were profitable (*Tempo* 1974:45), but it was with *Tiga Buronan*, an acclaimed hit, that Akup truly demonstrated a knack for negotiating the prickly borders between a critical cinematic politics of "Indonesianness" and success at the box office, in this case through a penchant for humor. He continued making popular films, mostly comedy-dramas, until his death at age fifty-nine. For more information, see http://filmindonesia.or.id/.

5. The psychiatric term "culture bound syndrome" refers to "disorders" that are believed to occur exclusively in certain geographic areas. Latah has been most closely studied in Indonesia and Malaysia but is also noted as frequently occurring in Thailand, Myanmar, and the Philippines, where the same behavior pattern is given locally specific names. While latah and a number of other culture-bound syndromes are categorized within a class of neuropsychiatric illnesses loosely related to Tourette's syndrome and obsessive-compulsive disorder, cultural psychiatrist Ronald Simons (2001:2) also reminds us that "in actuality . . . many are not syndromes at all. Instead, they are local ways of explaining any of a wide assortment of misfortunes."

6. Likewise, the film and popular culture magazine *Varia Baru* (*New Varia*) refers to the advent of "masa latah film Indonesia" (the latah era of Indonesian film); see *Varia Baru*, Dec. 20, 1970, 10.

7. Until 1963, much of what is now Malaysia was referred to as Malaya, including during British colonization prior to 1957. Singapore was part of both Malaya and the earliest iteration of Malaysia until Malaysia and Singapore split into separate republics in 1965.

8. The targeting of song and dance in this case is not random. *Tiga Buronan* was Akup's third film for Perfini. Akup was initially hired in 1952 as an assistant director, a position he continued to play on films directed by Ismail until *Tiga Buronan*. He was therefore closely involved in the production of Ismail's *Tiga Dara* (*Three Sisters*, 1956), a hit musical that saved Perfini from impending bankruptcy. Despite the film's success, however, Ismail privately expressed his embarrassment at *Tiga Dara*'s populist style (see chapter 3), which was intended to compete with the Malayan, Philippine, Indian, and Hollywood imports then flooding Indonesia's screens and was filled throughout with song-and-dance numbers. According to one of his colleagues, Ismail found it difficult "to accept the reality that he had been *forced* to make such a film" (Said 1991:57, emphasis added). Akup, known as a keen observer who mined real-life situations for comedic episodes in his films, appears to have turned Ismail's sense of compulsion into a more lighthearted approach to market-based formal prescription and mimicry in *Tiga Buronan*.

9. In this children's film, a ten-year-old's dream transports him into a cardboard cutout version of an Old West ranch. Sporting spurs and a ten-gallon hat, he emits a warbling, idiotic yodel and crosses his eyes. The scene also includes wooden horses that move on mechanical tracks and a shoot-out and peace-pipe reunion with another child, who is dressed in stereotypical Native American costume.

10. Akup's 1974 hit *Koboi Cengeng* (*Crybaby Cowboy*) develops his earlier ideas further, using the dissonance produced by applying stereotypical tropes of westerns to an entire film set in 1970s Indonesia as the main source of humor. In the decade following *Koboi Cengeng*, at least eight similarly themed western spoofs were released (including Akup's *Koboi Cilik* [*Little Cowboy*, 1977] and *Koboi Sutra Ungu* [*Purple Silk Cowboy*, 1981]), leading Hanan to speculate that with *Tiga Buronan*, Akup had innovated an entire Indonesian subgenre (2017:135–36). As I elaborate below, these regional variants also bear a certain resemblance to contemporary American western spoofs like Frank Tashlin's 1952 genre-bending comedy *Son of Paleface*, although with a critical difference in how the Southeast Asian films pointedly refuse to wrap things up at the end.

11. See chapter 2 for a more sustained engagement with Hansen's work and her concept of cinema as "vernacular modernism."

12. I build on David Hanan's (2009, 2017) analyses of classical Indonesian cinema as continuing to adapt and expand local traditions of representation, satire, and political engagement that extend back into local, precolonial modes of art and performance such as Javanese *wayang kulit* (shadow play).

13. See, e.g., Ismail (1983:96–98); Said (1991:59–75); and Sen (1994:41).

14. Gunning's (1986) formulation of an "exhibitionist" "cinema of attractions" in pre-1908 Europe and the U.S., before mainstream Western films became fixated on immersive, feature-length narratives. The clear difference is that Thai versioning took place during a completely different, and much longer historical period, and was not an obvious precursor to a more formally unified cinematic style. While typical film running times during the cinema of attractions were from three to fifteen minutes, Thai versioned films were generally feature length. The breakdown or nonvalidity of classical cinematic space and time in Thai versioning also did not preclude the ability for films to convey complex narratives. Here there appears to be an ability among viewers to concentrate on numerous stimuli at once without losing the thread of the story or feeling that the images onscreen have been denuded of their authenticity or naturality. Clearly, visuals are constructed and faked in numerous ways, but this only adds to their allure.

15. Although not consistent, there are notable instances in which the localized approach to film *was* referred to as classical or "classic," as in critic Sitor Situmorang's review of *Tarmina* (1954, dir. Sudjio) in the newspaper *Dunia Film* (*Film World*); see Situmorang (1955b).

16. Describing the relationship of the "makeshift" Thai popular apparatus to more mainstream global forms of cinema, Ingawanij draws on Francesco Casetti's (2015) application of Giorgio Agamben's "profanation" to film.

2. THE EMERGENCE OF ARCHIPELAGIC AESTHETICS

1. Krishna Sen, for example, has argued across several different analyses of Indonesian cinema history that Ismail and others in his camp were "deeply influenced by Hollywood cinema and consciously modeled their work on it" (1994:151). Because Ismail was

"enthralled by Hollywood" (Sen 2015:2), she suggests elsewhere, he and his films were also beacons of "liberal-democratic politics" (2003:151).

2. See, e.g., Armijn Pané (1953); Bienvenido Lumbera (1984, 2011); Tan Sooi Beng (1995); Misbach Yusa Biran (2008); Matthew Cohen (2006); Hassan Muthalib (2013); and May Ingawanij (2012, 2018).

3. As Tan Sooi Beng (1989:231–32) points out, the use of terms like *komedie* and *opera* was influenced by the regional popularity of vaudeville and also Chinese operas at the time.

4. See, e.g., Cohen (2006:232–33); Hatley (1979:4); and Pané (1953:30).

5. Nugroho and Herlina (2015:27–31) and Biran (2008), for example, list localized Javanese vernacular theaters like ketoprak and ludruk, along with regional forms like *sandiwara*, as influences on Indonesian filmmakers, although they do not explain the specific formal or stylistic elements that emerged as a result of the influence.

6. See Pané (1953); Cohen (2006); Muthalib (2013); and Ingawanij (2012, 2018).

7. See, e.g., Pané (1953:30); and Ruppin (2016:7).

8. Echoing Thai scholars, Muthalib claims as classical the basic approach to cinema taken by the majority of early Malayan films, despite their clear discrepancies with the global conception of classical cinema set by Hollywood.

9. The political history of Singapore as a key locale for the production of cinema only adds to the sense of fragmentation around ideals of national unity in the region: Singapore gained independence separately from Malaya in 1959, after which it became part of the new federation of Malaysia in 1963. Only two years later, however, it separated again, becoming the independent city-state it has been known as since, a move that had lasting effects on the Malaysian film industry.

10. Ironically, it was the new, literate, script-memorizing players who were known as "amateurs," while established actors trained in improvisation were called "professionals" (Tan 1993:52).

11. Even more so than in Indonesia, which also had a number of transnational players involved in filmmaking at the time, Singapore studios in the 1950s employed experienced directors, screenwriters, and cinematographers from India and the Philippines. Like India, the Philippines had established film studios in the 1930s, earlier than much of the rest of the region, and Filipino filmmakers were seen as having more experience at the time. See Galt (2021).

12. See Salim Said (1991:42–43, 57); Tanete Pong Masak (2016:286–89); and Adrian Jonathan Pasaribu (2020). Both Said and Masak claim that *Lewat Djam Malam* was a commercial success, while Pasaribu calls it a "minor box-office hit" that was "ultimately deemed too intellectual," the result of which was that "Ismail's potential audience dwindled to a few thousand" (n.p.). Misbach Yusa Biran claims that in 1954, Perfini was "entering a time of crisis because their quality films [which implicitly includes *Lewat Djam Malam*] weren't getting big enough audiences" (2008:85). A table in Masak shows the film in a weak fourth position among Indonesian movies released around the same time in a key city. More tellingly still, it lagged far behind the Indonesian box-office numbers of Singapore-produced Malay films, which sold between three and ten times the number of tickets as *Lewat Djam Malam* (Masak 2016:432). All three scholars agree that after *Lewat Djam Malam*, Ismail's Perfini was in deep financial trouble.

13. Siagian's youngest daughter, Bunga, told me (August 18, 2016, in Jakarta) that her father had often described his films as explicitly drawing on Hollywood conventions.

14. See Sen (1994); Said (1991); and Masak (2016).

15. See Barnard (2005, 2009); Galt (2021); and Tan (1989,1993).

3. ARCHIPELAGIC MODERNISM AND TRADITIONS OF GENDER

1. As I noted in chapter 2, Jason McGrath has argued that interwar leftist filmmakers in Shanghai were intentionally "jumpy" and critical of classical Hollywood naturalism in their formal approaches, while also deploying certain established American and European tropes or narrative arcs to attract more viewers (2023:105). As Ben Singer shows, throughout much of its history, Japanese cinema is well established as deploying narratively extraneous, stylistic "flourishes," although to what extent these make Japanese films qualitatively "nonrealist" or distinct from Western classical approaches is up for debate (2014:55–56). As I take up in more detail below, during the American occupation (1945–52) after Japan's loss to Allied forces in World War II (shortly after the interwar period that Hansen mainly refers to), its gender representation also shifted radically as locally made films were aligned with the U.S. drive to promote democracy and Western-style ideals of "freedom" (Saito 2014:329).

2. Based on studies in Indonesia of Achenese, Javanese, and Minang societies, for example, Nancy Tanner argues that "the structural features [of matrifocality] include women's important economic roles, women's extensive participation in decision making, and a residential pattern that enhances ties among kinswomen" (Tanner 1974:143). The idea of matrifocality is normally applied to groups that are not matrilineal or matriarchal, where women's dominant positions are generally uncontested. As in Tanner's study, however, it has been applied to the Minangkabau of Western Sumatra, Indonesia. The Minangkabau, a group with outsized representation among Indonesia's early national modernist artists and filmmakers, are matrilineal but have gone through processes of patriarchalization beginning in the mid-twentieth century.

3. See Andaya (2007); Hanan (2017:248–58); Karim (1995); King and Wilder (2003); Ong and Peletz (1995); and Roces (2022).

4. At the very end of *Ibu Mertuaku*, seeing that Kassim has blinded himself again (and more important, perhaps, realizing he knows she lied to him), Mansoor suddenly repents, crying hysterically and begging his forgiveness. This shift, however, appears as a forced, unnatural "resolution" that is completely out of character with Mansoor as we have seen her throughout the film—as a woman whose confidence in her power and outlook is unshakable. It also does nothing to change the tragic ending of the narrative, since Kassim has already blinded himself and is not hindered in his decision to disappear from the lives of his son and ex-wife.

5. As I take up in more detail below, a similar example can be found in Filipino cineaste Lamberto Avellana's *Anak Dalita* (*Child of Sorrow*, 1956), produced the same year as *Tiga Dara*.

6. Similar political and often ethnonationalist divisions were raising their heads in Indonesia, Thailand, the Philippines, and elsewhere, often causing major schisms and even bloodshed but generally without actual geopolitical division of territories. As in Malaysia, the role of communist parties and other leftist factions (and increasingly staunch opposition to them) was also on the rise, showcasing local engagements with, and interpretations of, the encroachment of global cold war politics. Separatist provinces and groups also challenged the sanctity of the new, vulnerable national borders that had been inherited from defeated postwar colonial parceling.

7. Further examples of radically gendered Western or non-Western films can almost certainly be found; my point is that they are likely to be formally or narratively unusual in the context of the mainstream or alternative cinemas in which they are embedded or possibly also juxtaposed against.

8. Even then, as Hansen shows, many of the earliest stage- and screen-women were of mixed-race backgrounds. The general perception of such women as "foreign" was used to justify their flaunting local mores governing women's public appearance. But at the same time, like the cross-dressing male actors who preceded them, they were often prized for their ability to performatively embody a pure "Indianness" and ideal femininity (1999:141–43).

9. Beginning in the nineteenth century, the strong matrifocal and matrilineal customs and legal systems of the Minangkabau were increasingly subject to debate, at times becoming the source of violent conflict (Wieringa 1997:246–47). At stake were precisely women's inheritance rights and the economic power based on them, both of which provided a platform for the Minangkabau's combination of strict adherence to Islam with "an egalitarian ideology and a strong belief in democracy" based in female leadership with significant male participation (1997:243). In this context, both P. Ramlee (the director of *Ibu Mertuaku*) and Usmar Ismail (the director of *Tiga Dara*) are descended from Minang families (Ramlee was raised in Malaysia in a Minang community. Ismail was born in Bukittinggi, West Sumatra, a center of Minang society, after which he moved to Java for his higher education).

10. Sanchai Chotirosseranee, deputy director of the Thai Film Archive, personal communication via email.

4. SIGNATURES OF THE INVISIBLE

1. As I discuss in chapter 5, the semi-illicit spectator interactions in these old movie theaters also mirror the performance of politicized, spiritual sex acts at certain ritual locales dedicated to the memory of various legendary "power couples." These sites and their basis in the human-spirit relations that define such power couples also resonate with the mortal-spectral romances and the supernatural political powers they generate in popular horror films of the 1970s, 1980s, and 1990s.

2. In Indonesia, for example, as Sen and Hill show, censorship guidelines instated in the 1970s had "only one direct reference to sex in its list of twenty-four criteria for banning or cutting films" (2000:141). Only in 1981 did regulations emerge where characters committing crimes or immoral acts would have to be shown to be punished in the end, meaning that throughout the 1970s, there were significant loopholes for indirect critique through figures whose identities, while only indirectly political, nonetheless made them read as subversive.

3. Because the situation in Malaysia and Singapore was so different during this period, I have mainly excluded them from comparative analysis in this chapter. As detailed in the previous chapters, after Malaysia's split with Singapore in 1965, film industries in both places experienced extreme lulls in production lasting until the late 1970s and beyond in the case of Singapore—precisely the opposite of what happened in the Philippines, Thailand, and Indonesia. In Malaysia, 95 percent of the films shown on local screens throughout the 1970s, for example, were foreign. Ethnic Malays often watched Indonesian films, and ethnic Chinese and Indians enjoyed imported fare in their own respective languages (mainly in Mandarin, Cantonese, Tamil, and Hindi, often with subtitles in English, Malay, or other Chinese dialects) (Frymus 2022:59–67).

4. For more on the killings, their aftermath, and the events leading up to them, including the imbrication of art and artists in the politics of the time, see, for example, Larasati (2013), Wieringa (2002), Roosa (2006, 2020), Robinson (1995), and Wardaya (2007).

5. See, e.g., Barker (2011) and Sen (1994, 2003, 2015).

6. Ever the poet, for "knee," Sani choses the word *lutut*, which also means to kneel or bow to authority, instead of the more common *dengkul*. I translated from the line "menggaruk kepala, sedangkan kita tahu betul yang gatal itu lutut." It is taken from the August 2, 1967, essay "Semua Hipokrisi Harus Puna" (All hypocrisy must pass) in the daily *Harian Kami*.

7. It is interesting that only in the late 1960s does Sani's view of Indonesia begin to come into closer alignment with that of Benedict Anderson (1983), who argues that from the beginning of nationalism in the nineteenth century, Southeast Asian nations have been imagined as communities that move in unison according to the dictates of mass media, developing "calendrically" in "homogeneous empty time." Sani's view of the later onset of "empty time" is also far more openly negative than Anderson's.

8. In light of regional traditions of positioning women in ways that most spectators could identify with in a "nonpathological" manner, I distinguish this from the uncomfortable or "forced" condition Laura Mulvey calls "transvestite" identification. Mulvey's term denotes what she argues is the only relation available to female spectators in the masculine-centered classical cinematic system, which mimics dominant patterns of identification in society: "for women (from childhood onwards) trans-sex identification is a habit that very easily becomes second nature. However, this Nature does not sit easily and shifts restlessly in its borrowed transvestite clothes" (1989:33). While refusing to draw broader conclusions about gender and representation, from his analysis of three films produced under the New Order (two of which deal with forms of prostitution), David Hanan likewise suggests that the films are "significantly different in the way that they represent women, from what is found in mainstream patriarchal cinema elsewhere" (2017:253).

9. For Deleuze, one of the most important examples of this crisis was the emergence of Italian neorealism after the Second World War. Films such as *Ladri di Bicilette* (*The Bicycle Thieves*, dir. Vittorio De Sica, 1948) and *Umberto D* (dir. Vittorio De Sica, 1952) employed lengthy tracking shots of the postwar poor wandering through the ruined outskirts of Rome.

10. In Indonesia, where inherited family names are not the norm, changing one's name is fairly common and legally uncomplicated. The Name-of-the-Father, which for Lacan functions as a symbolic foundation of male authority across generations, is hence more or less inoperative.

11. *Rear Window* is one of Laura Mulvey's (1975) main examples of how classical Hollywood films construct a dominant "male gaze" that implicates spectators in objectifying passive women.

12. See, e.g., Joel (2008); Tolentino (2012); Espiritu (2017); and Diaz (2021).

5. MONSTROUS FEMININE SUPERHEROES

1. The spread of Hinduism or Hinduized concepts in the Philippines is generally believed to have been indirect, occurring mainly through contact with the Sriwijaya and Majapahit empires in Sumatra and Java, respectively, between the seventh and fourteenth centuries. Systems of writing based in India were also in use in certain parts of the Philippines prior to Spanish colonization, which began in the fifteenth century. See, e.g., Evangelista (1965).

2. For a more detailed analysis and ethnographic description of this ritual, see Yngvesson (2016:89–126).

3. On the rituals at Parangkusumo and their official and socially based rules, see, e.g., Gottowik (2018, 2020); and Smith and Woodward (2016).

4. See, e.g., Florida (1992); Jordaan (1984, 1997); and Resink (1997).

5. The dynasty's third king took the more overtly Islamic title of sultan. In the eighteenth century, Mataram split into two factions: the Sunanate of Surakarta and the Sultanate of Yogyakarta. Both are still active in the present, and the sultan of Yogyakarta still serves as the unelected governor of the city and the large and sociopolitically influential region surrounding it.

6. See, e.g., Hefner (2011); Gottowik (2020); Ricklefs (2008a); and Weng (2017).

7. The room was set aside after the hotel's disastrous beachside opening ceremony in which President Soekarno and various other luminaries present were drenched by a sudden wave that also wrecked the new hotel's dining area. Locals said the wave was caused by the hotel's refusal to give offerings to Ratu Kidul to ensure the success of the ceremony and hotel, which borders her ocean territory (Strassler 2014:111). Even now, filmmakers around Yogyakarta are also sensitive to the issue of spirit portrayal without ritual permission. As contemporary writer-director Makbul Mubarak explained at a question-and-answer session for the screening of his short film *Ruah* (*The Malediction*, 2016) in 2018, his original intention to prominently feature a painting of Ratu Kidul in the film was strongly objected to by his local collaborators (Mubarak is originally from Sulawesi). To his surprise, they were not joking when they said they felt it would be too "risky" to portray the queen without proper permission. Rather than going through the potentially elaborate rituals to get permission, he changed the painting to one that roughly resembles the queen. This involved shifting the main color of her costume to purple from the typical green, which is known as the queen's favorite color.

8. In the recent documentary *Suzzanna: The Queen of Black Magic* (dir. David Gregory, 2024), Suzzanna's role in her films is discussed in detail in interviews with key industry players who worked with her during her heyday, including her second husband, the actor Clift Sangra.

9. The New Order takeover of Gunung Kemukus also aimed at exerting pressure on residents to allow their land to be flooded by way of a dam the government would construct nearby. But whatever the intention, the result was that the site itself expanded its ritual operations with only slight modifications to the mythical narratives attached to it, which did not alter its symbolic basis in a legendary "power couple." For more on the takeover and narrative alterations, see de Guzman (2006).

10. The inclusion of scenes of policemen and kiai turning to the camera to voice the narrower concerns of masculine officialdom mirror ritual elements such as a banner I observed at the event at Parangkusumo detailed above. Despite the fact that prostitution, a major facet of the event, is illegal in Bantul, the regency where Parangkusumo is located, the banner thanked "Polres *dan* Kabupaten Bantul" (the offices of the local government and police) for their sponsorship and implicitly for their flexibility and understanding. Clearly the authorities make exceptions when the queen of the South Sea, with her connections to the reigning sultan and governor, is invoked. During the shadow-play performance, the banner's message was also reiterated by the puppet master in a manner similar to the film's mocking "public service announcements," using special puppets associated with satire and direct audience address. Both film and shadow play in this case deploy one of the key archipelagic conventions that I have identified in previous chapters as

embedded in regional cinemas and live performance: an interactive mode of expression that pauses narrative flow in order to engage with elements of the surrounding public sphere, linking actual and diegetic spaces.

11. As in *Bernafas Dalam Lumpur*, the "unnatural" death of the central female character at the hands of unscrupulous men under an officially masculine regime unleashes an uncanny force—one that embeds itself in the film's diegesis while projecting from the screen into the spaces of viewers. In the case of *Sundelbolong*, however, as in many other supernatural horror films, the death of the central female character does not come at the end of the narrative but in the beginning or the middle, after which the power released by her death (in the form of a vengeful ghost) becomes the focus of the film. One can also draw similarities between *Sundelbolong* and *Bumi Makin Panas*, another earlier Suzzanna vehicle in which her prostitute character has an almost supernatural ability to survive attacks. In *Sundelbolong*, once Alisa becomes a sundel bolong, she is similarly positioned as an unstoppable force that acts at the intersection of gender and law, humanity and the superhuman, and officially authorized and unauthorized power.

12. It does not, however, unduly minimize the roles of the female part of the site's Oedipus-like legend. That role is played by the prince's mother, *Ibu* Ontrowulan, who misrecognizes and falls in love with him after a long separation. It is she that female pilgrims mimetically embody in the performance of ritual, and the ritual sex act makes a "blessing" of the normally taboo union.

13. The net result of this can be unclear. Base sexual desire often carries negative connotations in Javanese philosophy, while sex framed as a union and transfer of knowledge and spiritual power between two participants, as in the cases of the legendary "power couples" behind the above rituals, is generally lauded. In this case, it appears to be a combination, but the lust with which the women approach male characters (contrasting with the heroes' stoicism toward the women) is likely aimed to showcase a certain spiritual weakness.

14. There are certain exceptions to this, most notably the 1970s, 1980s, and 1990s films starring the pop musician Rhoma Irama as a kiai-type figure also imbued with mystical powers.

15. As Eric Sasono argues, *laga* films in which the setting is anticolonial struggle also mirror shadow play (*wayang kulit*) in the convention of presenting Dutch characters "with untrimmed facial hair [who] . . . always speak in coarse language to emphasize their impolite behaviour." Likewise, in many wayang narratives involving characters meant to represent the position of the Dutch, the puppets used are generally villainous, "ogre-like creatures . . . depicted with physical deformation and speaking with coarse language" (2014:41).

16. See, for example, the 1959 16 mm version of *Mae Nak Phra Khanong* available on YouTube (dir. Rungsri Tasapayak), in which the ending sequence conveys a similar message.

6. RECLAIMING AFFECT

1. Building on current trends in local-language films, however, three recent movies have attempted to resurrect and capitalize on the stage legacy of Srimulat, although with less success than *Warkop DKI: Finding Srimulat* (dir. Charles Gozali, 2013) and *Srimulat: Hil Yang Mustahal*, chapters 1 (dir. Fajar Nugros, 2022) and 2 (dir. Fajar Nugros, 2023).

2. I conducted an interview in 2015 with the adult children of the late Herry Koko, the director of Surya Group at their home in Sidoarjo, East Java, which is in a neighborhood adjacent to that of my in-laws. The background information about the group came from this meeting and conversation, as did the photograph of the Surya Group.

3. *DKI* stands for Dono, Kasino, and Indro, the names of the three core members, but also mimics the initials of *Daerah Khusus Ibukota* or "Special Region of the Capital City," as the administrative area that includes Jakarta is known. On Warkop's history and theatrical and filmic approaches, see Kristanto (2004:108–11).

4. See Imanjaya (2014) and Sasono (2014) on the status of Indonesian supernatural horror as global cult cinema.

5. In chapter 5, I also frame Soeharto's partnership with his politically and publicly active wife as a similar kind of power couple, not unlike the "conjugal dictatorship" of Ferdinand Marcos in the Philippines.

6. See, e.g., Gottowik (2020); Ricklefs (2008a); and Weng (2017).

7. See *Suzzanna: The Queen of Black Magic* (dir. David Gregory, 2024).

8. Versions of the film that have since been edited together with Sasanatieng's commercial are available online; see, e.g., https://www.youtube.com/watch?v=qW85GRkHhLg.

9. See Yngvesson (2015) for a detailed analysis of how Riza, Achnas, Lesmana, and Mantovani's breakout 1998 film *Kuldesak* performed its inability to separate itself from Indonesia's aesthetic past, despite its codirectors' stated goals of doing just that.

10. For more on the Thai new wave, their aesthetics, and their politics, see Harrison (2006, 2007, 2024); Ingawanij (2006); Knee (2003); and Sutton (2012).

11. The power of "wielding" two sexes or gender identities together and without sublating one into the other also recalls Ben Murtagh's (2013) analysis of New Order–era Indonesian films featuring dynamic *waria* characters, indicating the local formulation of male-to-female transgender identity.

12. On these assumptions, see also Mary Anne Doane (1987).

13. *KKN* stands for *Kuliah Kerja Nyata*, which means "real work study" but is often translated as "Student Study Service." KKN is a special program required of undergrads in many Indonesian universities. It involves proposing a project, often aimed at teaching new skills or improving infrastructure, to be carried out by a group of students in a remote, rural, or otherwise underserved area. In the film, students are tasked with improving water management infrastructure in a village in East Java. The story for the film comes from a viral narrative posted on Twitter in 2019 by the user SimpleMan, who claimed it was based on his actual experiences during a KKN project in 2009.

14. The term *satanic* or *Satan* in English is an inadequate translation for the concept of *setan* in the film's title. While *setan* can at times refer to the Satan or devil of Abrahamic religions, it more often indicates a local concept of a nefarious ghost or spirit that does not align with the figures known to Islam or Christianity. Because of the way spirits and *setans* are positioned and rendered in *Pengabdi Setan*, I believe it invokes the non-Abrahamic version, despite its English translation as "Satan's Slaves."

REFERENCES

Ainslie, Mary J. 2014. "The Supernatural and Post-War Thai Cinema." *Horror Studies* 5(2):157–69.

Ainslie, Mary J. 2018. "Post-War Thai Cinema: Audiences and Film Style in a Divided Nation." Pp. 303–24 in *Rural Cinema Exhibition and Audiences in a Global Context*, edited by Daniela Treveri Gennari, Danielle Hipkins, and Catherine O'Rawe. Cham, Switzerland: Palgrave Macmillan.

Ainslie, Mary J. 2020. "Ratana Pestonji and *Santi Vina*: Exploring the 'Master' of Thai Cinema during Thailand's 'American Era.'" In Khoo, Barker, and Ainslie:171–91.

Althusser, Louis. 1971. "Ideology and Ideological State Apparatuses." Pp. 127–88 in *Lenin and Philosophy and Other Essays*. Translated by Ben Brewster. London: New Left Books.

Andaya, Barbara. 2007. *The Flaming Womb: Repositioning Women in Early Modern Southeast Asia*. Manoa, HI: University of Hawai'i Press.

Andaya, Barbara Watson, and Leonard Y. Andaya. 2015. *A History of Early Modern Southeast Asia, 1400–1830*. Cambridge: Cambridge University Press.

Anderson, Benedict R. O'G. 1983. *Imagined Communities: Reflections on the Origin and Spread of Nationalism*. London: Verso.

Anderson, Benedict R. O'G. 1998. *The Spectre of Comparisons: Nationalism, Southeast Asia, and the World*. New York: Verso.

Anggraini, Sazkia Noor, Rahayu Harjanthi, and Tito Imanda. 2021. *Menuju Kesetaraan Gender Perfilman Indonesia: Analisis Data Terpilah-Gender dan Rekomendasi Rencana Aksi* (Moving toward gender equity in Indonesian filmmaking: An analysis of data and recommendations around gender). Yogyakarta, Indonesia: Asosiasi Pengkaji Film Indonesia.

Anisah, Siti. 2022. "Filmografi Ratna Asmara" (Ratna Asmara's Filmography). Pp. 143–53 in *Ratna Asmara: Perempuan di Dua Sisi Kamera* (Ratna Asmara: Woman on both sides of the camera), edited by Umi Lestari, Julita Pratiwi, Efi Sri Handatyani, Imedla Taurina

Mandala, Lisabona Rahman, and Siti Anisah. Yogyakarta, Indonesia: Indonesian Visual Art Archive.

Ariesti, Lovelli. 2008. "Didin Syamsudin: The Queen's Makeup Artist." *Jakarta Post*. Nov. 2.

Armes, Roy. 1987. *Third World Filmmaking and the West*. Berkeley: University of California Press.

Aspinall, Edward. 2013. "A Nation in Fragments: Patronage and Neoliberalism in contemporary Indonesia." *Critical Asian Studies* 45(1):27–54.

Barker, Thomas. 2011. "A Cultural Economy of the Contemporary Indonesian Film Industry." PhD diss., Department of Sociology, National University of Singapore.

Barker, Thomas. 2019. *Indonesian Cinema after the New Order: Going Mainstream*. Hong Kong: Hong Kong University Press.

Barnard, Timothy. 2005. "Sedih Sampai Buta: Blindness, Modernity and Tradition in Malay Films of the 1950s and 1960s." *Bijdragen tot de Taal-, Land- en Volkenkunde* 161(4):433–53.

Barnard, Timothy. 2009. "Decolonization and the Nation in Malay Film, 1955–1965." *South East Asia Research* 17(1):65–86.

Barnard, Timothy P. and Jan van der Putten. 2008. "Malay Cosmopolitan Activism in Post-War Singapore." Pp. 132–53 in *Paths Not Taken: Political Pluralism in Post-War Singapore*, edited by Michael Bar and Carl Trocki. Singapore: NUS Press.

Baumgärtel, Tilman, ed. 2012. *Southeast Asian Independent Cinema: Essays, Documents, Interviews*. Hong Kong: Hong Kong University Press.

Benjamin, Walter. 1968. "The Work of Art in the Age of Mechanical Reproduction." Pp. 217–53 in *Illuminations*, edited by H. Arendt. New York: Schocken.

Berg, C. C. 1955. "The Islamisation of Java." *Studia Islamica* (4):111–42.

Berg, C. C. 1965. "The Javanese Picture of the Past." In Soedjatmoko, Resink, and Kahin:87–118.

Bernards, Brian. 2015. *Writing the South Seas: Imagining the Nanyang in Chinese and Southeast Asian Postcolonial Literature*. Seattle: University of Washington Press.

Biran, Misbach Yusa. 2008. *Kenang-Kenangan Orang Bandel* (The life and times of a rebel). Jakarta, Indonesia: Komunitas Bamboo.

Boellstorff, Tom. 2005. *The Gay Archipelago: Sexuality and Nation in Indonesia*. Princeton, NJ: Princeton University Press.

Borsuk, Richard, and Nancy Chng. 2014. *Liem Sioe Liong's Salim Group: The Business Pillar of Suharto's Indonesia*. Singapore: ISEAS.

Brown, Graham K. 2007. "Making Ethnic Citizens: The Politics and Practice of Education in Malaysia." *International Journal of Education Development* 27(3):318–30.

Campos, Patrick F. 2016. *The End of National Cinema: Filipino Film at the Turn of the Century*. Quezon City, Metro Manila: University of the Philippines Press.

Campos, Patrick F. 2021. "Topos, Historia, Islas: Film Islands and Regional Cinemas." In Lovatt and Trice 2021b:163–68.

Capino, José B. 2020. *Martial Law Melodrama: Lino Brocka's Cinema Politics*. Berkeley: University of California Press.

Cassetti, Francesco. 2015. *The Lumière Galaxy: Seven Key Words for the Cinema to Come*. New York: Columbia University Press.

Chaiworaporn, Anchalee. 2001. "Thai Cinema since 1970." Pp. 141–62 in *Film in South East Asia: Views from the Region: Essays on Film in Ten South East Asia-Pacific Countries*, edited by David Hanan. Manila: SEAPAVAA (Southeast Asia-Pacific Audiovisual Archive Association).

Chulphongsathorn, Graiwoot. 2021. "The Cinematic Forest and Southeast Asian Cinema." In Lovatt and Trice 2021b:182–87.

Cohen, Matthew Isaac. 2006. *The Komedie Stamboel: Popular Theater in Colonial Indonesia, 1891–1903*. Athens: Ohio University Press.

Crofts, Steven. 1993. "Reconceptualizing National Cinema/s." *Quarterly Review of Film & Video* 14(3):49–67.

Cruz, Francis Joseph A. 2011. "Evolutions and Devolutions in Philippine Cinema: A Brief History of Cinema in the Philippines." Pp. 383–93 in *Southeast Asian Cinema/Le cinéma d'Asie du Sud-Est*, edited by Gaetan Margirier and Jean-Pierre Gimenez. Lyon, France: Asiexpo.

David, Joel. 2008. "The Cold War and Marcos Era Cinema in the Philippines." Pp. 1–29 in *Proceedings of the 8th ASEAN Inter-university Conference on Social Development* (CD-ROM), edited by Almond Pilar Aguila, Danilo Araña Arao, Alfonso Deza, Lourdes Portus, and Fernando Paragas. Quezon City, Philippines: University of the Philippines, Union Network International.

De Guzman, Orlando. 2006. "Apakah Ada Hubungan Antara G30S Dan Munculnya Mitos Pangeran Samodro Di Gunung Kumukus?" ("Is There a Relationship between G30S and the Emergence of the Myth of Prince Samudra at Gunung Kumukus?"). Malang, Indonesia: Department of Social Science and Political Science, Muhammadiyah University, Malang.

Deleuze, Gilles. 1989. *Cinema 2: The Time-Image*. Minneapolis: University of Minnesota Press.

Diaz, Josen Masangkay. 2021. "Chaos and Order in Lino Brocka's *Insiang* (1976)." In "Anti-Martial Law." Special issue, *Alon: Journal for Filipinx American and Diasporic Studies* 1(3):311–30.

Dieleman, Marleen. 2007. *The Rhythm of Strategy: A Corporate Biography of the Salim Group of Indonesia*. Amsterdam, the Netherlands: Amsterdam University Press.

Dieleman, Marleen. 2011. "Continuous and Discontinuous Change in Ethnic Chinese Business Networks: The Case of the Salim Group." Pp. 201–26 in *Chinese Indonesians and Regime Change*, edited by Marleen Dieleman, Juliette Koning, and Peter Post. Boston: Brill.

Doane, Mary Anne. 1987. *The Desire to Desire: The Woman's Film of the 1940s*. Bloomington: Indiana University Press.

Driskell, Jonathan, ed. 2022. *Film Stardom in Southeast Asia*. Edinburgh, UK: Edinburgh University Press.

Engchuan, Rosalia Namsai. 2021. "Landscapes of Possibility: Community Filmmaking in Indonesia as a Relational Process." *Bijdragen tot de Taal-, Land- en Volkenkunde* 177(2/3):221–33.

Espiritu, Talitha. 2017. "National Discipline and the Cinema." Pp. 84–115 in *Passionate Revolutions: The Media and the Rise and Fall of the Marcos Regime*. Athens: Ohio University Press.

Evangelista, Alfredo E. 1965. "Identifying Some Intrusive Archaeological Materials Found in Philippine Proto-historic Sites." *Asian Studies Journal* 3(1):86–102.

Film Indonesia. http://filmindonesia.or.id/.

Film in the Philippines: A Report by Tony Rayns (documentary film). 1983. Directed by Ron Orders. London: Channel Four. https://archive.org/details/vcfitp.

Florida, Nancy. 1992. "The Badhaya Katawang: A Translation of the Song of Kanjeng Ratu Kidul." *Indonesia* 53(April):20–32.

Francia, Luis H. 2002. "Side-Stepping History—Beginnings to 1980s." Pp. 346–64 in *Being & Becoming: The Cinemas of Asia*, edited by Aruna Vasudev, Latika Padgaonkar, and Rashmi Doraiswamy. New Delhi: Macmillan India.

Frymus, Agata. 2022. "Cinemagoing in Kuala Lumpur: Memories, Movies, and the Multiethnic City, 1970–1979." *Film History: An International Journal* 34(1):55–81. https://dx.doi.org/10.2979/filmhistory.34.1.03.

Fuhrmann, Arnika. 2009. "Nang Nak—Ghost Wife: Desire, Embodiment, and Buddhist Melancholia in a Contemporary Thai Ghost Film." In "Translation and Embodiment in National and Transnational Asian Film and Media." Special issue, *Discourse* 31(3):220–47.

Fuhrmann, Arnika. 2016. *Ghostly Desires: Queer Sexuality and Vernacular Buddhism in Contemporary Thai Cinema*. Durham, NC: Duke University Press, 2016.

Gabriel, Teshome H. 1982. *Third Cinema in the Third World: An Aesthetics of Liberation*. Ann Arbor, MI: UMI Research Press.

Galt, Rosalind. 2021. *Alluring Monsters: The Pontianak and Cinemas of Decolonization*. New York: Columbia University Press.

Galt, Rosalind. 2026. "Tales of Entrails: Animist Cult Horror in Southeast Asia." In *Global Cult Cinemas: Decolonising Cult Film Studies*, edited by Iain Robert Smith, Dolores Tierney, and Shruti Narayanswami. London: Bloomsbury.

Ganguly, Keya. 2010. *Cinema, Emergence, and the Films of Satyajit Ray*. Berkeley: University of California Press.

Geertz, Hildred. 1968. "*Latah* in Java: A Theoretical Paradox." *Indonesia* 5:93–104.

Gonzaga, Elmo. 2016. "Introduction: Archipelagic Intermediality." Introduction to special *Forum Kritika* section entitled "Strange Convergences: Intermedial Encounters in Southeast Asia," edited by Elmo Gonzaga, *Kritika Kultura* 27:92–102.

Gonzaga, Elmo. 2017. "The Cinematographic Unconscious of Slum Voyeurism." *Cinema Journal* 56(4):102–25.

Gonzaga, Elmo. 2024. *Monsoon Marketplace: Capitalism, Media, and Modernity in Manila and Singapore*. New York: Fordham University Press.

Gottowik, Volker. 2018. "Pilgrims, Prostitutes and *Ritual Seks*: Heterodox Ritual Practices in the Context of the Islamic Veneration of Saints in Central Java." *Bijdragen tot de Taal-, Land- en Volkenkunde* 174(4):393–421.

Gottowik, Volker. 2020. "Ritual, Sex and the Body: Heterodox Ritual Practices at Pilgrimage Sites in Central Java." *Asia Pacific Journal of Anthropology* 21(4):332–51.

Guelden, Marlane. 1995. *Thailand: Into the Spirit World*. Bangkok: Asia Books.

Guiness World Records. 2023. "Most Horror-Focused Film Industry (Country)." https://www.guinnessworldrecords.com/world-records/772733-most-horror-focused-film-industry-country.

Gunning, Tom. 1986. "The Cinema of Attractions: Early Cinema, Its Spectator and the Avant-Garde." *Wide Angle* 8(3–4):63–70.

Hamilton, Annette. 1992. "The Mediascape of Modern Southeast Asia." *Screen* 33(1):81–92.

Hanan, David. 2009. "A Tradition of Political Allegory and Political Satire in Indonesian Cinema." Pp. 14–46 in *Asian Hot Shots: Indonesian Cinema*, edited by Y. Michalik and L. Coppens. Marburg, Germany: Schüren.

Hanan, David. 2017. *Cultural Specificity in Indonesian Film: Diversity in Unity*. Cham: Palgrave Macmillan.

Hansen, Kathryn. 1999. "Making Women Visible: Gender and Race Cross-Dressing in the Parsi Theatre." *Theatre Journal* 51(2):127–47.

Hansen, Miriam. 1999. "The Mass Production of the Senses: Classical Cinema as Vernacular Modernism." *Modernism/Modernity* 6(2):59–77.

Hansen, Miriam Bratu. 2000. "Fallen Women, Rising Stars, New Horizons: Shanghai Silent Film as Vernacular Modernism." *Film Quarterly* 54(1):10–22.

Hansen, Miriam Bratu. 2012. "Tracking Cinema on a Global Scale." Pp. 601–26 in *The Oxford Handbook of Global Modernisms*, edited by Mark Wollaeger and Matt Eatough. Oxford: Oxford University Press.

Harrison, Rachel. 2006. "Amazing Thai Film: The Rise and Rise of Contemporary Thai Cinema on the International Screen." *Asian Affairs* 36(3):321–38.

Harrison, Rachel. 2007. "'Somewhere over the Rainbow': Global Projections/Local Allusions in *Tears of the Black Tiger/Fa Thalai Jone*." *Inter-Asia Cultural Studies* 8(2): 194–210.

Harrison, Rachel. 2024. "Global Aspirations/Local Affiliations: Exploring the Tensions of 'Post-Crisis' Thai Cinema, 1997–2004." In Zhen et al.:335–45.

Harvey, David. 2007. *A Brief History of Neoliberalism*. Oxford: Oxford University Press.

Hatley, Barbara. 1979. *Ketoprak Theatre and the Wayang Tradition*. Sydney: Department of Indonesian and Malay, University of Sydney.

Hefner, Robert. 2011. "Where Have All the Abangan Gone? Religionization and the Decline of Non-standard Islam in Contemporary Indonesia." Pp. 71–91 in *The Politics of Religion in Indonesia: Syncretism, Orthodoxy, and Religious Contention in Java and Bali*, edited by Michel Picard and Rémy Madinier. New York: Routledge.

Hermanu, ed. 2010. *Illustrasi Karya B. Margono* (Illustrations and works of B. Margono). Yogyakarta, Indonesia: Bentara Budaya.

Hewison, Kevin. 2005. "Neo-liberalism and Domestic Capital: The Political Outcomes of the Economic Crisis in Thailand." *Journal of Development Studies* 41(2):310–30.

Hinton, Devon. 2012. "Healing through Flexibility Primers." Pp. 121–63 in *The Oxford Handbook of Medical Ethnomusicology*, edited by Benjamin D. Koen. New York: Oxford University Press.

Huyssen, Andreas. 1986. "Mass Culture as Woman: Modernism's Other." Pp. 44–62 in *After the Great Divide: Modernism, Mass Culture, Postmodernism*. Bloomington: Indiana University Press.

Imanjaya, Ekky. 2014. "The Significance of Indonesian Cult, Exploitation, and B Movies." *Plaridel* 11(2):i–xi.

Imanjaya, Ekky. 2021. *Usmar Ismail: Mujahid Film*. Jakarta: Kineforum and Storial.

Ingawanij, May Adadol. 2006. "Transistor and Temporality: The Rural as Modern Thai Cinema's Pastoral." Pp. 80–97 in *Representing the Rural: Space, Place, and Identity in Films about the Land*, edited by Catherine Fowler and Gillian Helfield. Detroit, MI: Wayne State University Press.

Ingawanij, May Adadol. 2012. "*Mother India* in Six Voices: Melodrama, Voice Performance, and Indian Films in Siam." *BioScope* 3(2):99–121.

Ingawanij, May Adadol. 2018. "Itinerant Cinematic Practices in and around Thailand during the Cold War." *Southeast of Now: Directions in Contemporary and Modern Art in Asia* 2(1):9–41.

Ingawanij, May Adadol, and Benjamin McKay, eds. 2012. *Glimpses of Freedom: Independent Cinema in Southeast Asia*. Ithaca, NY: Southeast Asia Program, Cornell University.

Ismail, Usmar. 1983. *Usmar Ismail Mengupas Film* (Usmar Ismail unwraps film), compiled by J. E. Siahaan. Jakarta: Sinar Agape Press.

Izharuddin, Alicia. 2017. *Gender and Islam in Indonesian Cinema*. Singapore: Palgrave MacMillan.

Izharuddin, Alicia. 2020. "The Laugh of the Pontianak: Darkness and Feminism in Malay Folk Horror." *Feminist Media Studies* 20(7):999–1012.

Jackson, Yo, ed. 2006. *Encyclopedia of Multicultural Psychology*. London: Sage.

Jameson, Fredric. 1986. "Third-World Literature in the Era of Multinational Capitalism." *Social Text* 15(Autumn):65–88.

Jameson, Fredric. 1991. *Postmodernism, or, The Cultural Logic of Late Capitalism*. Durham, NC: Duke University Press.

Jenkins, Henry. 1992. *What Made Pistachio Nuts? Early Sound Comedy and the Vaudeville Aesthetic*. New York: Columbia University Press.

Jordaan, R. 1984. "The Mystery of Nyai Lara Kidul, Goddess of the Southern Ocean." *Archipel* 28:99–116.

Jordaan, R. 1997. Tara and Nyai Lara Kidul: Images of the Divine Feminine in Java. *Asian Folklore Studies* 56(2):285–312.

Jordaan, R., and P. de Josselin de Jong. 1985. "Sickness as a Metaphor in Indonesian Political Myths." *Bijdragen tot de Taal-, Land- en Volkenkunde* 141(2/3):253–74.

Juniarto, Damar. 2016. "Ada Apa Dengan *Tiga Dara?*" (What's up with *Tiga Dara?*). *Cinema Poetica*, August 11. http://cinemapoetica.com/ada-apa-dengan-tiga-dara/.

Karim, Wazir Jahan. 1995. "Introduction: Genderising Anthropology in Southeast Asia." Pp. 11–34 in *"Male" and "Female" in Developing Southeast Asia*, edited by Wazir Jahan Karim. Oxford: Berg.

Khoo, Gaik Cheng. 2006. *Reclaiming Adat: Contemporary Malaysian Film and Literature*. Vancouver: University of British Columbia Press.

Khoo, Gaik Cheng. 2024. "'Still Doing It Themselves, with a Little Help from Friends': Independent Filmmaking in Malaysia Two Decades Hence." In Zhen et al.:382–91.

Khoo, Gaik Cheng, Thomas Barker, and Mary J. Ainslie, eds. 2020. *Southeast Asia on Screen: From Independence to Financial Crisis (1945–1998)*. Amsterdam, the Netherlands: Amsterdam University Press.

King, Victor T., and William D. Wilder. 2003. *The Modern Anthropology of South-East Asia: An Introduction*. New York: Routledge.

Knee, Adam. 2003. "Gendering the Thai Economic Crisis: The Films of Pen-ek Ratanaruang." *Asian Cinema* 14(2):102–21.

Knee, Adam. 2014. "Reincarnating Mae Nak: The Contemporary Cinematic History of a Thai Icon." *Horror Studies* 5(2):211–31.

Kong, Rithdee. 2020. "Uncle Boonmee at 10." *Bangkok Post*, May 22. https://www.bangkokpost.com/life/social-and-lifestyle/1922384/uncle-boonmee-at-10.

Kristanto, J. B. 2004. *Nonton Film Nonton Indonesia* (Watching films watching Indonesia). Jakarta: Kompas Press.

Kurnia, Novi. 2014. "Women Directors in Post–New Order Indonesia: Making Film, Making a Difference." PhD diss., Department of Women's Studies, Flinders University.

Lacan, Jacques. [1966] 2002. *Écrits: A Selection*. Translated by Bruce Fink. New York: Norton.

Lacan, Jacques. 1998. *The Seminar of Jacques Lacan: Book XI*. New York: Norton.

Laclau, Ernesto. 2005. *On Populist Reason*. New York: Verso.

Larasati, Rachmi Diyah. 2013. *The Dance That Makes You Vanish: Cultural Reconstruction in Post-Genocide Indonesia*. Minneapolis: University of Minnesota Press.

Larkin, Brian. 2008. *Signal and Noise: Media, Infrastructure, and Urban Culture in Nigeria*. Durham, NC: Duke University Press.

Lestari, Umi. 2020. "Basuki Resobowo as a Jack of All Trades: The Intersectionality of Arts and Film in Perfini Films and Resobowo's Legacy in Indonesian Cinema." *Southeast of Now: Directions in Contemporary and Modern Art in Asia* 4(2):313–45.

Lestari, Umi, et al. 2022. "Ratna Asmara." Pp. 21–87 in *Ratna Asmara: Perempuan di Dua Sisi Kamera* (Ratna Asmara: Woman on both sides of the camera), edited by Umi Lestari, Julita Pratiwi, Efi Sri Handatyani, Imedla Taurina Mandala, Lisabona Rahman, and Siti Anisah. Yogyakarta, Indonesia: Indonesian Visual Art Archive.

Lieberman, Victor. 2010. *Strange Parallels*. Vol. 1, *Integration of the Mainland: Southeast Asia in Global Context, c. 800–1830*. Cambridge: Cambridge University Press.

Lim, Bliss Cua. 2009. *Translating Time: Cinema, the Fantastic, and Temporal Critique*. Durham, NC. Duke University Press.

Lim, David C. L., and Hiroyuki Yamamoto, eds. 2012. *Film in Contemporary Southeast Asia: Cultural Interpretation and Social Intervention*. New York: Routledge.

Lovatt, Philippa. 2021. "The Acoustics of the Archipelagic Imagination in Southeast Asian Artists' Film." In Lovatt and Trice 2021b:176–81.

Lovatt, Philippa, and Jasmine Nadua Trice. 2021a. "Theorizing Region: Film and Video Cultures in Southeast Asia." In Lovatt and Trice 2021b:158–62.

Lovatt, Philippa, and Jasmine Nadua Trice, eds. 2021b. "Theorizing Region: Film and Video Cultures in Southeast Asia." In Focus section of *Journal of Cinema and Media Studies* 60(3).

Lumbera, Bienvenido. 1984. *Revaluation: Essays on Philippine Literature, Cinema and Popular Culture*. Manila: Index Press.

Lumbera, Bienvenido. 2011. *Re-viewing Filipino Cinema*. Mandaluyong City, Philippines: Anvil.

Masak, Tanete Pong. 2016. *Sinema pada Masa Soekarno* (Cinema in the Sukarno era). Jakarta, Indonesia: FFTV-IKJ.

McGrath, Jason. 2023. *Chinese Film: Realism and Convention from the Silent Era to the Digital Age*. Minneapolis: University of Minnesota Press.

Moertono, Soemarsaid. 1981. *State and Statecraft in Old Java: Study of the Later Mataram Period, 16th to 19th Century*. Ithaca, NY: Cornell Modern Indonesia Project.

Mulvey, Laura. [1975] 1999. "Visual Pleasure and Narrative Cinema." Pp. 833–44 in *Film Theory and Criticism*, 5th ed., edited by L. Braudy and M. Cohen. New York: Oxford University Press.

Mulvey, Laura. 1989. "Afterthoughts on 'Visual Pleasure and Narrative Cinema' Inspired by King Vidor's *Duel in the Sun* (1946)." Pp. 29–38 in *Visual and Other Pleasures*. Bloomington: Indiana University Press.

Murtagh, Ben. 2013. *Genders and Sexualities in Indonesian Cinema: Constructing* Gay, Lesbi *and* Waria *Identities on Screen*. New York: Routledge.

Muthalib, Hassan. 2013. *Malaysian Cinema in a Bottle: A Century and a Bit More of Wayang.* Petaling Jaya, Malaysia: Merpati Jingga.

Normanda, Nosa. 2021. "Ibu Arkaik dan Bapak Yang Mati di Pengabdi Setan dan Perempuan Tanah Jahanam" (The Archaic Mother and the Dead Father in Pengabdi Setan and Perempuan Tanah Jahanam). *Esai Nosa* (blog). https://eseinosa.com/2021/09/17/ibu-arkaik-dan-bapak-yang-mati-di-pengabdi-setan-dan-perempuan-tanah-jahanam/.

Nguyen, Viet Thanh, and Janet Hoskins. 2014. "Introduction: Transpacific Studies: Critical Perspectives on an Emerging Field." Pp. 1–40 in *Transpacific Studies: Framing an Emerging Field,* edited by Janet Hoskins and Viet Thanh Nguyen. Honolulu: University of Hawai'i Press.

Nugroho, Garin, and Dina Herlina. 2015. *The Crisis and Paradox of Indonesian Film (1900–2012).* Yogyakarta, Indonesia: Provincial Office for Culture of Yogyakarta Province.

Ong, Aihwa, and Michael G. Peletz. 1995. "Introduction." Pp. 1–19 in *Bewitching Women, Pious Men: Gender and Body Politics in Southeast Asia,* edited by Aihwa Ong and Michael G. Peletz. Berkeley: University of California Press, 1995.

Pandji, Dhanurendra. 2021. "Candi Cetho: Manifestasi Ideologi Mistik Kejawen Orde Baru" (Candi Cetho: Manifestation of the New Order's mystical kejawen ideology). Pp. 22–28 in *Kanal Memori,* edited by Otty Widasari. Jakarta, Indonesia: Forum Lenteng.

Pané, Armijn. 1953. *Produksi Film Tjerita di Indonesia: Perkembangannja Sebagai Alat Masjarakat* (Narrative film production in Indonesia: Its development as a tool of people). Jakarta: Badan Musjawarat Kebudajaan Nasional.

Paramaditha, Intan. 2024. "Transnational Women's Cinema in Southeast Asia: Mouly Surya's *Marlina the Murderer in Four Acts.*" In Zhen et al.:70–81.

Pasaribu, Adrian Jonathan. 2020. "After the Curfew: A Nation of Dead Ends." Online essay for *Criterion Collection.* https://www.criterion.com/current/posts/7116-after-the-curfew-a-nation-of-dead-ends.

Pedoman. 1970. "Apa Jang Kau Tontonkan, Palupi?" (What Are You Watching, Palupi?). April 9.

Poedjosoedarmo, Gloria. 1983. "The Position of Women in Java." *Indonesia Circle. School of Oriental and African Studies. Newsletter* 11(32):3–9.

Pratiwi, Julia. 2022. "Kode Pelapukan dan Bahasa Keibuan dalam *Dr. Samsi.*" (The corrosion code and the language of motherhood in *Dr. Samsi*). Pp. 113–29 in *Ratna Asmara: Perempuan di Dua Sisi Kamera* (Ratna Asmara: Woman on both sides of the camera), edited by Umi Lestari, Julita Pratiwi, Efi Sri Handatyani, Imedla Taurina Mandala, Lisabona Rahman, and Siti Anisah. Yogyakarta, Indonesia: Indonesian Visual Art Archive.

Purwanto, Bambang, Abdul Wahid, Gerry van Klinken, Ireen Hoogenboom, Martijn Eickhoff, Roel Frakking, and Yulianti, eds. 2023. *Revolutionary Worlds: Local Perspectives and Dynamics during the Indonesian Independence War, 1945–1949.* Amsterdam, the Netherlands: Amsterdam University Press.

Rafael, Vicente L. 2005. *The Promise of the Foreign: Nationalism and the Technics of Translation in the Spanish Philippines.* Durham, NC: Duke University Press.

Rahmat, Ahmad Fuad. 2020. "Neither Here nor There: The Uneven Modernisation of Malay Masculinity." PhD diss., School of Media, Languages and Cultures, University of Nottingham, Malaysia.

Rajadhyaksha, Ashish. 2009. *Indian Cinema in the Time of Celluloid: From Bollywood to the Emergency*. Bloomington: Indiana University Press.

Reid, Anthony. 2011. *To Nation by Revolution: Indonesia in the 20th Century*. Singapore: National University of Singapore Press.

Reid, Anthony. 2015. *A History of Southeast Asia: Critical Crossroads*. West Sussex: Wiley Blackwell.

Resink, G. J. 1997. "Kanjeng Ratu Kidul: The Second Divine Spouse of the Sultans of Ngayogyakarta." *Asian Folklore Studies* 56:313–16.

Richardson, Thomas. 2016. "Interview with Chatrichalerm Yukol." *Medium* (blog). https://medium.com/@anticonsultant/interview-with-chatrichalerm-yukol-26d00b18c9b6.

Ricklefs, M. C. 2008a. "The Birth of the Abangan." *Bijdragen tot de Taal-, Land- en Volkenkunde* 162(1):35–55.

Ricklefs, M. C. 2008b. *A History of Modern Indonesia since c. 1200*. 4th ed. New York: Palgrave Macmillan.

Roberts, Martin. 2000. "Indonesia: The Movie." Pp. 162–76 in *Cinema and Nation*, edited by Mette Hjort and Scott Mackenzie. New York: Routledge.

Robinson, Geoffrey. 1995. *The Dark Side of Paradise: Political Violence in Bali*. Ithaca, NY: Cornell University Press.

Roces, Mina. 2022. *Gender in Southeast Asia*. Cambridge: Cambridge University Press.

Roosa, John. 2006. *Pretext for Mass Murder: The September 30th Movement & Suharto's Coup d'état in Indonesia*. Madison: University of Wisconsin Press.

Roosa, John. 2020. *Buried Histories: The Anticommunist Massacres of 1965–1966 in Indonesia*. Madison: University of Wisconsin Press.

Rudnyckyj, Daromir. 2009. "Spiritual Economies: Islam and Neoliberalism in Contemporary Indonesia." *Cultural Anthropology* 24(1):104–41.

Ruppin, Dafna. 2016. *The Komedi Bioscoop: Early Cinema in Colonial Indonesia*. Bloomington: Indiana University Press.

Said, Salim. 1991. *Shadows on the Silver Screen: A Social History of Indonesian Film*. Jakarta: Lontar Foundation.

Saito, Ayako. 2014. "Occupation and Memory: The Representation of Woman's Body in Postwar Japanese Cinema." Pp. 327–62 in *The Oxford Handbook of Japanese Cinema*, edited by Daisuke Miyao. Oxford: Oxford University Press.

Sani, Asrul. 1997. *Surat-Surat Kepercayaan* (Letters of faith), compiled by Ajip Rosidi. Jakarta, Indonesia: Pustaka Jaya.

Sasono, Eric. 2014. "The Raiding Dutchmen: Colonial Stereotypes, Identity and Islam in Indonesian B-movies." *Plaridel* 11(2):23–53.

Sedyaningsih, Endang R. 2010. *Perempuan-Perempuan Kramat Tunggak* (The women of Kramat Tunggak). Jakarta: Kepustakaan Populer Gramedia.

Sembiring, Edi. 2010. "Bermula Dari Ucapan Pelacur" (Beginning with the calls of prostitutes). *Jejak-jejak Meracau* (Delirious steps) (blog). Sept. 30. http://edisantana.blogspot.com/2010/09/bermula-dari-ucapan-para-pelacur.html.

Sen, Krishna. 1993. "Politics of Melodrama in Indonesian Cinema." Pp. 205–17 in *Melodrama and Asian Cinema*, edited by W. Dissanayake. Cambridge: Cambridge University Press.

Sen, Krishna. 1994. *Indonesian Cinema: Framing the New Order*. London: Zed.

Sen, Krishna. 2003. "What's 'Oppositional' in Indonesian Cinema?" Pp. 147–65 in *Rethinking Third Cinema*, edited by A. R. Guneratne and W. Dissanayake. New York: Routledge.

Sen, Krishna. 2015. "The Death of a Film Legacy: Remembering Indonesia's Bachtiar Siagian." *The Conversation*, Oct. 12. https://theconversation.com/death-of-a-film-legacy -remembering-indonesias-bachtiar-siagian-48444.

Sen, Krishna, and David T. Hill. 2000. *Media, Culture and Politics in Indonesia*. Oxford: Oxford University Press.

Shohat, Ella, and Robert Stam. 2014. *Unthinking Eurocentrism: Multiculturalism and the Media*. 2nd ed. London: Routledge.

Siagian, Bachtiar. 1957. "Prinsip-prinsip Pemilihan dan Pengorganisasian Material" (The principles of choosing material and organization). *Purnama* (22):9–10.

Siagian, Bachtiar, and Windu Yusuf. 2013. "Bachtiar Siagian Dan Misteri Realisme Sosialis Dalam Film Indonesia" (Bachtiar Siagian and the mystery of socialist realism in Indonesian film). *Indoprogress*, Nov. 5. https://www.tribunal1965.org/bachtiar-siagian-dan -misteri-realisme-sosialis-dalam-film-indonesia/.

Siegel, James T. 1986. *Solo in the New Order: Language and Hierarchy in an Indonesian City*. Princeton, NJ: Princeton University Press.

Sim, Gerald. 2020. *Postcolonial Hangups in Southeast Asian Cinema: Poetics of Space, Sound, and Stability*. Amsterdam, the Netherlands: Amsterdam University Press.

Simons, Ronald C. 2001. "Introduction to Culture-Bound Syndromes." *Psychiatric Times* 18(11). http://web.mnstate.edu/robertsb/306/Intro%20to%20Culture%20Bound %20Syndromes.pdf.

Singer, Ben. 2014. "Triangulating Japanese Film Style." Pp. 33–60 in *The Oxford Handbook of Japanese Cinema*, edited by Daisuke Miyao. Oxford: Oxford University Press.

Situmorang, Sitor. 1955a. "*Lewat Djam Malam, Tarmina, Hasil Dua Dunia*" (*After the Curfew, Tarmina, Result of Two Worlds*"). *Dunia Film* (Film world), May 15, 9–11.

Situmorang, Sitor. 1955b. *Tarmina*. Film review in *Dunia Film* (Film world), June 1, 6, 28.

Sjarief, Mardali. 1970. "Mau Kemana Engkau, Palupi?" (Where Are You Going, Palupi?). *Purnama*, April 19.

Smith, Bianca J., and Mark Woodward. 2016. "Magico-Spiritual Power, Female Sexuality and Ritual Sex in Muslim Java: Unveiling the Kesekten of Magical Women." *Australian Journal of Anthropology* 27:317–32.

Soedjatmoko, Mohammad Ali. 1965. "The Indonesian Historian and His Time." In Soedjatmoko, Resink, and Kahin:404–16.

Soedjatmoko, Mohammad Ali, G. J. Resink, and G. McT. Kahin, eds. 1965. *An Introduction to Indonesian Historiography*. Ithaca, NY: Cornell University Press.

Soh, Byungkuk. 2007. "In Search of 'Unity in Diversity': The Image of Women in New Order Indonesia. *International Area Review* 10(2):67–94.

Strassler, Karen. 2014. "Seeing the Unseen in Indonesia's Public Sphere: Photographic Appearances of a Spirit Queen." *Comparative Studies in Society and History* 56(1):98–130.

Sungsri, Patsorn. 2004. "Thai Cinema as National Cinema: An Evaluative History." PhD diss., Murdoch University, Australia.

Sunya, Samhita. 2022. *Sirens of Modernity: World Cinema via Bombay*. Berkeley: University of California Press.

Suryadinata, Leo. 1972. "Indonesian Chinese Education: Past and Present." *Indonesia* (14):49–71.

Sutandio, Anton. 2019. "The Politics of Religion in Sisworo Gautama Putra's and Joko Anwar's *Pengabdi Setan*." *Kata* 21(1):24–32.

Sutton, David. 2012. "Philosophy, Politics and Homage in *Tears of the Black Tiger*." Pp. 37–53 in *Deleuze and Film*, edited by David Martin-Jones and William Brown. Edinburgh: Edinburgh University Press.

Swestin, Grace. 2009. "In the Boys' Club: A Historical Perspective on the Roles of Women in the Indonesian Cinema, 1926–May 1998." *Jurnal Ilmiah SCRIPTURA* 3(2):103–11.

Tan, Sooi Beng. 1989. "From Popular to 'Traditional' Theater: The Dynamics of Change in Bangsawan of Malaysia." *Ethnomusicology* 33(2):229–74.

Tan, Sooi Beng. 1993. *Bangsawan: A Social and Stylistic History of Popular Malay Opera*. Singapore: Oxford University Press.

Tan, Sooi Beng. 1995. "Breaking Tradition: Women Stars of Bangsawan Theatre." *Bijdragen tot de Taal-, Land- en Volkenkunde* 151(4):602–16.

Tanner, Nancy. 1974. "Matrifocality in Indonesia and Africa and among Black Americans." Pp. 129–56 in *Woman, Culture, and Society*, edited by Michelle Z. Rosaldo and Louise Lamphere. Stanford, CA: Stanford University Press.

Tarling, Nicholas. 2004. *Nationalism in Southeast Asia: "If the People Are with Us."* New York: RoutledgeCurzon.

Tempo. 1974. "Ha, Ha, Ha, Buat Film Indonesia. Dari Seni Melucu S/D Air Seni" (Ha, ha, ha for Indonesian cinema: From comedy to artistic lineage). *Tempo*, July 27, 44–48.

Thevoideck. 2010. "Tears of the Black Tiger (2000) by Wisit Sasanatieng." *The Void Deck: A Flim Blog* (blog). Dec. 10. https://thevoideck.wordpress.com/2010/12/10/tears-of-the -black-tiger-2000-by-wisit-sasanatieng/.

Thomas, Rosie. 1985. "Indian Cinema: Pleasures and Popularity. An Introduction by Rosie Thomas." *Screen* 26(34):116–31.

Tofighian, Nadi. 2013. "Blurring the Colonial Binary: Turn-of-the-Century Transnational Entertainment in Southeast Asia." PhD diss., Stockholm University.

Tolentino, Roland. 2012. "Forum Kritika: A Closer Look at *Manila by Night*. Marcos, Brocka, Bernal, City Films, and the Contestation for Imagery of Nation." *Kritika Kultura* 19:115–38.

Trice, Jasmine Nadua. 2021. "Performing Region in Southeast Asian Film Industries." In Lovatt and Trice 2021b:188–93.

Trice, Jasmine Nadua. 2024. "Domestic Temporalities and Film Practice: Los Otros, Quezon City, and Forum Lenteng, Jakarta." In Zhen et al.:425–33.

van Heeren, Katinka. 2012. *Contemporary Indonesian Film: Spirits of Reform and Ghosts from the Past*. Leiden: KITLV Press.

van Wichelen, Sonja. 2007. "Embodied Contestations: Muslim Politics and Democratization in Indonesia through the Prism of Gender." PhD diss., University of Amsterdam.

van Wichelen, Sonja. 2010. *Religion, Politics and Gender in Indonesia: Disputing the Muslim Body*. New York: Routledge.

Vatsyayan, Kapila Malik. 1971. "Aesthetic Theories Underlying Asian Performing Arts." Pp. 15–27 in *The Performing Arts in Asia*, edited by James R. Brandon. Paris: UNESCO.

Vasudevan, Ravi. 1989. "The Melodramatic Mode and the Commercial Hindi Cinema: Notes on Film History, Narrative and Performance in the 1950s." *Screen* 30(3):29–50.

Vasudevan, Ravi. 1993. "Shifting Codes, Dissolving Identities: The Hindi Social Film of the 1950s as Popular Culture." *Journal of Arts and Ideas* (23–24):51–84.

Wardaya, Baskara T. 2007. *Membongkar Supersemar! Dari CIA Hingga Kudeta Meranggak Melawan Bung Karno* (Taking apart Supersemar! From the CIA to the creeping coup d'état against Sukarno). Yogyakarta, Indonesia: Galang Press.

Weintraub, Andrew N. 2022. "Padang Moonrise: The Birth of the Modern Indonesian Recording Industry, 1955–69." Liner notes published with *Padang Moonrise* (LP). London: Soundway Records.

Weng, Hew Wai. 2017. "Middle Class Competition and Islamic Populism." *New Mandala*, May 2. http://www.newmandala.org/competitions-among-middle-classes/.

Wessing, Robert. 1997. "A Princess from Sunda: Some Aspects of Nyai Roro Kidul." *Asian Folklore Studies* 56(2):317–53.

Wieringa, Saskia. 1997. "Matrilinearity and Women's Interests: The Minangkabau of Western Sumatra." Pp. 241–68 in *Subversive Women: Historical Experiences of Gender and Resistance*, edited by Saskia Wieringa. New York: Zed.

Wieringa, Saskia. 2002. *Sexual Politics in Indonesia.* Houndmills, Basingstoke: Palgrave Macmillan/Institute of Social Studies.

Williams, Linda. 1991. "Film Bodies: Gender, Genre, and Excess." *Film Quarterly* 44(4):2–13.

Wong, Ka F. 2000. "Nang Naak: The Cult and Myth of a Popular Ghost in Thailand." Pp. 123–42 in *Thai Folklore: Insights into Thai Culture*, edited by Siraporn Natalang. Bangkok: Chulalongkorn University Press.

Yeatter, Bryan L. 2007. *Cinema of the Philippines: A History and Filmography, 1897–2005.* Jefferson, NC: McFarland.

Yngvesson, Dag. 2011. "Let's Get Lost: Unmapping History and Reformasi in the Indonesian Film *Tiga Hari Untuk Selamanya*." *Jump Cut* 53. http://ejumpcut.org/archive/jc53.2011/DagIndonesia/index.html.

Yngvesson, Dag. 2014. "The Earth Is Getting Hotter: Urban Apocalypse and Outsider Women's Collectives in *Bumi Makin Panas*." *Plaridel* 11(2):53–84.

Yngvesson, Dag. 2015. "*Kuldesak* and the Inexorable Pulp Fiction of Indonesian Film History." *Indonesia and the Malay World* 43(127):345–77.

Yngvesson, Dag. 2018. "Sang Nyai: Modern Ghost and Indonesian Femme Fatale." In "Southeast Asian Noir." Special issue, *International Journal of Indonesian Studies* (Monash University, Australia):50–65.

Yngvesson, Dag. 2021. "Centering Peripheries: The Return of Regionalism in Indonesian Independent Cinema." In Lovatt and Trice 2021b:169–75.

Yngvesson, Dag, and Adrian Alarilla. 2020. "A Nation Imagined Differently: The Critical Impulse of 1950s Indonesian Cinema." In Khoo, Barker, and Ainslie:37–58.

Young, Damon R. 2018. *Making Sex Public and Other Cinematic Fantasies.* Durham, NC: Duke University Press.

Zhen Zhang. 2006. *An Amorous History of the Silver Screen: Shanghai Cinema, 1896–1937.* Chicago: University of Chicago Press.

Zhen Zhang, Debashree Mukherjee, Intan Paramaditha, and Sangjoon Lee, eds. 2024. *The Routledge Companion to Asian Cinemas.* London: Routledge

Žižek, Slavoj. 1989. *The Sublime Object of Ideology.* New York: Verso.

INDEX

Founded in 1893,
UNIVERSITY OF CALIFORNIA PRESS
publishes bold, progressive books and journals
on topics in the arts, humanities, social sciences,
and natural sciences—with a focus on social
justice issues—that inspire thought and action
among readers worldwide.

The UC PRESS FOUNDATION
raises funds to uphold the press's vital role
as an independent, nonprofit publisher, and
receives philanthropic support from a wide
range of individuals and institutions—and from
committed readers like you. To learn more, visit
ucpress.edu/supportus.